"Whether Claire Saffitz is teaching us to make a simple loaf cake or a complex croquembouche, you know just by reading her recipes that she's got only one aim: to make sure we succeed. This is a wonderful book for experienced bakers—there are plenty of surprises and challenges—and an ideal one for beginners. Look at the Recipe Matrix, choose an easy recipe that doesn't take much time, follow Claire's directions, and chalk up your first win. If you're not already a dessert person, Claire will make you one."

—**DORIE GREENSPAN**, author of *Dorie's Cookies* and *Everyday Dorie*

"Claire Saffitz is a skillful and imaginative baker with a knack for writing beautiful recipes. Her gorgeous book will unleash the inner dessert person in a novice and inspire those who know their way around a pastry kitchen. It certainly has a place on my shelf."

—**CLAUDIA FLEMING**, chef and author of *The Last Course*

"I've always been a fan of Claire's work at *Bon Appétit*, and I am most definitely a dessert person, so this book really appeals to me. Her recipes all have modern twists of flavor, but at their core they are the familiar bakes we always want to get into the kitchen for."

—**CLAIRE PTAK**, Violet Cakes director

"Dessert is last in a meal but first in many people's hearts. It also, beneath the sweetness, requires a sophisticated mix of time management, architectural thinking, visual seduction, and unexpected restraint. As these recipes prove, Claire Saffitz has all of that, and more."

—**QUESTLOVE**

"Who knew that baking could be even more fun than it already is? Claire Saffitz, that's who. Her brilliance shines through in a buttery, caramelized tart that pairs rosemary with salted nuts and irresistibly beguiling blondies made with an equal billing of halvah and white chocolate. Claire's easier take on the French galette des rois will win over those who want to make one with less fuss, and have more fun doing it. If anyone can turn you into a dessert person, it's Claire. You'll want to make everything in this book, as I do."

—**DAVID LEBOVITZ**, author *My Paris Kitchen* and *Drinking French*

"If you know Claire (and how could you not?), gourmet Doritos and Skittles may come to mind, but she's got so much more up her flour-dusted sleeve. From the subtle flavors of a pear-and-chestnut cake to miso-spiked buttermilk biscuits, *Dessert Person* is Claire's personal dissertation on baking. Which isn't to say it's a sugar fest all the way through— thanks to a substantial section on savory baking, even those without a well-developed sweet tooth can bake along, too."

—**STELLA PARKS**, author of *BraveTart: Iconic American Desserts*

"As a lover of all-things-dessert, I instantly identified the same in Claire—a sister in search for creative, delicious ingredients rooted in classic baking technique. She has that rare combination of creative generosity crossed with baking-professor that the very best authors can convey in a book, and it will make this one a classic."

—**ELISABETH PRUEITT**, founder, Tartine

"Does any chef have a more reassuring and trustworthy voice than Claire Saffitz? Equal parts tireless, hyper-organized technician and empathic cheerleader, Claire presents one of the most convincing arguments I've ever read for diving into the world of baking. If anybody can fell the wall that divides home cooks and home bakers, it's Claire, with her thoroughly modern yet classically elegant desserts."

—**NATASHA PICKOWICZ**, pastry chef

Dessert Person

Dessert Person

Recipes and Guidance for Baking with Confidence

Claire Saffitz

CLARKSON POTTER / PUBLISHERS

NEW YORK

Contents

Recipe Matrix

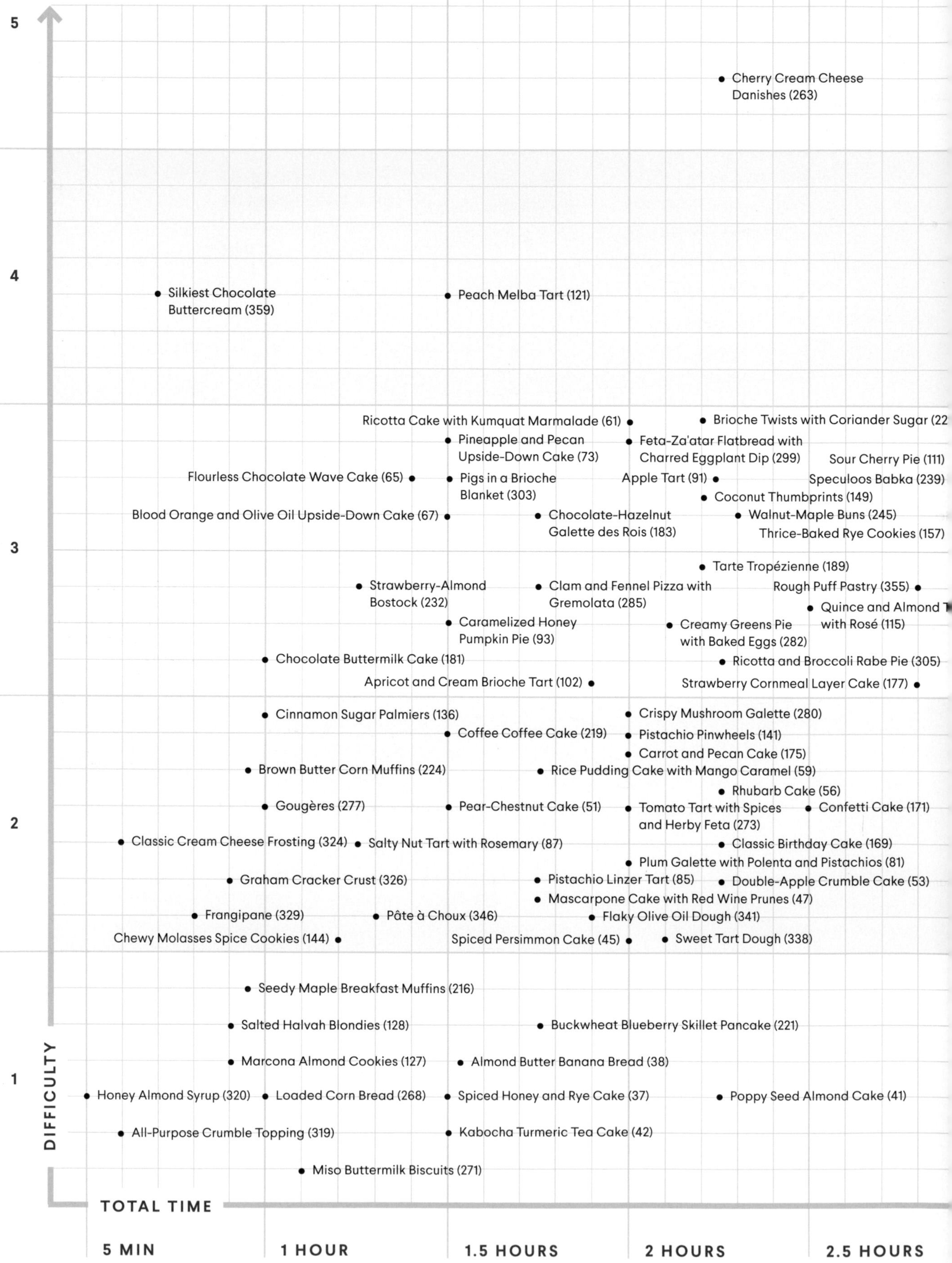

DIFFICULTY (vertical axis, values 1–5)

TOTAL TIME (horizontal axis: 5 MIN, 1 HOUR, 1.5 HOURS, 2 HOURS, 2.5 HOURS)

- Cherry Cream Cheese Danishes (263)
- Silkiest Chocolate Buttercream (359)
- Peach Melba Tart (121)
- Ricotta Cake with Kumquat Marmalade (61)
- Brioche Twists with Coriander Sugar (22)
- Pineapple and Pecan Upside-Down Cake (73)
- Feta-Za'atar Flatbread with Charred Eggplant Dip (299)
- Sour Cherry Pie (111)
- Flourless Chocolate Wave Cake (65)
- Pigs in a Brioche Blanket (303)
- Apple Tart (91)
- Speculoos Babka (239)
- Coconut Thumbprints (149)
- Blood Orange and Olive Oil Upside-Down Cake (67)
- Chocolate-Hazelnut Galette des Rois (183)
- Walnut-Maple Buns (245)
- Thrice-Baked Rye Cookies (157)
- Tarte Tropézienne (189)
- Strawberry-Almond Bostock (232)
- Clam and Fennel Pizza with Gremolata (285)
- Rough Puff Pastry (355)
- Quince and Almond T with Rosé (115)
- Caramelized Honey Pumpkin Pie (93)
- Creamy Greens Pie with Baked Eggs (282)
- Chocolate Buttermilk Cake (181)
- Ricotta and Broccoli Rabe Pie (305)
- Apricot and Cream Brioche Tart (102)
- Strawberry Cornmeal Layer Cake (177)
- Cinnamon Sugar Palmiers (136)
- Crispy Mushroom Galette (280)
- Coffee Coffee Cake (219)
- Pistachio Pinwheels (141)
- Carrot and Pecan Cake (175)
- Brown Butter Corn Muffins (224)
- Rice Pudding Cake with Mango Caramel (59)
- Rhubarb Cake (56)
- Gougères (277)
- Pear-Chestnut Cake (51)
- Tomato Tart with Spices and Herby Feta (273)
- Confetti Cake (171)
- Classic Cream Cheese Frosting (324)
- Salty Nut Tart with Rosemary (87)
- Classic Birthday Cake (169)
- Plum Galette with Polenta and Pistachios (81)
- Graham Cracker Crust (326)
- Pistachio Linzer Tart (85)
- Double-Apple Crumble Cake (53)
- Mascarpone Cake with Red Wine Prunes (47)
- Frangipane (329)
- Pâte à Choux (346)
- Flaky Olive Oil Dough (341)
- Chewy Molasses Spice Cookies (144)
- Spiced Persimmon Cake (45)
- Sweet Tart Dough (338)
- Seedy Maple Breakfast Muffins (216)
- Salted Halvah Blondies (128)
- Buckwheat Blueberry Skillet Pancake (221)
- Marcona Almond Cookies (127)
- Almond Butter Banana Bread (38)
- Honey Almond Syrup (320)
- Loaded Corn Bread (268)
- Spiced Honey and Rye Cake (37)
- Poppy Seed Almond Cake (41)
- All-Purpose Crumble Topping (319)
- Kabocha Turmeric Tea Cake (42)
- Miso Buttermilk Biscuits (271)

5

● Croquembouche (211)   ● Kouign-amann (257)   ● Spelt Croissants (253)

Fruitcake (193) (2 mos) ⟶

● Black Sesame Paris-Brest (203)   ● Gâteau Basque (197)

● Preserved Lemon Meringue Cake (206)

4

● All Allium Deep-Dish Quiche (309)   ● Blueberry Slab Pie (119)

● Pull-Apart Sour Cream and Chive Rolls (313)   ● A Little Bit of Everything Bagles (249)

● All Coconut Cake (201)

● Foolproof Tarte Tatin (107)

● Strawberry Rhubarb Pavlovas with Rose (187)

ackberry Caramel Tart (99)   ● Earl Grey and Apricot Hamantaschen (159)

leyer Lemon Tart (104)   ● Soft and Crispy Focaccia (289)

3

● Goat Cheese Cake with Honey and Figs (71)

● Minty Lime Bars (155)   ● Babkallah (235)   ● Brioche Dough (352)

● Apple and Concord Grape Crumble Pie (97)   ● Soft and Pillowy Flatbread (349)   ● Peanut Butter and Concord Grape Sandwich Cookies (163)   ● Oat and Pecan Brittle Cookies (151)

● St. Louis Gooey Butter Cake (243)

● Honey Tahini Challah (295)

● Malted "Forever" Brownies (139)   ● Aunt Rose's Mondel Bread (147)

● Brown Butter and Sage Sablés (131)   ● Classic English Muffins (227)

● Cranberry-Pomegranate Mousse Pie (79)

2

● Pastry Cream (321)

aramelized Endive Galette (278)   ● Flaky All-Butter Pie Dough (333)   ● Chocolate Chip Cookies (133)

● Lemon Curd (330)   ● Sweet Yeast Dough (344)

1

3 HOURS   3.5 HOURS   4 HOURS   6 HOURS   12 HOURS +

Introduction

I am a dessert person. I like cakes and cookies and pies and believe that no meal is complete without something sweet at the end. When a server asks me if I saved room for dessert, the answer is always "yes." I walk to the corner bodega late at night for a piece of chocolate on the rare occasion that I don't have any in my apartment. Whipped cream is my favorite food of all time.

My love of eating desserts is matched by my love of making them. The alchemy that turns butter, sugar, eggs, and flour into cake never ceases to astonish or delight me. I crave the tactile sensation of dough between my fingers. Rolling out a pie crust or cutting biscuits is my version of doing yoga. Dessert is in my DNA.

So when I hear people say, "I don't like sweets" or "I'm not a dessert person," it makes me a bit suspicious. Sweet is one of the five tastes, so how can anyone discount it entirely? While I, too, reject cloying desserts, I suggest that those who say they don't like sweets just haven't found the right one. Whether it's composed of chocolate or fruit, buttery pastry or creamy custard, there's a dessert for everyone. In short, I think anyone can be a dessert person, even people who think they're not.

Identifying as a dessert person isn't just about a love of baking and pastry and all things sweet. To me, it's an attitude; it's about embracing cooking and eating as fundamental sources of pleasure. This is a book about baking—most of it sweet, some of it savory—but, more broadly, it argues in favor of an approach to food that is celebratory, abundant, and at times a tad luxurious.

This book is a defense of baking.

Another thing I hear people say is "I'm a cook but I'm not a baker," as if cooking and baking are separate disciplines when, in fact, they are closely related. These kinds of statements reveal a bias against baking. While cooking is considered creative, passionate, and improvisational, baking gets labeled exacting, rigid, and nondeviating.

This book is a defense of baking. The recipes are modern interpretations of classic dishes and put unexpected twists on familiar flavors in an effort to demonstrate just how versatile and flexible baking can be (which is why you'll find an entire chapter on savory baking as well). As a whole, I wrote this book as a friendly rebuke to anyone who thinks of baking as a lesser art that affords fewer creative opportunities.

I started my career in the test kitchen at *Bon Appétit* magazine, where I still work as a video host and occasional contributor, even though I am no longer on staff full-time. Working in the test kitchen taught me to develop recipes with a sensitivity to the realities and limitations that home cooks face. As much as you or I might love being in the kitchen, I know that it can feel like work. It requires time and money to shop for ingredients. It requires washing dishes. It requires patience and attentiveness. Most significantly, it requires practice if you want to be even remotely good at it.

One reason I suspect people who cook say they don't, won't, or can't bake is because baking poses a particular challenge. Unlike cooking, where you can correct course and make adjustments as you go, baking is less forgiving. It requires an understanding of certain rules and principles. Ingredients combine and transform in unseen, mysterious ways inside the oven. Success never feels like a guarantee. It took years of practice for much of my anxiety about baking to abate, but despite all my professional experience, I sometimes still feel uneasy in the kitchen. Will the filling thicken enough? Is it browning too fast on the bottom? Did the center fully bake even though the tester came out clean? These feelings are normal, and *Dessert Person* is here to help!

I wrote this book to celebrate and defend my love of desserts, and also to empower reluctant home bakers to work with new ingredients, attempt new techniques, and bake with more confidence. Each recipe is carefully written to provide all the information necessary to achieve a successful result. I provide notes to help explain basic baking principles, like *why* the butter in pie dough should stay cold, or *how* to whip egg whites so they form firm peaks. My goal in explaining the hows and whys of each recipe is to demystify the baking process and make it more rewarding.

My approach to baking is similar to my approach to cooking, which means I use seasonal produce whenever possible. Fruit desserts are my preference, and I usually want whatever I'm making to check one or more of the following boxes: crispy, chewy, cakey, custardy, or buttery. Just like in cooking, I strive for balance in my sweets, which is why I especially love using bitter ingredients like tahini and unsweetened cocoa, since they combine with sugar in such interesting and delicious ways. By countering the sugar in my recipes with other bitter, sour, and salty flavors, I aim for desserts that are just sweet enough. A variety of pleasing textures is important, too, so you'll notice lots of crispy-edged, chewy-in-the-center cookies and flaky-bottomed, cream-filled tarts.

You won't find a lot of individually prepared desserts here, since composed dishes just aren't as fun as shareable ones. I treasure the tiny thrill of setting down a whole burnished pie, glistening tart, or fluffy layer cake on a table surrounded by friends, and the spectacle of cutting into it. Even when it turns out a little wonky, dessert is always a centerpiece, an attention-grabber, and an object of excitement.

You will not find these recipes overwrought in terms of styling, either. I see no need to try too hard, make a fuss, or be overly precious when it comes to presenting a dessert. If it tastes good, it usually looks good, too. I want a homemade dessert to look homemade, not social media–perfect. Every recipe should still be beautiful—an artful dollop of whipped cream here, a scattering of sparkly sugar there—but I'm guided by the principle that any decoration, embellishment, or garnish should also enhance flavor.

Some of the recipes feature clever, unexpected elements or flavor combinations, like the **Preserved Lemon Meringue Cake** (page 206) or **Brioche Twists with Coriander Sugar** (page 229). A lot will look familiar, too. For example, I rely on the tried-and-true mix of buttery pastry and brown sugar in my recipe for **Apple Tart** (page 91), since there's simply no improving this combination. Whether it's a recipe as unusual-sounding as **Kabocha Turmeric Tea Cake** (page 42), or as familiar as **Chocolate Chip Cookies** (page 133), I hope you'll want to make many of these recipes again and again.

From simple **Marcona Almond Cookies** (page 127) to a complex **Peach Melba Tart** (page 121), the breadth of desserts in this book means that everyone from the beginner to the veteran home baker will find a comfortable entry point. I rate the difficulty of each recipe on a scale from 1 (Very Easy) to 5 (Very Challenging). The easier recipes are designed to make even a novice baker feel like a pro without great effort, while the more challenging recipes are projects. For more on this ratings system, read How to Use This Book (and Be a Successful Baker) on page 17.

I've tried in each recipe, no matter the level of difficulty, to ease the burden for home bakers. I call for standard pan sizes whenever possible. Most ingredients are ones you can find at any well-stocked grocery store, and I make every attempt to minimize odds and ends. For example, a recipe will use the full 8 ounces of sour cream in a single container, rather than 7 or 9. I strive for each recipe to have a sense of self-containment and wholeness, meaning I won't call for two ingredients where one will do.

This book asks you to spend time in the kitchen, but it also tries to make that experience fun and interesting. I hope that it leads already committed home bakers down a path of experimentation, creative expression, and maybe even stress reduction. I hope it gives novices the confidence they need to start learning and to feel less intimidated. And finally, I hope that it persuades any skeptics that baking is more adaptable and multifaceted than they thought. There are no "just cooks" out there, only bakers who haven't yet been converted.

Self-identifying as a dessert person is my way of declaring that no foods are good or bad. Food holds no moral weight at all. Dessert is not "sinful," and I don't need permission from anyone, myself included, to enjoy it. This is a book filled with practical recipes for the home baker, but it's also my personal meditation on the benefits and pleasures of living less restrictively. I hope that you not only make something from this book, but that you enjoy it, guilt-free, with family and friends. I am a dessert person, and we are all dessert people.

There are no "just cooks" out there, only bakers who haven't yet been converted.

How to Use This Book
(and Be a Successful Baker)

As a recipe developer, I find it fascinating—and more than a little distressing—that even if a recipe works perfectly in one kitchen one day, it could fail miserably in another the next. Even though baking is often labeled a "science" because it involves chemistry and measuring ingredients precisely, kitchens are not laboratories. It's impossible to control all the variables, such as time, temperature, and humidity at all times. Even if I took an exhaustive approach to testing every recipe, working in different kitchens with different ingredients, equipment, and appliances to try to account for every possible variation in outcome, I am sure that the recipe would still fail some of the time.

Knowing that the truly foolproof recipe doesn't exist, I've thought long and hard about how I can reasonably maximize a home baker's chances of success. Often I find a recipe meets its doom when a home cook unwittingly takes a shortcut, makes a substitution, or skips a step, without realizing that doing so will compromise the outcome. While it might *seem* innocuous to replace the sour cream in a recipe with low-fat yogurt—maybe you've done it in another recipe and it worked out fine—there is a chance it'll backfire.

Home bakers need the reassurance of a recipe that will tell them, like a road map, where they can safely veer off and where they need to stay the course. The road to making a showstopping dessert can get treacherous—brown butter can sputter and burn if unattended, for example, and egg whites can get dry and curdy if overbeaten. Fear not, though, the recipes in this book will guide you, specifying where and when you can take a detour or make a stop, where you must keep moving forward as planned, and when to use caution.

As a navigator, I use a lot of words. I understand that for bakers of any level, a long, wordy recipe feels intimidating and off-putting. While recipe length is of course a direct reflection of how many steps it requires, in this book it's also reflective of my overall approach, which is to provide more information rather than less. I give lots of "indicators" to signal an end point. For example, I will never instruct you to bake a cake just until a tester inserted into the center comes out clean. To eliminate any guesswork or doubt, I will also tell you that it will look golden brown across the surface, feel springy to the touch in the center, and smell very fragrant.

I remember what it feels like to find baking arduous, but somewhere along my path, after much practice and learning, I crossed a threshold and began to see baking less as a series of tasks and more as a system of logical, interconnected processes. Pie dough, for example, isn't so much a "recipe" as it is a method of working cold fat into flour and using cold water to bring it together into a dough. To help home bakers discern these processes more easily, I begin each step with a boldfaced header to announce and summarize the objective of that step. If you make several loaf cakes from this book, for example, you'll see that they all come together using the same basic technique: First you mix the wet ingredients, then you mix the dry, then you mix the wet into the dry. Learning to recognize these types of patterns will make you a smarter, better, more intuitive baker.

All of the recipes in this book have a difficulty rating of 1 to 5. I've streamlined the steps as much as possible, so if a recipe asks you to bake in a water bath, for example, it's either because the recipe won't work without it, or because it will help you avoid doing even more work in the long run. Here is a breakdown of what each rating means:

---

1. Very Easy: A quick recipe that requires minimal technique and no special equipment. It's doable even for the person who has never baked before.

2. Easy: A recipe that involves a series of steps and may require some special equipment, but uses no finicky techniques. It's doable for beginners.

3. Moderate: A recipe that requires some technique, patience, and a piece or two of special equipment, but can still be completed by a beginner.

4. Challenging: A recipe that requires two or more components to assemble and uses more advanced techniques. These are more appropriate for the intermediate baker.

5. Very Challenging: A recipe with multiple components and that requires considerable time and equipment to complete. It may also employ multiple techniques and is best attempted by more confident and/or ambitious bakers.

Within each chapter, the recipes are ordered according to difficulty level, starting with the easiest and ending with the hardest. I designed it this way so bakers of every ability have a clear sense of how much they take on with each recipe. It's also designed so that the skills taught in each build upon one another—as bakers gain confidence with level 1 and 2 recipes, they can attempt ones rated 3 and 4, and eventually 5 if they desire. For example, once you master **Pâte à Choux** (page 346) and **Pastry Cream** (page 321), both rated level 2, you could combine them to make the level 4 **Black Sesame Paris-Brest** (page 203). Then you might have the confidence to try your hand at **Croquembouche** (page 211), one of the few level 5 recipes.

Note that a difficulty rating is not necessarily an indication of how long a recipe will take. Some easy recipes take a long time because they might need an overnight rest in the refrigerator, for example, while a difficult recipe might come together in a relatively short period of time. To understand what kind of time commitment is required, pay attention to the Active and Total Times listed for each recipe as well as the Recipe Matrix (page 8). The matrix will give you an overview of how difficult all the recipes are relative to how long they take. When you're making a recipe that calls for another recipe component to be prepared ahead of time—for example, the **Plum Galette with Polenta and Pistachios** (page 81) requires a pre-made **Flaky All-Butter Pie Dough** (page 333)—the Total and Active Times do not include the time it takes to prepare the component recipe (refer to the component recipe itself for Total and Active Times).

If you continue to work at it, eventually you'll look past the list of ingredients and the (many) words on the page and see the architecture of a recipe. You won't need to be told to chill pastry dough if it's getting warm and sticky—you'll pop it into the fridge automatically. If a recipe calls for room temperature egg whites and yolks, you'll know to separate the eggs cold so they're easier to handle. Once you reach this point, baking becomes a lot less scary and a lot more fun.

Here are some specific tips for baking with more confidence and maximizing your chances of success in the kitchen.

Be organized: Before you turn on the oven, check to make sure you have all your ingredients. Read through the entire recipe at least once, including all the helpful notes at the bottom of the pages. Make sure you have enough time to complete the recipe, and check for long pauses when something needs to rise or chill. I can't say I always follow this advice, but I always regret it when I don't.

Measure accurately: I've included weight measurements in grams and ounces for most ingredients because this is the absolute best and most accurate way to achieve consistent results. It's also so easy to place a bowl on the scale, zero it out, and then add ingredients to the bowl straight from the bag/container/jar/bottle they came in. However, if you're partial to measuring in cups, please use liquid measuring cups to measure liquids, reading the volume at eye level, and use dry cups to measure dry, leveling them with a straightedge (like the back of a knife). If you measure flour by volume, don't scoop directly from the bag with the measuring cup. This compacts the flour, increasing the amount you add to the recipe, which could lead to denser and drier baked goods. Instead, transfer the flour to a large lidded container, fluff it lightly with a fork, use a spoon or scoop to transfer the flour to a measuring cup, and then level it. Flour is the baking ingredient that's most prone to inaccurate measurement, and the one that's very likely to throw a recipe off.

Bake to the given indicator, not the time: For example, my recipe for **Malted "Forever" Brownies** (page 139) says to bake them "until the surface is shiny and puffed and the center is dry to the touch but still soft when pressed, 25 to 30 minutes." If after

30 minutes in your oven, though, they're still gooey in the center, don't take the brownies out! Continue to bake them until they match the description in the recipe, even if it takes 10 or 15 minutes longer. Pay attention first and foremost to the sensory indicator(s) or end point(s) given in the recipe, and keep going until you hit them. I cannot emphasize this principle enough. The time ranges in this book are suggestions, not dogma. They represent how long each recipe took in my particular oven/kitchen, on the particular days that I tested it, under particular weather conditions (yes, sometimes even the weather makes a difference), and with the particular ingredients I used. A peach grown in New Jersey is different in sweetness, juiciness, and

volume from a peach grown in Georgia or California. Ovens and bakeware can be wacky, and yours will behave differently than mine. Start checking for the indicator at the early end of the given range, but do rely on your senses. A cake that consistently took 25 minutes to bake in my oven might take 35 in yours, or a yeasted dough that needs 1 hour to rise in summer might need 3 hours in winter. It doesn't mean that you screwed up or that anything went wrong. Note how long the steps of a recipe take in your kitchen so you know for next time.

Know your oven: In my experience, the biggest variable in baking is oven performance. The professional oven I used for many years in the *Bon Appétit* test kitchen had twice the power of my home oven and would bake things much faster. Even if two ovens both register 350°F, they will transfer heat differently, affecting how (and how quickly) the items bake. The better you know the idiosyncrasies of your oven, the better able you'll be to make adjustments.

- **Check the temperature:** Use a freestanding, dial-face oven thermometer to verify the true internal temperature of your oven, since it's often different from what the knob (or digital panel) reads. Place the thermometer in the center of your preheated oven and let it sit for 20 minutes before you take the reading. Move the thermometer around and test a few different positions to identify any hot or cold spots (you can also toast slices of bread all over the oven and see what areas brown faster). If you do observe dramatic temperature fluctuations inside your oven, I recommend purchasing a couple of unglazed ceramic tiles from a home improvement store (they're cheap!) and placing them directly on the oven floor. These will absorb and radiate heat, helping to distribute it more evenly.

- **Know the heat source and adjust the racks accordingly:** Most gas and electric ovens have heating elements that run along the bottom and a separate broiler that runs along the top (some narrow gas models, like the one in my old apartment, have broiling drawers under the oven and a single burner beneath the oven floor). Knowing how your oven heats and adjusting the position of the racks accordingly will allow you to control how things bake. Baking on the lower rack means the baked good will develop more color on the bottom. This is useful when you're baking a fruit pie, for example, because the bottom layer of pastry needs more heat to help it brown. Baking on the top rack means more browning will occur on the surface. If you notice that things in your oven have a tendency to brown quickly on top, even when they're on the center rack, you can lower the rack and place a baking sheet on the top rack to absorb some of the heat like a shield (do this in reverse if the bottom tends to brown more quickly). The point is, once you know how your oven heats, you can strategically position the racks (and pans) to achieve the type of doneness you want.

- **Understand convection vs. conventional ovens:** Most home ovens are "conventional," meaning they contain a heating element that warms the air inside. A "convection" oven, alternatively, uses fans to circulate air and distribute heat evenly, eliminating hot and cold spots. Some conventional home ovens also come with a convection setting. While professional bakers tend to prefer convection ovens because they're faster and more efficient, most recipes for home bakers, including the ones in this book, have been developed for conventional ovens. If you have a convection oven or want to use the convection setting, lower all the baking temperatures in the recipes by 25°F.

Failure happens. Don't freak out. Keep trying. One or more of the recipes in this book might not work for you. I am sorry if that happens. The baking goddesses can be fickle, and know that even professionals—myself included—experience unexplained failure in the kitchen. The only thing we can do is try to learn from our mistakes. If you're committed to being a better baker, pick a few recipes—maybe even ones that seem intimidating—and make them each five or six or ten times. Take notes. I promise you will start to understand how small changes affect the outcome of a recipe, and in baking there's no better learning than that.

Techniques and End Points

This section gives a number of helpful visual references for key techniques and end points that are mentioned several times throughout the recipes. Take a look through the following photographs and refer back to them as frequently as you need if you're ever unsure of what a step should look like or how to do it.

HOW TO FILL A PASTRY BAG

Place a large plastic or reusable pastry bag (fitted with the desired tip if using one) upright inside a quart-sized container and fold the top of the bag down and over the sides of the container. Use a flexible spatula to transfer the mixture to the bag.

Unfold the ends of the bag and lift it out of the container. Lay the bag flat on the work surface and use the straight side of a bench or bowl scraper to scrape and push the mixture down, forcing it into the tip of the bag.

Gather the ends of the bag, pressing out any air, and twist several times until you have a tight bundle. Secure the end with a rubber band, if desired (to help keep it closed), and, if you're using a disposable plastic pastry bag (or a gallon-sized resealable bag), use scissors to snip an opening at the tip.

HOW TO LINE A ROUND CAKE PAN WITH PARCHMENT PAPER

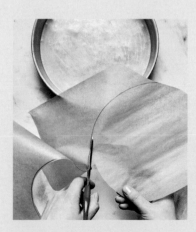  

Place the cake pan on a piece of parchment paper and trace around it with a marker or pencil. Use scissors to cut inside the line of the circle. Use a pastry brush to lightly coat the bottom and sides of the cake pan with room temperature or melted butter or oil.

Lay the round of parchment paper inside the bottom of the pan and smooth to eliminate air bubbles.

Lightly brush the parchment with more butter or oil.

HOW TO LINE A LOAF PAN WITH PARCHMENT PAPER

HOW TO SCRAPE A VANILLA BEAN

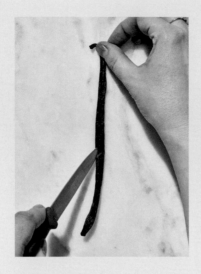

Lightly coat the bottom and sides of a loaf pan with room temperature or melted butter or oil. Cut a long rectangle of parchment paper that's as wide as the bottom length of the loaf pan, then lay the parchment in the bottom of the pan, pressing it up the sides and into the right angles, eliminating air bubbles.

Use a sharp paring knife to make a lengthwise slit from tip to tip down the vanilla pod, taking care to cut just one side and not all the way through.

Open up the pod along the slit and, starting from one tip, drag the dull side of the knife along the interior of the pod, pressing firmly to scrape out the seeds.

HOW TO FORM A LOG OF COOKIE DOUGH

HOW TO BROWN BUTTER

Place the cookie dough in the center of a piece of parchment paper. Fold one end of the parchment over the dough.

Holding a bench scraper nearly parallel to the work surface, place it on top of the parchment, angled slightly downward, and push toward the cookie dough, forcing the dough into a log. Roll up the log of dough in the parchment paper.

Place the butter in a saucepan (do not use nonstick or dark-coated) and cook over medium-low heat, stirring and scraping the bottom and sides often with a heatproof silicone spatula. It will bubble and sputter as the water boils off. Continue to cook the butter, stirring constantly, until it's very foamy and there are free-floating golden brown bits. Turn off the heat and let the butter cool, stirring occasionally. The solid bits will darken to a deep golden brown.

CREAM WHIPPED TO SOFT PEAKS

Softly whipped cream will be light and thickened just enough so the cream holds its shape and doesn't slide around inside the bowl. Cream that's under-whipped will settle back into the bowl and have a somewhat liquid consistency, but, if being used as a garnish, it's preferable to cream that has been beaten too much and contains curds of butterfat.

MERINGUE BEATEN TO STIFF PEAKS

When it's ready, the meringue should be stiff and dense but still smooth and spreadable. It will have a glossy (not matte) sheen, and when you lift the whisk out of the bowl, the meringue should create a sharp-pointed "peak" that doesn't droop.

EGGS BEATEN UNTIL RIBBONY

Ribbony eggs will have a satiny finish and a light, thick, voluminous, but still liquid consistency. When the mixture runs off the end of the whisk back into the bowl, it will fold onto itself in a three-dimensional trail or "ribbon" that sits above the surface for a second or two before settling back into the mixture.

EGG WHITES BEATEN TO SOFT PEAKS

Softly whipped egg whites will have an opaque white color and matte finish, and will hold their shape in droopy mounds in the bowl. Overbeaten egg whites will lose their smooth texture and have a dry, curdy look, making them difficult to incorporate into the recipe, so check them frequently as they whip.

Equipment

Having the right bakeware and tools in the kitchen dramatically increases your chances of baking success. I won't recommend any piece of equipment that only serves one function, so all of the essentials listed below are multipurpose. Webstaurant.com is an inexpensive resource for anyone trying to build up a kitchen arsenal. As your baking repertoire expands over time, you can add additional pieces of equipment as needed.

Essential Equipment

The recipes in this book presume home bakers have the following:

Bowl scraper and bench scraper. A flexible bowl scraper with a rounded edge is handy for scraping dough and batter off the sides of bowls, and a squared-off metal bench scraper is great for cleaning off a work surface, lifting and transferring ingredients, and portioning dough. Each is designed to keep your hands clean and, indeed, when using them, try to think of them as extensions of your hands!

Box grater. While not intuitively a baking tool, a box grater is good for shredding ingredients like butter (for rough puff pastry) and carrots (for carrot cake).

Fine-mesh sieve. I try to avoid the annoyance of straining anything in a recipe, but a fine-mesh sieve is useful for removing the seeds or solids from jam, or sifting lumpy ingredients like cocoa powder or cake flour.

Fine rasp-style grater. I like the Microplane brand, but any fine rasp grater works. Use it for finely grating citrus zest, ginger, cheese, and nutmeg.

Kitchen scale. Measuring ingredients by weight is by far the most accurate method—I include weight conversions for most of the volume measurements in the book—so a digital kitchen scale is crucial. A standard model by my preferred brand, Escali, will set you back about $25.

Large and small saucepans and skillets. Many recipes that are baked in the oven have at least one component that's first prepared stovetop, so you'll need these for cooking pastry cream, pâte à choux, jams, and compotes, and for poaching fruit (among other things).

Mixing bowls. Metal and tempered glass bowls are preferable to plastic, and a mix of both kinds is best. You need at least one large bowl, two or three medium and small bowls, and, ideally, a half dozen very small glass bowls.

Parchment paper and/or silicone baking mats. Both of these create a nonstick surface on any piece of bakeware. Use unbleached parchment paper (I find precut sheets more convenient than rolls) for lining cake and loaf pans, but consider investing in at least one reusable silicone baking mat for lining sheet pans.

Pastry brush. You'll want at least one brush with soft natural bristles and a head that's 1 to 1½ inches wide. Make sure you clean and dry it well between uses to preserve the bristles, especially if you use it for egg wash.

Pizza cutter or pastry wheel. A wheel cutter is great for trimming pastry dough cleanly and quickly and glides easily around curves.

Rolling pin. In a pinch you can use a wine bottle to roll out dough, but nothing replaces the ease and control of a sturdy wooden rolling pin, which you can also use for crushing nuts and ice. I prefer a straight, dowel-style rolling pin over a tapered or handled one because it allows me the most amount of control, but use whatever style feels the most comfortable to you.

Ruler. While it might seem painfully fussy to use a ruler in the kitchen, there are many instances where taking precise measurements or knowing exact dimensions are necessary (like cutting triangles of dough for rolling croissants).

Sheet pans. Every home baker should have at least two standard-sized rimmed half-sheet pans measuring 18 × 13 inches. They are inexpensive, indestructible, fit in 99 percent of home ovens, and are indispensable for baking cookies, galettes, breads, etc. While you could make do with smaller cookie sheets or jelly-roll pans, some recipes in this book, like the **Soft and Crispy Focaccia** (page 289), were developed to work best in a standard half-sheet pan. Quarter-sheet pans are inexpensive and durable like half-sheets; they are perfect for smaller tasks like toasting nuts.

Small offset spatula. A small offset spatula is the kitchen tool I cannot live without. I use it for everything from frosting a cake to spreading a filling to cutting around the sides of a pan.

Wet and dry measures. Invest in at least one set of stainless steel measuring spoons (I like the ones with a narrower scoop so they can fit inside most jars). For dry ingredients, I like a set of stainless steel cup measures, and for liquids, I recommend having both a 1- and 2-cup Pyrex measure.

Whisk. A medium-sized stainless steel balloon whisk is essential. Another large balloon whisk is useful for whipping cream by hand, while a small, narrow one is good for getting into the corners of a saucepan.

Wooden spoon and spatula. Have at least one wooden spoon and one flexible heatproof spatula for cooking and scraping. A large flexible spatula is also good for folding batters.

Special Equipment

I don't expect every home baker to have all of the equipment listed here, but the recipes in this book frequently call for one or more of the following:

Bakeware. Because having the right baking vessel is so important, I consider all bakeware specialized and call out any required pan at the top of each recipe. In general, I prefer pans made from anodized aluminum because they are nonreactive and promote even and consistent baking. When choosing a pan, look for ones with high sides, at least 2 inches, made of light-

colored metal. Try to avoid pans with dark, nonstick coatings because these cause baked goods to darken too quickly and rise unevenly. In most places I call for a 9-inch-diameter pan since I find this to be the most versatile size, but in some instances a recipe will require an 8- or 10-inch pan. All the recipes in this book, with the exception of pies, were tested in metal pans; glass heats more slowly than metal and retains heat longer, so by the time the center of a batter or dough is fully baked, the bottom and sides are overbaked and dry. If you only have a glass pan, reduce the oven temperature in the recipe by 25°F to encourage more even baking. Here are all the pieces of bakeware you might need:

- 8 × 8-inch metal baking pan
- Three 8-inch metal cake pans (for layer cakes)
- At least one 9-inch metal cake pan
- Standard 9-inch glass pie plate (glass makes it easy to monitor the browning of the bottom crust)
- 9-inch removable-bottom tart pan
- 9-inch metal springform pan
- 10-inch metal cake pan
- 10-inch metal springform pan
- Standard metal loaf pan (4½ × 8½ inches, measured across the top)
- 13 × 9-inch metal baking pan
- Standard 12-cup metal muffin tin
- 12-cup metal Bundt pan

Cookware. A 10-inch ovenproof skillet, preferably cast-iron, is often required for precooking some fillings and griddling English muffins, plus as a baking vessel for tarte Tatin, corn bread, and a few cakes. Additionally, a **large Dutch oven** (for boiling bagels, for example) and a **large roasting pan** (for baking in a water bath) are good to have.

Food processor. Many of the tasks a food processor performs can also be done by hand, but a food processor does it way faster. Look for one with an 11-cup capacity, which can handle large and small jobs and has a manageable footprint. I prefer Cuisinart food processors, which include disks for shredding and slicing.

Instant-read digital thermometer. A digital thermometer gives a quick and accurate reading for temperature-sensitive operations, like cooking lemon curd. (To confirm your thermometer is accurate, stick it in boiling water and see if it displays 212°F.) There are many inexpensive models available, and note that most digital thermometers can also do the job of a candy thermometer.

Miscellaneous. Each of the following items pop up in these pages once or twice at the most, but I'm generally glad to have all of these in my collection:

- Mandoline
- Cherry pitter with guard (my one violation of the "it must perform multiple functions" rule)
- Cardboard cake rounds
- Kitchen torch
- Melon baller
- Potato masher
- Spring-loaded ice cream scoop(s)
- Spray bottle filled with water

Pastry bag and tips. A pastry bag is one of those nonessential but extremely handy tools that has a number of cooking applications as well. I recommend a large bag (around 18 inches) you can wash and reuse rather than disposable ones. A few sizes of round and star pastry tips are versatile and the only shapes required here. In many cases, a gallon-sized resealable plastic bag will work as a pastry bag, but the plastic is weaker and it's harder to maneuver overall.

Pie weights or dried beans or rice. When parbaking any type of pastry crust, these are used to weight the dough and prevent it from puffing up in the oven. I don't bother with ceramic pie weights, since rice or dried beans work just as well and cost a fraction of the price. Make sure you have about 4 cups total, which is enough to completely fill a 9-inch pie plate. You can reuse them over and over again.

Set of stainless steel round cutters. These are handy for punching out rounds of cookie or bread doughs in various sizes. You can often find a quick substitute

in the kitchen, such as an upside-down glass, but a cutter will give the cleanest, sharpest edges.

Stand mixer or hand mixer. KitchenAid's Artisan stand mixer, with a tilt head, 5-quart capacity bowl, and three mixing attachments, is the standard in many home kitchens, including mine. It's an investment, but there is no piece of equipment that will expand your baking horizons more than a stand mixer, and it will last you for years (if not decades). You can use a hand mixer (my recommended brand: Oxo) in place of a stand mixer where noted in many recipes, but a hand mixer is much less powerful and will therefore take longer to reach the desired end point.

Standard blender or handheld blender. As far as this book is concerned, any countertop or handheld model works fine.

Pantry Ingredients

My recommendations for buying and storing the most common baking ingredients:

Flour. Because flour is considered shelf-stable, we easily forget that it's a plant-based product for which freshness and quality are important factors. While baking recreationally in my kitchen, I like to use flour that's grown and milled locally because it tends to be extra flavorful. However, local flours vary widely in terms of how much water they absorb and their protein contents, making them unpredictable. Consistency is key in recipe testing, so I always use King Arthur flour, a nationally available brand that makes many wheat and nonwheat options. Here are the types of flour I call for most often:

- **All-purpose flour** performs well in many applications (hence the name). It's a white flour, meaning the nutritious bran and germ have been removed, leaving only the starchy endosperm. This makes it more neutral in flavor and less likely to spoil, and leads to lighter, softer baked goods. To store, keep it in a large container with a tight-fitting lid in a cool, dry place. King Arthur flour, the all-purpose brand that I use, has a protein content of around 11.4%, which is slightly higher than other brands.

- **Whole wheat flour** generally contains all parts of the grain. It absorbs more water than all-purpose and will produce baked goods with a nuttier flavor and denser texture. Whole wheat flour has a tendency to turn rancid due to the oils in the germ, so store it in a resealable bag in the freezer up to 6 months to prevent spoiling.

- **Whole-grain buckwheat, spelt, and rye flours** have become easier to find due to the increasing popularity of whole-grain baking. Because they contain either a negligible amount of gluten or no gluten at all, these behave very differently from wheat flour. When added as a supplement to the all-purpose flour in a recipe, though, they produce a wonderfully complex flavor. Like whole wheat flour, they should be stored in the freezer.

Butter. Like flour, butter is a product that varies widely in terms of quality, and as with flour, you should use the best you can reasonably afford (although, know that I tested all the recipes in this book with relatively inexpensive, nationally available butter brands to make sure they still produced a good result). If you can spring for European-style butter, which has a higher fat content than standard American butter, your recipe will be the better for it. Note that different brands can vary dramatically in flavor and texture. For example, a softer European-style butter might roll out into streaky sheets in a pie dough, while a standard American one might stay in discrete bits (both will work fine!). Because I call for a precise amount of added salt in each recipe, unsalted butter is the default.

Sugar. I've noticed a trend toward less-sweet desserts in the last several years, and, indeed, I prefer desserts that keep sweetness in check. At the same time, many baked goods require a critical mass of sugar to achieve the right flavor and texture, so I add just what the recipe requires. I therefore don't recommend trying to cut the amount of sugar in any of these recipes, as it could adversely affect the outcome.

- **Granulated, light brown, dark brown, and powdered sugars:** Any brand of these will do. Remember to pay attention to the differences between light and dark brown sugars—even though you can usually substitute one for the other, doing so will slightly alter the flavor and texture.

- **Demerara and sanding sugars:** These consist of larger crystals and are used primarily as a garnish on top of a recipe to add a slight crunch, a sparkle, and a touch of extra sweetness. Demerara sugar is only partially refined and therefore has a subtle molasses flavor, while sanding sugar is refined and neutral in flavor.

Eggs. The labeling of eggs can be confusing, but buy the best quality you can afford, preferably from a brand that cares about chicken welfare (look for the Certified Humane seal). I use large eggs exclusively in baking. The size difference between large and extra-large eggs is significant, so don't try substituting them 1:1.

Kosher salt. Salt is crucial in baking because it enhances the flavors of all the other ingredients. A baked good lacking in salt will taste flat. Because these recipes don't rely on large amounts of sugar for flavor (sugar, like salt, is a flavor enhancer), I tend to call for a compensatory amount of salt, so don't be tempted to cut the amount or you may get a disappointingly bland result. I exclusively bake with kosher salt, since table salt has been stripped of its minerality and has a tinny flavor. I develop all my recipes with Diamond Crystal kosher salt, which I like for the fine, flaky texture of the crystals.

- **Diamond Crystal vs. Morton:** It's important to note that salt crystal structure varies between brands of kosher salt and can have a huge effect on the saltiness of a recipe. The pebbly crystals in Morton kosher salt, for example, pack together more densely than Diamond Crystal, *therefore, a teaspoon of Morton is saltier than a teaspoon of Diamond Crystal* (the difference would be even more dramatic if you used a teaspoon of table salt). *If you use Morton rather than Diamond, reduce the volume of salt by half to account for the difference in density.* Because these recipes are already generously seasoned, skipping this adjustment means your recipe could turn out unpleasantly salty.

Vanilla. Only buy **pure vanilla extract**, not imitation vanilla, and look for pungent-smelling **vanilla beans** that are plump and soft. In both cases, try to seek out a brand that is designated fair trade. Because beans are so expensive, I submerge the empty pods in a glass jar filled with vodka and a splash of vanilla extract. The beans infuse the liquid to make homemade vanilla extract, which keeps for years at room temperature (leave the pods submerged).

Chocolate and cocoa powder. Chocolate is another product that we consider a pantry item but is actually plant-based. It ranges in quality and price from cheap, industrially produced chips to handcrafted, single-origin bars that cost $12 apiece. When it comes to baking, look for chocolate that falls somewhere in the midrange.

- **Dark, milk, and white chocolates:** Stick with chocolate that's sold in disks or "féves" (a bean shape), or blocks. I like to bake with dark chocolate that's no more than 68% cacao, as anything higher is too bitter for my taste. I look for Guittard, Valrhona, and Callebaut brands. Avoid chips, as these have emulsifiers that affect the consistency and melting properties of the chocolate.

- **Unsweetened cocoa powder:** There are two main types of cocoa powder: raw and Dutch process. I prefer to bake with Dutch process cocoa, which is treated with alkali, a process that neutralizes some of the raw cocoa's natural acidity and deepens the flavor. Because the acidity levels of Dutch process and raw cocoa powders are different, they react with chemical leavening agents differently, so there's no easy rule for substituting one for the other. In general, stick with the type called for in the recipe. If you're not sure if your cocoa is "Dutched," check that "alkali" is listed as an ingredient.

Nuts and seeds. I bake with all variety of nuts and seeds, most commonly almonds, hazelnuts, pecans, walnuts, pistachios, coconut, poppy seeds, pumpkin seeds, and sesame seeds. Because nuts and seeds are high in fat, they turn rancid easily and should be stored in airtight containers in the freezer (ditto any nut flours). To that point, try to avoid buying any that look like they've been sitting on a shelf or in a bulk bin for months. In most instances, I take the time to toast nuts or seeds to develop their flavor before adding them to a recipe. Remember that frozen nuts and seeds will take a few minutes longer in the oven to toast.

Alcohol. I use brandy, rum, and whisky the most. Don't use a top-shelf brand, since the nuances that distinguish a fine liquor will be lost in baking, but do use something good quality that you'd drink in a cocktail. If you're not a drinker and don't want to buy a large bottle just to use a few tablespoons in a recipe, mini 50-milliliter bottles are a great option.

Leavening agents. These ingredients produce gasses during baking that provide "lift" in breads, cakes, and cookies, creating a lighter, airier texture.

- **Chemical leaveners:** Baking powder and baking soda are both chemical leaveners that react with other ingredients in the presence of water and heat to produce carbon dioxide. They react differently depending on the acidity of a recipe and cannot be substituted for each other. Try to use a brand of baking powder that's aluminum-free, but any baking soda is fine.

- **Yeast:** The most common form of commercial yeast is active dry, so I use it throughout this book. Because the flavor of yeasted dough improves over the course of a long, slow rise, I tend to call

for relatively small amounts of yeast and allow time to do its thing. Active dry yeast is perishable and should be refrigerated to maintain freshness. Before being added to a recipe, the granules should be dissolved in a warm liquid, usually water or milk, to activate them. In the presence of sugar (the lactose in milk, for example, or added sugar), the yeast will start to foam. This is known as "proofing" the yeast, since it confirms that the yeast is alive. In warm water, the yeast will dissolve and make the liquid cloudy, but it will not actively foam. In 99 percent of cases, the yeast is alive and well, so I instruct you to add it to the recipe without technically "proofing" it first. Be careful that you don't dissolve the yeast in a liquid hotter than about 120°F or you risk killing it. You can substitute an equal quantity of instant dry yeast for active dry, just skip the proofing step and add the yeast directly to the recipe (along with any liquid that would have been used to dissolve the yeast). Do not use any yeast labeled "fast-acting" as a substitute for active dry.

A Note on Seasonality and Sustainability

Central to my baking philosophy is using seasonal, locally grown produce whenever possible. While this book is not expressly about seasonal baking—in fact, the majority of the recipes are "evergreen," or makeable any time of the year—a significant portion of the recipes use fruits and vegetables only available during a certain window.

Not only does baking with the seasons make for a more mindful and vibrant practice, it's also friendlier toward the environment. Made in winter with berries from the southern hemisphere, the **Blackberry Caramel Tart** (page 99) is both less delicious *and* less sustainable. Throughout my baking and cooking career I've tried to lessen the environmental impact of my shopping and kitchen practices, but the intense amount of recipe testing I did for this book made it clear I could do more. While I understand it isn't possible to do all of these things all the time, many of the following suggestions are practical and easy to implement.

Buy locally and consciously whenever possible. Shopping at your local farmers' market can be more expensive than regular grocery stores, but in every other way it's a plus: You support local farmers, you know your food is fresh, and chances are it was grown organically or sustainably. In baking, ingredients are rarely presented fresh and whole, so buy blemished (but otherwise fine) produce wherever you shop to ensure it won't be thrown out. When it comes to buying ingredients that are only grown in tropical climates, such as chocolate, coffee, and vanilla, look for fair trade designations.

Try to reduce food and energy waste. Check if your community has a composting program where you can drop off food scraps (store them in the freezer in between donations), or start composting at home. Plan when you're going to shop for ingredients in advance of cooking and baking so they don't spoil. If you fear an ingredient is about to go bad, either cook it or freeze it to extend its life. Try to recycle all containers and avoid excessive packaging. Bring your own bags to the market and avoid putting each individual produce item in its own plastic bag.

Reduce single-use paper, plastic wrap, parchment paper, and aluminum foil. I call for plastic wrap, aluminum foil, and parchment paper frequently in recipes, but all are typically discarded after one use. Below are strategies I use at home for replacing them with reusable equipment.

- Switch to recycled paper towels and use cloth towels instead of paper whenever possible.

- Use a reusable pastry bag instead of disposable.

- Instead of using parchment paper to line baking sheets, invest in silicone baking mats (I recommend the Silpat brand). They can be pricey but will last forever and prevent sticking 99 percent of the time.

- Instead of using plastic wrap to cover a bowl, try using an inverted plate or variously sized fitted plastic covers (basically shower caps, available online) that can be washed and reused. To cover a baking sheet, place a damp kitchen towel on top, followed by a second sheet pan inverted like a lid. This will create a tight seal and prevent anything on the pan from drying out.

- When you do use aluminum foil or plastic wrap, try to wash and reuse the pieces as many times as possible before discarding.

Loaf Cakes and Single-Layer Cakes

An unfussy, single-layer or loaf cake is my favorite category of dessert. The cakes in this chapter are like a drapey jumpsuit—breezy and elegant, bordering on effortless. These are the types of cakes you could whip up without advance planning if you wanted to, yet they also happen to be dinner party–worthy. Many of them incorporate fresh fruit, another reason why these are my preferred recipes to bake, eat, and serve. For beginning bakers who want to make something simple but impressive—and all the advanced bakers who want the same—these cakes are for you.

MASCARPONE CAKE WITH RED
WINE PRUNES (PAGE 47)

Spiced Honey and Rye Cake

Makes 1 standard loaf

Special Equipment:
4½ × 8½-inch loaf pan, measured from the top

Neutral oil for the pan

1⅓ cups **all-purpose flour** (6.1 oz / 173g)

¼ cup **rye flour** (1.16 oz / 33g) [1]

1½ teaspoons **baking powder** (0.21 oz / 6g)

¾ teaspoon Diamond Crystal **kosher salt**

1 teaspoon **ground cinnamon**

¼ teaspoon **ground allspice**

¼ teaspoon **ground nutmeg** (preferably freshly grated)

⅛ teaspoon **ground cloves**

2 large **eggs** (3.5 oz / 100g), at room temperature

¼ cup **sugar** (1.8 oz / 50g)

2 teaspoons finely grated **lemon zest**

½ cup **honey** (6 oz / 170g), plus more for drizzling on top [2]

½ cup **neutral oil**, such as vegetable or grapeseed (4 oz / 113g)

½ cup unsweetened **applesauce** or **pear sauce** (3.5 oz / 100g)

Rosh Hashanah is the Jewish New Year, a holiday marked in part by the eating of apples dipped in honey to symbolize hope for a sweet year ahead. But I like to think of Rosh Hashanah as the time of year when Jews must endure honey cake, the always dry, universally terrible dessert traditionally consumed around the holiday. Taking inspiration from *pain d'épice*, a French spice bread made with rye flour and honey, I attempted to crack the honey cake code. It required swapping out some honey for granulated sugar, decreasing the proportion of rye flour to all-purpose, and adding applesauce or pear sauce for tenderness, but now I can say that this is a honey cake I'm proud to serve at Rosh Hashanah (or any time of year).

Preheat the oven and prepare the pan: Arrange an oven rack in the center position and preheat the oven to 350°F. Coat the bottom and sides of the loaf pan with oil. Line the bottom and two longer sides with a piece of parchment paper, leaving an overhang of an inch or two on each side, and set the pan aside.

Mix the dry ingredients: In a large bowl, whisk the all-purpose flour, rye flour, baking powder, salt, cinnamon, allspice, nutmeg, and cloves to combine. Set aside.

Mix the wet ingredients: In a separate large bowl, briefly whisk the eggs to break up the yolks and whites, then add the sugar, lemon zest, and ½ cup honey and whisk vigorously until the mixture is smooth and slightly thickened, about 30 seconds. Slowly stream in the ½ cup oil, whisking constantly, until it's incorporated, then whisk in the applesauce.

Mix the wet ingredients into the dry: Make a well in the center of the flour mixture and pour in the wet mixture. Whisk gently just until you have a smooth batter with no dry spots.

Fill the pan and bake: Pour the batter into the prepared loaf pan and bake until the top is risen and cracked and a cake tester or toothpick inserted into the center comes out clean, 50 to 60 minutes. Let the loaf cool in the pan for at least 20 minutes, then use a paring knife or small offset spatula to cut between the cake and the pan along the shorter sides. Use the parchment paper to lift out the loaf and let it cool completely on a wire rack.

Serve: Slice the cooled cake and drizzle with more honey.

DO AHEAD
The cake, well wrapped and stored at room temperature, will keep up to 4 days.

[1] Don't increase the proportion of rye flour to all-purpose, unless you really prefer the earthy, savory flavor of rye. You can, however, substitute spelt, buckwheat, or whole wheat flour for the rye for a slightly different flavor profile.

[2] Use a good-quality honey, the stronger the flavor the better, since much of the complexity of this cake comes from the honey itself. Just don't use buckwheat or chestnut honey, which are overpowering.

Almond Butter Banana Bread

Makes 1 standard loaf

Special Equipment:
4½ × 8½-inch loaf pan, measured from the top

Coconut oil for the pan

3 tablespoons plus ⅓ cup **almond butter** (4.6 oz / 130g) ①

1 tablespoon plus ⅔ cup **sugar** (5 oz / 143g)

1 teaspoon plus ½ cup **virgin coconut oil** (4 oz / 115g), gently warmed to liquefy ②

1⅓ cups **all-purpose flour** ③ (6.1 oz / 173g)

1 teaspoon **baking powder** (0.14 oz / 4g)

1 teaspoon **Diamond Crystal kosher salt** (0.11 oz / 3g)

½ teaspoon **baking soda**

¼ teaspoon **ground cardamom**

2 large **eggs** (3.5 oz / 100g), cold from the refrigerator

1 cup mashed **banana** (8 oz / 227g), from about 2 very ripe large bananas ④

⅓ cup plain whole-milk **Greek yogurt** (2.8 oz / 80g)

1 teaspoon **vanilla extract**

½ cup unsalted **roasted almonds** (optional), coarsely chopped (2.1 oz / 60g)

This straightforward banana bread perfectly illustrates the concept that the simplest things are often the hardest. Even though it only has a few main ingredients—ripe bananas, Greek yogurt, coconut oil, almond butter—I found that even slight variations in proportions produced very different results. It took lots of tweaking to strike the right balance between the elements, but I think this version hits all the notes: tender, moist, and pleasantly sweet but with a *slight* savory edge from the almond butter.

Preheat the oven and prepare the pan: Arrange an oven rack in the center position and preheat the oven to 350°F. Coat the bottom and sides of the loaf pan with coconut oil. Line the bottom and two longer sides with a piece of parchment paper, leaving an overhang of an inch or two on each side, and set the pan aside.

Mix the almond butter swirl: In a small bowl, stir together 3 tablespoons of the almond butter, 1 tablespoon of the sugar, and 1 teaspoon of the coconut oil until smooth. Set the almond butter mixture aside.

Mix the dry ingredients: In a large bowl, whisk together the flour, baking powder, salt, baking soda, and cardamom. Set aside.

Mix the wet ingredients: In a medium bowl, whisk the eggs to break up the yolks and whites. Add the remaining ⅔ cup sugar (4.6 oz / 130g) and whisk vigorously until the mixture is smooth and slightly thickened, about 30 seconds. Add the mashed banana, Greek yogurt, vanilla, remaining ⅓ cup almond butter (2.9 oz / 83g), and ½ cup coconut oil (3.9 oz / 110g) and whisk vigorously until the mixture is smooth (some banana lumps are okay).

Mix the wet ingredients into the dry: Pour the banana mixture into the bowl with the flour mixture and whisk gently just until you have a smooth batter with no dry spots. Add the almonds (if using) and fold the batter with a flexible spatula, scraping the bottom and sides of the bowl to make sure everything is well incorporated.

Fill the pan and make the swirl topping: Scrape the batter into the prepared pan and smooth the top. Dollop teaspoons of the reserved almond butter mixture all across the top of the batter and then use a toothpick or the tip of a paring knife to drag figure eights across the surface, making a swirl pattern.

DO AHEAD
The banana bread, well wrapped and stored at room temperature, will keep up to 4 days.

① Use an all-natural brand of almond butter and thoroughly stir it to incorporate the oil and solids before measuring it out for this recipe.

② Use refined coconut oil if you don't like the taste of coconut and prefer a more neutral flavor in the bread.

Bake and cool: Bake until the top is risen and split and a cake tester or toothpick inserted into the center comes out clean, 60 to 70 minutes. Remove the banana bread from the oven and set aside to cool in the pan for at least 20 minutes, then use a paring knife or small offset spatula to cut between the cake and the pan along the shorter sides. Use the parchment paper to lift out the banana bread and let it cool completely on a wire rack before slicing. ⑤

---

③ You can swap out half of the all-purpose flour for an equal amount of whole wheat flour. The loaf will be slightly denser, but also nuttier and more complex in flavor.

④ The banana bread needs the additional sweetness of truly overripe bananas, so let them sit on your counter for several days until they have lots of blackened spots.

⑤ For a snack, try griddling slices of the banana bread in a pan with more coconut oil, then slather with almond butter and top with flaky salt.

Poppy Seed Almond Cake

Makes 1 Bundt cake

Special Equipment:
Stand or hand mixer, 12-cup
Bundt pan ①

CAKE

Neutral oil and all-purpose flour
for the pan

2⅓ cups granulated sugar (16.4 oz / 465g)

2 tablespoons poppy seeds
(0.6 oz / 17g)

1½ teaspoons baking powder
(0.21 oz / 6g)

1 teaspoon Diamond Crystal kosher salt
(0.11 oz / 3g)

3 cups all-purpose flour
(13.8 oz / 390g)

1½ cups whole milk
(12.7 oz / 360g)

1⅓ cups neutral oil, such as vegetable
or grapeseed (10.2 oz / 288g)

3 large eggs (4.3 oz / 150g)

1½ teaspoons vanilla extract

1½ teaspoons almond extract

GLAZE

¾ cup powdered sugar
(3.2 oz / 90g)

¼ cup orange juice (2 oz / 57g)

2 teaspoons butter, melted

½ teaspoon vanilla extract

½ teaspoon almond extract

This cake is about as close to my heart as a recipe gets. Growing up, I ate this cake probably a thousand times, and it has never not been completely perfect. When she was pregnant with me, my mom got it from a family friend, a woman I only knew as Mrs. Grossman. The flavor of almond extract is prominent, so if you're not a big fan, this isn't the cake for you. The recipe calls for a lot of oil and sugar, which guarantee a tender and moist texture despite the easiest of methods: Put everything into the bowl and mix. I strongly encourage you not to change a thing.

Preheat the oven and prepare the pan: Arrange an oven rack in the center position and preheat the oven to 350°F. Generously brush the inside of the Bundt pan with oil. Dust flour all around the bottom, sides, and up the tube. Tap out the excess and set aside. ②

Combine the sugar and dry ingredients: In the bowl of a stand mixer fitted with the paddle attachment (or in a large bowl if using a hand mixer), mix together the granulated sugar, poppy seeds, baking powder, salt, and flour.

Add the wet ingredients and beat: Add the milk, oil, eggs, and vanilla and almond extracts to the bowl and beat on low just to combine. Increase the speed to medium-high and beat until the batter is very smooth and thick, about 2 minutes. (If using a hand mixer, beat about a minute longer.)

Fill the pan and bake: Scrape the batter into the prepared pan and bake until the top is risen, split, and deep golden brown and a cake tester or toothpick inserted into the deepest part of the cake comes out clean, 80 to 90 minutes. Let the cake cool in the pan for 15 minutes.

Invert the cake and poke holes: Use a butter knife or a small offset spatula to cut down and around the inner and outer edges of the Bundt pan. Invert it onto a wire rack and tap the rack sharply against the counter to release the cake. Remove the pan and poke holes all over the top of the cake with a skewer or toothpick. Set the rack over a rimmed baking sheet (to catch the drips of glaze) and set the cake aside.

Make the glaze and finish the cake: In a medium bowl, whisk the powdered sugar, orange juice, melted butter, and vanilla and almond extracts until smooth. Brush all of the glaze over the top of the cake, allowing it to absorb. Using the brush, collect any glaze that dripped onto the baking sheet and brush back over the cake. Let cool completely.

DO AHEAD
The cake, well wrapped and stored at room temperature, will keep up to 5 days.

① If you don't have a Bundt pan, you can use two standard loaf pans. Oil and line them with parchment paper, then divide

the batter evenly between the two. Bake side by side in the oven until a cake tester comes out clean, 75 to 80 minutes.

② Make sure you thoroughly coat the Bundt pan with oil, working it into every nook and cranny, and then flour to prevent

sticking. If you have an intricately patterned pan, use room temperature butter instead of oil, which will cling to the pan in a thicker layer and act as a better lubricant.

Kabocha Turmeric Tea Cake

Makes 1 standard loaf

Special Equipment:
4½ × 8½-inch loaf pan, measured from the top

Coconut oil for the pan

¼ cup hulled **pumpkin seeds** (1.4 oz / 40g)

1½ cups **all-purpose flour** (7 oz / 200g)

1½ teaspoons **baking powder** (0.21 oz / 6g)

1 teaspoon **ground turmeric**

¾ teaspoon **Diamond Crystal kosher salt**

½ teaspoon **garam masala** [1]

2 large **eggs** (3.5 oz / 100g), at room temperature

2 tablespoons **maple syrup** (1.2 oz / 35g)

1 teaspoon **vanilla extract**

¾ cup plus 2 tablespoons **sugar** (6.2 oz / 175g)

½ cup **virgin coconut oil** (3.9 oz / 110g), warmed slightly to liquefy [2]

1 cup mashed cooked **kabocha squash** (8.2 oz / 232g) [3]

I wanted a version of pumpkin bread that felt a bit more exciting, and kabocha was the answer. Here it's combined with turmeric and a bit of garam masala for an unexpectedly complex loaf cake. To cook the squash, I recommend roasting it whole. Poke a few holes through the leathery exterior and bake on a foil-lined baking sheet in a 425°F oven until a skewer slides easily into the flesh, about 90 minutes for a medium squash.

Preheat the oven and prepare the pan: Arrange an oven rack in the center position and preheat the oven to 350°F. Coat the bottom and sides of the loaf pan with coconut oil. Line the bottom and two longer sides with a piece of parchment paper, leaving an overhang of an inch or two on each side, and set aside.

Toast the pumpkin seeds: Spread the pumpkin seeds out on a small rimmed baking sheet and bake, shaking halfway through, until they're golden, puffed, and starting to pop, 5 to 7 minutes. Set aside to cool.

Mix the dry ingredients: In a large bowl, whisk the flour, baking powder, turmeric, salt, and garam masala. Set aside.

Mix the wet ingredients: In a separate large bowl, whisk the eggs briefly to break up the yolks and whites, then add the maple syrup, vanilla, and ¾ cup of the sugar (5.3 oz / 150g) and whisk vigorously until the mixture is smooth and slightly thickened, about 30 seconds. Slowly stream in the coconut oil, whisking constantly, until fully incorporated. [4] Whisk in the mashed kabocha squash until smooth (a few lumps are okay).

Mix the wet ingredients into the dry: Make a well in the center of the flour mixture and pour in the kabocha mixture. Whisk gently just until you have a smooth batter with no dry spots. Fold in the pumpkin seeds.

Fill the pan and bake: Scrape the batter into the prepared loaf pan and smooth the top. Sprinkle with the remaining 2 tablespoons sugar. Bake until the top is risen and cracked and a cake tester or toothpick inserted into the center comes out clean, 55 to 65 minutes. Let the cake cool in the pan for at least 20 minutes, then use a paring knife or small offset spatula to cut between the cake and the pan along the shorter sides. Use the parchment paper to lift out the loaf and let it cool completely on a wire rack.

DO AHEAD
The cake, well wrapped and stored at room temperature, will keep up to 4 days.

[1] Feel free to omit the garam masala if you can't find it (or if you don't care for the flavor) and use 1½ teaspoons cinnamon as a replacement.

[2] Use refined coconut oil or vegetable oil if you don't like the flavor of coconut.

[3] Substitute an equal amount of canned pumpkin for the kabocha to make this a zero-prep recipe. You can also use mashed roasted sweet potato.

[4] It's okay if the coconut oil solidifies when it hits the eggs and sugar mixture, forming small lumps (this might happen if the eggs are still a bit cold). Any lumps will smooth out in the oven.

Spiced Persimmon Cake

Makes 1 standard loaf

Special Equipment:
Standard or handheld blender; 4½ × 8½-inch loaf pan, measured from the top

Neutral oil and **demerara sugar** for the pan

1 cup **walnut halves** or **pecans** (4 oz / 115g)

2 large ripe **Hachiya persimmons** [1]

1 teaspoon **baking soda** (0.21 oz / 6g)

1¾ cups **all-purpose flour** (8 oz / 228g) [2]

2 teaspoons **Chinese 5-spice powder** [3]

1 teaspoon **Diamond Crystal kosher salt** (0.11 oz / 3g)

½ teaspoon **baking powder**

1 cup **granulated sugar** (7 oz / 200g)

½ cup **neutral oil**, such as vegetable or grapeseed (4 oz / 113g)

2 large **eggs** (3.5 oz / 100g)

1 teaspoon finely grated **orange zest**

¼ cup fresh **orange juice** (2 oz / 57g)

1 teaspoon **vanilla extract**

1 ripe medium **Fuyu persimmon** (optional), cut into about 8 very thin rounds

Demerara sugar, for sprinkling the top

My first introduction to orb-like persimmons was James Beard's persimmon bread, which I made several years ago after reading about the recipe on pastry chef and cookbook author David Lebovitz's website. I was intrigued by the persimmons themselves, which Lebovitz explained had to be left out on the counter until squishy and swollen like a water balloon before using (this is true for the more elongated, slightly tapered Hachiya persimmon; the rounder Fuyu persimmons stay firm when ripe). Beard's recipe sold me on using the jelly-like flesh to add moisture and natural sweetness to a quick bread, as I do here.

Preheat the oven and prepare the pan: Arrange an oven rack in the center position and preheat the oven to 350°F. Coat the bottom and sides of the loaf pan with oil. Line the bottom and two longer sides with a piece of parchment paper, leaving an overhang of an inch or two on each side. Oil the parchment paper, then sprinkle demerara sugar inside the pan, shaking it to coat the bottom and sides, and set the pan aside.

Toast the nuts: Place the walnuts on a rimmed baking sheet and toast, shaking halfway through, until the nuts are deeply browned and very fragrant, 7 to 9 minutes. Once they are cool, coarsely chop and set aside.

Make the persimmon puree: Cut the Hachiya persimmons in half through the stem and slice out the whitish core. Scoop out the translucent orange interior with a spoon (see photograph on page 46). Transfer it to a blender (or use a handheld blender) and puree until completely smooth. Measure out 1 cup of puree (9 oz / 256g) and transfer to a medium bowl. Thoroughly whisk the baking soda into the persimmon, then set aside for several minutes while you prepare the batter (as it sits, the baking soda will aerate and then "set" the puree into a solid).

Mix the dry ingredients: In a large bowl, whisk the flour, 5-spice powder, salt, and baking powder to combine. Set aside.

Mix the wet ingredients: Once the persimmon mixture has solidified, whisk in the granulated sugar, oil, eggs, orange zest, orange juice, and vanilla until thoroughly combined (there will be bits of persimmon floating around, which is okay; it'll all smooth out in the oven). (continues)

DO AHEAD
The cake, well wrapped and stored at room temperature, will keep up to 4 days.

[1] Unripe Hachiya persimmons are unpleasantly astringent, so pick ones that are shiny and heavy for their size, and let them sit on your counter until they feel very soft and jelly-filled and look slightly translucent, which can take up to 1 week.

[2] Swap ¾ cup (3.7 oz / 105g) whole wheat flour for the same amount of all-purpose for a slightly more wholesome loaf. Increase the bake time 10 to 20 minutes, until a tester comes out clean.

[3] If you can't find Chinese 5-spice powder, you can substitute the following blend of warm spices instead: 1 teaspoon ground cinnamon, ¾ teaspoon ground ginger, and ¼ teaspoon ground cloves.

Mix the wet ingredients into the dry: Make a well in the center of the flour mixture, then add the persimmon mixture to the dry ingredients. Whisking from the center of the bowl outward, incorporate the dry ingredients into the wet just until you have an evenly mixed batter with no dry spots. Add the walnuts and fold the batter several times with a flexible spatula to incorporate.

Fill the pan and bake: Scrape the batter into the prepared pan and smooth the top. Arrange the slices of Fuyu persimmon (if using) over the top of the batter, then sprinkle with demerara sugar. Bake until the cake has risen, the top is firm to the touch, and a cake tester or toothpick inserted into the center comes out clean, 60 to 75 minutes. Let cool in the pan for at least 20 minutes, then use a paring knife or small offset spatula to cut in between the cake and pan along the shorter sides to loosen and use the parchment to lift out the cake. Place on a wire rack and let cool completely before slicing.

Mascarpone Cake
with Red Wine Prunes

Serves 8

Special Equipment:
9-inch cake pan

RED WINE PRUNES

8 ounces (227g) pitted **prunes** (about 30 small or 15 large)

1½ cups **light red wine** (12 oz / 355g), such as gamay or pinot noir

¼ cup **sugar** (1.8 oz / 50g)

Pinch of **kosher salt**

2 (3-inch) **cinnamon sticks** or ½ teaspoon **ground cinnamon** [1]

1 whole **star anise** (optional)

MASCARPONE CAKE

Butter for the pan

1 cup **all-purpose flour** (4.6 oz / 130g)

¾ teaspoon **baking powder**

¾ teaspoon **Diamond Crystal kosher salt**

1 large **egg** (1.8 oz / 50g), at room temperature

2 large **egg yolks** (1.1 oz / 32g), at room temperature

1 cup **sugar** (7 oz / 200g)

½ cup **mascarpone** (4 oz / 113g), at room temperature, plus more for serving

4 tablespoons **unsalted butter** (2 oz / 57g), melted and cooled

2 teaspoons **vanilla extract**

2 teaspoons finely grated **lemon** or **orange zest**

This recipe has two major sources of inspiration: The first is the red wine prunes and mascarpone dessert at Frankies Spuntino in Brooklyn. It's a fantastically simple, delicious dessert—prunes cooked until soft and plump in a reduced red wine syrup, served over tangy mascarpone. The second is Marian Burros's famous plum torte, featuring fresh Italian plums baked into a simple butter cake. As a prune lover, I wanted the flavors of the Frankies dessert with the ease of Burros's cake, and so this mascarpone cake with red wine prunes was born. It might be the perfect dessert: delicious, elegant enough to bring to a dinner party, and so easy all you need are two mixing bowls to put it together.

Make the red wine prunes: In a small saucepan, combine the prunes, red wine, sugar, salt, cinnamon, star anise (if using), and ½ cup (4 oz / 113g) water. Bring to a simmer over medium heat, stirring to dissolve the sugar. Reduce the heat to a gentle simmer and cook, swirling the pan occasionally, until the prunes are very soft but not falling apart and the wine is reduced to a thick syrup, 40 to 50 minutes (you should have about ¼ cup syrup). Remove the saucepan from the heat and transfer the prunes and red wine syrup to a small heatproof bowl. Set aside to cool completely.

Preheat the oven and prepare the pan: Arrange an oven rack in the center position and preheat the oven to 350°F. Butter the bottom and sides of the cake pan, then line the bottom with a round of parchment paper. Butter the parchment and set the pan aside.

Mix the dry ingredients: In a medium bowl, whisk the flour, baking powder, and salt to combine. Set aside.

Mix the wet ingredients: In another medium bowl, whisk the whole egg, yolks, and sugar until the mixture is thick and pale, about 1 minute. Whisk in the mascarpone, melted butter, vanilla, and lemon zest until the mixture is smooth.

Mix the wet ingredients into the dry: Scrape the mascarpone mixture into the bowl with the flour mixture and whisk just until the batter is smooth. (continues)

DO AHEAD
The prune mixture can be made 4 days ahead. Let cool completely, then cover and refrigerate. The cake, well wrapped and stored at room temperature, will keep up to 2 days.

[1] Use any warm spices besides cinnamon and star anise in the prune mixture, such as cloves or cardamom (think mulled wine!).

Fill the pan and top with the prunes: Scrape the batter into the prepared pan and smooth it into an even layer (it will seem thin, but that's fine). Use a spoon to lift the prunes out of the syrup one at a time, letting any excess syrup drip back into the bowl, and dot them across the batter (if your prunes are large, cut them in half before arranging them over the batter). [2] Reserve the wine syrup for serving.

Bake: Bake the cake until the top is golden brown, firm to the touch, and a cake tester or toothpick inserted into the center comes out wet but mostly clean, 45 to 60 minutes. Tent the surface with a piece of foil if the prunes seem to be getting very dark toward the end of baking.

Cool the cake and serve: Let the cake cool completely in the pan. Cut around the sides with a small offset spatula or paring knife, then invert it onto a wire rack. Peel off the parchment, then invert again onto a serving plate. Slice and serve with a dollop of mascarpone. Drizzle the red wine syrup over the top.

[2] Try not to drizzle any of the red wine syrup over the batter when arranging the prunes if you can help it. The syrup has a tendency to burn before the cake is finished baking.

Pear Chestnut Cake

Serves 10

Special Equipment:
10-inch ovenproof skillet or 10-inch springform pan, ① stand mixer

Butter and **sugar** for the skillet or pan

3 firm-ripe **pears**, such as Bartlett or Comice (about 6 oz / 170g each)

1⅓ cups **all-purpose flour** (6.1 oz / 173g)

2 teaspoons **baking powder** (0.28 oz / 8g)

¼ teaspoon **baking soda**

10.4 ounces (300g) shelled whole **roasted chestnuts** (about 2 scant cups), from a bag or jar ②

2 teaspoons **vanilla extract**

1 teaspoon **Diamond Crystal kosher salt** (0.11 oz / 3g)

¾ cup plus 2 tablespoons **sugar** (6.2 oz / 175g)

10 tablespoons **unsalted butter** (5 oz / 142g), at room temperature

2 large **eggs** (3.5 oz / 100g), at room temperature

½ cup **crème fraîche** (4.2 oz / 120g), at room temperature, plus more for serving

2 tablespoons **fruit brandy** (preferably pear) or **dark rum** (1 oz / 28g)

My recipe development process typically starts with an ingredient or a flavor combination that sparks an idea. I loved the thought of pairing chestnuts and pears, both being somewhat mild and delicate in flavor. It's very gratifying when, after much trial and error, the reality of the recipe matches the hope. This cake employs the power of a stand mixer to work cooked, peeled chestnuts (the kind out of a bag or jar) into a coarse paste that adds texture as well as a subtle, earthy flavor to the batter. It's exactly what I envisioned, and exactly the kind of easy cake I want to make and eat come fall.

Preheat the oven and prepare the pan: Arrange an oven rack in the center position and preheat the oven to 350°F. Generously butter the bottom and sides of the ovenproof skillet or springform pan. Dust sugar all around the bottom and sides, then tap out the excess. Set aside.

Prepare the pears: Core and coarsely chop 1 pear and set it aside (you will fold this into the batter; you can peel the pear if you want, but it's not necessary). Core the remaining 2 pears and slice them very thinly lengthwise (these are for the top of the cake). Set aside.

Mix the dry ingredients: In a medium bowl, whisk the flour, baking powder, and baking soda to combine. Set aside.

Break down the chestnuts: In a stand mixer fitted with the paddle attachment, combine the chestnuts, vanilla, salt, and ¾ cup of the sugar (5.3 oz / 150g) and beat on low speed until the chestnuts are broken up into smaller pieces. Increase the speed to medium and continue to beat until the chestnuts and sugar have formed a coarse paste with some small bits of chestnuts throughout, about 2 minutes.

Cream the butter and chestnut mixture: Scrape down the sides of the bowl, add the butter, and beat on medium-high until the mixture is very light and fluffy, about 4 minutes.

Add the eggs: Add the eggs one at a time, beating well and scraping down the sides after each addition, until the mixture is light and smooth.
(continues)

DO AHEAD
The cake, well wrapped and stored at room temperature, will keep up to 4 days, but is best served on the first or second day.

① Make sure that the pan or skillet you're using has at least 2-inch-high sides to prevent overflow, as this recipe makes a lot of batter that bakes into a tall cake.

② Roasting and peeling your own chestnuts is a huge pain! The ones that come already cooked and peeled in a bag or jar save you lots of work and are soft enough that they'll blend into a batter.

Add the wet and dry ingredients: Reduce the mixer speed to low and slowly add half of the flour mixture. When you see the last trail of flour disappear into the batter, add the crème fraîche and mix just until incorporated. Add the remaining flour mixture, followed by the brandy, and continue to mix just until the batter is smooth and evenly combined.

Fold in the pear and fill the pan: Use a flexible spatula to fold the batter a few times, scraping the sides to incorporate any unmixed batter, then add the chopped pear and fold just until distributed throughout (gently, to avoid crushing the fruit). Scrape the batter into the prepared skillet or pan and smooth the top.

Arrange the fruit and bake: Working with 5 or 6 slices of pear at a time, fan out the slices and place on top of the batter in any arrangement, overlapping them slightly. Sprinkle the remaining 2 tablespoons sugar over the pears. Bake until the cake is golden brown around the edges, golden in patches between pear slices, the center is springy to the touch, and a cake tester inserted into the center comes out clean, 50 to 60 minutes. Let cool completely in the pan.

Serve: If you baked the cake in a springform pan, cut around the sides with a paring knife and carefully remove the outer ring. Serve slices of cake topped with more crème fraîche. ③

---

③ Beware of bits of chestnut that don't break down completely and harden in the baked cake. You certainly won't break a tooth, just know there might be a piece here or there depending on the softness of the chestnuts you're using.

Double-Apple Crumble Cake

Serves 10 to 12

Special Equipment:
9-inch springform pan ①

3 tablespoons **unsalted butter**
(1.5 oz / 43g)

4 medium **Pink Lady apples** (about
1¾ lb / 794g), peeled, halved, cored, and
cut into ¼-inch-thick slices ②

Butter for the pan

2 cups **all-purpose flour** (9.2 oz / 260g)

1½ teaspoons **ground cinnamon**

1½ teaspoons **baking powder**
(0.21 oz / 6g)

½ teaspoon **baking soda**

½ teaspoon **Diamond Crystal kosher salt**

1 cup **apple butter** (7.8 oz / 220g) ③

1 cup **sugar** (7 oz / 200g)

½ cup **crème fraîche** or **sour cream**
(4.2 oz / 120g)

¼ cup **neutral oil**, such as vegetable or
grapeseed (2 oz / 57g)

2 large **eggs** (3.5 oz / 100g)

2 teaspoons **vanilla extract**

All-Purpose Crumble Topping (page 319)

This double-apple crumble cake is so-called because it combines fresh apples and apple butter. The full cup of apple butter in the easy, stir-together batter means the cake bakes up extremely tender with a concentrated apple flavor. Even though it's an extra step, I sauté the fresh apples in a skillet before adding them to the batter to ensure they come out fully cooked. This precooking also helps eliminate some of the moisture in the fruit, which, given that there are four whole apples inside the cake, could otherwise make the interior wet and unappealing. This is the kind of cake I love: loaded with fruit, topped with a sweet, crunchy top, and oil-based so it never dries out.

Precook the apples: In a medium skillet, heat the 3 tablespoons butter over medium heat. When the butter starts to foam, add the apples and cook, tossing often, just until the slices have begun to soften and turn slightly translucent, 10 to 15 minutes (it's okay if some of them start to brown, which could happen if you're using drier, cold-storage apples). Remove the skillet from the heat and set aside to cool.

Preheat the oven and prepare the pan: Meanwhile, arrange an oven rack in the center position and preheat the oven to 350°F. Lightly coat the bottom and sides of the springform pan with room temperature butter, then line the bottom with a round of parchment paper, smoothing to eliminate air bubbles. Set the pan aside.

Mix the dry ingredients: In a large bowl, whisk the flour, cinnamon, baking powder, baking soda, and salt to combine. Set aside.

Mix the wet ingredients: In a medium bowl, whisk the apple butter, sugar, crème fraîche, oil, eggs, and vanilla until smooth.

Mix the wet ingredients into the dry: Make a well in the center of the flour mixture and pour in the apple butter mixture. Whisking from the center of the bowl outward, incorporate the dry ingredients into the wet just until you have an evenly mixed batter. (continues)

DO AHEAD
The cake, well wrapped and stored at room temperature, will keep up to 4 days.

① Use a 10-inch springform pan if you don't have a 9-inch. The cake will be slightly thinner, so start checking it for doneness after about 1 hour 15 minutes.

② Use whatever variety of apple you prefer, just as long as it's very firm and has some natural tartness. Try to avoid older apples that have been in cold storage for a long time and have a tendency to turn mealy when baked. To test an apple for freshness, press the tip of your thumb

firmly into the skin. If you can't make an indentation easily, it's a good apple.

③ Don't use an apple butter with added sugar or spices. Try to find one that lists apples as the sole ingredient.

Fold in the apples: Using a large flexible spatula, fold the cooled apples into the batter, leaving any liquid behind in the skillet and mixing thoroughly to distribute the apples evenly.

Fill the pan and top with the crumble: Scrape the batter into the prepared pan and smooth the top. Sprinkle the crumble topping evenly over the batter, breaking up any pieces larger than a marble.

Bake and cool: Bake until the crumble is browned and a cake tester or toothpick inserted into the center of the cake slides easily through the apple slices and comes out clean, 1 hour 20 minutes to 1 hour 30 minutes. Transfer to a wire rack and let cool completely.

Serve: Cut around the cake with a paring knife, then remove the ring. Use a serrated knife to cut the cake into slices.

Rhubarb Cake

Makes 1 standard loaf

Special Equipment:
4½ × 8½-inch loaf pan, measured from the top

1 pound (454g) **rhubarb stalks** [1]

½ teaspoon **baking soda**

Butter and **demerara sugar** for the pan

1¾ cups **all-purpose flour** (8 oz / 228g) [2]

2½ teaspoons **baking powder** (0.35 oz / 10g)

¾ teaspoon **Diamond Crystal kosher salt**

1¼ cups **granulated sugar** [3] (8.8 oz / 250g)

1 stick **unsalted butter** (4 oz / 113g), melted and cooled

2 large **eggs** (3.5 oz / 100g)

1½ teaspoons finely grated **orange zest**

⅓ cup plain whole-milk **Greek yogurt** (2.8 oz / 80g)

1 teaspoon **vanilla extract**

Demerara sugar, for sprinkling the top

I am a rhubarb person, but I know some people find it overrated. I imagine—and I'm speculating here—that rhubarb haters see it only as a harbinger of spring and not as an objectively tasty produce item. I couldn't disagree more, and in fact I love the puckeringly tart and subtly vegetal flavor that the long, shiny, ruby-red stalks bring to sweets. Whereas so many desserts just feature rhubarb on top for decoration, this recipe incorporates a half pound cooked down into mush and folded into the batter, plus more on top, giving it the flavor of rhubarb throughout—perfect for all my rhubarb people out there.

Preheat the oven and prepare the pan: Arrange an oven rack in the center position and preheat the oven to 350°F. Coat the bottom and sides of the loaf pan with butter. Line the bottom and two longer sides with a piece of parchment paper, leaving an overhang of several inches on each side. Butter the parchment paper, then sprinkle demerara sugar inside the pan, shaking it to coat the bottom and sides, and set the pan aside.

Prepare the rhubarb: Select the nicest, thinnest stalks of rhubarb and trim them to lengths of about 8½ inches until you have 4 or 5 pieces that length. If only some or none of the stalks are very thin, split 1 or 2 stalks lengthwise. Weigh the pieces: You should have about 4 ounces (113g)—remove or add accordingly! Set the trimmed stalks aside.

Make the rhubarb mush: Chop all of the remaining rhubarb into ½-inch pieces. Transfer two-thirds (8 oz / 227g) to a small saucepan and set the remaining one-third (4 oz / 113g) aside to fold into the batter later. Add 1 tablespoon water to the saucepan and cook the chopped rhubarb over medium heat, stirring often and mashing with the back of a wooden spoon, until the pieces have completely broken down into a smooth mixture that resembles applesauce, 5 to 7 minutes. Remove from the heat and set aside to cool completely (you should have about ⅔ cup [5.8 oz / 165g]).

Once the rhubarb mixture is cool, thoroughly stir the baking soda into the rhubarb (it will foam and turn a grayish tinge, which is normal). This will neutralize some of the acid and help the cake rise more predictably. Set the mixture aside.

DO AHEAD
The cake, well wrapped and stored at room temperature, will keep up to 5 days.

[1] Try to pick rhubarb stalks that are very firm and stiff (not flabby), dark red, and blemish-free. I like the more tender and flavorful thin stalks, but any size or color will work great.

[2] Stick with all-purpose flour in this recipe. Swapping in a whole-grain or whole wheat flour will make the loaf too dense.

Mix the dry ingredients: In a medium bowl, whisk the flour, baking powder, and salt to combine. Set aside.

Mix the wet ingredients: In a large bowl, vigorously whisk the granulated sugar, melted butter, eggs, and orange zest until the mixture is thick and light, about 1 minute. Whisk in the yogurt, vanilla, and rhubarb mush until smooth.

Mix the wet ingredients into the dry: Scrape the rhubarb mixture into the bowl with the flour mixture and whisk just until the dry ingredients disappear and the batter is evenly mixed. Switch to a flexible spatula and fold the reserved 4 ounces (113g) chopped rhubarb into the batter.

Fill the pan and bake: Scrape the batter into the prepared pan and smooth the top. Arrange the reserved rhubarb stalks over the top of the batter in parallel lines. Sprinkle the top generously with demerara sugar and bake, reducing the oven temperature to 325°F after 60 minutes, until the top is golden and crisp and a cake tester inserted into the center comes out clean, 80 to 90 minutes total. ④ Tent the top of the cake with a piece of foil if it starts to darken beyond a deep golden brown.

Cool and unmold the cake: Let the cake cool in the pan for 20 minutes. Cut along the short sides of the pan to release the cake and use the parchment to lift the cake from the pan. Let cool completely on a wire rack.

---

③ Don't be alarmed by the amount of sugar in this recipe. It's needed to balance out the tartness of the rhubarb; the final flavor of the cake is not overly sweet.

④ Err on the side of baking the loaf more rather than less. It's an extremely moist cake, and underbaking it even slightly could cause it to fall a bit as it cools (though it will still taste great).

Rice Pudding Cake
with Mango Caramel

Serves 10

Special Equipment:
Standard or handheld blender,
10-inch cake pan ①

MANGO CARAMEL SAUCE

1 cup **sugar** (7 oz / 200g)

1½ cups coarsely chopped fresh
mango (8 oz / 227g), from about
1 large mango ②

½ cup **heavy cream** (4.2 oz / 120g)

4 tablespoons **unsalted butter**
(2 oz / 57g), cut into ½-inch pieces

½ teaspoon **Diamond Crystal kosher salt**

RICE PUDDING CAKE AND ASSEMBLY

1 cup **Arborio** or **Carnaroli rice**
(7.1 oz / 200g)

3 cups **whole milk** (25.4 oz / 720g)

1 (12 oz / 340g) can **evaporated milk**

1 teaspoon **Diamond Crystal kosher salt**
(0.11 oz / 3g)

¾ cup **sugar** (5.3 oz / 150g)

¼ cup **dark rum** (2 oz / 57g)

½ teaspoon **ground cardamom**

Seeds scraped from 1 **vanilla bean**,
plus the pod

4 tablespoons **unsalted butter**
(2 oz / 57g), cut into ½-inch pieces, chilled

Butter for the pan

2 large **eggs** (3.5 oz / 100g)

3 large **egg yolks** (1.8 oz / 50g)

1 large **mango**, peeled and thinly sliced,
for serving

I love milky, lactose-rich desserts, which is why I find rice pudding irresistible. Think of this cake as rice pudding in sliceable form. Unlike "baked rice pudding" recipes where you cook the rice in the oven until thickened but still pudding-like, here you fully cook it on the stovetop, then beat in a couple of eggs and bake the mixture so it sets into a firm custard. I serve it with a mango caramel sauce and more fresh sliced mango on top, playing up the tropical hints of rum and vanilla already in the cake. It's a rich, comforting, fruity dessert that also happens to be gluten-free!

Make the mango caramel sauce: In a small saucepan, combine the sugar and ⅓ cup water (2.6 oz / 75g). Place the saucepan over medium heat and stir with a heatproof spatula to dissolve the sugar. Stop stirring when the mixture comes to a boil and cook, brushing down the sides of the pan with a wet pastry brush to dissolve any crystals and swirling the pan often, until the mixture turns a deep amber color, 7 to 10 minutes. Immediately remove the pan from the heat and carefully add the chopped mango. Return the saucepan to medium-low heat and cook, stirring occasionally, until the mango starts to release some liquid, about 5 minutes. Carefully add the heavy cream in a slow, steady stream, stirring constantly (the mixture may sputter), then stir in the butter a piece at a time until the mixture is smooth. Stir in the salt, then adjust the heat to a gentle simmer. Cook, stirring occasionally, until the caramel is slightly thickened, 5 to 10 minutes longer.

Blend and reserve the caramel: Remove the caramel mixture from the heat and let it cool slightly. Use a standard or handheld blender to blend until the sauce is completely smooth (you should have about 2 cups, but if you have less, stir in some more heavy cream). Set the caramel aside.

Cook the rice pudding mixture: In a medium saucepan, combine the rice, whole milk, evaporated milk, salt, sugar, rum, and cardamom. Add the vanilla seeds and throw in the pod, too. Bring it all to a simmer over medium heat, stirring often to dissolve the sugar and to (continues)

DO AHEAD
The caramel sauce, stored airtight in the refrigerator, will keep up to 1 week. The caramel will harden when cold; rewarm it in a small saucepan or microwave to liquefy. The rice pudding mixture can be cooked on the stovetop up to 2 days ahead. After stirring in the butter, cover and refrigerate. Bring the mixture to room temperature before adding the eggs and baking. The baked cake, covered and refrigerated, will keep up to 3 days but is best served on the first or second day.

① Use a 9-inch pan if you don't have a 10-inch pan, just note the cake layer will be thicker and might take several minutes longer to bake.

prevent the rice from sticking to the bottom. Reduce the heat to maintain a gentle simmer and continue to cook, stirring often, until the rice is translucent and tender and the liquid is thickened, 25 to 30 minutes. You'll know the rice is done when, rather than settling to the bottom of the pan, the individual grains float about suspended in the liquid. ③

Add the butter and cool: Remove the saucepan from the heat and stir in the 4 tablespoons butter, a few pieces at a time, until they have melted and incorporated into the liquid. Let the rice pudding mixture sit until it's warm but not hot, stirring occasionally to encourage cooling and to reincorporate any skin that forms on the surface (you can stir the pan over an ice bath to speed up this process).

Preheat the oven and prepare the pan: Arrange an oven rack in the center position and preheat the oven to 350°F. Butter the bottom and sides of the cake pan. Line the bottom with a round of parchment paper, then butter the parchment paper. Set the pan aside.

Beat and add the eggs: In a small bowl, beat the whole eggs and yolks until no streaks remain, then stir into the warm rice pudding mixture until thoroughly combined.

Bake and cool: Pour the entire mixture into the prepared cake pan (feel free to leave in the vanilla pod, which will continue to release flavor in the oven). Bake until the surface is lightly browned in spots and a cake tester or toothpick inserted into the center comes out clean, 40 to 50 minutes. Remove the cake from the oven and let it cool completely on a wire rack.

Serve: Cut around the sides of the pan with a small offset spatula or paring knife. Invert the cake onto a wire rack, peel off the parchment paper, then reinvert onto a serving plate. Rewarm the caramel sauce if necessary. Cut the cake into slices (remove the vanilla pod if you haven't) and serve with a drizzle of caramel and fresh sliced mango.

---

② You can use an equal weight of a fruit other than mango—like berries or banana—if you want to take this into another season or in a different flavor direction. If the fruit has seeds, like blackberries, you might want to strain the caramel after blending.

③ You want the rice to be fully cooked, since al dente rice will sink to the bottom of the custard rather than bake evenly throughout the cake. Make sure the grains are swollen and translucent before removing from the heat. Give it a taste to make sure!

Ricotta Cake
with Kumquat Marmalade

Serves 8

Special Equipment:
9-inch springform pan, food processor, hand or stand mixer

CAKE

Butter for the pan

2 cups fresh **whole-milk ricotta cheese** (16 oz / 452g) [1]

1 cup **heavy cream** (8.2 oz / 232g), chilled

4 large **eggs** (7 oz / 200g), separated

1 large **egg yolk** (0.6 oz / 16g)

1 tablespoon finely grated **lemon zest**

2 teaspoons **vanilla extract**

½ teaspoon plus a pinch of **Diamond Crystal kosher salt**

1 cup plus 1 tablespoon **sugar** (7.5 oz / 213g)

1 cup **all-purpose flour** (4.6 oz / 130g)

MARMALADE [2]

8 ounces (227g) **kumquats**, halved crosswise and seeded, sliced again crosswise if large

1 tablespoon fresh **lemon juice** (0.5 oz / 14g)

½ cup **sugar** (3.5 oz / 100g)

Seeds scraped from ½ **vanilla bean** or 1 teaspoon **vanilla extract**

This ricotta cake bakes into a texture that's hard to describe: eggy and creamy like a custard, but still light and cakey. It's extremely delicious on its own, but makes a wonderful canvas for any fruit preparation. I like making it in winter and pairing with a citrus component like this kumquat marmalade. The recipe *might* seem a bit fussy at first glance because it involves both a food processor and a hand or stand mixer, but there's very little other equipment needed—just a bowl and a spatula—and it comes together quickly.

Preheat the oven and prepare the pan: Arrange an oven rack in the center position and preheat the oven to 375°F. Butter the bottom (not the sides) of a 9-inch springform pan and line it with a round of parchment paper. Butter just the parchment paper and set the pan aside. [3]

Whip the ricotta and cream: In a food processor, combine the ricotta and heavy cream and process until the mixture is very thick, whipped, and completely silky smooth, about 1 minute.

Add the remaining wet ingredients: Add the 5 egg yolks, the lemon zest, vanilla, ½ teaspoon of the salt, and 1 cup of the sugar (7 oz / 200g) to the ricotta mixture. Pulse the food processor, scraping down the bowl once, until all of the ingredients are well combined and the mixture is smooth and fluid.

Add the flour: Add the flour and pulse just to combine. Transfer the ricotta mixture to a large bowl and set aside.

Whip the egg whites: In a stand mixer fitted with the whisk attachment (or in a large bowl if using a hand mixer), beat the egg whites and the pinch of salt on medium-low just to break them up. Increase the speed to medium-high and beat until the whites form soft peaks. Gradually sprinkle in the remaining 1 tablespoon sugar and continue to beat on high until the whites are shiny, quadrupled in volume, and hold a firm peak off the end of the beater, about 2 minutes. [4] (continues)

DO AHEAD
The cake, covered and refrigerated, will keep up to 4 days but is best served on the first or second day. Let it come to room temperature and top with the marmalade before serving. The marmalade, covered and refrigerated, will keep up to 2 weeks.

[1] Because the flavor of the cake is subtle, this recipe needs all the richness of full-fat ricotta, so don't try to substitute part-skim or other low-fat dairy. No need to drain the ricotta either—this recipe was designed to work using it straight out of the container.

[2] Skip the kumquat marmalade and use any seasonal fruit you like, such as fresh macerated berries in the summer, poached rhubarb in the spring (see **Strawberry-Rhubarb Pavlovas with Rose**, page 187), or poached quince in the fall (see **Quince and Almond Tart with Rosé**, page 115).

Fold in the egg whites: Scrape the egg whites into the bowl with the ricotta mixture and use a large flexible spatula to gently fold the mixture until no streaks remain.

Fill the pan and bake: Scrape the batter into the prepared pan and smooth the top. Bake until the edges are deeply browned and the center is risen, cracked, and golden brown and a cake tester or toothpick inserted into the center comes out clean, 40 to 45 minutes (it will still wobble quite a bit when done). Transfer the pan to a cooling rack. The cake will fall and crater immediately, which is normal. Let the cake cool completely in the pan.

Make the marmalade: While the cake is cooling, in a small saucepan, combine the kumquats, lemon juice, sugar, vanilla seeds, and 2 tablespoons water and bring to a boil over medium-low heat. Adjust the heat to maintain a gentle simmer and continue to cook, stirring often and skimming off any white foam that accumulates on the surface, until the liquid has thickened to the consistency of maple syrup and the kumquats are softened and mostly translucent, 15 to 20 minutes. Set aside and let the marmalade cool completely.

Serve: Use a small offset spatula or paring knife to cut around the sides of the pan to release the cake and remove the metal ring. Spread the cooled marmalade over the top of the ricotta cake (or serve alongside).

[3] Greasing the sides of the pan encourages the cake to form a "waist," meaning a sunken ring around the sides, as it falls, so it's best avoided. (If yours does get a waist, it's a cosmetic issue only. It will still taste delicious.)

[4] Try not to overbeat the whites to the point where they have lost their shine and have taken on a matte look and grainy texture. This will make it very difficult to incorporate them into the batter. If you're not sure, it's best to undershoot the mark slightly.

Blood Orange and Olive Oil Upside-Down Cake

Serves 8 to 10

Special Equipment:
10-inch springform pan, stand or hand mixer

Extra-virgin olive oil for the pan

4 medium **blood oranges** (about 1½ lb / 680g) ②

1⅓ cups **sugar** (9.3 oz / 263g)

1⅓ cups **cake flour** (5.5 oz / 156g)

½ cup **semolina flour** (2.8 oz / 82g)

2 teaspoons **baking powder** (0.28 oz / 8g)

½ teaspoon **Diamond Crystal kosher salt**

3 tablespoons **Grand Marnier** (1.5 oz / 43g)

1 tablespoon finely grated **orange zest**

1 teaspoon **orange blossom water** or **vanilla extract**

3 large **eggs** (5.3 oz / 150g)

1¼ cups **extra-virgin olive oil** (9.9 oz / 280g)

Plain **whole-milk yogurt**, lightly sweetened, for serving

You may have seen a blood orange upside-down olive oil cake before, and for good reason—they're so pretty, and the bitterness of blood orange marries well with olive oil. This is my version, spiked with a little orange blossom water and Grand Marnier for extra orange flavor, and semolina for texture. If you can't find blood oranges or you want something more neutral, you can skip the "upside-down" part, as this recipe makes an excellent olive oil cake on its own ①. Even though I like serving this with a little sweetened yogurt alongside, the cake itself is completely dairy-free. This allows you to safely "age" it on your counter, well wrapped, for several days since olive oil-based cakes improve in taste and texture the longer they sit.

Preheat the oven and prepare the pan: Arrange an oven rack in the center position and preheat the oven to 400°F. Coat the bottom and sides of the springform pan with oil. Line the bottom of the pan with a round of parchment paper and smooth it to eliminate air bubbles. Coat the parchment with more oil and set the pan aside.

Prepare the blood oranges: Position a blood orange on the cutting board so the "poles" are to your left and right and the fruit is resting on its side rather than upright. Use a sharp knife to cut off one of the poles, exposing a colorful round of fruit. Then slice the fruit as thinly as possible through the widest part, shaving off rounds that are no thicker than ⅛ inch. ③ Reserve the ends for squeezing juice. Remove and discard any seeds from the slices and repeat until all the oranges are sliced (you should have 25 to 30 slices total). Squeeze the reserved ends of the blood oranges into a medium bowl until you have 2 tablespoons of juice (save any remaining fruit for juicing or another use).

Build the upside-down layer in the pan: Add ⅓ cup of the sugar (2.3 oz / 66g) to the bowl with the juice and whisk until you have a smooth slurry. Pour the slurry into the bottom of the prepared pan and tilt in all directions to spread across the parchment. Arrange the orange slices in an overlapping pattern across the bottom of the pan (see photographs on page 68) and set aside. (continues)

DO AHEAD
The cake, well wrapped and stored at room temperature, will keep up to 5 days but is best served on the second or third days.

① To make a plain olive oil cake, skip the blood orange layer and just remember to omit the ⅓ cup of sugar that would have lined the bottom of the pan with the blood orange juice, only adding 1 cup to the cake itself. Otherwise, prepare the springform pan in the same way and proceed as written. Right before baking, I recommend sprinkling the top of the batter with more sugar for a sweet crunch. Let the cake cool completely in the pan and then carefully remove the metal ring.

Mix the dry ingredients: In a medium bowl, whisk the cake flour, semolina, baking powder, and salt to combine and eliminate any lumps.

Mix the wet ingredients: In a small bowl, stir together the Grand Marnier, orange zest, and orange blossom water and set aside.

Beat the eggs and sugar: In a stand mixer fitted with the whisk attachment (or in a large bowl if using a hand mixer), beat the eggs and the remaining 1 cup sugar (7 oz / 200g), starting on low to break up the eggs and gradually increasing to high, until the mixture is very light, thick, and pale, and it falls off the whisk or beaters back into the bowl in a slowly dissolving ribbon, about 5 minutes (with a hand mixer, this will take several minutes longer). See page 23 for a visual of ribbony eggs.

Beat in the oil: With the mixer still on high speed, gradually stream in the oil and beat until fully incorporated and the mixture is even thicker (it will be slightly reduced in volume). ④

Alternate adding wet ingredients and dry: Reduce the mixer speed to low and add the flour mixture in 3 additions, alternating with the Grand Marnier mixture in 2 additions, beginning and ending with the dry ingredients. After the final addition of flour, stop the mixer and use a large flexible spatula to fold the batter several times, scraping the bottom and sides of the bowl to make sure it's evenly mixed.

Fill the pan and bake: Gently pour the batter over the blood orange slices, making sure not to disturb them, and smooth the top. Transfer the cake to the oven and immediately reduce the temperature to 350°F. Bake until the top is golden brown, the center is firm to the touch, and a cake tester or toothpick inserted into the center comes out clean, 35 to 45 minutes.

Cool and unmold the cake: Transfer the pan to a wire rack and let the cake cool for 15 minutes. Run a thin knife around the edges of the cake and remove the outer ring (be careful, as some of the juices from the cake might run). Invert the cake onto a wire rack and remove the circular base. Carefully peel away the parchment and let the cake cool completely. For the best flavor and texture, wrap the cake in plastic and let it sit at room temperature for at least a day before serving.

Serve: Slice and serve with sweetened yogurt.

---

② You can substitute other citrus for the blood orange, such as tangerines or honey mandarins. Just make sure that whatever you use has a relatively thin skin, as thicker-skinned fruit can make the whole cake too bitter.

③ Try to slice the blood oranges as thinly as possible, or else the white pith will not fully soften during baking, not only leaving a bitter taste but also making the cake hard to cut. You want orange slices that are paper thin if possible.

④ Take your time streaming the oil into the egg/sugar mixture to make sure they emulsify, which helps maintain an airy and even texture in the final cake. Too much oil too soon would overwhelm the eggs and cause the mixture to break.

Goat Cheese Cake
with Honey and Figs

Serves 10

Special Equipment:
9-inch springform pan, roasting pan large enough to fit the springform pan, stand or hand mixer

Graham Cracker Crust (page 326), fully baked in a 9-inch springform pan and cooled

10.5 ounces (297g) fresh **goat cheese**, at room temperature

8 ounces (227g) full-fat **cream cheese**, preferably Philadelphia, at room temperature

⅔ cup **sugar** (4.6 oz / 130g)

Seeds scraped from 1 **vanilla bean** or 1 teaspoon vanilla paste

½ cup **heavy cream** (4 oz / 113g)

4 large **eggs** (7 oz / 200g), at room temperature

1 tablespoon finely grated **lemon zest**

2 tablespoons fresh **lemon juice** (1 oz / 28g)

1 pound (454g) fresh **figs**, quartered [1]

Honey, extra-virgin olive oil, and a **lemon wedge**, for serving

My relationship with the classic New York–style cheesecake is complicated. I love the first dense, smooth, ultrarich bite, but it's all downhill from there—usually there's too much filling for my taste, and it gets boring and heavy fast. I wanted one that was a little lighter, a bit more complex, and with a better proportion of filling to crust. Swapping in some goat cheese for the cream cheese was the game-changer, giving it all the unmistakable creaminess of Philadelphia (my one and only, as far as cream cheese is concerned) but with the added tang and slight funk of goat cheese. And less filling overall means every bite includes a bit of graham cracker crust.

Preheat the oven: Arrange an oven rack in the center position and preheat the oven to 325°F. Tightly wrap the outside of the springform pan (with the cooled baked **Graham Cracker Crust**) in a double layer of foil, making sure the foil extends at least 3 inches up the sides and all the way around to create a watertight seal. [2] Set the pan aside.

Make the filling: In a stand mixer fitted with the paddle attachment (or in large bowl if using a hand mixer), combine the goat cheese, cream cheese, sugar, and vanilla seeds and beat on medium-high until completely smooth. Add the heavy cream and beat on medium-low until smooth. Add the eggs, lemon zest, and lemon juice and mix until incorporated. Increase the speed to medium-high and beat, scraping down the sides of the bowl occasionally, until the filling is very light and smooth, about 3 minutes. Turn off the mixer.

Prepare the water bath: Bring 2 quarts of water to a boil on the stovetop. Place a roasting pan in the oven and carefully fill it with the boiling water to a depth of about 1 inch. This is your water bath for baking the cheesecake. [3]

Fill the crust and bake: Pour the batter into the graham cracker crust and smooth the top. Lightly tap the pan on the counter to pop (continues)

DO AHEAD
The cheesecake without the fig topping, well wrapped and refrigerated, will keep up to 3 days, although the crust will soften over time. Top with the figs just before serving, and store any leftover figs separate from the cheesecake in an airtight container in the refrigerator.

[1] Look for figs that are soft, unblemished, and starting to ooze nectar, indicating they're truly ripe. Unripe figs are flavorless and won't add much to the tart.

[2] Be diligent when covering the outside of the springform pan with foil, adding another layer if you see any gaps or tears, since leakage is a common problem when it comes to water baths. If you do notice that the water has breached the foil, don't worry too much— the cheesecake will still be fine (even if the crust is a tad soggy).

any air bubbles, then carefully place the springform pan inside the roasting pan so it's partially submerged in the water. Bake until the filling is set around the edges and slightly wobbly in the center, 30 to 35 minutes.

Turn off the oven and let the cheesecake cool in the water bath inside the oven with the door ajar for at least 2 hours (this will allow it to finish setting and to cool down gently, which helps prevent cracking on the surface).

Chill the cheesecake: Remove the cooled cheesecake from the water bath and peel away the foil. Transfer the pan to the refrigerator and chill the cheesecake for at least 2 hours (if chilling longer, cover the top of the pan with plastic wrap).

Arrange the figs on top: ④ Before serving, remove the cheesecake from the refrigerator and use a paring knife or small offset spatula to cut between the edges of the pan and the cheesecake to loosen it (the filling may have naturally shrunk away from the sides during cooling). Remove the outer ring. Place the cheesecake, still on the springform base, on a serving plate. Arrange the figs over the top and drizzle lightly with honey and extra-virgin olive oil. Squeeze the lemon wedge over the top and serve.

---

③ A helpful hint: Setting the roasting pan on the oven rack first and then filling it with the boiling water is much easier than trying to transfer a pan of sloshing boiling water from stovetop to oven.

④ Use any seasonal fresh fruit other than figs to serve on top, as goat cheese and fruit are always a good match: fresh macerated berries in the summer, poached rhubarb in the spring (see Strawberry-Rhubarb Pavlovas with Rose, page 187), or kumquat marmalade in the winter (see **Ricotta Cake with Kumquat Marmalade**, page 61).

Pineapple and Pecan Upside-Down Cake

Serves 8

Special Equipment:
9-inch cake pan, food processor, stand or hand mixer

PINEAPPLE CARAMEL LAYER

Butter for the pan

1 medium **pineapple** (about 3½ lb / 1.59kg) ①

½ cup packed **light brown sugar** (3.5 oz / 100g)

¼ cup **dark rum** (2 oz / 57g)

1 tablespoon **unsalted butter**

Pinch of **kosher salt**

TOASTED PECAN CAKE AND ASSEMBLY

1 cup **pecan halves** or **pieces** (4 oz / 113g)

1 cup **all-purpose flour** (4.6 oz / 130g)

1½ teaspoons **ground cinnamon**

1 teaspoon **Diamond Crystal kosher salt** (0.11 oz / 3g)

1 teaspoon **baking soda** (0.21 oz / 6g)

½ teaspoon **baking powder**

¼ teaspoon **ground nutmeg** (preferably freshly grated)

1 stick **unsalted butter** (4 oz / 113g), at room temperature

½ cup **granulated sugar** (3.5 oz / 100g)

¼ cup packed **light brown sugar** (1.8 oz / 50g)

2 large **eggs** (3.5 oz / 100g), at room temperature

1 teaspoon **vanilla extract**

½ cup **buttermilk** (4.2 oz / 120g), at room temperature

⅓ cup strained **apricot jam** (optional), warmed, for glazing

Despite being a great lover of upside-down cakes, I had never made a pineapple upside-down cake until I worked on this book. Totally unbeholden to the standard canned pineapple version, I wanted a cake that combined the tropical flavors of fresh pineapple, rum, brown sugar, vanilla, and warm spices. The balance between the nutty, fluffy, pecan-heavy cake and sweet-tart pineapple top leaves this cake wanting nothing, although a scoop of cinnamon, vanilla, or butter pecan ice cream on the side wouldn't be unwelcome at all.

Prepare the pan: Lightly butter the bottom and sides of the cake pan and line the bottom with a round of parchment paper. Set the pan aside.

Cut the pineapple: Working on a cutting board and using a large knife, place the pineapple on its side and cut crosswise to remove the stem end and base (discard). Stand the pineapple upright. Slice off the thick rind by cutting down and around the sides, following the contours of the fruit and rotating it as you go. Be generous as you cut, fully removing any and all of the knobby exterior (go back with a paring knife if necessary to remove any "eyes"). Cut the pineapple lengthwise into quarters, then lay each quarter flat on its side. Slice lengthwise along the spears to remove the fibrous inner core, ② then cut the pineapple crosswise into very thin fan-shaped slices that measure no more than ⅛-inch thick.

Poach the pineapple: In a large saucepan, combine the pineapple slices and any accumulated juices with the brown sugar and rum. Add just enough water so the pineapple is barely submerged. Bring the mixture to a simmer over medium-low heat, swirling the pan to dissolve the sugar. Adjust the heat to maintain a gentle simmer and cook, swirling the pan occasionally to ensure even cooking, until the pineapple slices are softened and translucent, 10 to 15 minutes. Carefully transfer the slices to a plate (they will be delicate), leaving the juices behind in the saucepan.

Make the caramel: Return the saucepan to medium heat and add the butter and a pinch of salt. Cook, swirling often, until the butter is melted and the liquid is bubbling and thick, 5 to 7 minutes. Pour the (continues)

DO AHEAD
The cake, well wrapped and stored at room temperature, will keep up to 3 days but is best served the day it's made. Glaze with the apricot jam just before serving.

① When picking a whole pineapple, smell the base end. A ripe one will have a fruity and floral scent. Alternatively, you can buy fresh whole, peeled, cored (but unsliced) pineapple if your grocery store offers it. Make sure you have about 1½ pounds (680g) of pineapple to start.

caramel into the bottom of the prepared cake pan and tilt to coat. Set the pan aside to cool.

Arrange the pineapple in the pan: Arrange the cooled pineapple slices across the bottom of the pan in a tight overlapping pattern (you may have some leftover pineapple). Set the pan aside while you make the cake.

Preheat the oven and toast the nuts: Arrange an oven rack in the center position and preheat the oven to 350°F. Place the pecans on a small rimmed baking sheet and bake, shaking halfway through, until darkened in color and very toasty smelling, 10 to 14 minutes. Remove from the oven and set aside to cool completely.

Mix the dry ingredients: In a food processor, combine the flour, cinnamon, salt, baking soda, baking powder, and nutmeg. Add the cooled pecans and process in long pulses until the nuts are finely ground. Set aside.

Cream the butter and sugars: In a stand mixer fitted with the paddle attachment (or in a large bowl if using a hand mixer), beat the butter, granulated sugar, and brown sugar on medium-high until light and fluffy, scraping down the sides of the bowl once or twice, about 4 minutes.

Add the eggs: Add the eggs one at a time, beating thoroughly after each addition. Beat in the vanilla.

Alternate the dry and wet ingredients: Reduce the mixer speed to low and add the flour mixture in 3 additions, alternating with 2 additions of the buttermilk, beating after each addition just until you have a smooth batter. Turn off the mixer and use a flexible spatula to fold the batter several times, scraping the bottom and sides, to ensure everything is evenly mixed.

Fill the pan and bake: Gently dollop the batter over the pineapple and use a flexible or small offset spatula to smooth it into an even layer (don't worry if some juices from the pineapple pool around the sides). Bake the cake until the surface is golden brown all over, springy to the touch, and a cake tester or toothpick inserted into the center comes out clean, 40 to 45 minutes.

Cool and glaze the cake: Set the pan on a wire rack and let the cake cool for 15 minutes. [3] Use an offset spatula or paring knife to cut around the sides of the pan to release the cake. Invert the cake onto the wire rack and slowly remove the pan. Peel off the parchment paper and let the cake cool completely. If desired, use a pastry brush to dab the warm apricot jam across the entire surface for a shiny finish.

---

[2] Make sure you remove the entire core of the pineapple, since it will remain tough and fibrous even after baking.

[3] Don't wait longer than 15 minutes to turn the cake out of the pan. The caramel will harden as the cake cools, making it more difficult to unmold it cleanly (even with a layer of parchment paper as insurance).

Pies and Tarts

Baking feels like an artistic practice to me, where the art just happens to be edible. Never do I experience this more than when I make a pie or tart. Rolling out the dough, lining a pie plate, folding and crimping an edge—all of these steps put me in a more meditative and creative frame of mind. Since every fruit pie or galette turns out unique, making one is a process of discovery. At the same time, it's also a lot of work. Pies and tarts (almost) always have a crust and filling, requiring more prep and overall work than a cake or cookie. Be prepared to bake any of the recipes in this chapter in stages, starting by making and chilling the pastry, preparing the filling, and then assembling and baking. The ends definitely justify the means—and you might even find some delight in the process.

SOUR CHERRY PIE, PAGE 111

Cranberry-Pomegranate Mousse Pie

Serves 8

Special Equipment:
9-inch pie plate, stand or hand mixer (optional)

2 wide strips **orange zest**, removed with a vegetable peeler

1 **cinnamon stick** or ¼ teaspoon **ground cinnamon**

Pinch of **kosher salt**

10 ounces (283g) fresh **cranberries** (about 2½ cups), plus 20 or so for garnish [1]

1½ cups **granulated sugar** (10.6 oz / 300g), plus more for garnish

4 tablespoons **pomegranate molasses** (3.5 oz / 100g) [2]

2 cups **heavy cream** (16 oz / 453g), chilled

1½ teaspoons **unflavored gelatin powder** (0.17 oz / 5g)

Graham Cracker Crust, Speculoos Variation (page 327), fully baked in a 9-inch pie plate and cooled [3]

2 tablespoons **powdered sugar**

As much as I love pumpkin and apple, *this* is the pie I want to eat after a big Thanksgiving meal: light, smooth, and very tart from cranberries and pomegranate molasses. It also has a no-bake filling, meaning your oven is freed up to accommodate everything else you're making for the Big Meal. However, there's no reason why a cranberry pie—or any cranberry dessert—can't make an appearance throughout fall and winter. It's that good.

Cook the cranberry compote: In a small saucepan, combine the orange zest, cinnamon, salt, cranberries, 1 cup of the granulated sugar (7 oz / 200g), 3 tablespoons of the pomegranate molasses (2.5 oz / 72g), and 1 cup water (8 oz / 227g). Bring the mixture to a boil and cook, stirring often with a heatproof spatula, until the cranberries have burst and the mixture is very thick and reduced to a jammy consistency, 10 to 15 minutes (it shouldn't immediately cover the line left by the spatula as you scrape it across the bottom of the pot). Remove from the heat.

Strain the mixture and stir in some cream: Set a fine-mesh sieve over a medium bowl and scrape the compote into the sieve. Set the saucepan aside to use again later. Use the spatula to force the mixture through the mesh into the bowl below, pressing on the solids (discard the solids). Whisk ⅓ cup of the heavy cream (2.7 oz / 76g) into the compote until the mixture is completely smooth. Cover with plastic wrap and refrigerate just until the cranberry mixture is cool, 25 to 30 minutes.

Soften the gelatin: Rinse and dry the reserved saucepan. Pour 3 tablespoons cold water (1.5 oz / 43g) into the saucepan and sprinkle the gelatin over it (don't stir). Set aside to allow the gelatin to soften, about 10 minutes.

Whip some of the cream to firm peaks: Meanwhile, pour 1 cup of the heavy cream (8 oz / 227g) into a stand mixer fitted with the whisk attachment (or into a large bowl if using a hand mixer) and beat, starting on medium-low and increasing the speed to medium-high as (continues)

DO AHEAD
The cranberry compote can be made up to 4 days ahead. Keep covered and refrigerated. The cranberry mousse can be assembled and chilled in the speculoos crust up to 1 day ahead. Keep covered and refrigerated. Whip the cream and top with sugared cranberries just before serving.

[1] You can use frozen cranberries instead of fresh in the compote, but note that you won't be able to use them for the sugared cranberry garnish, so skip that part.

[2] Look for pomegranate molasses at well-stocked supermarkets or Middle Eastern grocers. If you can't find any, omit it and replace the 1 cup water in the recipe with 100% unsweetened pomegranate juice. For the sugared cranberries, use ½ cup of the pomegranate juice in place of the water and pomegranate molasses.

the cream thickens, until you have firm peaks. You can also do this by hand with a whisk. Refrigerate the cream until it's time to assemble the mousse.

Melt the gelatin and whisk into the compote: Remove the cooled cranberry mixture from the refrigerator, uncover, and whisk to smooth it out. Place the saucepan with the gelatin over low heat and warm, swirling often, until the gelatin is melted into a clear liquid free of granules—you want to make sure it's completely melted or the mousse won't fully set. Whisk the gelatin into the cranberry mixture.

Assemble the cranberry mousse and chill in the crust: Remove the whipped cream from the refrigerator and scrape half of it into the bowl with the cranberry mixture. Fold until just a few streaks remain. ④ Fold in the remaining whipped cream until you have a light, uniform mixture, then scrape into the prepared crust. Smooth the top and refrigerate until the mousse is set, at least 4 hours. After the first hour in the refrigerator, cover the pie with plastic wrap to prevent a skin from forming.

Make the sugared cranberries: While the pie is setting, in a small saucepan, combine the remaining ½ cup sugar (3.5 oz / 100g), 1 tablespoon pomegranate molasses (0.9 oz / 25g), and ⅓ cup water (2.7 oz / 76g). Bring to a very gentle simmer over low heat, stirring to dissolve the sugar, and add the 20 cranberries. Simmer very gently just until the cranberries are softened and a few have burst, about 3 minutes. With a slotted spoon, remove the cranberries from the saucepan and transfer to a wire rack (discard any that have collapsed or lost their shape). Let sit until the cranberries are slightly tacky to the touch, about 1 hour. Toss the cranberries in some granulated sugar to coat them and return to the wire rack to continue drying at room temperature until the pie is set.

Whip the remaining cream and top the pie: Just before serving, remove the pie from the refrigerator and uncover. Whip the remaining ⅔ cup heavy cream as before until you have soft peaks. Beat in the powdered sugar and scrape the whipped cream on top of the pie. Spread over the filling, making swooshes and swirls, and dot with the sugared cranberries. Cut into wedges and serve.

---

③ If you can't find Biscoff cookies, just make a regular Graham Cracker Crust, or substitute gingersnap cookies.

④ Try to avoid mixing the mousse more than necessary as you fold in the whipped cream, otherwise it won't be as light. Only fold until no streaks remain, using a light hand to maintain as much airiness as possible.

Plum Galette
with Polenta and Pistachios

Serves 8

⅓ cup shelled **pistachios** (1.6 oz / 45g)

2 tablespoons coarse **polenta** or **cornmeal** (0.6 oz / 18g)

½ teaspoon **cornstarch**

Pinch of **kosher salt**

5 tablespoons **demerara sugar** (2.2 oz / 63g)

Flaky All-Butter Pie Dough (page 333)

All-purpose flour, for rolling out

1¼ pounds (567g) small **plums**, preferably Italian, halved and pitted ①

1 tablespoon **honey**, plus more for drizzling on top

1 large **egg**, beaten

The bittersweet feeling I get when summer fades into fall is made sweeter by the appearance of juicy, flavorful, bite-sized Italian plums. They're a great snacking fruit and even better for baking, since the heat of the oven concentrates their natural tartness, making a bit of added sugar extremely welcome. This plum galette feels simple and elegant in a *Call Me by Your Name* Italian-ish kind of way. Beneath the fruit is a layer of polenta, toasted pistachios, sugar, and cornstarch, and as the juices from the plums seep down, the polenta hydrates and tenderizes and the whole mixture thickens into a delicious, textured layer that also functions as a barrier between the soft, jammy fruit and the crisp pastry. It's a keeper of a recipe that should make an appearance at the end of each summer.

Preheat the oven and toast the pistachios: Arrange an oven rack in the center position and preheat the oven to 350°F. Scatter the pistachios on a small rimmed baking sheet and toast until they're golden and nutty smelling, shaking halfway through, 8 to 10 minutes. Remove from the oven and let the pistachios cool. Leave the oven on, increasing the temperature to 425°F.

Skin and chop the pistachios: Rub the warm pistachios between your fingers to remove any papery skins that may have loosened during toasting and discard (don't worry about removing every last bit). Finely chop the pistachios. Measure out 1 tablespoon of the nuts and set aside for sprinkling over the finished galette.

Mix the base layer: In a small bowl, combine the polenta, cornstarch, salt, 3 tablespoons of the demerara sugar (1.3 oz / 38g), and the chopped pistachios and toss to combine. Set the polenta mixture aside.

Roll out the pastry: Let the pie dough sit at room temperature for about 5 minutes to soften. Unwrap the dough and place it on a lightly floured surface. Use a rolling pin to beat the dough all across the surface to make it more pliable. Dust the top and underneath the dough with more flour, then roll it out, dusting with more flour as needed, into a 12-inch round. (continues)

DO AHEAD
The galette, covered and stored at room temperature, will keep up to 4 days but is best served on the first day while the crust is still crisp (it will soften as it sits).

① I start looking for Italian plums in early September when they're just coming into season and tend to be very small and tart. If you wait a few weeks and your plums are on the larger side, just cut them into smaller wedges before arranging them on the tart base. If you can't find Italian plums, you can use any variety as long as it tastes good out of hand.

Assemble the galette: Transfer the pastry to a large rimmed baking sheet lined with parchment paper. Sprinkle the polenta mixture evenly across the surface, leaving a 1½-inch border all the way around. Place the plum halves cut-side up on top of the polenta mixture, fitting them tightly and overlapping slightly. Drizzle the plums with the 1 tablespoon honey.

Fold up the pastry: Brush the border of the pastry with the beaten egg and then, using the parchment paper to help you, fold the border up and over the plums, leaving the center open and creating a series of evenly spaced pleats all the way around. Press firmly on the pleats to help the pastry adhere to itself, then brush the top of the pastry with more egg. Sprinkle the entire surface of the galette with the remaining 2 tablespoons demerara sugar.

Chill the galette: Transfer the galette to the refrigerator and chill until the pastry is firm, 10 to 15 minutes.

Bake and cool: Transfer the baking sheet to the oven and bake until the pastry is puffed and golden brown and the plums are soft and jammy, 55 to 65 minutes. [2] Remove from the oven and let cool at least 30 minutes.

Serve: Drizzle with more honey and sprinkle with the reserved tablespoon of chopped pistachios. [3] Slice and serve.

[2] Short of burning the whole thing, it's pretty hard to overbake a fruit pie or galette, so leave it until the pastry is a deep golden brown. The long bake time allows the juices from the plums to trickle down and hydrate and soften the polenta underneath, creating a sweet, textured layer between the fruit and pastry.

[3] Drizzle the baked galette generously with more honey if your plums are very sour, as baking some stone fruit, like plums and apricots, can actually intensify their tartness.

Pistachio Linzer Tart

Serves 8

Special Equipment:
9-inch round or 14 x 4-inch rectangular removable-bottom tart pan, food processor, pastry bag, large cake icer or other pastry tip (optional)

1 cup shelled **pistachios** (4.2 oz / 120g) [1]

Butter for the pan

1 cup **all-purpose flour** (4.6 oz / 130g)

½ teaspoon **ground cinnamon**

½ teaspoon **Diamond Crystal kosher salt**

½ cup **sugar** (3.5 oz / 100g)

10 tablespoons **unsalted butter** (5 oz / 142g), cut into ½-inch pieces, chilled

1 large **egg** (1.8 oz / 50g), cold

1 teaspoon **vanilla extract**

2 teaspoons finely grated **lemon zest**

⅔ cup store-bought **jam** (7 oz / 200g), such as raspberry, strawberry, cherry, or apricot [2]

2 teaspoons fresh **lemon juice**

One of my favorite spots in New York is Café Sabarsky, an impossibly charming Viennese-style café inside the Neue Galerie, a museum dedicated to German and Austrian art located in a mansion on Fifth Avenue and 86th Street in Manhattan. After viewing the Klimts and Schieles, I like to snag a table and order a *kaffee crème*, which comes on a little tray with bubbly water on the side, and a perfect slice of Linzertorte. A spiced nut-based tart that's filled with jam, Linzertorte is the epitome of a Viennese dessert: rich and a tad austere (in a good way!). This version uses a very stiff batter, assembled in the food processor, rather than a pastry dough that requires chilling and rolling, and pistachios instead of the typical hazelnuts and almonds. Half the batter is baked in the pan to create a bottom crust, then the filling (store-bought jam brightened with a bit of lemon juice) goes in and the remaining batter is piped over the top. There are a few steps, yes, but otherwise it's a fairly easy, very delicious dessert that somehow hits that sweet spot between low-key and fancy.

Preheat the oven and toast the pistachios: Arrange an oven rack in the center position and preheat the oven to 350°F. Scatter the pistachios on a small rimmed baking sheet and toast until they're golden and nutty smelling, shaking halfway through, 8 to 10 minutes. Remove from the oven (leave the oven on) and let the pistachios cool. Rub the warm pistachios between your fingers to remove any papery skins that may have loosened during toasting and discard (don't worry about removing every last bit).

Prepare the pan: Lightly coat the bottom and sides of the tart pan with butter and set aside.

Grind the nuts into the dry ingredients: In a food processor, combine the flour, cinnamon, salt, and cooled pistachios and process in long pulses until the nuts are finely ground. Transfer the flour mixture to a medium bowl and set aside.

Make the batter: In a food processor (no need to wash it after grinding the nuts), combine the sugar and chilled butter pieces and pulse, scraping the sides of the bowl once or twice, until the mixture is smooth and creamy. Add the egg, vanilla, and lemon zest and pulse again, scraping down the sides one more time, until incorporated (it's okay if it looks a little broken). Add the pistachio/flour mixture and pulse just until a thick, smooth batter forms. (continues)

DO AHEAD
The tart, well wrapped and stored at room temperature, will keep up to 3 days but is best served on the first or second day.

[1] Feel free to substitute an equal weight of almonds, hazelnuts, pecans, or walnuts for the pistachios (or a mix); just make sure any nut you use is well toasted.

[2] If you want to strain the jam to remove any seeds, go ahead, but it's not necessary. I rather like the texture they add!

Smooth half the batter into the pan: Carefully remove the blade from the food processor and scrape any batter back into the bowl. Mix the batter with a flexible spatula to make sure all of the ingredients are evenly incorporated, then scrape about half the batter into the prepared pan. Use a small offset spatula to smooth the batter into a thin, even layer across the bottom of the pan and all the way to the edges.

Bake and cool the first layer: Transfer the pan to the oven and bake until the batter is firm and set and just starting to turn golden around the edges, 15 to 20 minutes. Remove the pan from the oven and set aside to cool. (Leave the oven on.)

Transfer the remaining batter to a pastry bag (fitted with a large cake icer tip or other tip, if desired, to make a more decorative pattern). The batter will be thick, but do your best to eliminate air pockets as you place it inside the pastry bag, since they will make it harder to pipe it across the tart. If the bag is disposable, use scissors to snip a 1-inch opening off the end (you can do this with a resealable zip-top bag, too).

Mix the filling: In a small bowl, combine the jam and lemon juice and stir until smooth.

Assemble the tart: Spread the jam mixture in an even layer across the surface of the cooled tart bottom, leaving a ¼-inch border all the way around. Pipe tight, parallel rows of batter from one side of the pan to the other across the surface of the jam (or, really, in any pattern you want). Squeeze the pastry bag with even pressure and pipe slowly to coax the thick batter out of the bag. If the line of batter breaks or you hit an air pocket, just start again where you left off. Use all the remaining batter. [3]

Bake the tart: Bake again until the jam is bubbling gently and the edges of the tart are golden brown, another 25 to 30 minutes. Remove the pan from the oven and let the tart cool completely.

Serve: Carefully remove the tart base from the pan and slice.

---

[3] Try to pipe the batter as evenly as possible by applying constant pressure to the pastry bag and working slowly. The batter will puff only slightly during baking, so it comes out of the oven looking pretty much the same as it did going in.

Salty Nut Tart
with Rosemary

Serves 12

Special Equipment:
9 inch removable bottom tart pan, food processor (for the Sweet Tart Dough)

1 cup **pine nuts** (5 oz / 143g) ①

1 cup **walnuts** (4 oz / 113g), coarsely chopped

¼ cup **honey** (3 oz / 85g)

¼ cup **sugar** (1.8 oz / 50g)

¼ cup **heavy cream** (2 oz / 57g)

¼ cup **extra-virgin olive oil** (2 oz / 57g)

2 tablespoons **light corn syrup** (1.4 oz / 40g)

½ teaspoon **Diamond Crystal kosher salt**

½ teaspoon **vanilla extract**

½ teaspoon finely chopped fresh **rosemary**

Sweet Tart Dough (page 338), parbaked in a 9-inch removable-bottom tart pan and cooled ②

¼ teaspoon **flaky salt**, for serving

This luxe tart is one of those rare desserts whose looks and flavor belie its ease. The oven does all the work! The filling is a mixture of toasted pine nuts and walnuts stirred into a rosemary-spiked honey syrup that caramelizes as it bakes inside the tart crust—no stovetop caramel cooking required. The final tart is rich (thanks to the fatty pine nuts) and pleasingly sweet-savory. During the testing process it was a favorite among my family, all of whom thought it was delicious, and also a favorite of mine for how fancy yet unfussy it presents. Since caramel, nuts, and rosemary are all great accompaniments to cheese, this tart really shines when served with an aged cheddar, Comté, or a mild creamy blue.

Preheat the oven and toast the nuts: Arrange an oven rack in the center position and preheat the oven to 350°F. Scatter the pine nuts and chopped walnuts on a small rimmed baking sheet and toast, shaking halfway through, until they're golden brown and fragrant, 6 to 9 minutes. After 5 minutes keep a watchful eye since pine nuts burn easily! Remove them from the oven and set the nuts aside to cool. (Leave the oven on.)

Cook the filling: In a small saucepan, combine the honey, sugar, heavy cream, olive oil, and corn syrup and cook over medium-low heat, stirring gently with a heatproof spatula to dissolve the sugar. Increase the heat to medium and bring the mixture to a rapid simmer. Cook the mixture without stirring, swirling the pan often, until it has thickened slightly, about 5 minutes. This is an approximate end point—the idea is to cook off some moisture and make sure all the ingredients are well combined, not to cook it until it's caramel. The mixture will still be quite liquid. Remove the saucepan from the heat and stir in the kosher salt, vanilla, and ¼ teaspoon of the rosemary. Add the toasted nuts and stir well to combine. Set aside.

Fill the tart and bake: Place the cooled, parbaked tart crust on a large foil-lined rimmed baking sheet. Scrape the filling mixture into the tart, distributing all the nuts across the bottom so the liquid pools evenly around them. Bake until the filling around the nuts is (continues)

DO AHEAD
The tart, covered and stored at room temperature, will keep up to 4 days but is best served on the first or second day while the crust is still snappy. Make sure the tart is tightly wrapped to prevent the caramel from pulling moisture from the air and turning sticky (especially in humid weather).

bubbling and the surface is deep golden brown, 25 to 30 minutes. Remove from the oven and set the tart aside to cool slightly.

Top with rosemary salt: While the tart is still warm, in a small bowl, combine the flaky salt and remaining ¼ teaspoon rosemary and rub between your fingertips for a few seconds to release the fragrant oils. Sprinkle the mixture over the tart and let the tart cool completely (it will set as it cools).

Serve: Pop the tart out of the ring. Slide a thin metal spatula between the tart base and the bottom of the tart to loosen it, then carefully slide it onto a serving plate and cut into wedges.

---

1. Pine nuts are pricey, so feel free to substitute another nut, such as blanched almonds in their place. If you have the budget, though, and you can find them, I recommend Italian pine nuts, which are longer, more cylindrical, and generally tastier than the more ubiquitous, triangular Chinese pine nuts. Pine nuts are very high in fat and go rancid quickly, so keep them fresh in an airtight container in the freezer.

2. Double-check that your parbaked tart crust has no cracks, as the liquid filling will seep through even small ones. If you don't have any tart dough available for patching, mix together a small amount of flour and water to make a soft dough and use that like spackle to seal any cracks (no need to bake the crust again before filling).

Apple Tart

Serves 8

6 medium **Pink Lady** or any sweet-tart, firm **baking apples** (about 2½ lb / 1.13kg)

¼ cup packed **dark brown sugar** (1.8 oz / 50g)

6 tablespoons **unsalted butter** (3 oz / 85g)

Seeds scraped from ½ **vanilla bean**

¼ teaspoon **Diamond Crystal kosher salt**

2½ cups plus 4 tablespoons unfiltered unsweetened **apple cider** (22 oz / 624g)

½ recipe **Rough Puff Pastry** (page 355) or 1 sheet thawed frozen store-bought puff pastry ①

All-purpose flour, for rolling out

1 large **egg**, beaten

Demerara sugar, for sprinkling the top

½ cup **apricot jam** (5.6 oz / 160g)

I went to culinary school in Paris and lived in the 3rd arrondissement on rue du Temple, just a couple of blocks from an outpost of Poilâne, perhaps the most famed bread bakery in the world. Occasionally I'd stop in for one of their superlative apple tarts. It was a simple mix of apples, butter, brown sugar, and pastry, but on days when I'd catch them still warm from the oven, I was sure it was the best thing I'd ever eaten. That magical apple tart, plus the classic *tarte aux pommes* we made in culinary school, were the source materials for this one, which layers apple slices over the top of a caramelized apple compote. It will never taste exactly the way Poilâne's did, but warm out of the oven it comes reasonably close.

Cook the compote: Peel, halve, core, and coarsely chop 3 of the apples. In a medium saucepan, combine the brown sugar, 4 tablespoons of the butter (2 oz / 57g), the vanilla seeds, salt, and 1 tablespoon water (0.5 oz / 14g). Cook over medium-high heat, stirring often, until the sugar is dissolved and the mixture comes to a boil. Stop stirring and continue to cook, swirling the saucepan often, until the mixture is thick and the bubbles are large and slow to pop, about 2 minutes. Add the chopped apples and cook, stirring often and scraping the bottom of the saucepan with a wooden spoon or heatproof spatula to prevent scorching, until the apples are softened and starting to caramelize, 8 to 10 minutes. (If you are using particularly fresh or juicy apples, they may take quite a bit longer to take on color, but be patient and continue to cook until you see caramelization.)

Reduce the compote: Slowly stir in 2½ cups of the apple cider (20 oz / 567g), taking care because the mixture will sputter, and return it to a boil. Reduce the heat to keep the cider at a vigorous simmer and cook until it is reduced by about half, 8 to 12 minutes. Crush the apples with a potato masher or the back of a wooden spoon and continue to cook, stirring and mashing often, until the mixture is reduced to a thick, coarsely textured, deep golden brown applesauce, 12 to 18 minutes. Continue to cook, stirring constantly to prevent scorching, until nearly all of the moisture has been driven off and you have a thick compote that doesn't immediately cover the line left by the spoon as you drag it across the bottom of the pan, 5 to 8 minutes longer (you should have **(continues)**

DO AHEAD
The apple compote, covered and refrigerated, will keep up to 1 week. The apple tart, covered loosely and stored at room temperature, will keep up to 3 days but is best served on the first or second day.

① If you're using frozen puff pastry, let it thaw gently in the refrigerator overnight before using. I recommend Dufour brand, but any brand labeled "all-butter" will work. If your package of puff pastry contains two small sheets instead of one large, stack the sheets one on top of the other and roll out to the dimensions specified in the recipe.

between 1½ and 1¾ cups). Remove from the heat and let cool slightly. Transfer the compote to a bowl or container and refrigerate until cold.

Preheat the oven: Arrange an oven rack in the center position and preheat the oven to 425°F.

Roll out the pastry: Let the pastry sit at room temperature for about 5 minutes to soften. Roll it out on a lightly floured surface, dusting the pastry with more flour as needed to prevent sticking, into a large ⅛-inch-thick rectangle. ② Trim along the 4 sides to create a clean rectangle measuring about 13 × 9 inches (a little longer or wider is fine). If using thawed frozen puff pastry, gently roll out the pastry on a lightly floured surface just to smooth creases and lengthen or widen as needed. Transfer the pastry to a parchment-lined rimmed baking sheet.

Dock and egg wash the pastry: Leaving a 1-inch border around the edges, prick all across the surface of the pastry with the tines of a fork. Use a pastry brush to paint the 1-inch border of pastry with the beaten egg, then sprinkle the egg-washed area with a generous dusting of demerara sugar. Refrigerate the pastry while you slice the remaining apples.

Slice the remaining apples: With the 3 remaining apples positioned upright and stem pointing skyward, cut down and around the cores to remove the flesh in 4 lobes (you'll be left with a square-shaped core). Set the lobes flat-side down and slice lengthwise into thin slivers as evenly as possible, trying to keep the lobes together in their original shape.

Assemble the tart: Remove the pastry and apple compote from the refrigerator and spread the compote in an even layer across the pastry and inside the sugared border. Working with one lobe at a time, fan out the apple slices and arrange them over the compote, tightly shingling (you may not use all of the apple slices). Melt the remaining 2 tablespoons butter and combine with 2 tablespoons cider. Use a pastry brush to dab the butter mixture over the apple slices.

Bake the tart: Place the tart in the oven and reduce the temperature to 350°F. Bake the tart until the border is deeply browned and the apples are browned in spots, 40 to 55 minutes. Set the tart aside to cool.

Glaze and serve the tart: In a small saucepan, combine the jam and remaining 2 tablespoons cider and bring to a simmer over medium-low heat, stirring to combine. Press the mixture through a fine-mesh sieve to remove any solids and then dab the jam mixture over the apples to glaze them. ③ Serve slightly warm or at room temperature.

---

② If the pastry starts to soften and adhere to the rolling pin, return it to the refrigerator for several minutes to firm up. Working with warm pastry will reduce your chances of getting a shatteringly flaky, tender crust.

③ Try not to drag the pastry brush across the apples when glazing. Use a dabbing motion instead, which creates a smoother finish and won't disturb the apples.

Caramelized Honey
Pumpkin Pie

Serves 8

Special Equipment:
9-inch pie plate, pie weights or 4 cups dried beans or rice (for parbaking)

Flaky All-Butter Pie Dough
(page 333), parbaked in a 9-inch pie plate and cooled

5 tablespoons **unsalted butter**
(2.5 oz / 71g)

⅓ cup **honey** (4 oz / 113g) [1]

¾ cup **heavy cream** (6 oz / 170g), at room temperature

4 large **eggs** (7 oz / 200g), at room temperature

¼ cup packed **dark brown sugar**
(1.8 oz / 50g)

1 (15 oz / 425g) can unsweetened **pumpkin puree** (not pumpkin pie filling), preferably Libby's [2]

2 teaspoons **ground cinnamon**

1½ teaspoons **ground ginger**

1 teaspoon **vanilla extract**

1 teaspoon **Diamond Crystal kosher salt**
(0.11 oz / 3g)

½ teaspoon **ground allspice**

½ teaspoon **ground nutmeg** (preferably freshly grated), plus more for serving

¼ teaspoon **ground cloves** [3]

Softly whipped cream, for serving

There are thousands—maybe tens of thousands—of pumpkin pie recipes out there, and almost all of them contain a filling that follows this basic formula: pumpkin + eggs + sugar + dairy + warm spices. So why come up with yet another? Because so often the proportions are off between all these components. Sometimes it's an overwhelming amount of warm spice, other times too few eggs so the pie isn't custardy. Most often, there's too much sugar. I wanted a filling that set firmly into a custard and used strong flavors to balance out the vegetal quality of the pumpkin so I came up with browned butter for richness and caramelized honey (just honey that's cooked to intensify the flavor) for sweetness. I love this pie and would gladly eat it on any occasion, not just Thanksgiving.

Preheat the oven: Arrange an oven rack in the center position and preheat the oven to 325°F. Place the parbaked pie crust on a foil-lined rimmed baking sheet and set aside.

Brown the butter: In a small saucepan, cook the butter over medium-low heat, stirring and scraping the bottom and sides constantly with a heatproof spatula. The mixture will sputter as the water boils off. Continue to cook, stirring and scraping, until the sputtering subsides, the butter is foaming, and the solid bits turn a dark brown, 5 to 7 minutes.

Caramelize the honey: Remove the saucepan from the heat and immediately add the honey (to prevent the butter from burning), stirring to combine. Return the saucepan to medium heat and bring to a boil. Continue to cook, swirling often, until the mixture is darkened slightly and has a savory, nutty smell, about 2 minutes. Remove the saucepan from the heat and slowly stream in the heavy cream, stirring constantly (be careful—the mixture may sputter) until it's smooth. Set the warm honey mixture aside.

Make the pumpkin filling: In a large bowl, whisk the eggs to break up the whites and yolks, then add the brown sugar and whisk vigorously until the mixture has lightened in color by a shade or two, about 1 minute. Whisk in the pumpkin, cinnamon, ginger, vanilla, salt, allspice, nutmeg, and cloves until smooth. Slowly stream in the warm honey mixture, whisking constantly, until the filling is completely homogenous. (continues)

DO AHEAD
The pie, covered and refrigerated, will keep up to 3 days but is best served on the first or second day (the crust will soften over time).

[1] Use a good-quality, dark-hued honey. The more strongly flavored the better, so it stands out against the pumpkin. Just don't use buckwheat or chestnut honey, which are too intense.

[2] I don't bother making my own puree from fresh pumpkin since I've never found it worth the effort. Canned pumpkin like Libby's is lower in moisture and produces a perfectly smooth, flavorful pie.

Fill the crust and bake: Pour the filling into the parbaked crust all the way to the top. (Depending on the height of your crust, you may have some leftover filling, which I recommend you keep! ④) Ever so carefully transfer the pie to the center rack and bake until the filling is set and puffed around the edges and the center wobbles gently, 45 to 60 minutes.

Cool the pie gently: Turn off the oven and prop the door open with a wooden spoon. Let the pie cool completely in the oven. Doing so will allow it to cool gradually, which will prevent cracking on the surface.

Serve: Slice the pie into wedges and top each piece with softly whipped cream. Grate a bit of fresh nutmeg over the cream and serve.

---

③ I like this combination of warm spices, but if you are missing one, can't find them all at the store, or just don't like certain spices, feel free to come up with your own blend.

④ Bake any remaining pumpkin filling separately in a small ramekin. I like to do this to prevent ingredient waste, and also because it allows me to sample the filling prior to cutting into the pie!

Apple and Concord Grape Crumble Pie

Serves 8

Special Equipment:
9-inch pie plate, pie weights or 4 cups dried beans or rice (for parbaking)

2½ pounds (1.13kg) **Pink Lady** or any sweet-tart, firm **baking apples** (about 6 medium), peeled, cored, and thinly sliced

¼ cup packed **light brown sugar** (1.8 oz / 50g)

2 tablespoons fresh **lemon juice** (1 oz / 28g)

2 teaspoons **vanilla extract**

2 teaspoons **ground cinnamon**

½ teaspoon **Diamond Crystal kosher salt**

1 pound (454g) **Concord grapes** (picked from about 1 quart on the stem) ①

⅓ cup **granulated sugar** (2.3 oz / 66g)

3 tablespoons **cornstarch** (0.63 oz / 18g)

Flaky All-Butter Pie Dough (page 333), parbaked in a 9-inch pie plate and cooled ②

All-Purpose Crumble Topping, Buckwheat Variation (page 319)

Vanilla or **cinnamon ice cream,** for serving

Concord grapes have one of the most piercing, intense flavors in the entire fruit kingdom, and until a genius invents a seedless variety, I will endure the tedium of peeling them (for an explanation of why peeling is necessary, see page 163). It's more than worth it for this pie, which features apples and Concord grapes. Both are harbingers of fall at the farmers' market, and like most fruit that grows in the same season and in the same climate, grapes and apples pair extremely well together. This pie, topped with an earthy buckwheat crumble, might be one of my favorite flavor combinations ever.

Make the apple mixture: In a large bowl, toss together the apples, brown sugar, lemon juice, vanilla, cinnamon, and salt until the apples are evenly coated. Set the mixture aside and allow the apples to release their juices while you prepare the grape mixture.

Peel and cook down the Concord grapes: ③ Working over a small saucepan, grasp one grape at a time and squeeze it between your thumb and forefinger, stem end out, to pop the soft flesh into the saucepan, leaving the skin behind. Reserve the empty grape skins in a medium bowl. Place the saucepan of flesh over medium-low heat. Bring it to a simmer and cook, occasionally mashing the grapes against the side of the pan with the back of a wooden spoon, until the mixture is pulpy and broken down and the seeds are free-floating around the saucepan, 5 to 10 minutes. Remove the saucepan from the heat and let cool slightly.

Strain the flesh and combine with the skins and sugar: Set a fine-mesh sieve over the bowl with the reserved grape skins. Add the pulp to the sieve and press and scrape with a flexible spatula to force the pulp into the bowl below, leaving only the seeds behind. Transfer the pulp and grape skin mixture back to the same saucepan (discard seeds). Add the granulated sugar.

Reduce the apple juices: Pour any juices that have accumulated in the bowl with the apple mixture into the saucepan with the grape skin mixture and bring to a brisk simmer over medium heat. Cook, whisking occasionally, until the mixture starts to look syrupy and is reduced by about one-third, 8 to 10 minutes. Remove from the heat. (continues)

DO AHEAD
The pie, covered loosely and stored at room temperature, will keep up to 4 days but is best served on the first or second day.

① Take a whiff of the grapes at the market and pick ones that are particularly fruity smelling. More aroma means more flavor.

② To simplify this recipe considerably, skip the process of making and parbaking the **Flaky All-Butter Pie Dough** and turn this pie into a crumble. Follow all the same directions, baking it in a shallow 2-quart baking dish topped with the crumble.

Make a slurry and activate the cornstarch: Place the cornstarch in a small bowl and spoon 3 tablespoons of the hot grape mixture into the bowl. Stir with a fork until smooth, then whisk into the saucepan. Return the saucepan to medium heat and bring to a simmer again. Cook, whisking often, until the mixture has thickened, about 1 minute. Remove the saucepan from the heat and set aside to cool slightly.

Preheat the oven and prepare the pan: Arrange an oven rack in the center position and preheat the oven to 350°F. Line a rimmed baking sheet with foil and set aside.

Mix the filling and fill the pie: Pour the warm grape mixture over the apples and fold with a flexible spatula until all the apples are coated. Transfer half the mixture to the pie crust, arranging the apple slices so they fill in all the nooks and crannies around the bottom of the crust, then scrape the remaining filling on top, mounding it in the center.

Pack on the crumble topping: Sprinkle the crumble topping evenly over the apples. It will seem like a lot, but really pack all of it onto the apples and press firmly so it stays in place—packing the topping not only helps compress the filling and reduce air pockets, but it also forms the crumble into a solid layer that bakes into a firm lid and slices cleanly.

Tent with foil and bake: Place the pie on the lined baking sheet and loosely tent the top with a piece of foil (this will prevent it from darkening too quickly). Transfer the baking sheet to the oven and bake for 30 minutes. Remove the foil from the pie and continue to bake until the crumble topping is firm and browned and the juices are thick and bubbling around the sides, another 40 to 50 minutes. Remove from the oven and let the pie cool for at least 2 hours.

Serve: Cut the pie into slices and serve warm or at room temperature with ice cream.

---

[3] Please don't skip this part! It may seem unreasonably fussy to peel the grapes, but if you were to just cook down the whole grapes, you'd end up straining out the skins and therefore much of their flavor (not to mention all the color). I tested it this way to see if I could avoid peeling, and the result just doesn't compare.

Blackberry Caramel Tart

Serves 8

Special Equipment:
9-inch removable-bottom tart pan,
food processor (for the Sweet Tart
Dough)

⅔ cup **sugar** (4.6 oz / 130g)

2 tablespoons **light corn syrup**
(1.4 oz / 40g)

⅓ cup **heavy cream** (2.8 oz / 81g), at room
temperature

1 teaspoon **vanilla extract**

¼ teaspoon **Diamond Crystal kosher salt**

Sweet Tart Dough (page 338), fully
baked in a 9-inch removable-bottom
tart pan and cooled ①

18 ounces (510g) **blackberries** (about
3½ cups), rinsed and thoroughly dried

1 teaspoon **unflavored gelatin powder**
(0.11 oz / 3g)

When it comes to fruit desserts, if the dessert isn't as delicious as eating that fruit fresh out of hand, then something's wrong. I want to maintain the bright flavor and bursting-with-juices texture of summer blackberries, so in this tart I leave them mostly whole, surrounded by a blackberry caramel that highlights the natural flavor and sweetness of the fresh ones. It's set with gelatin, making the filling no-bake and the whole tart very easy to assemble ahead of time. As always, I recommend using peak-season blackberries, as out-of-season ones can be bitter and lacking in sweetness.

Make the blackberry caramel: In a medium heavy-bottomed saucepan, combine the sugar, corn syrup, and 3 tablespoons water (1.5 oz / 43g). Cook over medium heat, stirring with a heatproof spatula until the sugar is dissolved. Bring the mixture to a boil and stop stirring. Brush down the sides of the pan with a wet pastry brush as needed to dissolve any sugar crystals. Continue to cook, swirling the pan occasionally, until the syrup turns a medium amber color, 6 to 8 minutes (I normally advise cooking caramel to a deep, dark amber, but you actually want to stop short of this point; a lighter caramel will allow the flavor of the berries to shine). ② Immediately remove the saucepan from the heat and slowly stream in the heavy cream, stirring with a heatproof spatula until smooth (take care because the mixture will sputter). Stir in the vanilla, salt, and 6 ounces of blackberries (170g / about 1¼ cups). Return the saucepan to medium heat and bring to a lively simmer. Cook, stirring often and mashing the berries against the side of the saucepan until they're broken down and the mixture is slightly thickened, about 5 minutes. Remove from the heat and set aside to cool slightly.

Arrange the berries: Place the tart pan on a serving plate and arrange the remaining 12 ounces whole blackberries (340g / about 2¼ cups) inside the tart crust, spacing them evenly. Set aside.

Soften the gelatin: Place 2 tablespoons cold water (1 oz / 28g) in a small bowl and sprinkle the gelatin over the top (don't stir). Set aside to allow the gelatin to soften, about 10 minutes. (continues)

DO AHEAD
The tart, well wrapped and refrigerated, will keep up to 4 days but is best served on the first or second day (the crust will soften over time).

① Double-check that your tart crust has no cracks, as the caramel is liquid when it goes into the tart and will seep through even small ones. If you notice a crack and don't have any raw tart dough available to patch it, mix together a small amount of flour and water to make a soft dough and use that like spackle to seal any cracks (no need to bake the crust again).

Strain the caramel: Set a fine-mesh sieve over a medium bowl and scrape in the caramel (reserve the saucepan—you'll use it again in a minute). Press on the solids in the sieve with the spatula to extract as much juice and caramel as possible (discard the solids).

Melt the gelatin: Scrape the softened gelatin mixture, which by this point will have solidified and turned translucent, into the same saucepan you used for the caramel and place the pan back over low heat. Warm the pan, swirling until the mixture is completely clear and liquified and you see no traces of small granules. It's super important to make sure the gelatin is fully melted, otherwise it won't set the tart, so take your time and pay close attention. ③ At the same time, don't let the mixture come to a boil, as this could destroy the setting power of the gelatin!

Add the gelatin and cool down the filling: Stir the melted gelatin into the strained caramel and mix thoroughly. Fill a larger bowl one-third full with ice water and set the bowl of caramel inside. Stir constantly, scraping the sides of the bowl, until the caramel is thickened to the consistency of heavy cream, about 3 minutes.

Fill the tart and chill: Carefully and slowly pour the caramel into the crust, pouring in several places around the blackberries and allowing the caramel to settle and fill in the gaps. Use all the caramel, which should fill the tart and submerge the blackberries about halfway. Refrigerate the tart until the caramel is completely set, at least 2 hours. If chilling longer than 2 hours, cover with plastic wrap. Remove the tart from the ring and serve.

② Stay close to the caramel as it's cooking. It will look like nothing is happening for several minutes, but when the syrup starts to take on color, it goes from amber to dark amber to burned *very* quickly. Keep an eye on it!

③ Although it might seem like it would save a step to melt the gelatin directly into the hot caramel, it's difficult to tell if the gelatin is melted in the dark caramel, so it's best done by itself.

Apricot and Cream Brioche Tart

Serves 12

Special Equipment:
Stand mixer (for the Brioche Dough; optional, but recommended)

½ recipe **Brioche Dough** (page 352), chilled ①

All-purpose flour, for rolling out

½ cup **crème fraîche** (4.2 oz / 120g)

1 large **egg yolk** (0.5 oz / 15g)

½ cup **sugar** (3.5 oz / 100g)

16 fresh **apricots** (about 3¼ lb / 1.5kg), pitted and cut into ½-inch wedges ②

1 large **egg**, beaten

½ recipe **Honey Almond Syrup** (page 320)

Vanilla ice cream, for serving

The window for good apricots in the summertime is short, and even at the height of the season you might get a mealy dud or two, but a peak apricot is transcendent. I'd argue that a *baked* peak apricot is even better. I love how jammy and intensely sweet-tart they become. This massive tart is a spin on a version I made in pastry class in culinary school and a wonderful showcase for apricots. It's sweet enough to be dessert, especially served with vanilla ice cream, but it's also a superb breakfast pastry—like eating a piece of buttery brioche with apricot jam!

Roll out the brioche dough: Roll out the brioche dough on a lightly floured piece of parchment paper, dusting with more flour as needed to prevent sticking, into a thin, even rectangle that measures about 16 × 12 inches (you can also stretch it a bit with your fingertips). ③ Slide the parchment paper onto a rimmed baking sheet.

Reinforce the edges of the tart: Fold the edges of the brioche inward to create a reinforced wall that will act as the border of the tart. Press all the way around to make sure the dough sticks to itself.

Let the dough rise: Cover the dough with a damp kitchen towel and let it sit at room temperature until the dough is slightly puffed across the surface and the border springs back but leaves a slight imprint when poked with a floured finger, 25 to 35 minutes.

Preheat the oven: Meanwhile, arrange an oven rack in the upper third of the oven and preheat to 350°F.

Assemble the tart: Whisk the crème fraîche, yolk, and ¼ cup of the sugar (1.8 oz / 50g) in a small bowl until smooth. ④ Drizzle the mixture all across the surface of the dough, using the back of a spoon to gently and evenly spread it all the way to the borders. Arrange the apricot wedges in tight rows on top of the crème fraîche mixture, pressing down gently (you might not use all the wedges if the apricots are large). Brush the beaten egg all along the borders. Sprinkle the remaining ¼ cup sugar (1.8 oz / 50g) evenly across the entire surface of the tart.

DO AHEAD
The tart, covered and stored at room temperature, will keep up to 3 days but is best served the day it's made.

① I recommend making a full recipe of Brioche Dough even though this recipe only calls for a half quantity to make the tart. Bake the leftover dough into a loaf (instructions on page 354) or use it to make **Pigs in a Brioche Blanket** (page 303) or **Brioche Twists with Coriander Sugar** (page 229).

② Buy your apricots several days in advance so they can ripen on your countertop. When they're ripe, they should smell super fragrant and feel firm with a slight give when squeezed. Give the apricots a taste—if yours are very sweet, consider reducing the sugar by

Bake the tart: Bake the tart until the apricots start to brown at the points and are jammy and nearly collapsed and the brioche is a deep golden brown around the borders, 30 to 35 minutes.

Soak with syrup, cool, and serve: Remove from the oven and immediately and liberally brush the honey almond syrup over the apricots and around the edges of the tart. As the tart cools, about every 10 minutes, continue to brush it with more syrup until you've used it all. Slice the tart into squares and serve with vanilla ice cream.

2 tablespoons. You can also substitute an equal weight of another stone fruit, like nectarines or plums, for the apricots.

3 The dough will seem quite thin when you work it into the dimensions specified in the recipe, but it bakes up surprisingly tall in the oven!

4 Don't mix the crème fraîche, yolk, and sugar ahead of time—allowing it to sit will thin the texture of the crème fraîche and cause it to run across the fruit during baking. Only mix it right before assembling.

Meyer Lemon Tart

Serves 8 to 10

Special Equipment:
9-inch removable-bottom tart pan or 9-inch springform pan, instant-read thermometer, food processor (for the Sweet Tart Dough)

Lemon Curd, Meyer Lemon Variation (page 330) ①

½ cup plain whole-milk **Greek yogurt** (4.2 oz / 120g)

Sweet Tart Dough (page 338), parbaked in a 9-inch removable-bottom tart or springform pan and cooled

⅓ cup **raspberry** or **blackberry jam** (3.5 oz / 100g)

Citrus fruits are my natural antidote to seasonal affective disorder in the winter, and I get especially excited for the arrival of Meyer lemons. They have a floral, even slightly spicy flavor that makes a spectacular lemon curd and a very special tart. I spike the curd with a little yogurt to mellow out some of the lemon flavor and give the filling some body. It's still quite tart, though, which is how I prefer all my lemon desserts.

Mix the filling: In a medium bowl, whisk the curd and yogurt until smooth. Cover the bowl and set aside to allow the filling come to room temperature.

Preheat the oven: Arrange an oven rack in the center position and preheat the oven to 350°F.

Bake the jam layer: Place the parbaked tart crust on a foil-lined baking sheet. Spread the jam evenly across the bottom of the tart, working it all the way to the sides. Bake just until the jam is set, 5 to 7 minutes (this layer creates a seal between the curd and the crust so the latter stays crisp). Remove the tart from the oven. (Leave the oven on.)

Fill and bake the tart: Scrape the filling into the hot crust to the very top, then use an offset spatula to smooth the surface. (Depending on the height of your crust, you may have a tiny bit of curd left over; save it for another use. ②) Carefully transfer the tart to the oven and bake until the filling is set and puffed around the edges and the center wobbles gently (it will wobble as a cohesive mass, not ripple), 28 to 33 minutes.

Cool and chill the tart: Let the tart cool completely on a wire rack before removing the ring. Place the tart on a serving plate and chill until cold, at least 1 hour. Slice and serve.

DO AHEAD
The tart, covered and refrigerated, will keep up to 3 days but is best served the day it's made (the crust will soften over time).

① For a more classic lemon tart, substitute standard lemon curd here.

② Use any leftover curd to top scones, fill sandwich cookies, or dollop over a slice of cake.

Foolproof Tarte Tatin

Serves 8

Special Equipment:
10-inch ovenproof skillet

7 medium or 8 small **Pink Lady** or any sweet-tart, firm **baking apples** (about 3 lb / 1.36kg) ①

⅔ cup **maple syrup** (7 oz / 200g)

⅓ cup **brandy** (2.6 oz / 74g), preferably **apple brandy**

2 teaspoons **apple cider vinegar** (0.3 oz / 8g)

½ teaspoon plus a pinch of **Diamond Crystal kosher salt**

1 cup **sugar** (7 oz / 200g)

3 tablespoons **unsalted butter** (1.5 oz / 43g), cut into ½-inch pieces

½ recipe **Rough Puff Pastry** (page 355) or 1 sheet thawed frozen store-bought puff pastry

All-purpose flour, for rolling out

Vanilla ice cream, for serving

For a recipe that is often touted as "simple," tarte Tatin is remarkably easy to screw up. I have made tarts where the apples have overcaramelized and stuck to the skillet, stayed blond and released tons of moisture, or shrunk dramatically. Differences in the freshness and juiciness of apples was always the problem, so I developed a method of preroasting the apples to coax out some of the moisture, which helps to correct and account for this variation. Another advantage of this method is that the cold pastry gets placed atop cold apples, ensuring that it stays flaky. Is this recipe 100 percent foolproof? Probably not. But it's way more reliable than the traditional version and every bit as good.

Preheat the oven: Arrange an oven rack in the center position and preheat the oven to 275°F.

Roast the apples: Shave off a layer of flesh from the stem and bottom ends of the apples so they stand upright. Peel the apples, then cut them in half through the stem. Use a melon baller or round teaspoon measure to scoop out the cores and seeds, then slice out any remaining areas of core or stem. Stand the apple halves upright in a 10-inch ovenproof skillet (it will be a tight fit). Pour the maple syrup, brandy, and 1 teaspoon of the vinegar over the apples and add a pinch of salt. Cover the skillet with foil and crimp around the edges to create a steam-tight seal.

Transfer to the oven and roast the apples just until a cake tester or toothpick slides easily through the flesh, 1 hour 15 minutes to 1 hour 45 minutes, depending on firmness. They should be cooked just beyond "al dente," but not so much that they break apart and turn into mush. ② (If you're unsure, err on the side of slightly less cooked, but even slightly overcooked apples will still make a great tart.) The apples will turn brown during roasting, which is fine because they're going to caramelize in the tart.

Chill the apples: Leaving the juices in the skillet, carefully transfer the hot apples to a large plate and refrigerate uncovered until cold, at least 20 minutes and up to overnight (if chilling longer than 20 minutes, cover the apples). Don't clean the skillet—you'll use it in the next step. (continues)

DO AHEAD
The apples can be roasted up to 2 days ahead. Let cool on a plate, then cover and refrigerate. Reduce the cooking juices as directed, transfer to a container, and refrigerate until ready to use.
The tart, covered and stored at room temperature, will keep up to 3 days but is best served the day it's made.

① Pick an apple that you'd want to eat out of hand—not too sweet, not too tart. Pink Ladies are my go-to supermarket apple, while Gold Rush are the kind I look for at the farmers' market. You also want firm apples, ensuring they will hold their shape and not break down into applesauce in the tart. To test if an apple is firm enough to bake with, grip it and press your thumb into the flesh. It shouldn't leave an indent, or it should only do so with great pressure.

Cook down the apple juices to make the glaze: Place the skillet with the apple juices over medium-low heat and bring the juices to a vigorous simmer. Cook, swirling the skillet often, until the liquid is thick and syrupy, about 2 minutes. Transfer the syrup to a heatproof cup or container (you should have between ⅓ and ½ cup) and set aside for glazing. Rinse and dry the skillet.

Make the caramel: Sprinkle a few tablespoons of the sugar across the bottom of the skillet in an even layer. Cook undisturbed over medium heat until most of the granules are melted into a clear liquid, about 4 minutes. Sprinkle another layer of sugar on top of the first and cook, stirring around the sides of the skillet with a heatproof spatula to move the melted sugar toward the center, until mostly melted, another minute or so. Repeat a few more times until you've used the entire 1 cup sugar (7 oz / 200g) and all of it is mostly melted (there may be a solid clump here and there), 6 to 8 minutes. Continue to cook the sugar, stirring occasionally, until it turns a deep amber color, moves very fluidly, and releases wisps of smoke, about 5 minutes. Remove the skillet from the heat and slowly stir in the butter one piece at a time, taking care because the caramel will sputter, until the mixture is smooth. Stir in the salt and remaining 1 teaspoon vinegar and set the skillet aside to cool until the caramel is hardened, 10 to 15 minutes.

Arrange the apples in the skillet: Place the chilled apples rounded-side down in the skillet, overlapping them as needed to minimize gaps. Depending on the size of your apples, you might have an extra half left over, but try to fit them very tightly as they'll shrink some during baking. Refrigerate the skillet while you roll out the pastry.

Preheat the oven: Arrange an oven rack in the center position and preheat the oven to 425°F.

Roll out and cut the pastry: Remove the pastry from the refrigerator and let it soften at room temperature for about 5 minutes. Unwrap the dough and place it on a lightly floured surface. Use a rolling pin to beat the dough all across the surface to make it more pliable. Dust over top and underneath the dough with more flour, then roll out, dusting with more flour as needed, to a 12-inch round. If using thawed frozen puff pastry, gently roll out the pastry on a lightly floured surface to smooth any creases and widen so it's about 12 inches across in all directions. Set an 11-inch dinner plate (or an 11-inch parchment round) on top of the dough and cut around it with a sharp knife or a wheel cutter to create an 11-inch pastry round. Prick it all over with a fork.

Cover the apples with the pastry and chill: Drape the pastry over the apples and use a large spoon to tuck the edges of the pastry down between the apples and the sides of the skillet. Refrigerate the skillet for 10 to 15 minutes to firm up the pastry.

Bake the tart: Transfer the skillet to the oven and bake the tart for 20 minutes, then reduce the temperature to 350°F and bake until the pastry is puffed, golden brown all over, and the caramel is bubbling around the sides, another 35 to 45 minutes. Carefully remove the skillet from the oven and set it aside to rest for 5 to 10 minutes.

Invert the tart: Working over a sink to catch any flowing juices, carefully invert the skillet onto a wire cooling rack. Remove the skillet and scrape off any apples that may have stuck, pressing them back into place on the tart.

Glaze the tart and serve: While the tart is still warm, use a pastry brush to dab the reserved reduced juices over the apples to give them a high gloss (don't feel the need to use all the glaze). If the glaze is very thick, warm it briefly until it's more fluid. Slide the tart off the rack onto a plate, slice, and serve warm or at room temperature with vanilla ice cream.

---

[2] If you're using farmers' market apples, they may take much longer to roast. Very firm, fresh apples could take twice as long to soften as cold-storage apples from the supermarket.

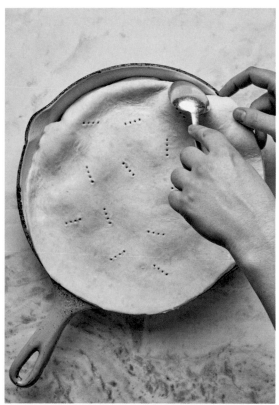

Season: Summer | Active Time: 45 minutes (not including pitting or making the Flaky All-Butter Pie Dough)
Total Time: 2 hours 45 minutes, plus time to cool | Difficulty: 3 (Moderate, mostly due to the lattice crust)

Sour Cherry Pie

Serves 8

Special Equipment:
Cherry pitter, 9-inch pie plate

2 recipes **Flaky All-Butter Pie Dough, Almond Variation** (page 337)

All-purpose flour, for rolling out

8 cups fresh pitted **sour cherries** (2.5 lb / 1.12kg), from about 3 pounds (1.36kg) [2]

1¼ cups **granulated sugar** (8.8 oz / 250g)

5 tablespoons **cornstarch** (1.6 oz / 44g)

2 teaspoons finely grated **lemon zest**

2 teaspoons **vanilla extract**

½ teaspoon **ground cinnamon**

¼ teaspoon **ground cardamom**

¼ teaspoon **Diamond Crystal kosher salt**

¼ teaspoon **almond extract**

1 large **egg**, beaten

Demerara sugar, for sprinkling the top

I grew up in a house that had a sour cherry tree in the front yard, and every summer my sisters and I would hang out a second-story window to pick the fruit so my mom could make pies. Now, I can't think of anything else I love to bake more than a sour cherry pie. Because they're only available during a short window in July, sour cherries are typically a farmers' market-only fruit (although sometimes you can find them frozen). Every summer I like to buy as many quarts as I can carry, then clean, pit, and freeze them in bags so I can make pies through the fall and winter. [1] This pie calls for more cornstarch and sugar than you might be used to adding to a pie, but both are necessary for a balanced, set filling.

Preheat the oven: Arrange an oven rack in the lowest position and preheat the oven to 425°F.

Roll out the pie dough: Remove one piece of pie dough from the refrigerator and let it soften at room temperature for about 5 minutes. Unwrap the dough and place it on a lightly floured surface. Use a rolling pin to beat the dough all across the surface to make it more pliable. Dust over top and underneath the dough with more flour, then roll it out, dusting with more flour as needed, until you have a round about 13 inches in diameter and ⅛ inch thick.

Lower the round into the pie plate, letting the pastry slump down the sides. Firmly press the pastry into the bottom and up the sides of the plate to ensure full contact. Use scissors to trim around the edge, leaving a ¾-inch overhang of dough. Refrigerate the bottom crust in the pie plate while you roll out the second crust just as you did the first. Cut the second round into 1-inch-wide strips. Transfer the strips to a dinner plate and refrigerate while you make the filling.

Mix the filling: In a large bowl, combine the cherries, granulated sugar, cornstarch, lemon zest, vanilla, cinnamon, cardamom, salt, and almond extract and toss to combine. (continues)

DO AHEAD
The pie, covered loosely and stored at room temperature, will keep up to 4 days but is best served on the first or second day while the pastry is still crisp.

[1] Even if you're pitting fresh cherries and plan to bake a pie straight away, it's still a good idea to freeze them. Frozen cherries keep the pastry cold (helping create an extra-flaky crust) and release their juices more slowly than fresh cherries, making it easier to assemble the pie.

[2] Taste the cherries when you bring them home to gauge their sweetness. If it's the very peak of the season, the cherries will be darker and sweeter, so you may want to decrease the sugar in the filling by about 2 tablespoons.

Assemble the pie: Remove the bottom crust and dough strips from the refrigerator and scrape the filling into the lined pie plate, mounding and pressing firmly on the cherries to eliminate air pockets. Use a pastry brush to dab beaten egg all around the edge of the pastry. Arrange the two longest strips of dough perpendicular to each other across the center of the pie. Start arranging the next longest strips parallel to the first two in both directions, spacing about ½ inch apart and weaving in an alternating under-over pattern. You'll have to fold every other strip up and back as you work, replacing them over each new strip placed in the opposite direction. Continue to weave the remaining strips, alternating the under-over motion to form a lattice. Press firmly where the strips come into contact with the egg wash on the bottom crust and then trim off the excess. Brush the overhang again with more egg and fold it up and inward onto itself. Pinch all the way around to seal the pastry, then crimp the edge, using floured hands if necessary to prevent sticking. Brush the top of the pie, including the entire lattice and crimped edge, with egg, then sprinkle generously with demerara sugar.

Bake the pie and cool: Set the pie on a foil-lined rimmed baking sheet (to catch drips—there *will* be drips!) and bake for 20 minutes. Reduce the oven temperature to 350°F and continue to bake, tenting any areas of the crust that are browning faster than everywhere else, until the juices are bubbling in the center of the pie, another 1½ to 2 hours. ③ Remove from the oven and let cool completely, at least 4 hours.

③ Wait to pull the pie until you absolutely see the juices bubbling in the center—as the recipe states, this could take upward of 2 hours! It's virtually impossible to overbake this pie unless you outright burn the top crust (tenting with foil helps prevent this). I prefer a pie that might have a few dark spots on top and a fully set filling rather than a pie with runny juices and a pale bottom crust.

Quince and Almond Tart
with Rosé

Serves 8

Special Equipment:
10-inch ovenproof skillet

1 (750 ml) bottle **dry rosé wine** [1]

1¼ cups **sugar** (8.8 oz / 250g)

1 teaspoon **vanilla extract**

1 **cinnamon stick**

1 whole **star anise**

Pinch of **kosher salt**

2 teaspoons **cocktail bitters** (optional)

1 **lemon**

2½ pounds (1.13kg) **quince**
(about 5 large), rinsed and rubbed
to remove any fuzz [2]

Neutral oil for the skillet

4 ounces (113g) **almond paste**
(not marzipan)

1 recipe **Flaky All-Butter Pie Dough**
(page 333) or ½ recipe **Rough Puff Pastry**
(page 355)

All-purpose flour, for rolling out

This book is filled with dear recipes, so forgive my frequent use of superlatives—I have lots of favorites! But actually, quince *really are* my favorite. These alluring fruits are easily mistaken for apples or pears at the farmers' market but have a completely unique flavor, redolent of lychee and pineapple. They have to be cooked to transform the hard, cottony flesh into a fragrant, juicy fruit. I like to poach them in rosé with a dash of cocktail bitters—both to enhance the naturally pink color they turn when cooked and to highlight their perfume—plus a few warm spices. Once the quince are poached, which you can do days ahead, the rest of the tart comes together quickly using an upside-down, Tatin-style method.

Make the poaching liquid: In a large saucepan or small Dutch oven, combine the rosé, sugar, vanilla, cinnamon stick, star anise, salt, and cocktail bitters (if using). Use a vegetable peeler to remove wide strips of lemon zest (just the yellow layer, avoiding the white pith) and add to the pan. Cut the lemon in half and squeeze both halves into the pan, seeds and all (discard the lemon halves). Bring the mixture to a simmer over medium heat, stirring once or twice to dissolve the sugar, then remove from the heat.

Prepare the quince: Working with one quince at a time, use a sharp knife to shave off the ends of the quince and then use a vegetable peeler to peel the fruit. Set aside the peels in a bowl and reserve for later. Halve the quince through the stems and use a melon baller or round teaspoon measure to scoop out the seeds and cores, adding them to the peels in the bowl. [3] As you work, drop each peeled and scooped quince half into the poaching liquid.

Poach the quince: Once all the quince are in the poaching liquid, add water to the pan if needed just to cover the fruit. Press a round of parchment paper onto the surface of the liquid, eliminating any air bubbles, then place a small plate on top—this will keep the quince fully submerged as they poach. Bring the mixture to a lively simmer over medium-high heat, reduce the heat to maintain a gentle (continues)

DO AHEAD
The poached quince and quince jelly can be refrigerated up to 2 weeks. The tart, covered and stored at room temperature, will keep up to 4 days but is best served on the first or second day (the crust will soften over time).

[1] Any inexpensive rosé wine will do for this recipe, just as long as it's decent enough that you wouldn't mind drinking it on its own.

[2] Quince will stay hard as a rock even when ripe, so the best indicators of ripeness are their color and scent. Look for quince that

are more yellow than green and give off a strong floral, tropical-fruity aroma. If they don't smell like anything, leave them on your counter—they're not ready yet!

[3] Be very careful when scooping the cores from the quince, as the raw flesh is very hard and slips happen easily.

simmer, and cook until the quince are tender but not mushy and a paring knife slides easily through the flesh, as little as 25 minutes for very ripe fruit but possibly as long as 1 hour. Check the quince every 10 minutes or so. Remove the pan from the heat and let the quince cool in the liquid until warm.

Make the quince jelly: Use a slotted spoon to remove the quince from the poaching liquid and transfer to a cutting board to continue to cool. Dump the reserved skins, seeds, and cores into the poaching liquid and bring to a boil over medium-high heat. Boil, stirring occasionally, until the mixture is very thick and syrupy and the bubbles are slow to pop, 20 to 25 minutes. Strain the syrup through a fine-mesh sieve into a heatproof bowl. Press on the solids with a heatproof spatula to force as much liquid through the sieve as possible (discard the solids). You should have about ⅔ cup liquid. If you have much more than this, transfer the strained liquid to a small saucepan and simmer until it's reduced to the right amount. Due to all the natural pectin in the seeds and peel of the quince, this liquid will solidify into a soft jelly when chilled. Cover and refrigerate the jelly.

Slice the quince: Cut the quince halves crosswise into thin slices between ¼ and ⅛ inch thick. If preparing the quince ahead of time, set them on a plate, cover, and refrigerate.

Preheat the oven and prepare the skillet: Arrange an oven rack in the center position and preheat the oven to 400°F. Lightly brush the bottom and sides of a 10-inch ovenproof skillet with a thin coating of oil. Line the bottom with a round of parchment paper, smoothing to eliminate any air bubbles. Brush the parchment very lightly with more oil and set aside.

Roll out the almond paste: Working on a separate piece of parchment paper, use the heel of your hand to flatten the almond paste into a round. Place another piece of parchment on top and use a rolling pin to roll the almond paste into a thin, even round measuring about 9 inches in diameter. Set aside.

Roll out the pastry: Remove the pie dough from the refrigerator and let soften at room temperature for about 5 minutes. Unwrap the dough and place it on a lightly floured surface. Use a rolling pin to beat the dough all across the surface to make it more pliable. Dust over top and underneath the dough with more flour, then roll it out, dusting with more flour as needed, into an 11-inch round. Use a sharp knife or a wheel cutter to cut the pastry into an even 10-inch round, tracing a dinner plate or a cake pan as a guide. Slide the pastry onto a plate and refrigerate until it's time to assemble the tart.

Assemble the tart: Spoon all but about 3 tablespoons of the chilled quince jelly into the bottom of the prepared skillet (reserve the remaining jelly for glazing the tart). Layer the quince slices over the jelly in the skillet, overlapping tightly into whatever pattern you like (rows, a rosette, or free-form!). Uncover the almond paste round and carefully place it in the skillet, centering over the quince. Remove the pastry from the refrigerator and slide it into the skillet, then use a spoon to tuck the edges of the pastry down between the quince and the sides of the skillet. Use a paring knife to make about 8 small slits across the pastry to allow steam to escape.

Bake: Transfer the skillet to the oven and bake for 20 minutes. Reduce the oven temperature to 350°F and continue to bake until the pastry is golden brown and the jelly is bubbling up around the sides and starting to turn golden, another 25 to 35 minutes. Remove the skillet from the oven and let cool for 5 minutes.

Turn out the tart and glaze: Working over the sink and using towels or mitts to protect your hands from hot flowing juices, place a rack over the skillet and invert. Give the rack a sharp tap on the counter to release the tart, then slowly remove the skillet. Peel away the parchment if stuck to the tart. Let cool for about 10 minutes, then while the tart is still warm, brush with the reserved jelly to glaze the fruit. Slide the cooled tart onto a platter and serve at room temperature.

Blueberry Slab Pie

Serves 24

Special Equipment:
Food processor, at least 2 half-sheet
pans (18 × 13 inches) [2]

DOUGH

7½ cups **all-purpose flour** (34 oz / 975g),
plus more for rolling out

4 tablespoons **granulated sugar**
(1.8 oz / 50g)

3 teaspoons **Diamond Crystal kosher
salt** (0.32 oz / 9g)

6 sticks **unsalted butter** (24 oz / 680g),
cut into ½-inch pieces, chilled

FILLING AND ASSEMBLY

3½ pounds (1.6kg) fresh or frozen
blueberries (about 11 cups) [3]

1 cup **granulated sugar** (7 oz / 200g)

7 tablespoons **cornstarch** (2.2 oz / 61g)

2 tablespoons finely grated
lemon zest

⅓ cup fresh **lemon juice** (2.7 oz / 76g)

2 teaspoons **vanilla extract**

2½ teaspoons **ground ginger**

1½ teaspoons **ground cinnamon**

½ teaspoon **ground cardamom**

½ teaspoon **Diamond Crystal kosher salt**

1 large **egg**, beaten

Demerara sugar, for sprinkling the top

Vanilla ice cream, for serving

Here's a hot take: A regular pie is great, but a slab pie might be even better.
For crust lovers, it has a superior ratio of crust to filling, plus it's fairly
forgiving and easy to cut and serve to a large crowd. However, there are
downsides: Rolling out such a large piece of pie dough can be challenging
for a beginner, plus you're handling a large sheet pan that's not easy to
maneuver or fit inside a fridge, so you also need to work efficiently. Then
there's the high potential for juices to overflow, burn, and set off your
smoke alarm. On the upside, this particular recipe uses blueberries, so
there's no extra labor like peeling or chopping fruit for the filling. If you
want to use another type of filling, see note [1] below for converting any
existing fruit pie recipe! Because you need so much dough for a slab pie,
I've included a scaled-up, streamlined crust recipe here.

Make the dough in the food processor: Prepare and refrigerate 1 cup of
ice water while you assemble the dough. In a food processor, combine
3¾ cups of the flour (17.2 oz / 488g), 2 tablespoons of the granulated sugar
(0.88 oz / 25g), and 1½ teaspoons of the salt (0.16 oz / 4.5g) and pulse a few
times to combine. [4] Add half of the butter pieces (12 oz / 340g) and toss
to coat in the flour mixture. Process the mixture in long pulses until the
butter is broken down into pieces no larger than a hazelnut. Transfer the
entire mixture to a large bowl.

Bring the dough together and chill: Place a large sheet of plastic wrap next
to you on a work surface for the dough. Measure out ¾ cup (12 oz / 340g)
ice water and slowly drizzle it over the flour mixture, tossing constantly
with a fork to distribute. Once all the water is added, switch to your
hands and toss the mixture several times, then knead until big, shaggy
pieces of dough form (there will still be unincorporated flour). Transfer
these shaggy pieces to the plastic wrap, leaving the dry bits behind.
Drizzle in more ice water 1 tablespoon at a time, mixing with a fork and
then your hands after each addition, until all the dough comes together.
It will still look floury and dry in many places but should hold together
when squeezed. [5] Transfer all the dough to the plastic wrap and press
into a single mass, then flatten into a ¾-inch-thick square. Wrap the
dough tightly in the plastic, eliminating any air pockets. Use a rolling pin
to firmly roll over the plastic-wrapped block of dough in both (continues)

DO AHEAD
The pie, covered and stored at room
temperature, will keep up to 4 days but
is best served on the first or second day.
The dough can be made and chilled
3 days ahead or frozen up to 2 months.
Thaw for at least 24 hours in the
refrigerator before using.

[1] To convert any standard-sized fruit pie
recipe, like **Sour Cherry Pie** (page 111),
into a slab pie, double the filling and use
this recipe for the dough and assembly.

[2] Having this exact size pan is important—
the quantities of dough and filling in this
recipe were developed to fit the specific
dimensions and volume of a standard
half-sheet pan (18 × 13 inches).

directions, forcing it into the corners and flattening into an even thickness. Transfer to the refrigerator. Repeat the entire dough-making process with the remaining 3¾ cups flour (17.2 oz / 488g), 2 tablespoons granulated sugar (0.88 oz / 25g), 1½ teaspoons salt (0.16 oz / 4.5g), 3 sticks of butter (12 oz / 340g), and more ice water. Chill both blocks of dough for at least 2 hours.

Roll out one piece of dough and cut strips: Let one block of dough sit at room temperature for 5 to 10 minutes to soften slightly. Unwrap the dough and place it on a lightly floured surface. Use a rolling pin to beat the dough all across the surface to make it more pliable. Dust over top and underneath with more flour, then roll it out, dusting with more flour as needed, into a giant rectangular slab about 18 × 15 inches. If any cracks appear in the dough while rolling, cut a small piece of dough from the edge and press it over the crack to patch, then carry on. Use a wheel cutter or chef's knife to cut the dough crosswise into strips measuring 1½ inches wide and 15 inches long. Place the strips on a parchment-lined baking sheet and refrigerate while you make the filling.

Preheat the oven: Arrange an oven rack in the lowest position and line the entire rack with overlapping sheets of foil. There will be lots of buttery juices that will bubble over and start to smoke if they hit the oven floor, so you definitely want the foil there to catch any drips. If you have a second 18 × 13-inch half-sheet pan (you also need one for the slab pie), place it on the rack on top of the foil. Preheat the oven to 425°F. You will bake the slab pie nested inside this preheated half-sheet pan, which will help the bottom brown and bake through more quickly—thanks to my friend Sue Li for this excellent baking tip!

Make the filling: In a large bowl, combine the blueberries, granulated sugar, cornstarch, lemon zest, lemon juice, vanilla, ginger, cinnamon, cardamom, and salt. Mix with a large flexible spatula or serving spoon until combined and set aside.

Roll out the bottom crust and fill: Follow the same instructions as above for rolling out the second piece of dough, this time rolling it into a slightly thinner slab measuring about 21 × 16 inches. Loosely fold the slab in half, then slide the dough onto an 18 × 13-inch half-sheet pan and unfold, positioning it so you have about ½ inch of overhang all the way around. Press the dough firmly into the bottom and against the sides. Brush the inside border of the overhang with some of the beaten egg, then scrape the blueberry filling into the crust and press it firmly into an even layer.

Arrange the top crust: Remove the strips of dough from the refrigerator and, starting at one end of the sheet pan, arrange them crosswise over the filling on a diagonal, overlapping the strips in a slight zigzag. Press the strips into the egg-washed border of the bottom crust and use scissors to trim off any excess. Brush the dough strips with egg and fold the overhang inward over the filling along all four sides. (The slab pie is already so labor-intensive at this point, I just leave the edge natural.) Brush more egg around the edges and generously sprinkle the entire top of the pie with demerara sugar. If your blueberries were not frozen, and if you have room in your refrigerator or freezer, chill the pie until the pastry is firm, 10 to 15 minutes (if not, the pie will be fine).

Bake the pie and serve: The slab pie is heavy, so carefully nest it inside the preheated sheet pan (or place directly on the foil) and bake for 20 minutes. Reduce the oven temperature to 350°F and continue to bake until the top is deep golden brown and the filling is bubbling, another 1 hour 15 minutes to 1 hour 30 minutes. Let the pie cool on a wire rack for at least 1 hour before serving warm or at room temperature with vanilla ice cream.

---

[3] If you're using frozen blueberries, don't thaw them first. Frozen berries actually help keep the bottom crust very cold, buying you more time to assemble the pie.

[4] 3¾ cups flour and 3 sticks of butter just about max out the capacity of an 11-cup food processor, which is why it's best to make the dough in two batches rather than a single batch that you divide in half.

(If you have a smaller food processor, you might have to work in more batches to pulse in the butter.) You can make the dough by hand, but be prepared for a workout. The volume of butter is so great that you might have a difficult time working it into the flour mixture with your fingers before it starts to soften. Either work in batches or ask someone to help you.

[5] The amount of water you use to make the pie dough can vary dramatically, especially if you're using flour that's been sitting in your cabinet or on a store shelf for many months (and losing moisture during that time). I once made this dough with flour of unknown origin, likely *very* old, and used nearly 50 percent more water than usual.

Peach Melba Tart

Serves 8

Special Equipment:
Large Dutch oven or straight-sided skillet

1 cup **granulated sugar** (7 oz / 200g)

½ cup **dry white wine** (4 oz / 113g)

1 teaspoon **vanilla extract**

Pinch of **kosher salt**

1 **lemon**, halved crosswise

1½ lb (680g) firm ripe **peaches** (about 6–10 small), halved, skins and pits left on ①

½ recipe **Rough Puff Pastry** (page 355) or 1 sheet thawed frozen store-bought puff pastry ②

All-purpose flour, for rolling out

1 large **egg**, beaten

6 ounces (170g) **raspberries** (about 1⅓ cups)

Pastry Cream (page 321)

When I was a graduate student studying French food history, I came across an old French newspaper clipping about the true origins of the dessert known as peach Melba, a dish of vanilla ice cream topped with peaches and raspberry sauce. According to the paper, the real story was not the popular one told about Auguste Escoffier, the most famous French chef of the late nineteenth and early twentieth centuries, creating the dessert to honor the Australian opera singer Nellie Melba. Actually, it explained, Melba had been badmouthing Escoffier's cooking all over Paris, and, knowing that Melba was not a fan of peaches, the chef named the dessert for her out of spite. This whole account seems dubious, mostly because I can't imagine anyone disliking peaches, but either way peach Melba is a phenomenal dessert. This tart swaps in vanilla pastry cream for the ice cream and layers the pastry cream, poached peaches, and crushed raspberries in a buttery pastry shell (besides the pastry, it's no-bake!). All these components require effort and planning (see Do Ahead below for how to space out the work), but I can't think of a better way to express summer in a dessert.

Poach the peaches: In the bottom of a large Dutch oven or straight-sided skillet, combine the sugar, wine, vanilla, salt, and 2 cups of water (16 oz / 454g). Squeeze the lemon halves into the Dutch oven and toss the rinds in as well. Set the Dutch oven over medium heat and stir occasionally until the sugar is dissolved. Bring the poaching liquid to a very gentle simmer, then add the peach halves cut-sides up, arranging them in a single layer so they are all submerged. Continue to cook over medium heat until the poaching liquid comes back to a simmer and is bubbling very gently, about 4 minutes. Remove the Dutch oven from the heat and turn the peaches over. Cover the Dutch oven and set aside to allow the peaches to poach gently as the mixture cools.

Preheat the oven: Arrange an oven rack in the center position and preheat the oven to 400°F. (continues)

DO AHEAD
The poached peaches, stored in their poaching liquid in the refrigerator, will keep up to 3 days. The baked, unfilled crust, well wrapped and stored at room temperature, will keep up to 1 day. The tart is best served the day it's made but will keep, covered and refrigerated, up to 2 days (the pastry will soften over time).

① Buy peaches at least 2 or 3 days ahead to allow them to ripen at room temperature. They should be firm and yield to light pressure. If the peaches don't soften enough by the time you want to poach them, go ahead and peel them before poaching since the peels won't easily release once cooked.

② If using frozen puff pastry as a substitute, just make sure to let it thaw gently in the refrigerator overnight before using. I recommend Dufour brand, but any brand labeled "all-butter" will work. If your package of puff pastry contains two small sheets instead of one large, stack the sheets one on top of the other and then roll out to the dimensions in the recipe.

Roll out the pastry and form the crust: Let the pastry sit at room temperature for about 5 minutes to soften. Roll out on a lightly floured surface, dusting over top and underneath with more flour as needed, to a large rectangle measuring about 15 × 11 inches and ⅛ inch thick.

If you're using thawed frozen puff pastry, roll out the pastry on a lightly floured surface to the same dimensions. Transfer the pastry to a parchment-lined rimmed baking sheet and trim with a knife to straighten the edges so you have a squared-off rectangle measuring about 14 × 10 inches. Slice off ½-inch-wide strips of pastry from all four sides of the rectangle. Brush around the border of the pastry rectangle with some of the beaten egg, then place the strips over the egg wash, aligning them so they're flush with the edges of the rectangle. Trim off any overhang at the corners, then press along the borders to help the pastry adhere to itself. Brush the borders with more egg wash, then use a fork to prick the surface of the pastry all over.

Bake the pastry: Bake the pastry until the surface is puffed and deep golden brown all over, 20 to 25 minutes. Remove from the oven and press down on the surface of the pastry with the back of a spoon to flatten if it's puffed up in places. Let cool completely.

Peel and pit the peaches: Meanwhile, remove the peaches from the cooled poaching liquid one piece at a time and gently peel the skin away from the flesh and discard. With truly ripe in-season peaches, this should happen easily. Gently pull out any pits and discard. Transfer the peeled and pitted halves to a plate. Reserve ¼ cup of the poaching liquid (if you have more fruit poaching to do down the road, reserve and chill the remaining poaching liquid; it's super flavorful!).

Crush the raspberries: In a small bowl, combine half the raspberries and the ¼ cup reserved poaching liquid and crush the berries with the back of a spoon until you have a saucy consistency. Fold in the remaining berries and set aside.

Assemble the tart: Whisk the pastry cream until smooth, then spoon between 1½ and 2 cups onto the surface of the pastry (don't use all the pastry cream, or you'll overfill the tart; save any leftover for serving with other summer fruits). Spread the pastry cream all the way to the edges in an even layer, then arrange the peach halves over the pastry cream (you may have one or two peach halves left over). Spoon the raspberry mixture over the peaches and serve immediately, or chill the tart, loosely covered, until ready to serve.

Bars and Cookies

Cookies are not my forte compared to cakes and pies. They don't typically incorporate fresh ingredients, making them less exciting to me. Plus, I don't love forming and baking individual pieces. All of that said, I know how useful it is to have several cookie recipes up one's sleeve. They're portable, giftable, and freezable, and there is never a party or gathering where cookies are not welcome. When I do make cookies, I gravitate toward those that are either a combination of buttery, tender, and crisp, like sablés, or chewy, butterscotchy, and brown sugary, like a classic chocolate chip. I try wherever possible to make the forming process unfussy, which means lots of slice-and-bake and bar cookies, and no complicated decorating. Every cookie here is on my short list, and, happily, one or two even include fruit.

CHEWY MOLASSES SPICE
COOKIES, PAGE 144

Marcona Almond Cookies

Makes about 24 small cookies

Special Equipment:
Food processor

4 ounces (118g) **Marcona almonds**, plus about 24 whole almonds for topping ①

1 (7 oz / 198g) tube **almond paste** (not marzipan), coarsely crumbled

¼ cup **sugar** (1.8 oz / 50g)

1 teaspoon **vanilla extract**

2 large **eggs** (3.5 oz / 100g)

I used to live in Carroll Gardens, Brooklyn, a historically Italian-American neighborhood with several beloved Italian bakeries all within a few blocks of one another and my apartment. I'd occasionally stop by Monteleone, Court Pastry, Caputo's Bake Shop, or Mazzola Bakery on my way home from the subway to buy a pignoli cookie—chewy, sweet, almondy, and by far my favorite Italian cookie. When thinking about a pignoli-inspired cookie for this book, it clicked that Marcona almonds, with their rich, toasty flavor, were a great swap for the pine nuts. Grinding some of the almonds into the dough lends texture and balance, the saltiness of the nuts tempering the sweetness of the almond paste. They're quick, easy, adorable, and super delicious.

Preheat the oven and prepare the baking sheet: Arrange an oven rack in the center position and preheat the oven to 400°F. Line a large rimmed baking sheet with parchment paper and set aside.

Make the dough: In a food processor, pulse the 4 ounces (118g) of almonds until coarsely chopped. Add the almond paste, sugar, vanilla, and 1 whole egg and 1 egg white (place the yolk in a small bowl) and process in long pulses until you have a smooth dough. Add 2 teaspoons of water to the yolk, beat with a fork to combine, then set aside to use as an egg wash.

Scoop the dough and top: Transfer the dough to a pastry bag (or a resealable zip-top bag) and snip a 1-inch opening. Pipe the dough onto the prepared baking sheet in 1½-inch-diameter rounds, spacing them about 1½ inches apart (the cookies will spread only slightly). (Alternatively, you can use a ½-ounce scoop or rounded tablespoon measure to portion dough into uniform mounds.) Use a pastry brush to cover the entire surface of each cookie with a thin layer of the egg wash, then press a whole almond into the center of each cookie.

Bake: Bake the cookies until they're puffed and golden brown all over, 10 to 12 minutes. Remove from the oven and let cool completely on the baking sheet before carefully peeling the cookies off the parchment paper.

DO AHEAD
The cookies, stored in an airtight container at room temperature, will keep up to 5 days. The baked cookies can also be frozen up to 2 months.

① Marcona almonds' very high fat content makes them turn rancid quickly, so store them in the freezer to maintain freshness. If you can't find Marconas (hint: they're usually in the cheese section of the grocery store), you can use salted roasted cashews, another high-fat nut.

Salted Halvah Blondies

Makes 16 blondies

Special Equipment:
8 × 8-inch pan (preferably metal)

Butter for the pan

1¼ cups **all-purpose flour** (5.6 oz / 163g)

1 teaspoon **Diamond Crystal kosher salt** (0.11 oz / 3g)

½ teaspoon **baking powder**

6 ounces (170g) **white chocolate**, coarsely chopped (1 cup)

1 stick **unsalted butter** (4 oz / 113g)

¼ cup **tahini** (2.5 oz / 70g)

½ cup packed **light brown sugar** (3.5 oz / 100g)

1 large **egg** (1.8 oz / 50g)

2 large **egg yolks** (1.1 oz / 32g)

1 tablespoon **vanilla extract**

4 ounces (113g) **halvah**, crumbled (about ½ cup) ①

2 tablespoons **sesame seeds** (0.63 oz / 18g)

Flaky salt, for sprinkling the top

As a sesame lover, I was psyched when sesame seeds and all their derivative products started appearing on supermarket shelves many years ago. I have an affinity for sesame because its strong, bitter flavor marries particularly well with sweet flavors, producing desserts that are intense but well balanced. Halvah is a Middle Eastern candy made with sugar and ground sesame that has a crumbly, dissolving texture. It's perfect folded into these white chocolate–based, tahini-laced blondies. Topped with a blanket of sesame seeds and a bit of flaky salt for texture, they make an unexpected (and super delicious) bar cookie.

Preheat the oven and prepare the pan: Arrange an oven rack in the center position and preheat the oven to 350°F. Line an 8 × 8-inch pan with 2 sheets of foil, crossing one over the other and pressing the foil into the corners and up the sides. Butter the foil generously and set the pan aside.

Mix the dry ingredients: In a medium bowl, whisk together the flour, salt, and baking powder to combine. Set aside.

Melt the white chocolate mixture: In a large heatproof bowl, combine the white chocolate, butter, and tahini and set it over a medium saucepan filled with about 1 inch of simmering (not boiling) water. Warm the mixture gently, stirring occasionally, just until the white chocolate and butter are melted and the mixture is smooth. Remove the bowl from the heat and let cool slightly.

Add the sugar and eggs: Whisk the brown sugar into the white chocolate mixture. It will look grainy and you might see some of the fat start to separate from the rest of the mixture, which is normal. Add the whole egg, egg yolks, and vanilla and whisk vigorously until the mixture comes back together and looks very thick, smooth, and glossy and is starting to pull ever so slightly away from the sides of the bowl.

Add the dry ingredients and halvah: Add the flour mixture and stir with a flexible spatula just until the dry ingredients are evenly incorporated into the batter. Add the crumbled halvah and fold in gently to avoid breaking it into smaller bits.

Bake the blondies: Scrape the batter into the prepared pan, spreading it in an even layer all the way to the corners. Sprinkle the sesame seeds

---

DO AHEAD
The blondies, stored in an airtight container at room temperature, will keep up to 5 days or can be frozen up to 2 months.

① Use any flavor of halvah you like, such as vanilla, marble, or pistachio.

② When they're finished baking, the blondies will look slightly underdone but will set as they cool. Try not to bake them longer, which could dry them out.

across the surface of the batter, then top with flaky salt. Bake until the blondies are puffed across the surface, golden brown around the edges, and slightly jiggly in the center, 20 to 25 minutes. ②

Let cool and serve: Allow the blondies to cool completely in the pan. Use the ends of the foil to lift the blondies out of the pan and slice into 16 bars.

Brown Butter
and Sage Sablés

Makes about 36 cookies

Special Equipment:
Stand or hand mixer

2 sticks **unsalted butter** (8 oz / 227g)

4 large fresh leafy **sage sprigs**
(0.5 oz / 14g)

1¾ cups **all-purpose flour** (8 oz / 228g)

¼ cup **cornstarch** (1.2 oz / 35g) [1]

1 teaspoon **Diamond Crystal kosher salt**
(0.11 oz / 3g)

¾ cup **granulated sugar** (5.3 oz / 150g)

1 teaspoon finely grated **lemon zest**

2 large **egg yolks** (1.1 oz / 32g)

2 teaspoons **vanilla extract**

½ cup **demerara sugar**

I love the sandy, dissolving texture of traditional sablé cookies—like a lighter, more tender shortbread. Besides being buttery, sablés are pretty much a blank canvas. I wasn't sure if the flavors of brown butter and sage would work in a sweet cookie, since they're typically used in savory recipes, but they totally do, adding a slightly grown-up complexity to the humble sablé.

Cook the sage and butter: In a small saucepan, combine the butter and sage and cook over medium-low heat, stirring occasionally, until the butter comes to a boil. Continue to cook, scraping the bottom and sides constantly with a heatproof spatula, until the sage leaves sizzle and fry and the butter sputters, foams, and eventually you see browned bits floating about, 5 to 8 minutes. [2]

Cool the sage butter: Pour the butter and sage mixture into the bowl of a stand mixer (or into a large bowl if using a hand mixer), making sure you scrape in all the browned bits. Pluck out all of the sage, letting any excess butter drip back into the bowl, and set the sprigs aside for later. Let the butter cool completely to room temperature, stirring occasionally, until it starts to solidify. (To speed this process along, submerge the bottom of the bowl in ice water and stir the butter until it turns opaque, but take care to not let it harden.) [3]

Mix the dry ingredients: While the butter is cooling, in a medium bowl, whisk together the flour, cornstarch, and salt and set aside.

Cream the butter and sugar: Set the bowl of solidified butter on the mixer and attach the paddle. Add the granulated sugar and lemon zest and beat on medium until the mixture is thoroughly combined and pale, about 2 minutes.

Beat in the egg yolks and vanilla: Use a flexible spatula to scrape down the sides of the bowl and add the egg yolks and vanilla. Beat on medium until just combined, about 30 seconds.

Add the flour mixture: Turn off the mixer and add all of the flour mixture, then mix on the lowest speed just until the dry ingredients are (continues)

DO AHEAD
The cookies, stored airtight at room temperature, will keep up to 4 days but are best served the day they're made. The dough, rolled into logs and refrigerated, will keep up to 3 days or can be frozen up to 2 months (thaw the

logs in the refrigerator for 1 day before slicing and baking). If you're making cookies from dough that was made more than 2 days ahead, it's best to fry a fresh batch of sage leaves and mix with demerara sugar just before baking so the sugar is fresh and fragrant.

[1] Feel free to use an additional ¼ cup of all-purpose flour (1.2 oz / 33g) if you don't have cornstarch; just note that the final texture won't be as light.

incorporated and you have a smooth dough. Fold the dough by hand with a flexible spatula several times to make sure everything is well mixed and no floury spots remain.

Form the dough into logs: Divide the dough in half and place each half on a 10-inch-long sheet of parchment paper. Roll each piece of dough into a tight 8-inch-long cylinder (see page 22 for a visual guide to rolling dough into logs). Wrap each parchment log in plastic wrap and refrigerate until the dough is firm, at least 2 hours or up to 2 days.

Make the sage sugar: Meanwhile, pick the reserved sage leaves from the stems and add half of the leaves to a small bowl with the demerara sugar. ④ Massage the mixture with your fingertips until the sage has broken down into tiny bits throughout the sugar.

Preheat the oven and prepare the pans: Arrange two oven racks in the upper and lower thirds of the oven and preheat to 350°F. Line two rimmed baking sheets with parchment paper.

Roll the dough in sugar and slice: Remove one log of dough from the refrigerator and unwrap. Gently sprinkle about half of the sage sugar across a clean work surface or cutting board, then roll the log in the sugar, pressing down very firmly as you roll so the sugar adheres. Continue to roll and press until the entire log is coated. Use a sharp, thin-bladed knife to cut the log crosswise into ¼- to ½-inch-thick coins, rotating the log as you cut to avoid flattening one side. You should get about 18 cookies per log. Transfer the coins to one of the prepared baking sheets, spacing them about 2 inches apart. Refrigerate the first sheet of cookies while you repeat the process with the second log and remaining sage sugar, slicing and arranging the cookies on the second prepared baking sheet.

Bake: Bake the cookies on the upper and lower racks until they're golden around the edges, 16 to 20 minutes, switching racks and rotating the sheets front to back halfway through. Remove from the oven and let the cookies cool completely on the baking sheets.

② Don't leave the butter unattended while it's bubbling in the saucepan. It will begin to sputter violently onto your stove or bare skin, and you risk burning the milk solids.

③ Only proceed when the butter has cooled completely and begun to set up in the bowl, otherwise you will compromise the cookies' sandy texture.

④ Save the remaining sage leaves and sprinkle them over pastas, potato dishes, soups, or roast chicken.

Chocolate Chip Cookies

Makes about 18 large cookies

2 sticks **unsalted butter** (8 oz / 227g), cut into tablespoons

2 tablespoons **heavy cream, half-and-half, or whole milk** (1 oz / 28g)

2 cups **all-purpose flour** (9.2 oz / 260g) [1]

2 teaspoons **Diamond Crystal kosher salt** (0.22 oz / 6g)

1 teaspoon **baking soda** (0.21 oz / 6g)

¾ cup packed **dark brown sugar** (5.3 oz / 150g)

¾ cup **granulated sugar** (5.3 oz / 150g)

2 large **eggs** (3.5 oz / 100g), cold from the refrigerator

1 tablespoon **vanilla extract**

5 ounces (142g) **bittersweet chocolate disks**, half coarsely chopped

5 ounces (142g) **milk chocolate disks**, half coarsely chopped [2]

A chocolate chip cookie recipe is fascinating to develop because every single ingredient has a distinct impact on the outcome of the recipe, so you change one thing and you change the final cookie. It's all about achieving the right proportions. This is the recipe I've tweaked over several years to get everything I want in a chocolate chip cookie: crisp-chewy edges, a soft chocolaty center, and lots of butterscotchy notes enhanced by a healthy amount of salt. This particular cookie requires a few steps along the way—browning some of the butter, using both milk and dark chocolate disks (not chips), and resting the dough in the refrigerator to improve both flavor and texture—but it's still eminently makeable (no mixer required!). The hardest part is letting the dough chill before baking.

Brown the butter: Measure out 4 ounces (113g) of the butter and set aside in a large bowl. In a small saucepan, cook the remaining 4 ounces (113g) butter over medium-low heat, stirring frequently, until the butter comes to a boil. Continue to cook, scraping the bottom and sides of the pan constantly with a heatproof spatula, until the butter sputters, foams, and eventually you see browned bits floating about, 5 to 7 minutes. Add the browned butter to the bowl with the other butter, making sure you scrape in all the browned bits, then add the heavy cream (no need to stir). Set aside to cool. [3]

Mix the dry ingredients: In a medium bowl, whisk together the flour, salt, and baking soda to combine. Set it aside.

Mix the batter: To the bowl with the browned butter mixture (it can be slightly warm, just make sure it's not hot), add the brown and granulated sugars and whisk vigorously until the mixture is very smooth and thick, about 45 seconds (since we're not going for a light and cakey cookie texture, you don't need a mixture that's light and fluffy). Add the eggs and vanilla and whisk until the mixture is satiny, about 45 seconds. Add the flour mixture and whisk until the batter is smooth and well combined. It will look a little loose—this is normal. Switch to a flexible spatula to scrape down the bowl, folding to make sure everything is well incorporated. (continues)

DO AHEAD
The cookies, stored airtight at room temperature, will keep up to 5 days or can be frozen up to 1 month. The cookie dough can be portioned and refrigerated up to 2 days ahead or frozen up to 2 months. If freezing, allow the portioned dough to chill in the refrigerator for at least 2 hours before transferring the entire sheet to the freezer. Once the balls are frozen solid, pack the pieces into a resealable plastic freezer bag and store. Bake the cookies directly from the freezer without thawing first, but keep in mind you may need to add a minute or two to the bake time.

[1] If you like, substitute whole wheat flour for half of the all-purpose flour. This will make the cookies a bit nuttier and more savory in flavor, but also slightly less chewy.

Add both the chocolates (whole disks and chopped) and mix to combine. ④ Set the batter aside for 5 minutes to firm up slightly.

Scoop and chill the dough: Using a 2-ounce scoop or ¼-cup measure, scoop level portions of dough and place on a parchment-lined baking sheet as close together as possible (you'll space them out before baking). Cover the sheet tightly with plastic wrap and refrigerate for at least 12 hours and up to 48 (if you're pressed for time, a couple of hours in the refrigerator will do—just note the baked cookies won't be as chewy or wrinkly-looking). ⑤

Preheat the oven and prepare the pans: When you're ready to bake, arrange two oven racks in the upper and lower thirds of the oven and preheat to 350°F. Line two rimmed baking sheets with parchment paper.

Bake the first batch of cookies: Place 6 pieces of chilled cookie dough on each of the prepared baking sheets, spacing them so they're at least 3 inches apart. ⑥ Bake the cookies on the upper and lower racks until they are dark golden brown around the edges, 18 to 22 minutes, switching racks and rotating the sheets front to back after 12 minutes. Allow the cookies to rest for 5 minutes on the baking sheets, then use a metal spatula to transfer the cookies to a wire rack to cool.

Bake the remaining cookies: Carefully move one of the oven racks to the center position, place the remaining dough on one of the baking sheets (it's okay if it's still warm), and bake on the center rack (this last sheet might bake a bit faster than the first two).

② You can add only one variety of chocolate rather than the mix of milk and dark, just note that doing so will change the balance of sweetness (all dark chocolate making it less sweet, all milk chocolate making it more). Seek out chocolate disks or féves, like the ones by Guittard or Valrhona, since they melt into wonderful gooey puddles inside the cookies. If you can't find disks, opt for a block or bar of chocolate and coarsely chop all of it yourself. If possible, avoid chips, since they typically contain emulsifiers that prevent them from melting.

③ If you're pressed for time, you can skip browning the butter, although I highly recommend this step for the deep butterscotchy flavor it adds. If skipping, omit the heavy cream entirely and gently melt both sticks of butter together in a saucepan. Let it cool before proceeding with the recipe as written.

④ You can also add 1 cup chopped toasted nuts (4.2 oz / 120g), such as walnuts, almonds, or pecans, to the batter along with the chocolate.

⑤ Always scoop the dough before chilling it, as a single mass of cold dough will be very firm and therefore difficult to portion. If you can't avoid chilling the dough all together, wait for it to come to room temperature before scooping.

⑥ Sprinkle some flaky salt on top of the cookies prior to baking if you're a salty dessert person. Even though the dough contains a whopping 2 teaspoons of kosher salt, it's mainly there to bring out the flavors of the other ingredients; the baked cookies don't taste noticeably salty.

Cinnamon Sugar Palmiers

Makes 16 palmiers

½ cup **demerara sugar** (3.5 oz / 100g)

2 teaspoons **ground cinnamon** [1]

Pinch of **kosher salt**

½ recipe **Rough Puff Pastry** (page 355) or 1 recipe **Flaky All-Butter Pie Dough** (page 333)

All-purpose flour, for rolling out

1 large **egg**, beaten

One of my favorite things about living in Paris during my time in culinary school was, not surprisingly, *pâtisserie* culture. Even the humblest bakeries manage to display a remarkably enticing selection of sweets in their storefronts, from huge clouds of meringue to glossy fruit tarts to flaky escargot pastries (Parisians really excel in the art of window dressing). What always got me were the palmiers, or elephant ears: giant double spirals of crispy, caramelized, *bien cuit* puff pastry that shatter into buttery shards with one bite. Palmiers are one of my favorite "cookies," if you can call them that, and I make them frequently at home with leftover pie dough or puff pastry. Once you have the pastry, it's a quick and easy recipe with lots of payoff.

Make the cinnamon sugar: In a small bowl, toss together the demerara sugar, cinnamon, and salt to combine.

Roll out the pastry and dust with cinnamon sugar: Let the pastry sit at room temperature for a few minutes to soften slightly. Roll it out on a lightly floured piece of parchment paper, lifting and dusting with more flour as needed, into a rectangle measuring 12 × 10 inches and ¼ inch thick. Use a pastry brush to dust any excess flour off the top or underside of the dough. Brush the entire surface with a thin layer of the beaten egg and then sprinkle half of the cinnamon sugar over the top, pressing it gently into the surface of the pastry.

Roll up the pastry: Starting at one of the longer sides of the slab and using the parchment paper to help you, tightly roll the pastry into a spiral just until you reach the midline. Rotate the parchment paper 180 degrees and repeat from the other side of the pastry so you have two tight spirals of equal thickness that touch. Firmly pinch the two sides together along the entire length of the pastry, compressing the spirals (the pastry will puff in the oven, causing the spirals to unwind a bit). Slide the pastry off the parchment, then brush the outsides of the pastry with more egg and sprinkle with the remaining cinnamon sugar, making sure every bit of surface is coated.

Freeze until firm: Wrap the piece of parchment paper you used for rolling out the pastry around the sugared log and again squeeze firmly up and down the length to help keep the two spirals together. Transfer the log to the freezer and chill until the pastry is very firm but not frozen solid, 20 to 25 minutes.

DO AHEAD
The palmiers, stored airtight at room temperature, will keep up to 3 days.

[1] Use any warm spice such as cardamom or, less obviously, coriander in place of the cinnamon here. You can also massage any of the following ingredients into the ½ cup demerara sugar in the recipe to make a flavored sugar, and use that instead:

- **Vanilla:** seeds scraped from ½ vanilla bean
- **Citrus:** 1 teaspoon finely grated citrus zest
- **Lavender:** ½ teaspoon very finely chopped culinary-grade dried lavender

Preheat the oven and prepare the baking sheet: Arrange an oven rack in the center position and preheat the oven to 375°F. Line a large rimmed baking sheet with parchment paper and set aside.

Cut the palmiers and bake: Remove the pastry log from the freezer and place on a cutting board. Use a sharp knife to trim away the ragged ends of the pastry, making crosswise slices about ½ inch in from each end. Cut the log in half crosswise and then in half again to make four equal pieces, then slice each quarter into four equal pieces so you have 16 palmiers measuring between ½ and ¾ inch thick. Transfer the palmiers to the prepared baking sheet cut-sides down, spacing them evenly, and bake until they are puffed and golden brown and the sugar has melted and caramelized into glassy puddles on the baking sheet, 25 to 30 minutes. Let cool completely on the baking sheet.

Malted "Forever" Brownies

Makes 16 brownies

Special Equipment:
8 × 8-inch pan (preferably metal) ①

Butter for the pan

¼ cup **Dutch process cocoa powder** (0.7 oz / 20g)

5 ounces (142g) **semisweet chocolate** (preferably 64 to 68% cacao), coarsely chopped

6 tablespoons **unsalted butter** (3 oz / 85g), cut into pieces

¼ cup **neutral oil**, such as vegetable or grapeseed (2 oz / 56g)

½ cup **granulated sugar** (3.5 oz / 100g)

½ cup packed **dark brown sugar** (3.5 oz / 100g)

1 large **egg** (1.8 oz / 50g)

2 large **egg yolks** (1.1 oz / 32g)

1½ teaspoons **vanilla extract**

¾ cup **all-purpose flour** (3.5 oz / 100g)

2 tablespoons **malted milk powder** ② (0.63 oz / 18g) (optional)

1 teaspoon **Diamond Crystal kosher salt** (0.11 oz / 3g)

6 ounces (170g) **milk chocolate**, coarsely chopped (1 cup)

I didn't have a go-to brownie recipe before writing this book, and since they're such an oft-requested, universally loved treat, I set out to develop one. This felt like a simple task since brownies, almost by definition, are easy to make, but I botched a lot of batches. It was the chewiness that eluded me, and because I was determined to keep these hand-makeable and weeknight-friendly, I didn't want to pull out any crazy stops. After much tweaking—and realizing that chilling them is an essential step— this is the winning formula. I call them my "forever" brownies, since I don't think I'll make any other brownie recipe again.

Preheat the oven and prepare the pan: Arrange an oven rack in the center position and preheat the oven to 350°F. Line an 8 × 8-inch pan ③ with 2 sheets of foil, crossing one over the other and pressing the foil into the corners and up the sides. Lightly butter the foil and set aside.

Bloom the cocoa: In a large heatproof bowl, whisk the cocoa powder and ¼ cup boiling water (4 oz / 113g) until smooth (this will bring out the flavor of the cocoa).

Melt the chocolate, butter, and oil: Add the semisweet chocolate, butter, and oil to the bowl with the cocoa mixture and set it over a medium saucepan filled with about 1 inch of simmering (not boiling) water (make sure the bottom of the bowl isn't touching the water). Warm the mixture gently, stirring occasionally, until the chocolate and butter are melted and the mixture is smooth. Remove the bowl from the heat and let cool until lukewarm.

Add the sugars and egg: Whisk the granulated and brown sugars into the chocolate mixture. It will look grainy and you might see some of the fat start to separate from the rest of the mixture, which is normal. Add the whole egg, egg yolks, and vanilla and whisk vigorously until the mixture comes back together and looks very thick, smooth, and glossy.

Add the dry ingredients: Add the flour, malted milk powder (if using), and salt and whisk slowly until everything is combined, then whisk more vigorously until the batter is very thick, a full 45 seconds. (continues)

DO AHEAD
The brownies, stored airtight at room temperature, will keep up to 5 days or can be frozen up to 2 months. Freeze the brownies separated by sheets of parchment paper.

① If you don't have an 8 x 8-inch pan, double the recipe and bake these in a 13 × 9-inch. If doubling the recipe makes more than you need, freeze the rest!

② Malted milk powder is available in most grocery stores (look for the Carnation brand). If you can't find it, you can substitute 6 ounces (170g) coarsely chopped malted milk balls (my favorite candy!) for the milk chocolate.

Fold in the chocolate and bake: Add the milk chocolate to the batter and fold with a flexible spatula to distribute. Scrape the batter into the prepared pan, spreading in an even layer all the way to the corners. ④ Bake the brownies until the surface is shiny and puffed and the center is dry to the touch but still soft when pressed, 25 to 30 minutes.

Cool, chill, and cut: Allow the brownies to cool in the pan until they are no longer hot, about 1 hour, then refrigerate until the bottom of the pan feels cold, about 1 hour longer (this results in a chewier texture). Use the ends of the foil to lift the brownies out of the pan and transfer to a cutting board. Slice the brownies into 16 squares.

VARIATIONS

- **Mint:** Omit the malted milk powder and add ½ teaspoon peppermint extract to the batter. Swap in 6 ounces (170g) of chopped Andes Chocolate Mints for the milk chocolate.

- **Nuts:** Add 1 cup coarsely chopped toasted walnuts, hazelnuts, or pecans (3.9 oz / 110g) to the batter along with the milk chocolate.

- **Whole grain:** Substitute ¼ cup buckwheat, rye, whole wheat, or spelt flour (1.2 oz / 33g) for ¼ cup of the all-purpose flour (1.2 oz / 33g).

---

③ Use a glass pan if it's the only one you've got, but note that this will affect the way the brownies bake. Glass takes longer than metal to heat up and cool, which means the brownies will continue to bake once they're out of the oven and possibly overshoot that medium-rare mark. To avoid possible overbaking, reduce the oven temperature by 25°F and keep a watchful eye.

④ Sprinkle flaky salt on top of the batter prior to baking if you're a salty dessert person.

Pistachio Pinwheels

Makes 32 cookies

Special Equipment:
Food processor

⅔ cup shelled **pistachios** (3.2 oz / 90g) ①

12 tablespoons **unsalted butter**
(6 oz / 170g), cut into ½-inch pieces, at
room temperature

¾ cup plus 2 tablespoons **powdered
sugar** (3.7 oz / 105g)

2 large **egg yolks** (1.1 oz / 32g)

½ teaspoon **almond extract**

1 cup **all-purpose flour** (4.6 oz / 130g)

½ teaspoon **Diamond Crystal kosher salt**

1⅓ cups **almond flour** (5.6 oz / 160g)

½ cup **demerara sugar**, for rolling

This is one of those ace-up-your-sleeve, slice-and-bake cookie recipes
every baker needs. The pinwheels are super tasty, need no decoration,
and require no major assembly. These buttery, nutty, shortbready cookies
achieve the highest calling for any recipe: They look and taste as if they
are harder to make than they are.

Grind the pistachios: In a food processor, pulse the pistachios until they're
very finely ground but not yet forming a paste, about 25 pulses. Transfer
the ground pistachios to a small bowl and set aside.

Make the dough in the food processor: To the same food processor (no
need to wash after grinding the pistachios), add the butter and powdered
sugar and process until the mixture is smooth and creamy. Add the yolks
and almond extract and process until the mixture is smooth and light.
Add the flour and salt and pulse, scraping down the sides of the bowl
once or twice, until you have a stiff, uniform dough.

Mix the almond dough: Transfer two-thirds of the dough to a medium
bowl and add the almond flour to the bowl (if you want to weigh the
dough, it should be about 10 oz / 283g). Use a flexible spatula to work the
almond flour into the dough until you have a uniform mixture.

Work the almond dough into a slab: Scrape the almond dough onto a piece
of parchment paper. Pat it down with your hands into a thinner layer,
then place a piece of parchment paper on top. Roll out the dough between
the sheets of parchment into a slab measuring about 12 × 8 inches and
¼ inch thick (uncover the dough and use a small offset spatula to shape
the dough into a rectangle if necessary). Slide the parchment paper onto
a baking sheet and refrigerate the slab until firm, 10 to 15 minutes.

Mix the pistachio dough: Meanwhile, add the ground pistachios to the
food processor with the remaining dough and pulse until the mixture
is thoroughly blended and the dough has taken on a green color, about
7 pulses. Set aside at room temperature until the almond dough is firm.
(continues)

DO AHEAD
The pinwheels, stored airtight at room
temperature, will keep up to 5 days or
can be frozen up to 2 months. The log of
dough, well wrapped and unsliced, can
be refrigerated up to 2 days and frozen
up to 2 months. Thaw 24 hours in the
refrigerator before slicing and baking.

① Look for blanched pistachios, which
have the papery skins removed,
although unblanched pistachios will
also work. Do look for pistachios that
are as green as possible for maximum
contrast with the almond layer.

Form the pinwheels: Remove the almond dough from the refrigerator and plop tablespoon-sized pieces of the pistachio dough across the surface of the slab. Use the offset spatula to spread the pistachio dough across the length of the slab in an even layer, leaving a ½-inch border along the longer sides. Starting at one of the longer sides and using the parchment paper to help you, roll the dough into a tight spiraled log. Wrap the log in parchment paper and transfer to the refrigerator. Chill until the dough is very firm, at least 1 hour.

Prepare the pans and preheat the oven: Meanwhile, arrange two oven racks in the upper and lower thirds of the oven and preheat to 350°F. Line two large rimmed baking sheets with parchment paper and set aside.

Roll the log in the demerara sugar and slice: Sprinkle the demerara sugar across a cutting board. Remove the log from the refrigerator, unwrap, and roll across the board in the sugar, pressing down very firmly as you roll so the sugar adheres. Continue to roll and press until the entire log is coated. Using a sharp knife, shave a thin crosswise slice off of each end so you have straight sides with the full spiral exposed. Cut the log in half crosswise, then cut each half in half again to make quarters, and cut each quarter in half again for eighths. As you cut, rotate the pieces on the cutting board to prevent the pinwheels from gaining a flat side and losing their round shape. Cut each piece into 4 equal slices to make 32 cookies.

Bake: Arrange the cookies flat, dividing them between the two prepared baking sheets and spacing evenly. Bake the cookies on the upper and lower racks until they are golden around the edges, 15 to 20 minutes, switching racks and rotating the sheets front to back halfway through baking. Remove from the oven and let cool completely on the baking sheets.

Chewy Molasses Spice Cookies

Makes about 42 cookies

Special Equipment:
Stand or hand mixer

3¾ cups **all-purpose flour** (17 oz / 488g)

1 tablespoon **baking soda** (0.63 oz / 18g)

2½ teaspoons **ground ginger**

½ teaspoon finely ground **black pepper**

½ teaspoon **ground allspice**

½ teaspoon **Diamond Crystal kosher salt**

¼ teaspoon **ground cloves**

1½ sticks **unsalted butter** (6 oz / 170g), melted and cooled to room temperature

1½ cups packed **dark brown sugar** (10.6 oz / 300g)

2 large **eggs** (3.5 oz / 100g), at room temperature

½ cup **unsulfured molasses** (5.6 oz / 160g)

2 teaspoons **apple cider vinegar** (0.33 oz / 9g)

2 teaspoons **vanilla extract**

½ cup **demerara sugar**, for rolling

A good molasses cookie should achieve harmony between the sweetness of brown sugar, the bitterness of molasses, and the gentle heat of spices. This cookie does all that, but where it really delivers is the texture: perfectly soft and chewy. The dough can be portioned and frozen ahead of time, making these your all-purpose holiday cookie.

Mix the dry ingredients: In a large bowl, whisk together the flour, baking soda, ginger, pepper, allspice, salt, and cloves. Set aside.

Make the dough: In a stand mixer fitted with the paddle attachment (or in a large bowl if using a hand mixer), beat the butter and brown sugar on medium speed until slightly pale, about 1 minute. Add the eggs one at a time, beating thoroughly after each addition until fluffy, about 1 minute. Add the molasses, vinegar, and vanilla and beat until combined. Reduce the mixer speed to low and gradually add the flour mixture, beating just until the last trace of flour disappears. The dough will be very soft and sticky.

Chill the dough: Divide the dough in half, wrap each half in plastic, and press into a 6 × 6-inch square. Refrigerate the dough until firm, at least 1 hour and up to 2 days.

Preheat the oven and prepare the pans: Arrange two oven racks in the upper and lower thirds of the oven and preheat to 350°F. Line two rimmed baking sheets with parchment paper.

Roll the dough into balls: Place the demerara sugar in a small bowl. Remove one square of dough from the refrigerator, portion into 1-ounce (28g) pieces, and roll each into a ball (they should be about 1¼ inches in diameter). Toss the balls in the demerara sugar to coat all over, then place on the prepared baking sheets, spaced about 3 inches apart (the cookies will spread during baking). Refrigerate any balls that don't fit on the baking sheets.

Bake: Bake on the upper and lower racks until the edges are firm to the touch but the centers are still very soft and slightly shiny, 12 to 14 minutes, switching racks and rotating the sheets front to back halfway through. ①
Remove from the oven and cool for 15 minutes on the baking sheets before using a thin spatula to transfer them to a wire rack. Repeat the rolling and baking process with the remaining dough and demerara sugar.

DO AHEAD
The cookies, stored airtight at room temperature, will keep up to 5 days. The dough can be refrigerated up to 3 days. You can also roll the dough into balls and toss in sugar, then arrange them in tight rows on a parchment-lined baking sheet, and freeze solid. Transfer the balls to a resealable plastic freezer bag and keep frozen up to 2 months. No need to thaw before baking, but extend the bake time by a couple of minutes.

① The cookies will look nearly raw in the center when you pull them out of the oven, but they will continue to set as they cool. The key to the soft and chewy texture of these cookies is, simply, underbaking them. If you like a crispier spice cookie, bake them 2 minutes longer.

Aunt Rose's Mondel Bread

Makes about 36 cookies

Special Equipment:
Stand mixer

2 tablespoons **ground cinnamon**

1½ cups **sugar** (10.6 oz / 300g)

2 cups slivered **almonds** (8 oz / 227g)

1 tablespoon plus 1 cup **neutral oil**, such as vegetable or grapeseed (8.4 oz / 238g) ①

1 tablespoon plus 4 cups **all-purpose flour** (18.6 oz / 528g)

2 teaspoons **baking powder** (0.28 oz / 8g)

½ teaspoon **Diamond Crystal kosher salt**

3 large **eggs** (5.3 oz / 150g)

1 teaspoon **vanilla extract**

I learned recently that before emigrating to the United States, my great-grandfather worked as a baker. That explains the handful of recipes passed down on my mother's side. One of my favorites is this mondel bread, named for my mother's Aunt Rose. Mondel bread is a kind of almond cookie that I describe as Jewish biscotti, although it's only baked once. Like a lot of Jewish baked goods, it uses oil instead of butter to keep it pareve (compatible with both milk and meat, according to kosher rules). The cookie is not very sweet, save for the generous coating of cinnamon sugar on the outside, and very nutty from well-toasted almonds, with a dry, crumbly texture. Maybe I'm not selling it, but the cookie is delicious and very worth savoring with a cup of tea or coffee. I resisted any urge to tweak the recipe and, except for the addition of a little salt, have faithfully reproduced Aunt Rose's version here. If four generations of baking are any indication, this one's a keeper.

Make the cinnamon sugar: Toss the cinnamon and ½ cup of the sugar (3.5 oz / 100g) in a small bowl until the mixture is uniform. Set aside.

Preheat the oven and toast the almonds: Arrange an oven rack in the center position and preheat the oven to 350°F. Place the almonds on a small rimmed baking sheet and toss with 1 tablespoon of the oil to coat. Bake until the almonds are deep golden brown and fragrant, shaking halfway through, 8 to 10 minutes. ② Remove from the oven and let cool, then toss with 1 tablespoon of the flour to coat. (Turn off the oven.)

Mix the dry ingredients: In a medium bowl, whisk together the baking powder, salt, and remaining 4 cups flour (18.3 oz / 520g) to combine.

Mix the cookie dough: In a stand mixer fitted with the paddle attachment, mix the eggs, remaining 1 cup sugar (7 oz / 200g), and remaining 1 cup oil (8 oz / 224g) on medium-high speed until smooth and homogenous, about 1 minute. Reduce the speed to low and add the vanilla and cooled toasted almonds, followed by the flour mixture. Continue to mix on low speed just until you have a smooth dough, about 45 seconds. (continues)

DO AHEAD
The cookies, well wrapped and stored at room temperature, will keep up to 5 days. The cookies can also be frozen up to 2 months.

① You can use olive oil in place of the neutral oil, but note that it will lend the cookies a slight grassy bitterness (in a good way).

② Make sure the almonds go a shade or two past golden brown before pulling them from the oven. You want them really well toasted, since most of the flavor of the cookie comes from this step.

Chill the dough: Use a flexible spatula to scrape any dough from the paddle back into the bowl, then fold the dough several times to ensure it's well mixed. Refrigerate the bowl uncovered for 4 hours. (My mom says it has to be exactly 4 hours, but an hour less or more is fine.)

Preheat the oven: Arrange an oven rack in the center position and preheat the oven to 350°F.

Form the dough into loaves: Remove the chilled dough from the refrigerator and divide it into 3 equal portions (if you have a scale, each portion should be about 1 lb / 454g). Space out the 3 mounds of dough on an unlined, ungreased baking sheet. Pat each portion of dough into a smooth loaf measuring about 8 × 3 inches and 1½ inches tall. The exact dimensions aren't important, but the loaves should all be about the same size. The dough will spread in the oven, so make sure you space them several inches apart.

Score and sugar the loaves: Use a serrated knife to make ½-inch-deep score marks crosswise along each loaf at ¾-inch intervals. (These marks completely disappear when you bake the loaves but, according to Aunt Rose and my mom, they help you slice the cookies more easily after baking.) Using one-third of the cinnamon sugar, sprinkle it over the tops of all the loaves.

Bake the loaves: Transfer the baking sheet to the oven and bake until the loaves are set and the tops are golden brown, about 30 minutes. Remove from the oven and, using a fish spatula, metal bench scraper, or other broad metal spatula, very carefully turn each loaf over so the sugared side is down. The loaves are only partially baked and fragile at this point—try to be gentle so they don't break. Sprinkle half of the remaining cinnamon sugar over the loaves and return to the oven. Bake for another 15 minutes, then remove from the oven and turn the loaves again. Sprinkle with the remaining cinnamon sugar and bake for a final 15 minutes. Remove the pan from the oven. Let the loaves cool slightly on the baking sheet, 10 to 15 minutes.

Slice the cookies: When the loaves are cool enough to handle but still very warm, slide the metal spatula beneath the loaves and transfer them, one at a time, to a cutting board. Use a serrated knife in a sawing motion to slice the loaves into ¾-inch-thick cookies. The score marks will have disappeared during baking, so you're making fresh cuts. Let the cookies cool completely.

Coconut Thumbprints

Makes about 50 two-bite cookies

Special Equipment:
Stand mixer

COCONUT DOUGH

14 tablespoons **unsalted butter**
(7 oz / 200g), at room temperature

¾ cup **powdered sugar** (3.1 oz / 90g)

Pinch of **Diamond Crystal kosher salt**

2 large **egg yolks** (1.1 oz / 32g)

1½ cups **all-purpose flour** (7 oz / 200g)

2 cups unsweetened finely shredded
dried coconut (6.6 oz / 188g)

COCONUT CARAMEL [1]

½ cup **granulated sugar** (3.5 oz / 100g)

2 tablespoons **light corn syrup**
(1.4 oz / 40g)

¼ cup unsweetened full-fat **coconut milk**
(2.2 oz / 61g)

2 tablespoons **virgin coconut oil**
(1 oz / 28g)

½ teaspoon **Diamond Crystal kosher salt**

I am always on a search for cookies that look decorated but don't actually require me to painstakingly pipe royal icing, which is one reason I appreciate these thumbprint cookies. Thumbprint cookie dough typically contains a high proportion of flour, making it stiff and more likely to hold an impression in the oven, but this can also make thumbprints dry. This coconut dough works better than most because the shredded coconut adds stiffness while also adding flavor, texture, and fat so the cookies don't dry out. Between the buttery, shortbread cookie itself and the oozy, rich coconut caramel filling, these two-bite thumbprints are a dream for coconut lovers like me.

Prepare the baking sheets: Line two large rimmed baking sheets with parchment paper and set aside.

Make the dough: In a stand mixer fitted with the paddle attachment, beat the butter on medium until smooth. Add the powdered sugar and salt and pulse the mixer several times to incorporate the sugar, then beat on medium-low until the mixture is light and creamy, about 1 minute. Add the yolks and beat on medium until the mixture is a bit fluffier, about 1 minute more. Add the flour and shredded coconut and mix on low until you have a stiff dough, about 30 seconds more. Scrape down the sides and bottom of the bowl and then pulse the mixer just to make sure everything is well incorporated.

Form the thumbprints: Use a ½-ounce scoop or tablespoon measure to scoop level portions of dough. Roll the portions between your palms to make balls, then place them on the prepared baking sheets, spacing them about 1 inch apart (they don't spread much during baking). Flatten each ball slightly, then use your thumb or the end of a wooden spoon handle to make a deep impression in the center of each piece of dough, almost but not quite pressing through to the baking sheet. Use your fingertips to widen the impression all the way around so it's about 1 inch across—the dough will slump a bit in the oven, so the impressions won't be as deep or wide after baking. If the dough cracks when you're making the impression, just squeeze it back together. (continues)

DO AHEAD
The thumbprints, stored airtight at room temperature, will keep up to 5 days. The baked but unfilled cookies can be frozen in a resealable plastic freezer bag up to 1 month. The dough can be formed into cookies with the impression and then covered and refrigerated for 24 hours or frozen up to 1 month. The caramel, covered and refrigerated, will keep up to 1 week. Warm over low heat until fluid before using to fill the cookies.

[1] Substitute store-bought dulce de leche for the coconut caramel if you want a fast, prefab filling. Since dulce de leche out of a jar or can is very thick, warm it gently and thin with some coconut milk or heavy cream for easier filling of the thumbprints.

Chill the dough and preheat the oven: Transfer the baking sheets to the refrigerator and chill until the cookies are very firm to the touch, 15 to 20 minutes. Meanwhile, arrange two oven racks in the upper and lower thirds of the oven and preheat to 350°F.

Bake the cookies: Bake the cookies on the upper and lower racks, switching racks and rotating the sheets front to back after 12 minutes, until they're golden all over, 20 to 25 minutes total. Remove the baking sheets from the oven and set aside to cool while you make the caramel.

Make the coconut caramel: In a small heavy-bottomed saucepan, combine the granulated sugar, corn syrup, and 3 tablespoons of water (1.5 oz / 43g). Cook over medium heat, stirring with a heatproof spatula until the sugar is dissolved. Bring the mixture to a boil and cook, swirling the pan occasionally instead of stirring, and brushing down the sides with a wet pastry brush to dissolve any sugar crystals, until the syrup turns a deep amber color, 6 to 8 minutes. Immediately remove the saucepan from the heat and slowly stream in the coconut milk, stirring with a heatproof spatula and taking care because the mixture will sputter. Add the coconut oil and salt and stir until smooth. Let the caramel cool, stirring occasionally, until it is thickened but still warm and pourable, 20 to 25 minutes (you can stir it over an ice bath to speed this up).

Fill the thumbprints: Use a teaspoon to carefully drizzle the liquid caramel into the depression of each cookie, filling them as generously as possible. (Alternatively, you can transfer the caramel to a piping bag and use that to fill the cookies for a bit more control.) Let the cookies sit until the caramel is set, about 10 minutes.

Oat and Pecan Brittle Cookies

Makes about 18 large cookies

Special Equipment:
Stand mixer, food processor

PECAN BRITTLE

1¼ cups coarsely chopped **pecans**
(5 oz / 142g)

¾ cup **granulated sugar** (5.3 oz / 150g)

4 tablespoons **unsalted butter** (2 oz / 57g)

½ teaspoon **baking soda**

½ teaspoon **Diamond Crystal kosher salt**

COOKIES

2 sticks **unsalted butter** (8 oz / 227g),
cut into tablespoons

1⅓ cups **all-purpose flour** (6.1 oz / 173g)

2 teaspoons **Diamond Crystal kosher salt**
(0.22 oz / 6g)

1 teaspoon **baking soda** (0.21 oz / 6g)

2 cups old-fashioned **rolled oats**, not
quick-cooking (7 oz / 200g)

¾ cup packed **dark brown sugar**
(5.3 oz / 150g)

½ cup **granulated sugar** (3.5 oz / 100g)

2 large **eggs** (3.5 oz / 100g), cold from the
refrigerator

1 tablespoon **vanilla extract**

A guiding principle for this book is that I will not ask bakers to perform tons of steps or generate excessive dishes for a recipe if it's not absolutely essential. In certain cases, though, the ends do justify the means, like these oatmeal cookies. I ask you to go through the process of toasting nuts, making a brittle (you can use store-bought toffee instead to save a step), browning butter, grinding oats and bits of brittle into the dry ingredients, and *then* resting the dough in the refrigerator, because I am confident that these are the best oatmeal cookies you will ever make (oh—and you have to use both a food processor and stand mixer). It's somewhere between a very chewy oat cookie and a lacy one, and just so *so* good. If you want a quick and easy oat cookie, this is not it (for that I actually recommend the recipe on the back of the Quaker Oats container—it's a winner!). But the point of jumping through all these baking hoops is that you'll be happy you put in the effort.

Preheat the oven and toast the pecans: Arrange an oven rack in the center position and preheat the oven to 350°F. Scatter the pecans on a small rimmed baking sheet and toast, tossing halfway through, until they're golden and nutty smelling, 8 to 10 minutes. Remove the baking sheet from the oven and set aside to allow the pecans cool.

Make the brittle: ① Meanwhile, line a small rimmed baking sheet with parchment paper and set aside. In a small saucepan, combine the granulated sugar, butter, and 2 tablespoons of water (1 oz / 28g) and cook over medium-low heat, stirring gently with a heatproof spatula to dissolve the sugar. Increase the heat to medium and bring the syrup to a rapid simmer. Cook without stirring, swirling the pan often, until the syrup turns a deep amber color, 8 to 10 minutes. Immediately remove the saucepan from the heat and stir in the pecans. Once the pecans are well coated, add the baking soda and salt and stir quickly to incorporate—the mixture will rapidly foam and sputter as the baking soda aerates the caramel. Quickly scrape the brittle out onto the prepared baking sheet and spread into a thin layer, if possible, before it starts to harden (which happens very quickly). Set the baking sheet aside until the brittle is completely cooled, 5 to 10 minutes. Chop the brittle into pea-sized bits and set aside. (continues)

DO AHEAD
The cookies, stored airtight at room temperature, will keep up to 5 days and can be frozen up to 1 month. The cookie dough can be portioned and refrigerated up to 2 days or frozen up to 2 months.

Allow the portioned dough to chill in the refrigerator for at least 2 hours before transferring the entire sheet of dough to the freezer; once the dough is frozen solid, you can pack the pieces into a resealable plastic freezer bag. Bake the

cookies directly from the freezer without thawing first, but keep in mind you may need to add a minute or two to the bake time.

Brown the butter: Measure out 4 ounces (113g) of the butter, place in the bowl of a stand mixer, and set aside. Place the other 4 ounces (113g) butter in a small saucepan and cook over medium-low heat, stirring frequently, until the butter comes to a boil. Continue to cook, scraping the bottom and sides of the pan constantly with a heatproof spatula, until the butter sputters, foams, and eventually you see browned bits floating about, 5 to 7 minutes. Add the browned butter to the stand mixer bowl, making sure you scrape in all the browned bits. Set the bowl aside to cool until the butter begins to resolidify, about 30 minutes.

Blitz the dry ingredients: In a food processor, combine the flour, salt, and baking soda, then add half of the pecan brittle bits and 1 cup (3.5 oz / 100g) of the oats. Blitz the mixture in long pulses until the oats and brittle are broken down and finely ground. Set aside.

Mix the batter: Set the bowl of cooled butter on the mixer and attach the paddle. Add the dark brown and granulated sugars and beat on medium speed until the mixture is light and smooth but not fluffy, about 2 minutes. Scrape down the sides of the bowl, add the eggs and vanilla, and continue to beat until you have a very light and satiny mixture, about 1 minute. Scrape down the sides of the bowl and add the flour/oat/brittle mixture and beat on low until no dry spots remain and you have a soft, evenly mixed dough. Add the remaining pecan brittle bits and 1 cup (3.5 oz / 100g) oats and mix on low again just until dispersed. Fold the batter several times with a flexible spatula to ensure everything is evenly mixed.

Scoop and chill the batter: Using a 2-ounce scoop or ¼-cup measure, scoop level portions of dough and place on a parchment-lined baking sheet as close together as possible (you'll space them out before baking). Cover the dough tightly with plastic wrap and refrigerate for at least 12 hours and up to 48. (If you're pressed for time, a couple of hours in the refrigerator will do. Just note the baked cookies won't be as chewy.)

Preheat the oven and prepare the pans: When you're ready to bake, arrange two oven racks in the upper and lower thirds of the oven and preheat to 350°F. Line two large rimmed baking sheets with parchment paper.

Bake the first batch of cookies: Place 6 pieces of chilled cookie dough on each of the prepared baking sheets, spacing so they're at least 3 inches apart. Bake the cookies on the upper and lower racks until they are dark golden brown around the edges, 16 to 20 minutes, switching racks and rotating the sheets front to back after 12 minutes. Allow the cookies to rest for 5 minutes on the baking sheets, then use a metal spatula to transfer the cookies to a wire rack to cool.

Bake the remaining cookies: Carefully move one of the oven racks to the center position, place the remaining dough on one of the baking sheets (it's okay if it's still warm), and bake on the center rack (this last sheet might bake a bit faster than the first two).

---

① If you'd like to skip the step of making the pecan brittle, you can add 8 ounces (227g) of toffee bits, such as Heath brand "Bits o' Brickle" (often found in the baking aisle of the supermarket), to the dough instead. You should still toast the pecans and grind half into the flour mixture, then add the rest to the dough along with the toffee bits and remaining oats.

Minty Lime Bars

Makes 16 bars

Special Equipment:
8 × 8-inch pan ① (preferably metal),
instant-read thermometer

SHORTBREAD CRUST

Butter for the pan

2 tablespoons finely grated **lime zest**
(from about 3 limes)

¼ cup **granulated sugar** (1.8 oz / 50g)

1 cup **all-purpose flour** (4.6 oz / 130g)

2 tablespoons finely chopped
fresh **mint**

¼ teaspoon **baking powder**

Pinch of **Diamond Crystal kosher salt**

1 stick **unsalted butter** (4 oz / 113g),
cut into ½-inch pieces, chilled

LIME CURD FILLING

¾ cup fresh **lime juice** (6 oz / 170g), from
about 7 limes

¼ cup fresh **lemon juice** (2 oz / 57g), from
about 1 large lemon

1 teaspoon **cornstarch** (0.11 oz / 3g)

Pinch of **Diamond Crystal kosher salt**

1 cup **granulated sugar** (7 oz / 200g)

5 large **egg yolks** (2.6 oz / 80g)

1 large **egg** (1.8 oz / 50g)

6 tablespoons **unsalted butter**
(3 oz / 85g), cut into tablespoons, chilled

Powdered sugar and finely grated **lime
zest**, for serving

Other than Key lime pie, there aren't a lot of desserts that put limes at center stage, but there should be. Swapping in lime juice for lemon in these bars—plus lots of zest and fresh mint in the shortbread crust—elevates them to a cookie that, in the best way, still reminds me of my elementary school bake sales. It was important to me that the filling in these be a little puckering (thus the addition of some lemon juice), silky smooth, and fully set so the bars could be sliced. The only way I found to achieve this was to make a curd for the filling, to which I add just a bit of cornstarch for more setting power, so the lime bars are firm enough to stack. It's more work than the classic stir-together fillings of most lemon bars, but worth it in the end.

Preheat the oven and prepare the pan: Arrange an oven rack in the center position and preheat the oven to 350°F. Line the 8 × 8-inch pan with two sheets of foil, crossing one over the other and pressing the foil into the corners and up the sides. Butter the bottom and sides of the foil and set the pan aside.

Make the shortbread crust: In a medium bowl, use your fingertips to massage the lime zest into the granulated sugar until the fragrant oils are released and the mixture looks like wet sand. Add the flour, chopped mint, baking powder, and salt and toss to combine. Add the pieces of chilled butter and toss to coat in the flour mixture. Use your fingertips to smash the butter completely into the flour mixture, working until you have lots of moist crumbs that hold together easily when squeezed.

Bake the crust: Transfer the shortbread dough to the prepared pan and scatter the crumbs evenly across the bottom. Use your hands to flatten the crumbs into an even layer, working it into the corners and against the sides. Bake the shortbread until lightly golden across the surface, 25 to 30 minutes. Remove the pan from the oven. (Leave the oven on and reduce the temperature to 300°F.) Let the crust cool while you make the filling. (continues)

DO AHEAD
The lime bars, stored airtight in the refrigerator, will keep up to 5 days but are best served on the first or second day. If making ahead, wait to sprinkle with powdered sugar and lime zest until just before serving. The shortbread crust can be baked up to 1 day ahead. Let the crust cool, then store well wrapped at room temperature. The lime curd can be made up to 3 days ahead. Pour it into a plastic or glass container (not stainless steel, which will give the curd a tinny taste), press a sheet of plastic wrap directly onto the surface of the curd, and refrigerate. Let the curd come to room temperature before whisking to loosen, pouring into the crust, and baking.

Make the lime curd filling: In a small saucepan, combine the lime juice, lemon juice, cornstarch, salt, and ½ cup of the granulated sugar (3.5 oz / 100g) and cook over medium heat, whisking occasionally, to dissolve the sugar. When the mixture comes to a boil, whisk constantly until it thickens slightly from the cornstarch, about 1 minute, then remove the saucepan from the heat.

In a medium bowl, vigorously whisk the egg yolks, whole egg, and remaining ½ cup sugar (3.5 oz / 100g) until the mixture is smooth, thick, and has paled in color a couple of shades, about 1 minute. ② Whisking constantly, slowly drizzle the hot citrus mixture into the eggs a tablespoon at a time to slowly raise the temperature, until you've added about half the citrus mixture to the eggs.

Whisk the egg mixture back into the saucepan, then set back over medium-low heat and cook, whisking constantly, until the curd turns opaque, is thick enough to coat the back of a spoon, and barely holds the marks of the whisk (it will also register 170°F on an instant-read thermometer), 3 to 5 minutes.

Remove the curd from the heat and whisk in the butter a piece at a time, waiting until each piece melts before adding the next, until the mixture is smooth.

Bake the bars: Pour the hot curd over the crust and shake the pan gently so it settles in an even layer. Bake the bars until the sides have puffed and the center is set but still a bit wobbly when you shake the pan, 30 to 35 minutes. Remove from the oven and let the bars cool completely in the pan.

Chill before serving: Transfer the cooled pan to the refrigerator and chill until the bottom of the pan is cold to the touch, about 1 hour. This will harden the butter in both the curd and crust, making it easier to remove the bars from the pan and slice. Use the edges of the foil to lift the bars out of the pan, then peel down the sides of the foil and slide a metal spatula underneath to loosen the crust from the foil. Slide the bars off the foil onto a cutting board and slice into 16 squares. Dust with powdered sugar and top with more lime zest before serving.

---

① To convert this recipe into a tart, use a 9-inch removable-bottom tart pan instead of the 8 × 8-inch pan. Pat the shortbread into the bottom and up the sides of the buttered (unlined) pan and use the bottom of a 1-cup dry measure to smooth it. The crust will seem rather crumbly, but just do your best to eliminate any gaps and don't worry if it looks a bit rustic. Proceed with the recipe as written for parbaking the crust and then adding the curd—you might have a bit left over after filling the tart—and bake until set but slightly wobbly in the center, 35 to 40 minutes. Instead of the shortbread crust, you could use the **Sweet Tart Dough** (page 338) and follow the instructions for parbaking it.

② Wait to mix the sugar and eggs until you have the lime mixture at a boil. Letting the sugar/egg mixture sit could lead to a lumpy curd.

Thrice-Baked
Rye Cookies

Makes several dozen cookies, depending on how you cut them

1 cup **all-purpose flour** (4.6 oz / 130g)

1 cup **rye flour** (4.5 oz / 130g) ①

1½ teaspoons **Diamond Crystal kosher salt** (0.16 oz / 5g)

1 teaspoon **baking powder** (0.14 oz / 4g)

2 **hard-boiled egg yolks** (1 oz / 30g)

8 ounces (227g) **unsalted butter**, preferably European-style, at room temperature

¾ cup **granulated sugar** (5.3 oz / 150g)

2 teaspoons **vanilla extract**

1 large **egg**, beaten

Demerara sugar, for sprinkling the top

When I worked at the now-shuttered Spring restaurant in Paris, I learned a cookie recipe that contained two of the best nuggets of baking knowledge I've ever acquired. One was sieving hard-boiled egg yolks and adding them to the dough, which creates an unbelievably tender cookie. The second was baking flour in a hot oven to toast it, which adds major depth of flavor. The toasting also inhibits gluten formation, so combining toasted flour and the sieved yolk produces a cookie that dissolves almost instantly into buttery crumbs in your mouth. That genius cookie from Spring was the inspiration for these cookies, rife with earthy flavor from toasted rye flour. They're "thrice-baked" because the recipe requires three trips to the oven: once to toast the flour, a second time to bake the slab of dough, and a third to bake the individual cookies after they're cut from the slab. It's step-y, but the dough is quick and the result is a cookie unlike any other.

Preheat the oven and toast the flour: Arrange an oven rack in the center position and preheat the oven to 425°F. Sprinkle the all-purpose and rye flours evenly across a large rimmed baking sheet and transfer to the oven. Bake, stirring the flour once, until the flour is browned and very toasty smelling (it will release wisps of steam as it bakes), 8 to 12 minutes. Remove from the oven and let it cool completely on the baking sheet. (Turn off the oven.)

Sift the dry ingredients and yolks: Set a fine-mesh sieve over a medium bowl and add the salt, baking powder, and cooled toasted flour mixture and use your fingertips to rub the dry ingredients through the sieve into the bowl. Place the egg yolks in the sieve and use the back of a spoon to press them through the sieve and into the flour mixture. Stir to combine and set aside.

Mix the dough: Place the butter in a large bowl and beat it a few times with a flexible spatula to make sure it's smooth and spreadable. Add the granulated sugar and vanilla and beat vigorously with the spatula until the mixture is light and creamy, about 1 minute. Fold in the flour mixture until you have a soft, homogenous dough.

Chill the dough: Scrape the dough onto a sheet of plastic wrap and form it into a square. Wrap tightly in the plastic and refrigerate until the dough is firm, about 1 hour. (continues)

DO AHEAD
The cookies, stored airtight at room temperature, will keep up to 5 days. The dough can be made and refrigerated up to 3 days.

① You can use any other whole-grain flour like spelt, whole wheat, barley, or buckwheat in place of the rye.

Preheat the oven and roll out the dough: Arrange an oven rack in the center position and preheat the oven to 350°F. Allow the block of dough to sit at room temperature for several minutes to soften slightly, then roll out the dough between two sheets of parchment paper, peeling off and repositioning both pieces of parchment periodically to prevent wrinkling, to a thin slab that is between ¼ and ⅛ inch thick (make sure the shape of the slab fits inside the dimensions of whatever baking sheet you're using).

Cut and bake the cookies: Remove the top sheet of parchment and brush the surface of the dough with a thin layer of the beaten egg, then sprinkle generously with the demerara sugar. Use a knife or wheel cutter to cut the dough into diamonds or rectangles of any size, but leave the pieces in place. Slide the parchment paper (and the dough along with it) onto a large rimmed baking sheet. Bake until the cookies are puffed and the edges are browned, 18 to 22 minutes. Remove from the oven and, while the cookies are still hot, retrace the lines from the cuts you made earlier with the knife or wheel cutter, cutting all the way through the dough. Allow the cookies to cool. (Leave the oven on and rearrange the racks so they're in the upper and lower thirds.)

Break the cookies apart and bake again: When the cookies are cool enough to handle, separate them and place half on a second parchment-lined baking sheet. Evenly space the cookies apart and transfer the sheets to the upper and lower racks. Bake until the cookies are browned all over, another 10 to 12 minutes, switching racks and rotating the sheets front to back after 6 minutes (they will seem soft when they come out of the oven, but will crisp as they cool). Let the cookies cool completely on the baking sheets.

Earl Grey and Apricot
Hamantaschen

Makes about 20 cookies

Special Equipment:
Food processor, 3½-inch round cutter [1]

EARL GREY APRICOT FILLING [2]

6 ounces (170g) **dried apricots**, coarsely chopped (about 1 rounded cup)

3 tablespoons **honey** (2.3 oz / 64g)

2 **Earl Grey tea** bags

Finely grated **zest of 1 lemon**

1 tablespoon fresh **lemon juice**
(0.5 oz / 15g)

DOUGH AND ASSEMBLY

12 tablespoons **unsalted butter**
(6 oz / 170g), cut into ½-inch pieces, at room temperature

4 ounces (113g) **cream cheese**, cut into ½-inch pieces, at room temperature

½ cup **powdered sugar** (2.1 oz / 60g)

1 large **egg yolk** (0.6 oz / 16g)

2 teaspoons **vanilla extract**

2 teaspoons finely grated
lemon zest

½ teaspoon **Diamond Crystal kosher salt**

1 teaspoon **baking powder** (0.14 oz / 4g)

2 cups **all-purpose flour** (9.2 oz / 260g), plus more for rolling out

1 large **egg**, beaten

Poppy seeds and **demerara sugar**, for sprinkling the top

Hamantaschen are triangle-shaped cookies with fruit or poppy seed–filled centers baked for the Jewish holiday of Purim. Unfortunately, the hamantaschen you get in most bakeries aren't very good, because the dough requires a lot of flour to help the cookies maintain their triangular shape in the oven and not unfold into wonky circles with exposed filling. This can lead to dry, tasteless cookies. In my version, I spike the dough with cream cheese and lemon zest for tang, and just enough flour so it holds its shape. These are filled generously with an apricot filling scented with Earl Grey, a slight spin on my favorite traditional flavor.

Make the filling: In a medium saucepan, bring 2 cups of water (16 oz / 454g) to a boil. Remove from the heat and add the apricots, honey, and tea bags and let the mixture steep uncovered for 10 minutes. Remove the tea bags and set the mixture over medium heat. Bring to a boil and then reduce the heat to cook at a gentle simmer, stirring and mashing the apricots often with the back of a wooden spoon or a potato masher, until you have a thick paste that doesn't immediately cover the line left by the spoon as you scrape it across the bottom of the pan, 25 to 30 minutes (the thicker the filling, the less likely the hamantaschen will be to open up during baking). Remove from the heat and scrape the apricot mixture into a heatproof glass measuring cup. You should have between 1 and 1¼ cups—a bit less is fine, but if you have more than an extra tablespoon or two, return it to the saucepan and cook it a bit longer. Stir in the lemon zest and juice. Let cool completely, then cover and refrigerate until you're ready to fill the cookies.

Make and chill the dough: In a food processor, combine the butter, cream cheese, powdered sugar, egg yolk, vanilla, and lemon zest and process in long pulses, scraping down the sides of the bowl once or twice, until the mixture is smooth and creamy, about 20 pulses total. Scrape down the sides and add the salt, baking powder, and 2 cups flour. Pulse until a dough forms around the blade, about 10 pulses. Divide the dough in half, wrap each half in plastic, and press into a ¾-inch-thick rectangle. Refrigerate until the dough is firm, at least 2 hours and up to 2 days.
(continues)

DO AHEAD
The filling, stored airtight and refrigerated, will keep up to 1 week. The hamantaschen, stored in an airtight container at room temperature, will keep up to 5 days. The dough can be

refrigerated up to 2 days or frozen up to 1 month (allow frozen dough to thaw 24 hours in the refrigerator before rolling out).

[1] You can use a smaller cutter, like a 3 inch or even a 2½ inch, if that's what you've got. Just remember to scale down the amount of filling and note that smaller hamantaschen might bake slightly faster than the larger ones.

Preheat the oven and prepare the baking sheets: Arrange an oven rack in the center position and preheat the oven to 350°F. Line two rimmed baking sheets with parchment paper and set aside.

Roll out and cut the dough: Remove one piece of dough from the refrigerator and let it sit at room temperature for about 5 minutes to soften slightly, then roll out on a lightly floured surface, dusting the top and underside of the dough with more flour as needed, into a ⅛-inch-thick slab (any size is fine). Use a 3½-inch round cutter to punch out rounds, cutting them as close together as possible to maximize the yield. Place the rounds on one of the prepared baking sheets. Gather the scraps, quickly mash them back together, and roll out again with more flour. Cut as many rounds as you can from the scraps and place on the baking sheet; discard any remaining dough scraps. Space all the rounds equally on the baking sheet—you should have about 10.

Fill and fold the hamantaschen: Dollop a scant tablespoon of filling in the center of each dough round. Working one at a time, use a pastry brush to paint the perimeter of each round with a thin layer

of beaten egg. Fold the dough over the filling on three sides to make an equal-sided triangle, leaving an opening about ½ inch wide in the center and pinching very firmly at the three points to make sure the dough sticks to itself. Repeat until all the rounds have been filled and folded into triangles. Brush all three sides of each hamantaschen with more egg and sprinkle with poppy seeds and demerara sugar. Transfer the baking sheet to the refrigerator and chill the hamantaschen, uncovered, for at least 10 minutes before baking. [3] Meanwhile, repeat the rolling, cutting, filling, shaping, and chilling process with the second piece of dough and remaining filling and egg, placing the hamantaschen on the second baking sheet.

Bake and cool: Remove the first baking sheet from the refrigerator and bake until the hamantaschen are golden brown all over, 22 to 27 minutes. They may open up slightly while baking, but should maintain their triangular shape. When the first batch comes out, transfer the second batch from the refrigerator to the oven and bake. Allow the hamantaschen to cool completely on the baking sheets before removing them from the parchment paper.

---

[2] To save time, use your favorite store-bought fruit preserves or jam instead of making the apricot filling (recommended: fig preserves or bitter orange marmalade). Just be sure to pick a jar of something that is thick and concentrated, like a compote with pieces of actual fruit or a fruit butter.

[3] Chilling the hamantaschen before baking them is an important step, since letting the dough rest in the refrigerator helps relax the gluten and makes them less likely to open up in the oven. One or two triangles per batch might unfold slightly, particularly if they were cut from rerolled scraps. No worries, they will still taste great, and you can consider them a perk for the baker.

Peanut Butter and Concord Grape Sandwich Cookies

Makes about 30 sandwich cookies [1]

Special Equipment:
Stand mixer, ¾-inch round or small decorative cutter (optional, for Linzers), instant-read thermometer (for the grape jam)

2½ cups **all-purpose flour** (11.4 oz / 325g)

½ teaspoon **baking soda**

1½ teaspoons **Diamond Crystal kosher salt** (0.16 oz / 5g), plus more for sprinkling the tops

2 sticks **unsalted butter** (8 oz / 227g), at room temperature

½ cup packed **light brown sugar** (3.5 oz / 100g)

½ cup **granulated sugar** (3.5 oz / 100g), plus more for sprinkling the tops

1 cup natural **crunchy peanut butter** [3] (9 oz / 260g)

2 large **eggs** (3.5 oz / 100g)

1 teaspoon **vanilla extract**

Concord Grape Jam (recipe follows)

I try to stay away from any techniques that feel excessively fussy in the kitchen (who has the time?!), but I make an exception for Concord grapes. In order to extract the most of their piercing flavor, the grapes must be peeled. It's not as crazy as it sounds—all you have to do is squeeze the grape till the flesh slips right out of the skin. This allows you to cook the flesh into a pulp and strain out the seeds before recombining it with the skins, where much of the flavor lies. I cook this mixture down into a jam, which I use as the filling of these Linzer-esque cookies—my take on PB&J. If you want to skip the Concord jam, go ahead and use store-bought instead. [2]

Mix the dry ingredients: In a medium bowl, whisk together the flour, baking soda, and 1½ teaspoons of the salt (0.16 oz / 5g). Set aside.

Cream the butter, sugars, and peanut butter: In a stand mixer fitted with the paddle attachment, beat the butter, brown sugar, and ½ cup of the granulated sugar (3.5 oz / 100g) on medium speed, scraping down the sides occasionally, until the mixture is light and just a little bit fluffy, about 2 minutes. Add the peanut butter and continue to mix on medium until the mixture is smooth and creamy, about 1 minute.

Add the eggs and dry ingredients: Add the eggs one at a time, beating well and scraping down the sides after each addition until the mixture is smooth. Turn off the mixer, add all of the flour mixture and the vanilla, and pulse the mixer on low just to incorporate the flour. Gradually increase the mixer to medium and beat, scraping down the sides if necessary, until you have a thick, smooth, homogenous dough, about 30 seconds.

Form the dough into logs: Divide the dough in half and, using two sheets of parchment paper, roll each half into a tight, even 2-inch-thick cylinder (see page 22 for a visual guide to forming dough into logs). Wrap the logs in plastic and refrigerate until the dough is firm, at least 2 hours or up to 2 days. (This would be a good time to make the Concord grape jam.)

(continues)

DO AHEAD
These cookies are very delicate, so even though they will keep, covered at room temperature, up to 4 days or more, they will start to soften once filled with the

jam. They are best served the day they're made. The baked cookies, unfilled and stored in an airtight container at room temperature, will keep up to 4 days.

[1] For a lower yield, feel free to make a half recipe of dough, since all the quantities halve easily.

Preheat the oven and prepare the baking sheets:
Meanwhile, arrange two oven racks in the upper and lower thirds of the oven and preheat to 350°F. Line two rimmed baking sheets with parchment paper.

Slice and punch out the cookies: Remove one log of dough from the refrigerator and unwrap. Place on a cutting board and use a sharp knife to trim off the ends. Slice the dough crosswise into ⅛-inch-thick coins, trying to make them as thin as possible but, more importantly, trying to get them the same thickness so they bake evenly. Rotate the log every couple of slices to maintain a cylindrical shape. Transfer each slice to a prepared baking sheet, spacing them about 1 inch apart. You should get about 30 slices per log, enough to fill both sheets. To make Linzer cookies instead of regular sandwich cookies, use a ¾-inch cutter to punch out the centers of half of the cookies—these will be the "tops" (you can reserve the small cutouts and bake them later). Sprinkle the "tops" (or half the cookies if you're not making Linzers) with sugar and just a few extra grains of salt.

Bake and repeat: Bake the cookies on the upper and lower racks until lightly browned around the edges, 13 to 15 minutes, switching racks and rotating the sheets front to back after 10 minutes. Remove from the oven and let cool completely. Repeat the slicing and baking process with the second log of dough.

Fill the cookies: Stir the Concord grape jam to loosen it and smooth out any lumps. If making Linzers, turn the "bottom" cookies with no cutout (or, if not, the un-sugared cookies) over and spread a thin layer of jam all the way to the edges. Top with the remaining "tops" for Linzers (or regular sugared cookies) and press gently so the cookies adhere.

² Use 1½ cups of a good-quality store-bought jam to fill the cookies instead of making your own Concord grape jam. Or, omit the jam entirely and serve these as plain peanut butter cookies. In that case, don't forget to sprinkle all of the cookies with more sugar and a bit of salt before baking.

³ Use a brand of peanut butter that lists roasted peanuts and salt as the only ingredients because this will give the cookies the most intense peanutty flavor. If you use a brand that's particularly salty, the final cookies will have an extra-salty kick (not a bad thing, in my opinion).

Concord Grape Jam

Makes about 1½ cups

1 pound (454g) **Concord grapes**
(picked from about 1 quart on the stem)

½ cup **sugar** (3.4 oz / 100g)

2 tablespoons fresh **lemon juice**
(1 oz / 28g)

Peel and cook down the Concord grapes: Working over a small saucepan, grasp one grape at a time and squeeze it between your thumb and forefinger, stem end out, to pop the soft flesh into the saucepan, leaving the skin behind. Reserve the empty grape skin in a separate medium bowl. Repeat with all the grapes, placing all the flesh in the saucepan and all the skins in the bowl. Set aside the grape skins and place the saucepan of flesh over medium-low heat. Bring it to a simmer and cook, occasionally mashing the grapes against the sides of the pan with the back of a wooden spoon, until the mixture is pulpy and broken down and the seeds are free-floating around the saucepan, 5 to 10 minutes. Remove the saucepan from the heat and let cool.

Strain the flesh and combine with the skins: Set a fine-mesh sieve over the bowl with the reserved grape skins. Add the cooked pulp to the sieve and press down and scrape with a flexible spatula to force the pulp into the bowl below, leaving only the seeds behind (discard seeds). Transfer the pulp and grape skin mixture back to the same saucepan. If you like jam with a smooth consistency, you can puree this mixture, or leave it as is for a coarser texture.

Make the jam: Add the sugar and lemon juice to the saucepan and bring the mixture to a boil over medium-high heat, stirring to dissolve the sugar. Adjust the heat as needed to maintain a boil and cook, stirring occasionally, until the jam is reduced and syrupy and registers 220°F on an instant-read thermometer, 15 to 20 minutes.

Let it set: Pour the hot jam into a clean 1-pint jar, cover, and refrigerate until set, at least 2 hours.

DO AHEAD
The jam, refrigerated, will keep up to 1 month.

Layer Cakes and Fancy Desserts

Be advised: If you're a beginner baker, this chapter probably isn't the best starting point (may I suggest the **Loaf Cakes and Single-Layer Cakes** chapter, page 34, as the better place to dip your toes in the cake-making waters?). Even though the recipes in this chapter require multiple components, most of the work lies in the architecture and assembly (I'm looking at you, croquembouche), while the components themselves remain relatively straightforward. The **Chocolate Buttermilk Cake** on page 181, for example, is my ideal chocolate cake: a construction of three tender layers separated by a silky, smooth frosting. And that's it. I can get a little fancy at times, using an extra filling here and a bit of torched meringue there, but don't expect elaborate decoration—when you have good cake and frosting, it just isn't necessary.

PRESERVED LEMON MERINGUE
CAKE, PAGE 206

Classic Birthday Cake

Serves 10

Special Equipment:
Stand mixer, three 8-inch cake pans [1]

Butter for the pans

3 cups **cake flour** (12.7 oz / 360g) [2]

2 teaspoons **baking powder** (0.28 oz / 8g)

1½ teaspoons **Diamond Crystal kosher salt** (0.16 oz / 5g)

½ teaspoon **baking soda**

2 sticks **unsalted butter** (8 oz / 226g), at room temperature

1¾ cups **sugar** (12.3 oz / 350g)

¼ cup **neutral oil**, such as vegetable or grapeseed (2 oz / 57g)

5 large **egg yolks** (2.6 oz / 80g)

2 large **eggs** (3.5 oz / 100g)

1 tablespoon **vanilla extract**

1 cup **buttermilk** (8.5 oz / 240g), at room temperature

Classic Cream Cheese Frosting, Chocolate Variation (page 324)

Sprinkles, for decorating

There are certain occasions where the only cake that will do is a yellow cake with chocolate frosting. It's the quintessential birthday cake combination, and this particular yellow cake is extremely buttery, tender, and light (thank you, cake flour!). It's good enough to eat on its own, but a chocolate variation on **Classic Cream Cheese Frosting** manages to make it way, way better.

Preheat the oven and prepare the pans: Arrange two oven racks in the upper and lower thirds of the oven and preheat to 350°F. Butter the bottoms and sides of the cake pans and line the bottoms with rounds of parchment paper, smoothing to eliminate air bubbles. Set the pans aside.

Mix the dry ingredients: In a large bowl, whisk together the flour, baking powder, salt, and baking soda to combine. Set aside.

Cream the butter, sugar, and oil: In a stand mixer fitted with the paddle attachment, combine the butter, sugar, and oil and beat on low until smooth. Increase the speed to medium-high and continue to beat, scraping down the sides once or twice, until the mixture is very light and fluffy, about 4 minutes.

Add the eggs and vanilla: Reduce the mixer speed to medium and add the egg yolks, a few at a time, beating well after each addition, followed by the whole eggs. Beat on medium-high until the mixture is very light and thick, about 1 minute. Beat in the vanilla. Stop the mixer and scrape down the sides.

Alternate the dry and wet ingredients: Add about one-third of the flour mixture and mix on low speed until the flour has almost disappeared. Add half of the buttermilk, mixing just until incorporated, then add the remaining flour mixture in 2 additions, alternating with the remaining buttermilk. When the last traces of flour disappear, stop the mixer and remove the bowl. Use a flexible spatula to scrape down the sides and fold the batter several times to make sure it's evenly mixed.

Fill the pans and bake the layers: Divide the batter among the three pans (if you have a scale, weigh out 17 oz / 482g of batter per pan). (continues)

DO AHEAD
The cake, well wrapped and refrigerated, will keep up to 3 days. Once frosted, refrigerate the cake until the frosting is hardened and then cover loosely with plastic wrap. Allow the cake to sit at room temperature for several hours before serving. The cake layers, covered tightly and stored at room temperature, will keep up to 2 days or can be frozen up to 3 weeks. When you're ready to use the layers, frost them frozen, then refrigerate the assembled cake loosely wrapped until the layers are completely thawed, at least 24 hours prior to serving.

Smooth the batter in an even layer all the way to the sides. Transfer the pans to the oven, placing two on the upper rack and one on the lower rack, staggering so the pan below doesn't have another pan directly above it. Bake until the cakes are risen and just starting to pull away from the sides, the tops are golden brown, and a cake tester or toothpick inserted into the centers comes out clean, 30 to 35 minutes, switching racks and rotating the pans front to back after 25 minutes.

Cool the cakes and level the layers: Remove the cakes from the oven and let them cool completely in the pans. Cut around the sides with a paring knife or offset spatula, then invert the layers onto a wire rack and peel away the parchment paper. Reinvert the layers onto a cardboard cake round or cutting board. Use a long serrated knife and long, even strokes to slice off the domed tops of the cakes, keeping the blade parallel to the work surface. (Snack on the cake scraps.) This creates level layers for easier stacking and assembly.

Stack and frost the cake: Place the first cake layer cut-side down on a cake round, serving plate, or cake stand and slide several strips of parchment partially underneath and all around the cake to cover and protect the plate or stand during frosting. Using a small offset spatula, spread ¾ cup of the frosting over the cake in an even layer all the way to the edges, then top with another layer, cut-side down, and cover with another ¾ cup frosting. Place the third layer on top, cut-side down, and cover the top and sides of the entire layer cake with 1 cup of the frosting in a very thin, even layer. This is the "crumb coat," which is just a base layer of frosting, so don't worry if the cake shows through in several places. Refrigerate the cake until the frosting has hardened, 10 to 15 minutes, then cover all the surfaces with the remaining frosting. Decorate with sprinkles as desired.

Serve: Slide the parchment strips out from underneath the cake before cutting into slices.

---

[1] If you don't have three 8-inch pans, you can bake the batter in two 9-inch pans, filling each with about 1 pound 11 ounces (765g) of batter. Bake the pans side by side in the center of the oven for 30 to 35 minutes, rotating the pans front to back and left to right, after 25 minutes.

[2] If you don't have or can't find cake flour, in a pinch you can substitute an equal amount of all-purpose flour: Just replace 1 tablespoon flour with 1 tablespoon cornstarch per 1 cup flour called for in the recipe (so, in this case, you'd measure out 3 cups of all-purpose flour, remove 3 tablespoons, and add 3 tablespoons of cornstarch).

Confetti Cake

Serves 16

Special Equipment:
Stand mixer, three 9-inch cake pans

Butter for the pans

5½ cups **cake flour** (23.3 oz / 660g) [2]

2⅓ cups **sugar** (16.4 oz / 466g)

4½ teaspoons **baking powder**
(0.63 oz / 18g)

1½ teaspoons **Diamond Crystal kosher
salt** (0.16 oz / 5g)

¾ teaspoon **baking soda**

3 sticks **unsalted butter** (12 oz / 340g), at
room temperature [3]

1½ cups **buttermilk** (12.7 oz / 360g)

⅓ cup **neutral oil**, such as vegetable or
grapeseed (2.6 oz / 75g)

3 large **eggs** (5.3 oz / 150g), at room
temperature

6 large **egg whites** (7.4 oz / 210g), at room
temperature

1 tablespoon **vanilla extract**

½ teaspoon **almond extract** (optional)

½ cup store-bought **rainbow sprinkles**
(3.3 oz / 93g), plus more for decorating [4]

Classic Cream Cheese Frosting
(page 324)

I started my baking career making boxed cake mixes at a young age.
I know I'm not alone when I write that my favorite was the Pillsbury
Funfetti Cake. It's basically a white cake with sprinkles mixed into
the batter, but the flavor is pure nostalgia. When my sister requested
a Funfetti cake for her wedding, I took it as an opportunity to dial in a
recipe for a homemade version. This is her cake, scaled to make three
generous 9-inch layers. [1] Rather than the standard mixing technique
that starts with creaming together butter and sugar, followed by the
addition of eggs, liquids, and dry ingredients, this recipe uses an
alternative technique called "reverse creaming"—pioneered by cake
maven Rose Levy Beranbaum—that mixes the fat and liquids directly
into the dry ingredients. This method leads to layers that bake flatter
with a very uniform crumb. I haven't tried the Pillsbury mix since I was a
kid, but this is just how I remember it tasting.

Prepare the pans and preheat the oven: Butter the bottom and sides of the
cake pans. Line the bottoms with rounds of parchment paper, smoothing
to eliminate air bubbles, and set aside. Arrange two oven racks in the
lower and upper thirds of the oven and preheat to 350°F.

Mix the dry ingredients: In a stand mixer bowl with at least a 5-quart
capacity, [5] combine the flour, sugar, baking powder, salt, and baking
soda. Mix on the lowest speed with the paddle attachment just to
combine (beware of flying flour).

Mix in the fat and some of the liquid: Add the butter, buttermilk, and oil
and beat on low just until the flour is moistened. Gradually increase the
speed to medium-high and beat, scraping down the sides of the bowl
once or twice, until the mixture is completely smooth, about 1 minute.

Whisk the egg mixture and add the remaining ingredients: In a medium
bowl, thoroughly whisk the whole eggs, egg whites, vanilla, and almond
extract (if using) until no streaks remain. With the mixer on medium-low,
add the egg mixture to the flour mixture in 2 additions, beating well after
each addition. Increase the speed to medium and continue to beat until
the batter is very light and thick, about 2 minutes. (continues)

DO AHEAD
The cake, well wrapped and refrigerated,
will keep up to 3 days. Once frosted,
refrigerate the cake until the frosting is
hardened and then cover loosely with
plastic wrap. Allow the cake to sit at
room temperature for several hours
before serving. The cake layers, covered

tightly and stored at room temperature,
will keep up to 2 days or can be frozen up
to 3 weeks. When you're ready to use the
layers, frost them frozen, then refrigerate
the assembled cake loosely wrapped
until the layers are completely thawed, at
least 24 hours prior to serving.

Fold in the sprinkles: Remove the bowl from the stand mixer and add the sprinkles; fold them into the batter with a large flexible spatula to distribute evenly. Try not to mix too much or the color of the sprinkles will start to bleed.

Fill the pans and bake: Scrape the batter into the prepared pans, dividing evenly (for uniform layers, use a scale and weigh out 1 lb 12 oz / 785g batter per pan). Smooth the batter in an even layer all the way to the sides. Transfer the pans to the oven, placing two on the upper rack and one on the lower rack, staggering so the pan below doesn't have another pan directly above it. Bake until the tops are golden brown, the centers spring back when pressed, and a cake tester or toothpick inserted into the centers comes out clean, 35 to 40 minutes, switching racks and rotating the pans front to back after 30 minutes.

Cool the cakes and level the layers: Remove the cakes from the oven and let them cool completely in the pans, then use a small offset spatula or paring knife to cut around the sides. Invert onto a wire rack, remove the parchment paper, then reinvert the layers onto a cardboard cake round or cutting board. Use a long serrated knife and long, even strokes to slice off the domed tops of the cakes, keeping the blade parallel to the work surface. (Snack on the cake scraps.) This creates level layers for easier stacking and assembly.

Stack and frost the cake: Place the first cake layer, cut-side down, on a cake round, serving plate, or cake stand and slide several strips of parchment partially underneath and all around the cake to cover and protect the plate or stand during frosting. Using a small offset spatula, spread 1 cup of frosting over the cake in an even layer all the way to the edges, then top with another cake layer, cut-side down, and cover with another 1 cup frosting. Place the third layer on top, cut-side down, and cover the top and sides of the entire layer cake with another 1½ cups frosting in a very thin, even layer. This is the "crumb coat," which is just a base layer of frosting, so don't worry if the cake shows through in several places. Refrigerate the cake until the frosting has hardened, 10 to 15 minutes, then cover the top and sides of the cake with the remaining frosting. Decorate the outside of the cake with more sprinkles.

Serve: Slide the parchment strips out from underneath the cake and let it come to room temperature before slicing.

1 You can make cupcakes with this recipe, but note that the yield is 36, which means you'll need three muffin tins. Feel free to halve the recipe and just make 18. You can also bake the cake as a sheet, buttering and lining a half-sheet pan (18 × 13 inches) with parchment and filling it with the entire volume of batter. Bake it in the center of the oven until the top is evenly golden brown and springy to the touch, 35 to 40 minutes. You can frost it as is, in a single layer, or cut it crosswise into two rectangular layers and stack them for a two-layer cake.

2 If you don't have or can't find cake flour, in a pinch you can substitute an equal amount of all-purpose flour: Just replace 1 tablespoon of flour with 1 tablespoon of cornstarch per 1 cup flour called for in the recipe.

3 Make sure the butter is fully room temperature before mixing the batter. It should be soft and very spreadable but not greasy looking (warm butter isn't good either). I recommend leaving the butter at room temperature for several hours and even overnight before mixing the batter, but you can also quickly temper cold butter by zapping it in the microwave in 20-second intervals on 30 percent power. With reverse creaming, the butter needs to fully incorporate so it coats the flour particles (this prevents gluten formation once the liquid ingredients are added, yielding a tender cake), and butter that's even the least bit cool won't do this easily.

4 Don't use fancy sprinkles made with vegetable-based coloring because they will disappear into the batter during baking. You want the waxy, tasteless, brightly colored, artificial ones.

5 Don't make this cake using a stand mixer with less than a 5-quart capacity, as the volume of batter will be too great. If you want to make this recipe with a hand mixer, you can, but I would strongly recommend halving all the quantities. A hand mixer lacks power compared to a stand mixer and won't be able to effectively mix such a large volume of batter.

Carrot and Pecan Cake

Serves 10

Special Equipment:
Stand mixer, three 8-inch cake pans

1½ cups **pecan** or **walnut** pieces and/or halves (5.3 oz / 150g)

Neutral oil for the pans

1 pound (454g) **carrots** (about 5 large), peeled and coarsely grated (about 3 cups)

1 cup **buttermilk** (8.5 oz / 240g), at room temperature

1 tablespoon finely grated **fresh ginger**

2 teaspoons **vanilla extract**

2½ cups **all-purpose flour** (11.4 oz / 325g)

2½ teaspoons **ground cinnamon**

2 teaspoons **baking powder** (0.28 oz / 8g)

2 teaspoons **Diamond Crystal kosher salt** (0.21 oz / 6g)

1 teaspoon **baking soda** (0.21 oz / 6g)

1 teaspoon **ground ginger**

¼ teaspoon **ground cloves**

4 large **eggs** (7 oz / 200g), at room temperature

¾ cup **granulated sugar** (5.3 oz / 150g)

¾ cup packed **dark brown sugar** (5.3 oz / 150g)

1 cup **neutral oil**, such as vegetable or grapeseed (8 oz / 226g)

Classic Cream Cheese Frosting, Brown Butter Variation (page 324)

When I was growing up, my mom made a carrot cake out of *Bach's Lunch,* the Junior Committee of the Cleveland Orchestra's Community Cookbook, published in 1971. Like a lot of recipes we often eat in childhood, it became the benchmark against which all carrot cakes were forever judged. This is a very different recipe—with lots of toasted pecans, buttermilk, and fresh ginger—but the spirit is the same. It's a rich, tender, moderately spiced cake loaded with carrots. Don't make it without the brown butter variation of the **Classic Cream Cheese Frosting** (page 324).

Preheat the oven and toast the pecans: Arrange two oven racks in the upper and lower thirds of the oven and preheat to 350°F. Scatter the pecans on a small rimmed baking sheet and bake on the lower rack, shaking halfway through, until the nuts are deep golden brown and very fragrant, 8 to 10 minutes. Remove and set aside to cool.

Prepare the pans: Lightly brush the bottoms and sides of the three cake pans with oil and line the bottoms with rounds of parchment paper, smoothing to eliminate air bubbles. Set the pans aside.

Mix the wet ingredients: In a medium bowl, stir together the carrots, buttermilk, fresh ginger, and vanilla to combine. Set aside. [1]

Crush the pecans: Place about two-thirds of the cooled pecans in a resealable plastic bag and seal, pressing out all the air. Use a rolling pin to lightly beat the nuts, breaking them up into smaller pieces. Open the bag and transfer the broken-up nuts to a small bowl and set aside. Place the remaining nuts in the same bag and seal, then beat thoroughly with the rolling pin to finely crush the nuts into a coarse meal. Transfer the nut meal to a medium bowl.

Mix the dry ingredients: To the medium bowl with the nut meal, add the flour, cinnamon, baking powder, salt, baking soda, ground ginger, and cloves and whisk to combine. Set aside. (continues)

DO AHEAD
The cake, well wrapped and refrigerated, will keep up to 3 days. Once frosted, refrigerate the cake until the frosting is hardened and then cover loosely with plastic wrap. Allow the cake to sit at room temperature for several hours before serving. The cake layers, covered tightly and stored at room temperature, will keep up to 2 days or can be frozen up to 3 weeks. When you're ready to use the layers, frost them frozen, then refrigerate the assembled cake loosely wrapped until the layers are completely thawed, at least 24 hours prior to serving.

[1] If you can, prepare the carrot and buttermilk mixture ahead of time (anywhere from 15 minutes to several hours), since the buttermilk will tenderize the carrots and lead to a more tender cake.

Beat the eggs and sugar to ribbon: In a stand mixer fitted with the whisk attachment, combine the eggs and granulated and brown sugars. Beat first on medium-low to break up the eggs, then increase to medium-high and beat until the mixture falls off the end of the whisk back into the bowl in a slowly dissolving ribbon, about 4 minutes (see page 23 for a visual of this step).

Stream in the oil: With the mixer on medium-high, very slowly stream in the oil until the mixture is smooth and emulsified (it will deflate some).

Alternate the dry and wet ingredients: Replace the whisk with the paddle attachment. Add about one-third of the flour mixture and mix on low speed until the flour has almost disappeared. Scrape in half of the carrot mixture, mixing just until incorporated, then add the remaining flour in 2 additions, alternating with the remaining carrot mixture. When the last traces of flour disappear, stop the mixer and remove the bowl. Use a flexible spatula to scrape down the sides and fold the batter several times to make sure it's evenly mixed, then fold in the pecan pieces.

Fill the pans and bake the layers: Divide the batter among the three prepared cake pans (if you have a scale, weigh out 1 lb 5 oz / 595g of batter per pan). Transfer the pans to the oven, placing two on the upper rack and one on the lower rack, staggering so the pan below doesn't have another pan directly above it. Bake until the cakes are springy to the touch in the center and a cake tester or toothpick inserted into the centers comes out clean, 25 to 30 minutes, switching racks and rotating the pans front to back after 20 minutes.

Cool the cakes: Remove the cakes from the oven and let cool completely in the pans. Use a small offset spatula or paring knife to cut around the sides. Invert onto a wire rack and peel off the parchment paper. Reinvert onto another rack, cutting board, or plate. [2]

Stack and frost the cake: Place a single cake layer upside down on a cake round, serving plate, or cake stand and slide several strips of parchment partially underneath and all around the cake to cover and protect the plate or stand during frosting. Using a small offset spatula, spread about 1 cup of the frosting across the surface, working all the way to the edges. Place another upside-down layer on top, centering it and pressing gently to level, then repeat with another 1 cup frosting. Place the third layer upside down on top and press gently. Cover the top and sides of the entire layer cake with another 1½ cups frosting in a very thin, even layer. This is the "crumb coat" which is just a base layer of frosting, so don't worry if the cake shows through in several places. Refrigerate the cake until the frosting has hardened, 10 to 15 minutes, then cover the entire cake with a generous layer of frosting, working it across the top and down the sides in loose strokes (depending on how thick a layer you like, you may have ½ to 1 cup frosting leftover). Refrigerate the cake just until the frosting is set, 10 to 15 minutes.

Serve: Slide the parchment strips out from underneath the cake before cutting into slices.

---

[2] These layers bake fairly flat, but for a truly level cake, use a serrated knife to slice off the domes. You might not get a clean cut due to all the carrots and pecans, though, so I usually don't bother!

Strawberry Cornmeal Layer Cake

Serves 8

Special Equipment:
9-inch springform pan or 9-inch cake pan with 2-inch sides, stand mixer

CORNMEAL CAKE

Butter for the pan

½ cup **yellow cornmeal** (2.6 oz / 75g) [1]

1 cup **buttermilk** (8.5 oz / 240g), at room temperature

1 teaspoon **vanilla extract**

1½ cups **all-purpose flour** (7 oz / 200g)

1 tablespoon **baking powder** (0.42 oz / 12g)

½ teaspoon **baking soda**

¾ teaspoon **Diamond Crystal kosher salt**

¾ cup **sugar** (5.3 oz / 150g)

2 teaspoons finely grated **lemon zest**

10 tablespoons **unsalted butter** (5 oz / 142g), at room temperature

2 large **eggs** (3.5 oz / 100g), at room temperature

ASSEMBLY

1½ pounds (681g) **strawberries**, hulled (about 4 cups) [2]

¼ cup **sugar** (1.8 oz / 50g)

2 teaspoons fresh **lemon juice**

2 cups **heavy cream** (16 oz / 454g)

This cake is my platonic ideal of a spring or summer dessert—uncomplicated, light, and fruit-forward. It's a hybrid of two other strawberry desserts I like quite a bit, the French layer cake known as *fraisier* and a classic strawberry shortcake. *Fraisier* is fussy to make and the sponge is usually nothing to write home about, while shortcakes tend to stale quickly and require quick hands to work in the cold butter. This simple cake has none of these drawbacks, and it's now my vehicle of choice for fresh berries and their juices.

Preheat the oven and prepare the pan: Arrange an oven rack in the center position and preheat the oven to 350°F. Butter the bottom and sides of the springform pan or cake pan. Line the bottom of the pan with a round of parchment paper and butter the parchment paper. Set aside.

Hydrate the cornmeal: In a small bowl or 2-cup measuring cup, stir together the cornmeal, buttermilk, and vanilla (this softens the cornmeal so it's not too crunchy in the baked cake). Set aside.

Mix the dry ingredients: In a medium bowl, whisk together the flour, baking powder, baking soda, and salt. Set aside.

Make the batter: In the bowl of a stand mixer, combine the sugar and lemon zest and massage the mixture with your fingertips to work the zest into the sugar until the mixture is very fragrant and resembles wet sand. Place the bowl on the mixer, attach the paddle, and add the butter. Beat on medium-high until very light and fluffy, scraping down the sides of the bowl once or twice, about 4 minutes. Add the eggs one at a time, beating well after each addition and scraping down the sides of the bowl as needed, until the mixture is very pale and light, another 2 minutes. Reduce the mixer to low and add the flour mixture in 3 additions, alternating with the buttermilk mixture in 2 additions, mixing just until the batter is smooth and homogenous. Stop the mixer and fold the batter several times by hand with a flexible spatula, scraping the bottom to make sure everything is well mixed. Scrape the batter into the prepared pan and smooth the top. (continues)

DO AHEAD
The assembled cake can be refrigerated, loosely covered, up to 8 hours. Let it sit at room temperature for 2 hours before serving. The baked cake layers, covered tightly and stored at room temperature, will keep up to 1 day.

[1] Use any grind cornmeal you have, just note that a finer cornmeal will result in a more lightly textured cake that rises a bit higher. Coarse cornmeal will add a pleasant crunch.

[2] Swap in an equal weight of halved blackberries or whole raspberries for the strawberries, macerating them as written, since either of these pair great with cornmeal. (Just make sure to crush a few of the raspberries with the back of a spoon to help release their juices.)

Bake: Bake the cake until the surface is deeply browned, the sides have started to pull away from the pan, the center springs back when pressed, and a cake tester or toothpick inserted into the center comes out clean, 40 to 50 minutes. ❸ Remove the cake from the oven and set it aside to cool in the pan for at least 20 minutes. Cut around the sides of the cake with a paring knife or small offset spatula to loosen and invert it onto a plate. Remove the parchment paper and invert again onto a wire rack so the cake is right-side up. Let it cool completely.

Macerate the berries: Select 5 of the largest strawberries you have, trim them so they're all the same height, and set aside. Slice the remaining berries lengthwise, halving the smallest and cutting the rest into ¼-inch-thick slices. Toss the sliced berries into a large bowl with the sugar and lemon juice and let sit until juices have accumulated, at least 15 minutes.

Whip the cream: Meanwhile, in a stand mixer fitted with the whisk attachment, beat the heavy cream, starting on medium-low and increasing the speed gradually to high as the cream thickens, until you have soft peaks. (Alternatively, beat the cream in a large bowl with a hand mixer.) Refrigerate the cream until you're ready to assemble the cake (but not for more than 1 hour, or the cream will deflate).

Split the cake into two layers: ❹ Using a serrated knife, score a horizontal line all around the side of the cake at the midway point. Then, using long, even strokes and positioning the knife parallel to the work surface, follow the shallow cut as a guide all the way around the cake to slice it into two even layers. Lift the top layer off the cake and set aside.

Assemble the cake: Carefully transfer the bottom layer to a cake stand or serving plate, cut-side up. Arrange the 5 trimmed berries that you set aside hulled-side down over the bottom layer, placing one in the center and the other 4 spaced evenly around. These are going to act like stilts to keep the top layer elevated so you don't squish out all the cream as you slice the cake. Spoon two-thirds of the sliced berries and any juices over the bottom layer, arranging them around the whole berries. Remove the whipped cream from the refrigerator and spoon half over the berries, spreading all the way to the edges of the cake. Carefully place the top layer of cake onto the bottom layer, cut-side down. Spread the remaining whipped cream over the top of the cake, making decorative swooshes and swirls. Spoon the remaining berries and juices on top and serve.

---

❸ Pay close attention to all the cake doneness indicators in the recipe to make sure the cake is fully baked, since it will sink slightly if underdone. Don't be afraid to bake the cake until the surface is deeply browned (it won't dry out even if you bake it an extra few minutes).

❹ If you don't feel like splitting the cake into layers, cut or break up the cake into 1-inch pieces and layer with whipped cream and berries in a dish like trifle.

Chocolate Buttermilk Cake

Serves 10

Special Equipment:
Stand mixer, three 8-inch cake pans, ① candy or instant-read thermometer (for the buttercream)

Butter and flour for the pans

2⅓ cups all-purpose flour (10.6 oz / 300g)

2½ teaspoons baking powder (0.35 oz / 10g)

2 teaspoons Diamond Crystal kosher salt (0.21 oz / 6g)

½ teaspoon baking soda

6 ounces (170g) semisweet chocolate, coarsely chopped (about 1 cup)

⅔ cup brewed coffee (5.5 oz / 157g) or 1 teaspoon instant coffee dissolved in ⅔ cup water

½ cup Dutch process cocoa powder (1.4 oz / 41g)

⅔ cup buttermilk (5.6 oz / 160g), at room temperature

2 teaspoons vanilla extract

1½ sticks unsalted butter (6 oz / 170g), at room temperature

1 cup granulated sugar (7 oz / 200g)

1 cup packed light brown sugar (7 oz / 200g)

¼ cup neutral oil, such as vegetable or grapeseed (2 oz / 57g)

3 large eggs (5.3 oz / 150g), at room temperature

Silkiest Chocolate Buttercream (page 359) or Classic Cream Cheese Frosting, Chocolate Variation (page 324)

I am sensitive to chocolate recipes that are so chocolaty they make me feel like I need to take a sip of water with every bite. This is the kind I prefer: a cake tender from buttermilk, moist from brown sugar, and just the right amount of intensity from a combination of melted chocolate and cocoa. To really celebrate the chocolate lovers in my life, I make this cake with the **Silkiest Chocolate Buttercream** (page 359), an incredibly smooth, rich frosting that *could* be too much if combined with an ultrachocolaty cake. If you don't want to attempt such a technical buttercream (it requires a thermometer and precise timing), this cake is still extremely delicious with the chocolate variation of the **Classic Cream Cheese Frosting** (page 324).

Preheat the oven and prepare the pans: Arrange two oven racks in the upper and lower thirds of the oven and preheat to 350°F. Butter the bottoms and sides of three 8-inch cake pans and line the bottoms with rounds of parchment paper, smoothing to eliminate air bubbles. Butter the parchment, then sprinkle the pans generously with flour. Shake and rotate the pans to coat the bottoms and sides, then tap out the excess. Set the pans aside.

Mix the dry ingredients: In a large bowl, whisk together the flour, baking powder, salt, and baking soda and set aside.

Melt the chocolate mixture: In a separate large heatproof bowl, combine the chopped chocolate, coffee, and cocoa powder. Set the bowl over a medium saucepan filled with about 1 inch of simmering (not boiling) water and heat, whisking occasionally, until the chocolate is melted and the mixture is completely smooth. Remove from the heat and whisk in the buttermilk and vanilla. Set aside.

Cream the butter, sugars, and oil: In a stand mixer fitted with the paddle attachment, combine the butter, granulated sugar, brown sugar, and oil and beat on low speed until smooth. Increase the speed to medium-high and continue to beat, scraping down the sides once or twice, until the mixture is very light and fluffy, about 5 minutes. (continues)

DO AHEAD
The cake, well wrapped and refrigerated, will keep up to 3 days. Allow the cake to sit at room temperature for several hours before serving. The cake layers, covered tightly and stored at room temperature, will keep up to 2 days or can be frozen up to 3 weeks. When you're ready to use the layers, frost them frozen, then refrigerate

the assembled cake loosely wrapped until the layers are completely thawed, at least 24 hours prior to serving (let the frosting firm up in the refrigerator before wrapping the cake).

① Bake this cake in two 9-inch cake pans with 2-inch sides if that's what you have. Bake to the same end point, which will take 40 to 45 minutes. The layers will be very tall, so split them horizontally if you want to make a four-layer cake. You'll need closer to 1 cup of frosting between the layers when you assemble the cake, but follow the rest of the assembly instructions as written.

Add the eggs: Reduce the mixer speed to medium and add the eggs one at a time, beating well after each addition. Stop the mixer and scrape down the sides.

Alternate the dry and wet ingredients: Add about one-third of the flour mixture and mix on low speed until the flour has almost disappeared. Add half of the cooled chocolate mixture, mixing just until incorporated, then add the remaining flour in 2 additions, alternating with the remaining chocolate mixture. When the last traces of flour disappear, stop the mixer and remove the bowl. Use a flexible spatula to scrape down the sides and fold the batter several times to make sure it's evenly mixed and no chocolate streaks remain.

Fill the pans and bake the layers: Divide the batter among the three pans (if you have a scale, weigh out 18 oz / 510g of batter per pan), smoothing the batter into an even layer. Transfer the pans to the oven, placing two on the upper rack and one on the lower rack, staggering so the pan below doesn't have another pan directly above it. Bake until the cakes are risen and just starting to pull away from the sides, the top is firm to the touch, and a cake tester or toothpick inserted into the centers comes out clean, 30 to 40 minutes, switching racks and rotating the pans front to back after 25 minutes.

Cool the cakes: Remove the cakes from the oven and let cool completely in the pans. [2] Use a small offset spatula or paring knife to cut around the sides of the pans to release the cakes, then invert the cakes onto a wire rack and peel off the parchment paper.

Level the layers (if necessary): Reinvert the cooled layers onto a cardboard cake round or cutting board. If the cakes have pronounced domes, or if you're a stickler for flat, even layers, use a large serrated knife and long, even strokes to slice horizontally through the very top of the cakes, keeping the blade parallel to the work surface, to remove the dome (snack on the cake scraps). This creates a flat top for easier stacking and assembly. If the cakes have just a slight dome, you can leave them as is.

Stack and frost the cake: Place the first cake layer on a cake round, [3] serving plate, or cake stand upside down (also cut-side down if you leveled the layers) and slide several strips of parchment partially underneath and all around the cake to cover and protect the plate or stand during frosting. Using a small offset spatula, spread ¾ cup of the chocolate frosting over the cake in an even layer all the way to the edges, then top with another upside-down cake layer and cover with another ¾ cup frosting. Place the third layer on top, upside down, and cover the top and sides of the entire cake with 1 cup of the frosting in a very thin, even layer. This is the "crumb coat," which is just a base layer of frosting, so don't worry if the cake shows through in several places. Refrigerate the cake until the frosting has hardened, 10 to 15 minutes, then cover the top and sides with the remaining frosting.

Serve: Slide the parchment strips out from underneath the cake before cutting into slices. [4]

---

[2] Be patient here. If the layers are even the least bit warm, the butter in the frosting will immediately start to melt as you try to frost them, and the whole cake will slide around.

[3] Building the cake on a cardboard cake round will make moving it around much easier. I keep a stack of them at home, but you can also make one by tracing the cake pan on a piece of cardboard, cutting it out, and covering it in foil.

[4] If you opt for the **Silkiest Chocolate Buttercream** and want to make the cake ahead of time, make sure you pull it out of the refrigerator with plenty of time to allow the cake to come to room temperature before serving—2 to 4 hours is a good time frame. If the cake is even slightly chilled, the butter-based frosting will be hard rather than smooth and creamy, and therefore much less delicious.

Chocolate-Hazelnut Galette des Rois

Serves 8 to 10

Special Equipment:
Food processor (for making the Frangipane)

Rough Puff Pastry (page 355) or 2 sheets thawed frozen store-bought puff pastry

All-purpose flour, for rolling out

¼ cup **chocolate-hazelnut spread** (2.3 oz / 65g) [1]

Frangipane, Chocolate-Hazelnut Variation (page 329) [2]

1 large **egg**, beaten

2 tablespoons coarsely chopped toasted **hazelnuts**

1 tablespoon **demerara sugar**

Galette des rois is a fancy French dessert that appears in bakeries following the holidays. But, less intimidatingly, you can just think of it as a free-form, double-crust tart made using puff pastry. The filling is typically an almond frangipane, but this chocolate-hazelnut riff feels even more special and tastes extra-delicious, thanks in part to a swipe of chocolate-hazelnut spread on the bottom. Don't let its association with the holidays deter you from making this impressive, easy-to-prep-ahead-of-time dessert all year long.

Preheat the oven and prepare the baking sheet: Arrange an oven rack in the center position and preheat the oven to 400°F. Line a large baking sheet with parchment paper and set aside.

Roll out the pastry: Remove one piece of pastry from the refrigerator and let it sit at room temperature for 5 minutes to soften slightly. Unwrap the dough and place it on a lightly floured surface. Use a rolling pin to lightly beat the dough all across the surface to make it more pliable, then dust the top and underside with more flour and roll out, dusting with more flour as needed, into a round a little larger than 10 inches in diameter. Transfer the pastry (this will be the top layer) to a dinner plate and refrigerate while you roll out the other piece. Remove the second piece of pastry from the refrigerator and repeat the rolling process. Transfer it to the prepared baking sheet. (If using thawed frozen store-bought puff pastry, lightly roll out the sheets of pastry on a floured surface to smooth any creases and make sure you have enough clearance to cut a 10-inch round.)

Fill the pastry: [3] Invert a 9-inch cake pan and press it down onto the pastry on the baking sheet to leave a circular impression, making sure it's centered so you have a ½ inch of clearance all the way around. Scrape the chocolate-hazelnut spread into the center of the pastry and use a spoon or small offset spatula to spread it in an even layer all the way to the edges of the round. Transfer the chocolate-hazelnut frangipane to a pastry bag or resealable plastic bag and snip a ¾-inch opening. Starting in the center of the round, pipe the frangipane into a tight spiral that fully covers the chocolate-hazelnut spread. If you run out (continues)

DO AHEAD
The galette, covered at room temperature, will keep up to 3 days but is best served on the first or second day (the pastry will soften over time). The

chocolate-hazelnut frangipane, stored in an airtight container in the refrigerator, will keep up to 2 days. Let it come to room temperature before using.

[1] Look for Rigoni di Asiago Nocciolata, an Italian brand of chocolate-hazelnut spread that is very smooth and not too sweet. Of course, Nutella works great, too.

before you get to the edges of the round, just spread the frangipane in a thinner layer with an offset spatula so it reaches the margins.

Egg wash the pastry and place the second layer on top: Brush the egg over the pastry in a circle around the frangipane. Remove the pastry from the refrigerator and drape it gently over the frangipane, making sure there's overlap all the way around. Press firmly around the edges of the round, carefully eliminating air pockets, to seal the two layers of pastry together.

Trim and seal pastry: Use a wheel cutter or sharp knife to cut around the filled pastry, leaving a ½-inch margin around the frangipane, to make a 10-inch round (you can trace around a 10-inch dinner plate or cake pan if you want it very even). Discard the pastry scraps. Holding a paring knife upright, press the tip (the dull side, not the blade side) into the cut sides of the pastry to crimp it lightly, working all the way around and spacing the crimps about ½ inch apart. Brush the top of the galette with more egg, then sprinkle with the chopped hazelnuts and demerara sugar. Use the tip of the paring knife to cut a couple of small vents in the top of the crust.

Chill to firm up: Transfer the baking sheet to the refrigerator and chill until the pastry is firm, about 15 minutes.

Bake: Transfer the baking sheet to the oven and bake until the pastry is puffed and the surface is a deep golden brown, 35 to 40 minutes, rotating the pan front to back after 25 minutes. Remove from the oven and let cool completely on the baking sheet before transferring to a serving plate and cutting into slices.

---

[2] Use any variation on frangipane that you prefer. You can also omit the chocolate-hazelnut spread.

[3] Try to keep the pastry as cold as possible throughout the assembly process to ensure the flakiest result. Return it to the refrigerator as needed if it starts to soften and become difficult to handle.

Strawberry-Rhubarb Pavlovas
with Rose

Makes 8 individual pavlovas

Special Equipment:
Stand mixer [1]

MERINGUES [2]

1 teaspoon fresh **lemon juice**,
plus a **lemon wedge** for rubbing the bowl

6 large **egg whites** (7.4 oz / 210g)

Pinch of **kosher salt**

1 cup **granulated sugar** (7 oz / 200g)

1¾ cups **powdered sugar** (7 oz / 200g)

1 teaspoon **vanilla extract**

**STRAWBERRY-RHUBARB TOPPING
AND ASSEMBLY**

¾ cup **granulated sugar** (5.3 oz / 150g)

¼ cup dry **white wine** (2 oz / 57g)

Pinch of **kosher salt**

½ **lemon**

½ **vanilla bean**, split lengthwise

1 pound (454g) **rhubarb**, thick stalks
halved lengthwise, cut crosswise into
1½-inch pieces

1 pound (454g) **strawberries**, hulled,
halved if small, sliced lengthwise if large

½ teaspoon **rose water**

2 cups **heavy cream** (16 oz / 448g)

If there is a more satisfying textural dessert than crispy-on-the-outside, marshmallowy-on-the-inside meringues, topped with whipped cream and fruit, then I have yet to find one. When I worked at the now-closed Spring restaurant in Paris, I made mini teardrop-shaped meringues first thing every morning. The recipe we used in the restaurant produced a gorgeously glossy, dense, stable meringue that baked into airy, crispy-shelled pillows—perfect for Pavlova—so I've adapted it here. It takes quite a bit of sugar to achieve that desired texture, so I like to balance it out with tart rhubarb and unsweetened whipped cream. Rose water, which I add to the rhubarb and strawberry mixture, is divisive. Used in too large amounts, it makes anything taste like potpourri, so the trick is using just a bit to add a floral note. If you hate the taste and smell of rose, of course feel free to leave it out.

Preheat the oven and prepare the pans: Arrange two oven racks in the upper and lower thirds of the oven and preheat to 200°F. Line two rimmed baking sheets with parchment paper and set aside.

Make the meringue: Rub the inside of a stand mixer bowl with the cut part of a lemon wedge to remove any grease or residue (this helps the egg whites whip up more easily). Place the egg whites and salt in the bowl and beat with the whisk attachment on low speed just to break up the whites. Increase the speed to medium-high and beat until the mixture is foamy and white. With the mixer running, very gradually add the granulated sugar, only allowing a thin, steady stream of granules to cascade into the bowl. Incorporating all the sugar will take 2 to 3 minutes, so be patient, as you want the egg whites to whip slowly. [3]

Once you've incorporated all the granulated sugar, you should have a dense and glossy meringue. Increase the speed to high and continue to beat until the meringue forms a stiff peak off the end of the whisk, about another minute. Stop the mixer and add about one-third of the powdered sugar. Beat on low to incorporate, then stop the mixer and repeat two more times with the remaining powdered sugar until it's (continues)

DO AHEAD
The meringues, wrapped very well and stored at room temperature, will keep up to 2 days. The rhubarb, stored airtight in the poaching liquid in the refrigerator, will keep up to 4 days. Assemble the Pavlovas right before serving.

[1] Don't attempt to make the meringue with a hand mixer. A hand mixer doesn't have the power required to sufficiently beat a stable meringue, plus you need a free hand to steadily stream in the sugar.

[2] Use plain store-bought meringue cookies as a shortcut. Break them into large pieces and layer with the cream and fruit mixtures in glasses for a spin on the classic British dessert Eton Mess.

completely incorporated into the meringue. The addition of the powdered sugar will cause the meringue to lose a bit of volume, so increase the mixer to high after adding all of it and beat once more until you have very stiff, glossy peaks, about 1 minute. Beat in the vanilla and 1 teaspoon lemon juice, then remove the bowl from the mixer.

Form the meringues: ④ Use a large spoon to make 8 equal dollops of meringue spaced out evenly across the two prepared baking sheets, 4 dollops per sheet. Use the back of a smaller spoon to create deep depressions about 3 inches wide in the center of each dollop. Don't worry about manipulating the shape of the dollops too much; they look best when left in their natural form, plus the meringue will relax and puff slightly in the oven.

Bake the meringues: Bake the meringues on the upper and lower racks until they are dry to the touch, very crisp on the outside, and soft and marshmallowy on the inside, about 2 hours, switching racks and rotating the pans front to back after 1 hour. Test their doneness by peeling a meringue off the parchment paper—it should release cleanly from the parchment (if it sticks, keep baking). Turn off the oven, prop the door open with a wooden spoon, and allow the meringues to cool in the oven for at least 1 hour and up to 2. ⑤

Poach the rhubarb: In a large saucepan or medium Dutch oven, combine the granulated sugar, wine, salt, and 1 cup water (8 oz / 227g). Squeeze the lemon half into the saucepan and toss in the rind as well. Scrape in the vanilla seeds and add the pod. Set the saucepan over medium heat and stir occasionally until the sugar is dissolved, about 2 minutes. Bring the poaching liquid to a very gentle simmer, then add the rhubarb. Continue to cook over medium heat, swirling the pan gently (don't disturb the rhubarb too much—you want it to keep its shape), just until you see the mixture start to bubble around the edges of the pan. ⑥ Remove from the heat and set the pan aside to cool completely; the rhubarb will slowly poach from the residual heat.

Macerate the strawberries: In a large bowl, combine the strawberries and rose water. Spoon 3 tablespoons of the warm rhubarb poaching liquid into the bowl with the strawberries, toss gently, and set aside while the rhubarb finishes cooling.

Whip the cream: In a stand mixer fitted with the whisk attachment, beat the heavy cream, starting on medium-low and increasing the speed gradually to high as the cream thickens, until you have soft peaks. (Alternatively, beat the heavy cream in a large bowl with a hand mixer.)

Assemble the Pavlovas: Arrange the meringues on individual plates and top them with the whipped cream and the strawberry mixture (plus juices), dividing evenly. Using a slotted spoon, top the Pavlovas with the poached rhubarb. Serve immediately.

---

③ You want to add the sugar very slowly to the egg whites so it dissolves completely. This produces a more stable and stiffer meringue that is resistant to weeping. (Weeping is when the meringue leaches out a clear, sticky syrup during baking, and is usually a result of undissolved sugar.)

④ You can make a single large-format Pavlova rather than individuals. Cover the better part of a parchment-lined rimmed baking sheet with the meringue, spreading it into a rough 13 x 9-inch rectangle and making several divots all across the surface so there are lots of peaks and valleys to hold the cream and fruit. Bake in the center of the oven for 2½ to 3 hours. Assemble on the baking sheet and cut into pieces to serve.

⑤ Wrap the meringues tightly in plastic if you're making them ahead, especially if it's humid. The sugar in the meringue will pull moisture from the air and cause them to soften, so creating an airtight and moisture-tight seal is key.

⑥ Don't allow the poaching liquid to boil or you will risk overcooking the rhubarb and turning it to mush.

Tarte Tropézienne

Serves 8

Special Equipment:
9-inch cake pan, stand mixer (for making Brioche Dough)

Butter for the pan

½ recipe **Brioche Dough** (page 352) ①

All-purpose flour, for rolling out

1 large **egg**, beaten

Demerara sugar, for sprinkling the top

½ recipe **Honey Almond Syrup** (page 320)

Pastry Cream (page 321), chilled

1 cup **heavy cream** (8.2 oz / 232g), chilled

Tarte Tropézienne is one of those French desserts with a charming backstory: a Polish baker working in St. Tropez in the 1950s invented the dessert and served it to Brigitte Bardot, who was there filming a movie. She, as the story goes, fell in love with it and dubbed the dessert "tarte Tropézienne." Not so much a tart as a big, cream-filled brioche sandwich, tarte Tropézienne isn't well known in the United States, but those who do know it are fierce devotees. The contrast between the bready, less-sweet brioche and the sweet vanilla-scented cream makes it particularly alluring. There are several components to prepare, but you can do them all ahead of time and then simply assemble the dessert the day you want to serve it.

Prepare the pan: Lightly butter the bottom and sides of the cake pan. Line the bottom with a round of parchment paper and set aside.

Roll out and cut the brioche: Use your fist to punch down the cold brioche dough and knock out some of the gas that built up during the first rise. Turn the brioche out onto a lightly floured surface and roll it into a 10-inch round. Place the cake pan over the dough and use a wheel cutter to cut around the pan, making a smooth round (try to work quickly so the brioche doesn't soften too much). Lift the round of dough and place it inside the cake pan, centering it so all the edges are flush.

Proof the brioche: Cover the cake pan and let the brioche sit at room temperature until it's puffed and a finger poked gently into the dough leaves only a slight imprint, 45 to 60 minutes.

Preheat the oven: Arrange an oven rack in the center position and preheat the oven to 350°F.

Bake the brioche: Uncover the pan and brush the surface of the dough with the beaten egg, then sprinkle generously with demerara sugar. Bake the brioche until the surface is domed, golden brown, and firm to the touch, 20 to 25 minutes. Remove from the oven and let cool in the pan for 15 minutes, then turn the brioche out onto a wire rack. Remove the parchment, turn it right-side up, and let it cool completely. (continues)

DO AHEAD
The tart, covered and stored in the refrigerator, will keep for several days but is best served the day it's made. The brioche, unsliced, well wrapped, and stored at room temperature, will keep for 1 day.

① Prepare a full recipe of brioche dough and use the other half to make **Brioche Twists with Coriander Sugar** (page 229) or **Pigs in a Brioche Blanket** (page 303).

Split the brioche: Using a serrated knife and holding it horizontally, make a shallow cut around the brioche right at the point where the straight side meets the edge of the dome. Then, using long, even strokes and positioning the knife parallel to the work surface, follow the shallow cut as a guide all the way around the brioche to slice it in half horizontally. Lift the top layer off the brioche and carefully set it cut-side up on a cutting board. Place the bottom half on a serving plate.

Soak the brioche and preslice the top: Use a pastry brush to dab a generous layer of the honey almond syrup across the surface of the bottom layer of the brioche and set aside. Soak the cut side of the top layer the same way, then turn it over so it's cut-side down on the cutting board. Use the serrated knife to cut the top layer into 8 equal wedges (like a pie; preslicing it will make serving the tart much easier). Set aside.

Whip the cream and fold into the pastry cream: Transfer the chilled pastry cream to a medium bowl and whisk briefly to smooth any lumps. In a large bowl, vigorously beat the chilled heavy cream with a whisk until it forms very firm peaks and clearly holds the marks of the whisk. The cream needs to be very stiff, otherwise the filling will be too loose and will ooze out of the tart. Whisk about one-third of the whipped cream into the pastry cream, then add the rest of the whipped cream and use a spatula to gently fold it in. [2]

Fill and chill the tart: Dollop the pastry cream mixture onto the soaked bottom layer of brioche and smooth it gently to make an even layer. Place the cut pieces of the top layer of brioche over the cream, reassembling it into a round. Place the assembled tart in the refrigerator and chill for at least 20 minutes. If chilling for more than 20 minutes, cover the tart loosely with plastic wrap.

Serve: Slice down between the wedges of the brioche with the serrated knife (without the precut top, much of the cream would smush out during slicing).

---

[2] Try not to overmix the pastry cream/ whipped cream mixture, as this could deflate it and make it more likely to ooze as you dollop it over the brioche. You want it as light and thick as possible, so use a gentle touch when folding in the whipped cream. If the mixture gets too runny and a dollop won't hold its shape, put it back in the refrigerator and let it set up for 15 minutes before spreading onto the brioche.

Fruitcake

Makes two 9-inch cakes (each serves at least 20)

Special Equipment:
Two 9-inch cake pans with 2-inch sides, stand mixer, two 9-inch cardboard cake rounds, pastry bag

FRUIT MIXTURE [1]

8 ounces (227g) **dried cranberries** (about 1⅔ cups)

8 ounces (227g) **dried currants** (about 1⅔ cups)

8 ounces (227g) **golden raisins** (about 1½ cups)

8 ounces (227g) **dried apricots**, chopped (about 1⅓ cups)

12 ounces (340g) **dried cherries** (about 2⅓ cups)

4 ounces (113g) **crystallized ginger**, chopped (about ¾ cup)

⅓ cup **brandy**, whisky, or Grand Marnier (2.7 oz / 77g)

¼ cup fresh **orange juice** (2 oz / 57g)

2 tablespoons fresh **lemon juice** (1 oz / 28g)

CAKE

4 ounces (113g) **walnuts** or **macadamia nuts** (about 1 cup)

Butter for the pans

3¼ cups **all-purpose flour** (15 oz / 423g)

1 cup plus 2 tablespoons **almond flour** (4.8 oz / 135g)

1 teaspoon **Diamond Crystal kosher salt** (0.11 oz / 3g)

1 teaspoon **ground allspice**

(ingredients continue)

PSA: If you're reading this recipe in December thinking you might want to make it for the holidays, I'm sorry to tell you, you're too late! This style of fruitcake must be "aged" for 2 months before it's ready to serve, which means baking it in October. The cake is "fed" weekly with a couple of tablespoons of brandy to preserve it and build flavor, then it's hermetically sealed in layers of jam, marzipan, and royal icing (uncut, the finished cake will literally keep for years). The result is an ultrarich, dense, and complex dessert that will forever dispel the stereotype of fruitcake as leaden and terrible. I adapted this recipe from a traditional English fruitcake recipe given to me by a friend, Joanna Keohane. Jo, a Brit, has had the recipe in her family for generations. I definitely Americanized it, swapping in dark brown sugar for muscovado, molasses for black treacle, fresh citrus zest instead of candied peel, and adding cranberries. (The macadamia nuts, also an American touch, are an homage to a late family member who was a great fan of this fruitcake and preferred macadamias over any other nut; you can swap in whatever kind you like.) While this is the most time-consuming recipe in the book, it's not overly technical and makes a fun and rewarding project.

Prepare the fruit mixture and macerate overnight: In a large bowl, toss the cranberries, currants, raisins, apricots, cherries, and crystallized ginger, breaking up any clumps. Pour the brandy, orange juice, and lemon juice over the fruit and toss to coat. Cover the bowl tightly with plastic wrap and let sit at least 8 hours and up to 24.

Toast the nuts: Preheat the oven to 350°F. Place the nuts on a small rimmed baking sheet and bake, shaking halfway through, until deep golden brown and very fragrant, 8 to 10 minutes. Remove the nuts from the oven and let cool, then coarsely chop and set aside.

Drop the oven temperature: Reduce the temperature of the oven to 275°F. These are very dense cakes with no leavening, so they bake for a long time at a low temperature to ensure the centers fully cook without the surfaces darkening too much. (continues)

DO AHEAD
The cakes, covered in royal icing, will keep for several years (seriously!). Once cut, the cakes, well wrapped and stored in the refrigerator, will keep for several weeks.

[1] Because this recipe contains as much dried fruit as it does cake, use the best quality dried fruit you can find.

[2] While you are adding a large volume of brandy to the cakes, the raw burn of alcohol dissipates so there isn't a pronounced alcohol flavor.

[3] I recommend setting a calendar reminder so you don't forget to "feed" the cakes once a week.

3 sticks **unsalted butter** (12 oz / 340g), at room temperature

1⅔ cups packed **dark brown sugar** (12 oz / 340g)

¼ cup **unsulfured molasses** (2.8 oz / 80g)

Finely grated **zest of 1 orange**

Finely grated **zest of 2 lemons**

7 large **eggs** (12.3 oz / 350g), at room temperature

2 teaspoons **vanilla extract**

4 tablespoons **brandy, whisky,** or **Grand Marnier**, plus 2 cups more so you can feed the cakes 2 tablespoons a week for 2 months ②

ASSEMBLY

16 tablespoons **raspberry jam** (11.3 oz / 320g)

24 ounces (680g) **marzipan**

8 cups (2 lb / 907g) **powdered sugar**, plus more for rolling out

5 large **egg whites** (6.2 oz / 175g)

Pinch of **kosher salt**

2 tablespoons **lemon juice**

Prepare the pans: Butter the cake pans and line the bottoms with rounds of parchment paper. Line all the way around the insides of the pans with a double thickness of parchment paper, which should be an inch taller than the pan itself (this helps shield the surfaces of the cakes from the heat). Set the pans aside.

Prepare the dry ingredients: In a medium bowl, whisk the all-purpose flour, almond flour, salt, and allspice. Set aside.

Make the cake: In a stand mixer fitted with the paddle attachment, combine the butter, brown sugar, molasses, orange zest, and lemon zest and beat on low until smooth. Increase the speed to medium-high and continue to beat, scraping down the sides once or twice, until the mixture is light and fluffy, about 3 minutes. With the mixer on low, add the eggs one at a time, increasing the speed just to incorporate each egg before decreasing to low and adding the next, until the mixture is very smooth. Beat in the vanilla, then, on low speed, add the flour mixture and mix just until it disappears.

Fold in the fruit and nuts: Remove the bowl from the mixer and tip in the entire dried fruit mixture (it should have absorbed all the liquid, but if there is still some liquid, go ahead and add it) and the toasted nuts. Use a large spatula to fold in the fruit and nuts until they're distributed evenly throughout the batter. It will seem like an enormous amount of fruit relative to the batter, but it's correct.

Fill the pans: Scrape the batter into the prepared pans, dividing evenly, working the batter all the way to the sides, and smoothing the top in an even layer. Make a shallow, wide depression in the center of the batter; the cakes will dome slightly in the oven, so this helps keep the tops flat and level.

Bake and cool: Bake the cakes side by side until the surfaces are deeply browned and a cake tester or skewer inserted into the centers comes out clean, 2½ to 3 hours, rotating the position of the pans after 1½ hours. If you notice that the fruit on the surface is starting to burn, tent it loosely with a piece of foil. Remove from the oven and let the cakes cool completely in the pans.

"Feed" the cakes and turn them out: Poke holes all across the surfaces of the cakes with a skewer. Slowly pour 2 tablespoons brandy over the top of each cake, allowing it to absorb. Turn the cakes out of the pans onto a rack, leaving all the parchment paper on the cakes. Reinvert the cakes and wrap them in another layer of parchment paper, then in a layer of foil, then place inside an airtight container. Store in a cool, dark place where you will age the cakes.

"Feed" once a week for 2 months: ③ Once a week, carefully unwrap the cakes and drizzle the surface of each with 2 tablespoons brandy. This will gradually preserve the cakes and give them a deep, rich flavor. Rewrap the cakes, using the same parchment and foil, place back in the airtight container and return to their resting place.

Cover the cakes: After 2 months, unwrap the cakes and place them on a wire rack. Working with one cake at a time, use a small offset spatula to spread 5 tablespoons of the jam across the top and down and around the sides of the cake in a very thin layer. Roll out 6 ounces (340g) of the marzipan between two sheets of parchment paper, occasionally peeling off the paper and dusting both sides with powdered sugar to prevent sticking, until you have a thin round measuring about 12 inches across. Remove the top piece of parchment, invert and center the round over the coated cake, and peel off the second piece of parchment so the marzipan is draped over the cake. Smooth the top to eliminate air bubbles and then work it down and around the sides, pressing firmly so it sticks to the jam. Repeat with the second cake, using another 5 tablespoons of the jam and 6 ounces (340g) of the marzipan.

Invert each cake onto a parchment-lined baking sheet so the uncovered surfaces are exposed. Coat the uncovered surface of one cake with 3 tablespoons of the jam in a thin, even layer. Roll out 6 ounces (340g) of the marzipan into a thin round the same way as before and drape it over the jam, smoothing so it meets and overlaps with the first layer of marzipan (some folds and creases are okay, but the entire cake should now be covered). Dip a finger in warm water and rub along the folds and seams between the layers of marzipan to seal them. Repeat with the second cake and the remaining 3 tablespoons jam and 6 ounces (340g) marzipan.

Let the covered cakes sit out at room temperature for at least 4 hours and up to 24, carefully turning once, to allow the marzipan to dry out.

Seal the cakes with royal icing: In a stand mixer fitted with the whisk attachment, beat the egg whites and pinch of salt on medium until frothy. Turn off the mixer, add 4 cups (1 lb / 454g) of the powdered sugar, and pulse the mixer several times until the sugar is incorporated. Increase the speed to medium and beat until the mixture is smooth and glossy, about 30 seconds. Turn off the mixer and add the remaining 4 cups (1 lb / 454g) powdered sugar and the lemon juice and pulse again. Beat the icing on high until it's very thick, glossy, opaque, and holding a firm peak, another 45 seconds.

Spread a thin layer of the royal icing across the top of each cake, then place the cardboard cake rounds on top of the royal icing, centering them, and invert the cakes onto the rounds so the iced side is down (this will "glue" the cake to the board). Scrape the remaining royal icing over top of the two cakes, dividing it evenly, and use a small offset spatula to spread the icing across the top and down the sides so it's covering every bit of the marzipan. You can smooth the icing or make swooshes and swirls, or pipe the icing into a decorative pattern. Let the cakes sit at room temperature, uncovered, for 24 hours to allow the royal icing to fully dry. Whew—you made it! They're done!

Serve: Cut the cakes into thin slices to serve.

Gâteau Basque

Serves 8

Special Equipment:
9-inch removable-bottom tart pan, stand or hand mixer

CHERRY COMPOTE

12 ounces (340g) fresh or frozen pitted **sweet cherries** (about 2½ cups)

2 tablespoons **kirsch**, **brandy**, or **rum**

3 tablespoons **sugar**

2 tablespoons fresh **lemon juice**

¼ teaspoon **cornstarch**

2 teaspoons finely grated **lemon zest**

PASTRY CRUST AND ASSEMBLY

2 cups **all-purpose flour** (9.2 oz / 260g), plus more for rolling out

1 teaspoon **baking powder** (0.14 oz / 4g)

¾ teaspoon **Diamond Crystal kosher salt**

10 tablespoons **unsalted butter** (5 oz / 142g), at room temperature

⅔ cup **sugar** (4.6 oz / 130g)

1 large **egg yolk** (0.53 oz / 16g)

2 large **eggs** (3.5 oz / 100g)

½ teaspoon **almond extract**

Butter and **flour** for the pan

Pastry Cream (page 321)

Gâteau Basque is my favorite kind of dessert: simple in concept (if not in execution; it's a long recipe), not too sweet, and suitable for any occasion or time of the day. It's essentially a sturdy tart, native to the French Basque country, comprising a layer of either pastry cream or cherry preserves baked inside a cookie-like double crust. For this version, I combine a sweet cherry compote with the pastry cream in a best-of-both-worlds hybrid. It's a great entertaining dessert, and highly transportable.

Make the cherry compote: ① In a small saucepan, combine the cherries, kirsch, and sugar and cook over medium-low heat, stirring occasionally to dissolve the sugar, until the cherries have released their juices, about 5 minutes. Continue to simmer briskly, swirling the saucepan occasionally and adjusting the heat if necessary, until the cherries are soft and the juices are reduced to a thick syrup, 10 to 15 minutes. In a small bowl, stir it together the lemon juice and cornstarch with a fork until smooth, then stir it into the cherry mixture. Bring to a simmer again and cook for 20 seconds to activate the cornstarch. Remove the compote from the heat, stir in the lemon zest, and transfer to a 2-cup heatproof glass measuring cup. You should have about 1¼ cups of compote—a bit less is fine, but if you have more than an extra tablespoon or two, return it to the saucepan and cook it a bit longer. Cover and refrigerate until the compote is cold and thickened, at least 1 hour or up to 1 week.

Make the pastry: In a medium bowl, whisk together the flour, baking powder, and salt to combine. Set aside.

In a stand mixer fitted with the paddle attachment (or in a large bowl if using a hand mixer), combine the butter and sugar and beat on medium-high speed, scraping down the sides of the bowl occasionally, until the mixture is light and fluffy, about 4 minutes. Turn off the mixer and scrape down the sides of bowl, then add the yolk, 1 whole egg, and the almond extract. Beat on medium-high until the mixture has increased in volume and paled slightly, about 2 minutes. Reduce the mixer speed to low and add the flour mixture in 2 additions, beating briefly in between to incorporate. Continue to mix just until no floury spots remain. (continues)

DO AHEAD
The tart, covered and refrigerated, will keep up to 4 days but is best served on the first or second day (the pastry will soften over time). The cherry compote, covered and refrigerated, will keep up

to 1 week. The tart dough, wrapped and refrigerated, will keep up to 2 days or can be frozen up to 1 month. Let the frozen dough thaw overnight in the refrigerator before using.

① Use good-quality cherry preserves in place of the cherry compote if you feel like eliminating this step.

Chill the dough: Knead the dough inside the bowl a couple of times to make sure it's homogenous, then divide it in half, making one piece slightly larger than the other. Wrap the pieces in plastic, pressing the dough into ½-inch-thick disks, and refrigerate until cold, at least 2 hours or up to 2 days. **②**

Prepare the pan: Lightly butter the bottom and sides of the tart pan, then dust it all over with flour. Tap out the excess and set the pan aside.

Press the bottom crust into the tart pan: Remove the larger piece of dough from the refrigerator (you're going to press this piece into the bottom of the pan; leave the other piece of dough in the refrigerator for the top). Use a knife or bench scraper to cut the dough in half, then cut one half into 6 pieces. Roll the pieces beneath your palms on the work surface to form ropes that are about ½ inch thick, then arrange the ropes around the sides of the prepared pan, overlapping slightly so there are no gaps. Using a lightly, floured straight-sided 1-cup dry measure, press the dough against the sides all the way around so it extends slightly above the top of the pan. Using lightly floured hands, press the other half of the dough into and across the bottom of the pan in an even layer. Where the bottom meets the sides, smooth and press the dough together to seal. For an extra-smooth surface, or if you notice any unevenness, use the bottom of the 1-cup measure to flatten the dough. Refrigerate the pan until the pastry is cold, about 20 minutes.

Roll out the top crust: Meanwhile, roll out the second disk of dough on a lightly floured piece of parchment paper into a 10-inch round, frequently flipping the dough and dusting with more flour as needed (this dough is delicate and will soften quickly; if it starts to stick, put it back in the refrigerator). Slide the dough, still on the parchment paper, onto a plate and refrigerate while you assemble the tart.

Preheat the oven: Arrange an oven rack in the center position and preheat the oven to 350°F. Line a rimmed baking sheet with foil.

Assemble the tart: **③** Scrape the cold cherry mixture into the bottom of the chilled tart crust, arranging the cherries and syrup evenly across the surface. Whisk the pastry cream until it's smooth, and then dollop it over the cherries, spreading it with the back of a spoon or a small offset spatula into an even layer all the way to the edges (it's okay if some syrup pools around the sides). Beat the remaining whole egg in a small bowl. Use a pastry brush to lightly coat the inner edge of tart dough with a thin layer of egg (just above the pastry cream). Remove the cold dough round from the refrigerator and slide it off the parchment paper onto the tart. Press gently starting in the center and moving outward to eliminate air pockets between the pastry and the cream. Press firmly around the edge so the top crust adheres to the sides, and pinch off the overhang. Brush more egg across the surface of the pastry, then gently scrape the tines of a fork across the top to create a decorative crosshatch pattern. Refrigerate the tart again until cold (I know, it's a process!), 15 to 20 minutes.

Bake the tart: Bake the tart on the prepared baking sheet until the top of the tart is shiny and deep golden brown, 45 to 55 minutes. Let the tart cool completely (preferably up to a full day!) before removing the outer ring and serving.

---

② I recommend making and chilling each component at least 1 day ahead to lighten the workload, so all you have to do on baking day is assemble. Plus, working with well-chilled pastry and filling is much easier.

③ Hold onto your dough scraps to patch any cracks that might occur on the surface of the tart during assembly, and don't worry if the top layer of pastry has a few imperfections prior to baking. The baking powder in the pastry causes it to puff in the oven, which will help hide flaws.

All Coconut Cake

Serves 10

Special Equipment:
Stand mixer, three 8-inch cake pans, food processor

COCONUT CAKE LAYERS

Coconut oil for the pans

3 cups **cake flour** (12.7 oz / 360g) [2]

1 tablespoon **baking powder** (0.42 oz / 12g)

1½ teaspoons **Diamond Crystal kosher salt** (0.16 oz / 5g)

2 sticks **unsalted butter** (8 oz / 227g), at room temperature

3 tablespoons **virgin coconut oil** (1.4 oz / 40g), at room temperature

1¾ cups **granulated sugar** (12.3 oz / 350g)

4 large **eggs** (7 oz / 200g), at room temperature

2 teaspoons **vanilla extract**

1 (13.5 oz / 383g) can unsweetened full-fat **coconut milk**, well shaken

ASSEMBLY

5 ounces (142g) unsweetened large **coconut flakes** (about 2½ cups)

Pastry Cream, Coconut Variation (page 322)

5 ounces (142g) fresh **coconut meat** [3]

½ recipe **Classic Cream Cheese Frosting** (page 324)

Years ago I made a coconut cake recipe by the late chef Paul Prudhomme that began with me struggling to crack open five whole coconuts in my tiny New York City apartment kitchen. The finished cake, which I brought to a party, is still talked about by the people who ate it. I don't recall many details about the recipe itself, but what I do remember—that it was composed of several thin cake layers separated by coconut custard and packed with real coconut—firmly established my idea of what a coconut cake should be. While many recipes call for white cake and frosting flavored only with coconut extract, I wanted to take advantage of the many forms of real coconut now easily found in most grocery stores: oil, milk, fresh, and dried. They're all in here, and the end result is a celebratory cake I guarantee people will talk about (but won't require you to crack open any coconuts).

Preheat the oven and prepare the pans: Arrange two oven racks in the upper and lower thirds of the oven and preheat to 350°F. Brush the bottoms and sides of the cake pans with melted coconut oil and line the bottoms with rounds of parchment paper, smoothing to eliminate air bubbles. Brush the parchment with more oil and set the pans aside.

Mix the dry ingredients: In a large bowl, whisk together the flour, baking powder, and salt to combine. Set aside.

Cream the butter, oil, and sugar: In a stand mixer fitted with the paddle attachment, combine the butter, coconut oil, and granulated sugar and beat on low until smooth. Increase the speed to medium-high and continue to beat, scraping down the sides once or twice, until the mixture is very light and fluffy, about 5 minutes.

Add the eggs and vanilla: Reduce the mixer speed to medium and add the eggs one at a time, beating well after each addition. Beat on medium-high until the mixture is very light and thick, about 1 minute, then beat in the vanilla. Stop the mixer and scrape down the sides.

Alternate the dry and wet ingredients: Add about one-third of the flour mixture and mix on low speed until the flour has almost disappeared. Add ½ cup (4.2 oz / 120g) of the coconut milk, mixing just until (continues)

DO AHEAD
The cake, well wrapped and refrigerated, will keep up to 3 days. Once frosted, refrigerate the cake until the frosting is hardened and then cover loosely with plastic wrap. Allow the cake to sit at room temperature for several hours before serving. The cake layers, covered tightly and stored at room temperature, will keep up to 2 days.

[1] To cut down on the labor of this recipe, skip the coconut pastry cream filling and instead spread a thin layer of cream cheese frosting between the layers (follow the rest of the recipe as written). If you want to do this, be sure to make a full recipe of the **Classic Cream Cheese Frosting** rather than just a half.

incorporated, then add the remaining flour in 2 additions, alternating with another ½ cup (4.2 oz / 120g) coconut milk (reserve the remaining coconut milk for soaking the layers). When the last traces of flour disappear, stop the mixer and remove the bowl. Use a flexible spatula to scrape down the sides and fold the batter several times to make sure it's evenly mixed.

Fill the pans and bake the layers: Divide the batter among the three pans (if you have a scale, weigh out 1 lb / 454g of batter per pan). Smooth the batter in an even layer all the way to the sides. Transfer the pans to the oven, placing two on the upper rack and one on the lower rack, staggering so the pan below doesn't have another pan directly above it. Bake until the cakes are risen and just starting to pull away from the sides, the tops are lightly golden, and a cake tester or toothpick inserted into the centers comes out clean, 30 to 35 minutes, switching racks and rotating the pans front to back after 25 minutes.

Cool the cakes: Remove the cakes from the oven and let cool completely in the pans. (Leave the oven on.)

Prepare the coconut: While the cakes are cooling, spread the large coconut flakes on a small rimmed baking sheet and bake until the flakes are deep golden brown but still pale along one edge, about 5 minutes. Set aside to cool. If the fresh coconut is in large pieces, chop it up so the pieces are about the size of a quarter. Put it in the food processor and pulse, scraping down the sides, until it's very finely chopped. Transfer to a small bowl and set aside (you should have about 1¼ cups).

Split the layers: Use a small offset spatula or paring knife to cut around the sides of the pans to loosen the cakes. Invert them onto a wire rack, peel off the parchment, then reinvert onto a cardboard cake round or cutting board. The cakes should bake very

flat so you won't need to level them. You are, however, going to split the layers in half horizontally to make six thinner layers out of the three.

Holding a serrated knife horizontally, mark the midway point around the side of a cake by making shallow score marks all the way around. Then, using long, even strokes and positioning the knife parallel to the work surface, follow the shallow cut as a guide all the way around the cake to slice it into two even layers. Lift the top layer off the cake and set aside. Repeat with the remaining layers so you have six total.

Fill and stack the layers: Place a cake layer, cut-side up, on a cake round, serving plate, or cake stand and slide several strips of parchment partially underneath and all around the cake to cover and protect the plate or stand during frosting. Use a pastry brush to dab some of the reserved coconut milk across the surface of the cake to soak the layer. Using a small offset spatula, spread ½ cup of the pastry cream evenly over the top of the cake layer, leaving a ¼-inch border around the cake. Evenly sprinkle about ¼ cup (1 oz / 28g) of the chopped fresh coconut over the cream, then place another cake layer on top, making sure it's positioned cut-side up and centered. Press gently to level, then brush with more coconut milk, spread with another ½ cup coconut pastry cream, and top with another ¼ cup fresh coconut. Repeat until you've soaked, stacked, and filled all the layers, placing the final layer cut-side down.

Frost the cake: Use a small offset spatula to spread the cream cheese frosting around the top and sides of the stacked cake, smoothing the top. Press the cooled toasted coconut flakes into the sides and top of the cake so they adhere to the frosting.

Serve: Slide the parchment strips out from underneath the cake before cutting into slices.

---

[2] Don't worry if you don't have or can't find cake flour. In a pinch, you can substitute an equal amount of all-purpose flour: Just replace 1 tablespoon flour with 1 tablespoon cornstarch per 1 cup flour called for in the recipe.

[3] Sample both the dried and fresh coconut before you start baking. Coconut goes rancid extremely quickly, so make sure the ingredients taste fresh.

Black Sesame Paris-Brest

Serves 8

Special Equipment:
Stand mixer (for the Pâte à Choux), three pastry bags

Pâte à Choux (page 346), transferred to a pastry bag

1 large egg, beaten

Demerara sugar, for sprinkling the top

Black sesame seeds, for sprinkling the top

1⅓ cups **heavy cream** (11 oz / 312g), chilled

Pastry Cream, Black Sesame Variation (page 322) ①

Paris-Brest is a French pastry made of a ring of *pâte à choux* filled with praline cream. It is named for the former bike race between Paris and the city of Brest (and is meant to resemble a bike wheel). Praline, a smooth paste ground from caramelized almonds and hazelnuts, is completely delicious but also expensive and hard to find, so I love using black tahini instead. The black sesame adds depth of flavor and bitterness, and without it the recipe could definitely lean a bit sweet. Plus, it looks incredible in the Paris-Brest, contrasted against a layer of whipped cream and accented by black sesame seeds on top. Here's a textbook example of my most prized dessert recipes: familiar yet a bit unexpected.

Preheat the oven and prepare the baking sheet: Arrange an oven rack in the center position and preheat the oven to 400°F. Line a standard half-sheet pan (18 × 13 inches) with parchment paper and place a 9-inch cake pan in the center. Trace around it with a pencil, then turn the parchment over (you should still be able to see the line).

Pipe the *pâte à choux* ring: Snip a 1-inch opening in a pastry bag with the *pâte à choux* and, applying constant pressure to the bag, pipe the pastry along the traced line to make a circle with a slight overlap at the point where the pastry begins and ends. ② Pipe another ring of pastry just inside the first so the two are flush, but starting and ending at a different point. Make a third ring, piping it on top of and nestling it between the first two, starting at yet a different point (you should use all or nearly all of the dough).

Decorate the ring: Brush all around the *pâte à choux* ring with the egg. Following the contours of the ring, lightly drag the tines of a fork around, inside, and on top of the dough to make score marks and blend the rings together. Generously sprinkle demerara sugar and black sesame seeds over the ring.

Bake the *pâte à choux*: Transfer the half-sheet pan to the oven and bake for 10 minutes. Reduce the oven temperature to 350°F and bake until the pastry is puffed and deep golden brown, 45 to 55 minutes longer. You want to make sure the pastry is thoroughly baked or it could collapse, so if you're not sure, bake it a few minutes longer.   (continues)

DO AHEAD
The pastry cream and *pâte à choux* can be prepared in advance (see the respective recipe's Do Ahead for details), but the pastry ring should be baked and filled just before serving.

① Look for black tahini at Whole Foods or at a Middle Eastern grocer. You can also order it online, but feel free to substitute regular tahini if you can't find it. You won't have the cool charcoal gray color, and the flavor will be different, but the Paris-Brest will still be delicious.

② The ring of *pâte à choux* will puff dramatically in the oven, so don't pipe a ring larger than 9 inches, otherwise it will expand beyond the dimensions of a standard half-sheet pan.

Remove the baking sheet from the oven, poke several holes around the side of the pastry with a paring knife to release steam, and return it to the turned-off oven with the door propped open for 10 minutes (this will dry it out and help the dough maintain its shape).

Split the pastry ring: Let the ring of *pâte à choux* cool completely at room temperature, then slide the ring off the parchment paper onto a large cutting board. Holding a serrated knife parallel to the work surface, insert it through the hollow part of the pastry at any point around the ring, sliding it all the way through so the tip of the knife is right at the center of the ring. Using a sawing motion, cut horizontally all the way around the circle, rotating the pastry, so you separate a narrower ring of pastry from the wider base below. Carefully lift off the ring and place it next to the base. Cut the ring in half, then into quarters, and then into eighths. Scoop out and discard some of the wet, doughy innards from the ring base.

Whip the cream: In a stand mixer fitted with the whisk attachment, beat the heavy cream, starting on medium-low and then increasing to high as it thickens, until firm peaks form (or, beat with a whisk by hand or with a hand mixer in a large bowl). Refrigerate.

Assemble the Paris-Brest: Transfer the pastry cream to a large pastry bag, snip a ½-inch opening, and pipe big teardrop-shaped dollops inside the base, distributing evenly (use all of the pastry cream). Remove the whipped cream from the refrigerator and transfer it to another pastry bag. Snip a 1-inch opening and pipe dollops of whipped cream in a ring on top of the pastry cream (use all the whipped cream). Gently arrange the pieces of the pastry ring on top of the cream, fitting them back into a circle.

Serve: To slice, use a serrated knife to cut down in between the pieces of the upper ring through the pastry base (the cut top prevents you from squishing out the filling as you slice).

Preserved Lemon
Meringue Cake

Serves 10

Special Equipment:
Stand mixer, standard or handheld blender, three 8-inch cake pans, candy or instant-read thermometer, kitchen torch (optional)

PRESERVED LEMON CAKE

Butter for the pans

3 whole small **preserved lemons** (about 6 oz / 170g)

¾ cup plain whole-milk **Greek yogurt** (6.3 oz / 180g), at room temperature

2 tablespoons fresh **lemon juice** (1 oz / 28g)

2 teaspoons **vanilla extract**

Finely grated **zest of 1 lemon**

3⅓ cups **cake flour** (14 oz / 400g) ①

1 tablespoon **baking powder** (0.42 oz / 12g)

¼ teaspoon **baking soda**

2 sticks **unsalted butter** (8 oz / 227g), at room temperature

⅓ cup **neutral oil**, such as vegetable or grapeseed (2.6 oz / 75g)

2 cups **sugar** (14 oz / 400g)

5 large **eggs** (8.8 oz / 250g), at room temperature

ITALIAN MERINGUE AND ASSEMBLY ②

Lemon Curd (page 330)

3 large **egg whites** (3.7 oz / 105g)

½ teaspoon fresh **lemon juice**

Pinch of **kosher salt**

¾ cup **sugar** (5.3 oz / 150g)

1 teaspoon **vanilla extract** or **orange blossom water**

Preserved lemons, a staple of North African and Middle Eastern cuisines, add a pungent lemony flavor to savory dishes without the puckering acid of fresh lemons. The best way to infuse a baked good with lemon flavor, I've found, is to add a large amount of fresh grated lemon zest, but this gets impractical quickly. Instead, it occurred to me that preserved lemons might be a cool and interesting way to flavor a cake. As a test, I blended the rind of a few preserved lemons (generally the only part you use, even though the whole fruit is preserved) into some plain yogurt and added it to a batter, and the resulting flavor was complex and floral and even better than I expected. Preserved lemons are cured in salt and therefore very salty, so there's no need to add additional salt to the cake recipe. Look for them jarred in Middle Eastern grocery stores or well-stocked supermarkets.

Preheat the oven and prepare the pans: Arrange two oven racks in the upper and lower thirds of the oven and preheat to 350°F. Lightly butter the bottoms and sides of the cake pans and line the bottoms with rounds of parchment paper, smoothing to eliminate air bubbles. Butter the parchment and set the pans aside.

Blend the lemon into the wet ingredients: Halve the preserved lemons and pull out and discard the pulpy innards and seeds, leaving only the rind. Rinse and coarsely chop the halves, then weigh and measure the amount. You should have about 3 ounces / 85g or a scant ½ cup. In a blender, combine the chopped preserved lemons, yogurt, lemon juice, vanilla, and grated zest and blend on low speed to liquefy, then on high until the pieces of lemon rind disappear and the mixture is smooth. Set the mixture aside.

Mix the dry ingredients: In a medium bowl, whisk together the flour, baking powder, and baking soda and set aside.

Cream the butter, oil, and sugar: In a stand mixer fitted with the paddle attachment, combine the butter, oil, and sugar and beat on low until smooth. Increase the speed to medium-high and continue to beat, scraping down the sides occasionally, until the mixture is very light and fluffy, about 5 minutes.

DO AHEAD
The cake layers, well wrapped and stored at room temperature, will keep up to 2 days or can be frozen up to 1 month (split them in half horizontally before freezing). Fill and stack the frozen cake layers, then cover and let the cake thaw overnight in the refrigerator before covering with the meringue. The cake layers can be filled and stacked 1 day ahead; keep covered in the refrigerator. Let the cake come to room temperature and cover with the meringue just before serving. The coated cake will keep at room temperature for at least 1 day, but the meringue will deflate over time.

Add the eggs: Reduce the mixer speed to medium and add the eggs one at a time, beating well after each addition. Beat on medium-high until the mixture is very light and thick, about 1 minute.

Alternate the dry and wet ingredients: With the mixer on low speed, add about one-third of the flour mixture and mix until the flour has almost disappeared. Scrape in half of the yogurt mixture, mixing just until incorporated, then add the remaining flour in 2 additions, alternating with the remaining yogurt mixture. When the last traces of flour disappear, stop the mixer and remove the bowl. Use a flexible spatula to scrape down the sides and fold the batter several times to make sure it's evenly mixed.

Fill the pans and bake the layers: Divide the batter among the three prepared pans (if you have a scale, weigh out 1 lb 3 oz / 539g of batter per pan). Smooth the batter in an even layer all the way to the sides. Transfer the pans to the oven, placing two on the upper rack and one on the lower rack, staggering so the pan below doesn't have another pan directly above it. Bake the cakes until the centers spring back when pressed, the surface is golden, and a cake tester or toothpick inserted into the centers comes out clean, 25 to 30 minutes, switching racks and rotating the pans front to back after 20 minutes.

Cool the cakes: Remove the cakes from the oven and let them cool completely in the pans.

Split the layers: Use a small offset spatula or paring knife to cut around the sides of the pans to loosen the cakes. Invert them onto a wire rack, peel off the parchment, then reinvert onto a cardboard cake round or cutting board. The cakes should bake very flat so you won't need to level them. You are, however, going to split the layers in half horizontally to make six thinner layers out of the three.

Holding a serrated knife horizontally, mark the midway point around the side of a cake by making shallow score marks all the way around. Then, using long, even strokes and positioning the knife parallel to the work surface, follow the shallow cut as a guide all the way around the cake to slice it into two even layers. Lift the top layer off the cake and set aside. Repeat with the remaining layers so you have six total.

Stack, fill, and chill the layers: Place a cake layer, cut-side up, on a cake round, serving plate, or cake stand and slide several strips of parchment partially underneath and all around the cake to cover and protect the plate or stand during frosting. Using a small offset spatula, spread a slightly heaping ⅓ cup cold lemon curd across the surface, leaving a ½-inch border. Place another layer on top, cut-side up, making sure it's centered. Press gently to level, then spread with another slightly heaping ⅓ cup curd. Repeat until you've stacked all six layers and used all the curd, placing the final layer cut-side down. The layers might start to slide around, so cover the cake with plastic wrap and carefully transfer it to the refrigerator to chill until the curd has firmed up and the layers are stable, about 20 minutes. You can also stick a skewer down the center of the cake through all the layers to hold them in place.

Make the Italian meringue: In a clean stand mixer bowl fitted with the whisk attachment (make sure all the mixer parts are free of grease, or the meringue won't whip up), combine the egg whites, lemon juice, and salt. In a small saucepan, combine the sugar and ¼ cup water (2 oz / 57g) and set over medium heat, stirring with a heatproof spatula to dissolve the sugar. When the syrup comes to a boil, stop stirring and wash down the sides of the pan with a wet pastry brush to dissolve any sugar crystals. Clip a candy thermometer to the side of the pan (or use an instant-read thermometer) and cook the syrup, (continues)

---

[1] If you don't have or can't find cake flour, in a pinch you can substitute an equal amount of all-purpose flour: Just replace 1 tablespoon flour with 1 tablespoon of cornstarch per 1 cup flour called for in the recipe.

[2] For a simpler spin on this cake, skip the Italian meringue and instead coat the layers in stiffly whipped, lightly sweetened cream just before serving.

gently swirling the pan often, until it reaches 244°F. While the sugar syrup is cooking, turn the mixer on medium-high speed to begin to whip the egg whites—you want them foamy and softly whipped right as the sugar hits 244°F. Immediately remove the saucepan from the heat and, with the mixer still on medium-high, very slowly stream the hot sugar syrup into the egg whites. Try to stream the sugar down the side of the bowl to avoid hitting the moving whisk and splattering the sugar.

Beat the meringue and cover the cake: Once all the sugar syrup has been added, increase the mixer to high and continue to whip until the meringue is very glossy and forms a firm peak off the end of the beater. Be careful not to overbeat or the meringue will become dry and take on a curdy texture, making it hard to smooth over the cake. Beat in the vanilla. Remove the cake from the refrigerator and uncover. Scrape all of the meringue over the top of the cake and smooth it across the surface and down the sides with an offset spatula, covering the entire cake and making lots of swirls.

Torch, if desired, and serve: Slide the parchment strips out from underneath the cake. If desired, use a kitchen torch to toast the meringue all over before cutting the cake into slices and serving.

Croquembouche

Serves 14

Special Equipment:
Pastry bag fitted with ¼-inch round tip, 1-inch round cutter

CRAQUELIN

1 stick **unsalted butter** (4 oz / 113g), at room temperature

¾ cup packed **light brown sugar** (5.3 oz / 150g)

1 cup **all-purpose flour** (4.6 oz / 130g)

Pinch of **kosher salt**

ASSEMBLY

Pâte à Choux (page 346), transferred to a pastry bag

Pastry Cream, Chocolate Variation (page 322) ①

1 cup **crème fraîche** (8.5 oz / 240g)

3¼ cups **granulated sugar** (23 oz / 650g)

My sister likes to tell the story of when I made my first croquembouche. It was pre-culinary school, pre-working in a restaurant, and pre-understanding of just how much work it requires. I burned the caramel while assembling it in her kitchen, and—as she recalls—had to frantically send her out to buy more sugar. I have since improved my croquembouche skills and collected a few strategies for making the process as smooth as possible, but just know it's a colossal amount of work and you'll need to set aside a block of several hours to get it all done. And for your own sake, make the pastry cream and *pâte à choux* in advance. This recipe also has you make something called *craquelin*, a simple cookie-like dough that's cut into rounds and baked onto each puff, giving them a round, even, lightly textured appearance. I like to use the *craquelin* because it makes the puffs more uniform overall, which means they're easier to stack. If you want to skip the *craquelin*, that's fine, too, just brush the puffs with a bit of beaten egg before baking. Godspeed to all the brave bakers who go for this one.

Make the *craquelin*: In a medium bowl, combine the butter and brown sugar and mix with a flexible spatula until you have a smooth, creamy mixture. Add the flour and salt and stir until no floury spots remain and you have a stiff dough. Fold the dough onto itself several times in a light kneading motion to make sure it's very evenly mixed, then divide it in half.

Roll out the *craquelin* and punch out the rounds: Roll out one piece of *craquelin* dough between two sheets of parchment paper to a ⅛-inch thickness (it helps to periodically peel off and reposition both pieces of parchment paper for wrinkle-free rolling). Slide the parchment onto a baking sheet and refrigerate until the dough is firm, 10 to 15 minutes. Remove the dough from the refrigerator and peel off the top layer of parchment. Use a 1-inch round cutter to punch out as many rounds of dough as you can fit. Transfer the rounds to a plate, cover, and refrigerate. Repeat the rolling and cutting process with the second half of the dough and any scraps until you have about 70 rounds. Keep them covered and refrigerated until ready to bake (discard any remaining scraps).

Bake the puffs: Follow the directions in the *pâte à choux* recipe (page 347) for piping out plain cream puffs, omitting the egg wash and instead placing a round of *craquelin* on top of each mound of piped *pâte à choux*. Transfer to the oven and bake and cool as directed. (continues)

DO AHEAD
The croquembouche should be assembled within a couple of hours of serving to ensure the caramel is crunchy and the *choux* are crisp. Keep it uncovered at room temperature in a cool, dry place. Even though the croquembouche will keep for 1 day, over time the caramel will soften and become sticky. The *craquelin* dough, covered and refrigerated, will keep up to 3 days. The baked, unfilled puffs, stored airtight at room temperature, will keep for 1 day.

① Instead of chocolate, use plain vanilla pastry cream or the black sesame variation to fill the cream puffs. The flavor is up to you!

Prepare your base: Cover a 9-inch cake round, the circular bottom of a springform or removable tart pan, or an inverted 9-inch cake pan with foil. Place this on a larger serving plate or cake stand and set it next to you on the work surface.

Mix the pastry cream and fill the puffs: In a large bowl, combine the chocolate pastry cream and crème fraîche and whisk until smooth. Transfer to a large pastry bag fitted with a ¼-inch round tip. Twist the bag to seal, pressing out air. Insert the pastry tip into the bottom of each puff and squeeze the bag firmly to fill the puff. You want it filled completely, but not to the point where the puff bursts or the filling squeezes back out of the opening. Fill as many puffs as you can with the pastry cream mixture—for a croquembouche with a base ring of 11 cream puffs, you will need around 66, possibly a few more or less. Arrange all the filled puffs across two wire racks. Line two large rimmed baking sheets with parchment paper, then set the racks inside the baking sheets.

Make the first batch of caramel: Place a clean, dry heatproof 2-cup measure or a similarly sized heatproof container next to the stove. In a small saucepan, combine 2 cups of the sugar (14 oz / 400g) and ½ cup water (4 oz / 113g). Cook over medium heat, stirring with a heatproof spatula until the sugar is dissolved. When the mixture comes to a boil, stop stirring and wash down the sides of the pan with a wet pastry brush to dissolve any sugar crystals. Cook, swirling the pan often, until the mixture starts to turn golden around the sides. Reduce the heat to medium-low and cook, swirling, until the caramel is a medium amber color (you don't want to make it too dark since it will continue to darken off the heat). Immediately remove the pan from the heat and carefully pour the caramel into the measuring cup. Let the caramel sit for a minute so it starts to set and thicken slightly.

Dip all the puffs: [2] Grasp one puff at a time from the bottom and carefully dip it, rounded-side down, into the caramel so there's a dome of caramel covering the *craquelin*-topped surface of the puff. Let the excess

drip off, then carefully place the puff caramel-side up back on the rack so it can cool and harden. Repeat with all the puffs. Try to work quickly, because eventually the caramel will thicken and set making it hard to dip, but also work carefully to avoid a sugar burn!

Make the second batch of caramel: Once you've coated all the puffs, rinse the saucepan and measuring cup with lots of hot water to dissolve any remaining caramel. Dry them thoroughly, then repeat the caramel-making process, this time with the remaining 1¼ cups sugar (8.8 oz / 250g) and ⅓ cup water (2.7 oz / 76g). Pour it into the same clean measuring cup.

Lay out the first ring of cream puffs and dip: Arrange 11 filled, dipped puffs around the foil-lined base in a ring so they're touching. One at a time, dip one side of each puff into the fresh caramel and stick it back on the base rounded-side out, pressing the dipped edge into the base. Hold it in place until the caramel hardens, which should only take a few seconds. Repeat with all the puffs on the base to make the first ring of the croquembouche.

Build the croquembouche: Repeat the dipping process, building successive rings of cream puffs and decreasing the number of puffs in a ring by one with each layer to create a tall, hollow cone. Try to position each puff in the little space between the two below it, angling it slightly inward to create an even slope building to a peak. [3] Set aside some smaller puffs to fill in any small gaps. You may end up using more or fewer puffs in a layer in order to make a full ring. Finish the croquembouche with a single cream puff on top.

Make caramel threads (optional): If the caramel hasn't fully set, dip a fork into the measuring cup and let the caramel drip off back into the cup until it falls in a thin thread. Move the fork in a circle around the croquembouche, wrapping the threads around it from top to bottom. Repeat as desired until the caramel is too hardened to drizzle. Arrange any leftover dipped, filled puffs around the base and serve, encouraging everyone to break off the puffs with their hands.

---

[2] Be very careful while working with the caramel to avoid sugar burns (I usually get one or two minor ones every time I make a croquembouche). Minimize the risk by wearing a double layer of powder-free latex gloves or a dishwashing glove on your dipping hand.

[3] Stand back to take a look at your progress as you build the croquembouche to make sure you're working evenly. And don't worry if it's not a perfect cone—the end result will impress no matter what!

Breakfast and Brunch

My breakfast usually consists of coffee and, if I'm lucky, a yogurt on the go. I bet most home bakers are like me and only take the time to prepare a breakfast or brunch dish when they have friends coming over. That makes this chapter special, since it's about spending time with others over a meal you'd only make for guests. Many of the recipes in this chapter use yeast, which works to a home baker's advantage because it means you can prepare the recipe the day before, refrigerate it overnight, and bake the next morning. Even though I'm not a big breakfast eater, I thoroughly enjoy breakfast baking, so the mere thought of **A Little Bit of Everything Bagels** (page 249) or **Walnut-Maple Buns** (page 245), ready to go in the oven, is enough to pull me out of bed in the morning. As a bonus, many of the sweet recipes in this chapter like **Speculoos Babka** (page 239) and **St. Louis Gooey Butter Cake** (page 243) can be served again later as dessert.

WALNUT-MAPLE BUNS,
PAGE 245

Seedy Maple Breakfast Muffins

Makes 12 muffins

Special Equipment:
12-cup muffin tin, muffin liners

⅓ cup plus 2 tablespoons hulled **pumpkin seeds** (2.3 oz / 65g)

¼ cup plus 1 tablespoon hulled **sunflower seeds** (1.6 oz / 45g)

2 tablespoons **flax meal** (0.46 oz / 13g) ①

1 tablespoon **demerara sugar**

1 teaspoon **white** or **black chia seeds**

1 teaspoon **poppy seeds**

1 cup **all-purpose flour** (4.6 oz / 130g)

½ cup **whole wheat flour** (2.5 oz / 70g)

2¼ teaspoons **baking powder** (0.32 oz / 9g)

1½ teaspoon **ground cinnamon**

¾ teaspoon **Diamond Crystal kosher salt**

1 cup **unsweetened applesauce** (8.6 oz / 243g)

½ cup **virgin** or **refined coconut oil** (4 oz / 113g), warmed gently to liquefy

⅓ cup packed **light brown sugar** (2.3 oz / 65g)

¼ cup **maple syrup** (2.8 oz / 80g)

2 teaspoons **vanilla extract**

1 cup frozen **blueberries** (5 oz / 140g) ②

Though my negative feelings about muffins are documented elsewhere in this book, I do credit muffins for being quick and easy to make and portable, so I was motivated to engineer one that felt like a truly wholesome breakfast item (and that wasn't also dry or weird or overly healthful). That these muffins turned out so light, so tasty, so pleasantly crunchy from all the seeds, *and* vegan was actually a surprise to me. I don't develop a lot of vegan recipes primarily because omitting eggs in baking is exceptionally tricky, but the method of making an egg replacement with ground flaxseeds and water works beautifully here. I'm happy to report that not only would I make, serve, and eat these for breakfast myself, but I fed them to my two-year-old nephew during the testing process—and he happily ate two!

Preheat the oven and toast the seeds: Arrange an oven rack in the center position and preheat the oven to 350°F. Scatter ⅓ cup of the pumpkin seeds and ¼ cup of the sunflower seeds on a small rimmed baking sheet and toast, shaking halfway through, until they're golden and nutty smelling, 6 to 8 minutes. Remove them from the oven and set aside to cool. (Leave the oven on for the muffins.)

Prepare the muffin tin: Line 12 cups of a muffin tin with paper liners and set aside.

Make the flax "egg": In a medium bowl, whisk together the flax meal and ¼ cup (2 oz / 57g) boiling water and set aside until it's warm to the touch but not hot, about 5 minutes.

Mix the topping: Meanwhile, in a small bowl, toss together the demerara sugar, chia seeds, poppy seeds, the remaining 2 tablespoons pumpkin seeds, and the remaining 1 tablespoon sunflower seeds to combine. Set the topping aside.

Mix the dry ingredients: In a large bowl, whisk together the all-purpose flour, whole wheat flour, baking powder, ground cinnamon, and salt to combine. Set aside.

Mix the wet ingredients: To the bowl with the flax "egg," add the applesauce, coconut oil, brown sugar, maple syrup, and vanilla and whisk until the mixture is smooth.

DO AHEAD
The muffins, stored in an airtight container at room temperature, will keep up to 5 days but are best served on the first or second day. The muffins can also be frozen up to 1 month.

① You can make your own flax meal by grinding flaxseeds in a spice grinder. Store flaxseeds or flax meal in the freezer, since their high fat content causes them to go rancid quickly.

② Use fresh blueberries if you've got them, but I find that frozen work better in muffins because they don't burst or turn to mush when you mix them into the batter.

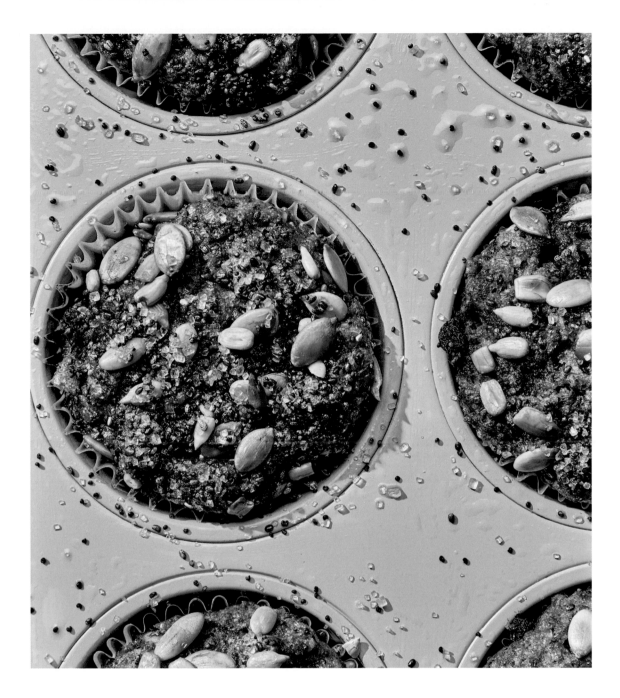

Mix the wet ingredients into the dry: Make a well in the center of the flour mixture and pour in the applesauce mixture. Starting in the center and working outward, whisk gently until everything is combined and you have a thick, even batter.

Fold in the solids: Use a flexible spatula to fold the blueberries and toasted pumpkin and sunflower seeds into the batter until they're evenly incorporated.

Portion, top, and bake the muffins: Using a 4-ounce scoop or ½-cup measure, drop a scant ½ cup of batter into each muffin cup. Sprinkle the muffins with the reserved topping mixture. Bake the muffins until the tops are firm and spring back when pressed lightly, 25 to 30 minutes. Remove the muffins from the oven and set aside to cool in the pan for 10 minutes, then turn them out onto a wire rack. Set the muffins upright and let cool completely.

Coffee Coffee Cake

Serves 15 to 20

Special Equipment:
13 × 9-inch pan (preferably metal), [1]
stand mixer

Butter for the pan

COFFEE RIBBON

3 tablespoons packed **light brown sugar**

2 teaspoons **ground cinnamon**

1 tablespoon **instant coffee granules** [2]

COFFEE CRUMB TOPPING

1¼ cups **all-purpose flour** (5.6 oz / 160g)

½ cup packed **light brown sugar**
(3.5 oz / 100g)

2 teaspoons **instant coffee granules**

¾ teaspoon **ground cardamom**

¼ teaspoon **Diamond Crystal kosher salt**

1 stick **unsalted butter** (4 oz / 113g), cut
into pieces, at room temperature

CAKE

3½ cups **all-purpose flour** (16 oz / 455g)

2½ teaspoons **baking powder**
(0.35 oz / 10g)

1½ teaspoons **Diamond Crystal kosher
salt** (0.16 oz / 6g)

½ teaspoon **baking soda**

⅔ cup **sour cream** (6 oz / 170g)

½ cup **strong brewed coffee** (4 oz / 113g)

1 tablespoon **instant coffee granules**

2 teaspoons **vanilla extract**

12 tablespoons **unsalted butter**
(6 oz / 170g), at room temperature

¼ cup **neutral oil**, such as vegetable or
grapeseed (2 oz / 57g)

1 cup **granulated sugar** (7 oz / 200g)

¾ cup packed **light brown sugar**
(5.3 oz / 150g)

4 large **eggs** (7 oz / 200g), at
room temperature

This coffee-flavored cake is like eating a bite of good cake with a sip of milky coffee—a little bitter, a little sweet, and the right amount of rich. Coffee is one of my favorite flavors in the world and could stand to find its way into more desserts, in my opinion. It has a subtle presence in this very tender, perfect-any-time-of-day cake, lending some floral and pleasantly bitter flavors in a way that both enhances and balances it. You don't need a strong cup of coffee with it, but it's still a good idea.

Preheat the oven and prepare the pan: Generously butter the bottom and sides of a 13 × 9-inch pan and set aside. Arrange an oven rack in the center position and preheat the oven to 350°F.

Make the coffee ribbon: In a small bowl, toss together the brown sugar, cinnamon, and instant coffee. Set the coffee ribbon mixture aside.

Make the coffee crumb topping: In a medium bowl, toss together the flour, brown sugar, coffee granules, cardamom, and salt. Add the butter and toss to coat, then use your fingertips to smash the butter into the dry ingredients until no visible bits of butter remain and the mixture is crumbly but holds together when squeezed. Set the crumb topping aside.

Combine the dry ingredients: In a medium bowl, whisk together the flour, baking powder, salt, and baking soda to combine and set aside.

Combine the wet ingredients: In a separate medium bowl, whisk together the sour cream, brewed coffee, instant coffee granules, and vanilla until smooth and set aside.

Cream the butter, oil, and sugars: In a stand mixer fitted with the paddle attachment, beat the butter, oil, granulated sugar, and brown sugar on low just until smooth, then increase the speed to medium-high and beat, scraping down the sides of the bowl once or twice, until the mixture is very light and fluffy, about 5 minutes. [3]

Add the eggs: Reduce the mixer speed to medium and add the eggs one at a time, beating well after each addition. Stop the mixer and scrape down the sides. (continues)

DO AHEAD
The cake, tightly covered and stored at room temperature, will keep up to 3 days. The individual squares can also be wrapped well and frozen. Let thaw completely at room temperature.

[1] You can use a glass baking pan if you don't have a metal one, but bake the cake at 325°F rather than 350°F to promote more even baking (in glass, the sides tend to overcook). It will take about the same amount of time in the oven, 40 to 45 minutes.

Alternate the dry and wet ingredients: Add about one-third of the flour mixture and mix on low speed until the flour has almost disappeared. Add half of the sour cream mixture, beating just until incorporated, then add the remaining flour in 2 additions, alternating with the remaining sour cream mixture. When the last traces of flour disappear, stop the mixer and remove the bowl. Use a flexible spatula to scrape down the sides and fold the batter several times to make sure it's evenly mixed.

Assemble the cake: Scrape half of the batter into the prepared pan and smooth it into an even layer, working it into the corners. Sprinkle the coffee ribbon mixture all across the batter, trying to cover every bit of surface area. Dollop the remaining batter all over, then smooth it into an even layer. Scatter the crumb topping over the batter, covering the entire surface.

Bake: Bake the cake until the top is puffed and golden brown and a cake tester or toothpick inserted into the center comes out clean, 40 to 45 minutes (be careful not to overbake it; the cake will still wobble in the center when a tester comes out clean). Remove the cake from the oven and let it cool completely on a wire rack. Cut into squares and serve.

[2] Don't use instant espresso powder as a substitute for the instant coffee granules, as instant espresso is finer and stronger in flavor, and your cake will be unpleasantly bitter.

[3] Really take your time creaming the butter, oil, and sugars together in the mixer, as the cake gets a lot of its lift from the air you're working in during this step. Rushing this process might result in a slightly denser, less fluffy cake.

Buckwheat Blueberry
Skillet Pancake

Serves 4 [1]

Special Equipment:
10-inch ovenproof skillet (preferably cast-iron), standard or handheld blender

5 tablespoons **unsalted butter** (2.5 oz / 71g)

1 cup **whole milk** (8 oz / 227g), at room temperature

½ cup **all-purpose flour** (2.3 oz / 65g)

¼ cup **buckwheat flour** (1.1 oz / 30g)

3 large **eggs** (4.3 oz / 150g), at room temperature

3 tablespoons **sugar** (1.3 oz / 38g)

¼ teaspoon **Diamond Crystal kosher salt**

¼ teaspoon **ground cardamom**

6 ounces (170g) fresh or frozen **blueberries** (about 1¼ cups)

Maple syrup, for serving

I've never been a lover of pancakes, not even as a kid (I wasn't into breakfast, especially sweet breakfast, and usually opted for the previous night's leftovers instead). As an adult, I still dislike traditional pancakes because not only am I terrible at flipping them, but they have a way of turning into syrup-soaked gut bombs. However, I do enjoy pancake-adjacent foods, such as Dutch babies and crepes, so this buckwheat skillet pancake mostly takes its cues from those somewhat lighter, crispy-edged dishes. Like a Dutch baby, the brown butter and buckwheat batter in this pancake puffs and browns dramatically in the oven. The texture isn't fluffy but is rich and custardy, similar to a clafoutis. My favorite part is the way the tart blueberries burst from the high heat and turn into a jammy topping. And because the pancake is only a tiny bit sweet, this is one breakfast where a drizzle of maple syrup is actually welcome.

Brown the butter: In a small saucepan, cook 4 tablespoons of the butter (2 oz / 57g) over medium-low heat, stirring and scraping the bottom and sides constantly with a heatproof spatula, until the butter sputters, foams, and eventually the solid bits turn a dark brown, 5 to 7 minutes. Scrape the butter and all the toasted bits into a heatproof bowl and set aside to cool.

Blend the batter and let it rest: In a blender, combine the milk, all-purpose flour, buckwheat flour, eggs, sugar, salt, and cardamom and blend on high until all the ingredients are thoroughly incorporated and you have a thin, smooth batter. (Alternatively, combine the ingredients in a medium bowl and blend with a handheld blender until smooth.) With the motor running, stream in the cooled browned butter and blend until incorporated. Cover the batter and set aside at room temperature to rest for at least 1 hour, or refrigerate up to 24 hours. (continues)

DO AHEAD
The batter, covered and stored in the refrigerator, can be made 1 day ahead.

[1] If you have a crowd to feed, double the recipe for the batter and bake the pancake in a 13 × 9-inch baking dish (preferably metal or ceramic). You won't preheat the pan on the stove the way you do the skillet, but follow these baking instructions: Arrange an oven rack in the center position and preheat the oven to 350°F. Thoroughly butter the bottom and sides of the dish, then pour in one-third of the batter and let it settle all the way into the sides and corners. Bake just until the surface is set and matte and the center

springs back gently when pressed, about 4 minutes. Carefully remove the pan from the oven and pour in the remaining batter, then scatter 12 ounces (340g) blueberries over the batter. Return it to the oven and bake until the edges are puffed and browned and the center is risen and set but still jiggly, another 45 to 55 minutes. It won't soufflé as dramatically as it does in a preheated skillet, but will be more clafoutis-like. Cut it into pieces and serve with maple syrup.

Preheat the oven and reblend the batter: Arrange an oven rack in the center position and preheat the oven to 450°F. Briefly blend the batter again to recombine any ingredients that have settled.

Heat a skillet and add the batter and blueberries: Heat a 10-inch ovenproof skillet (preferably cast-iron), over medium-high heat. Add the remaining 1 tablespoon butter to the skillet and swirl to coat the surface. Add about one-third of the batter to the skillet and cook until the top of the batter is set and goes from shiny to matte, about 2 minutes (this step creates a platform for the berries, so they don't sink to the bottom of the skillet). Add the remaining batter to the skillet and scatter the blueberries on top (no need to thaw first if using frozen berries).

Bake: Immediately transfer the skillet to the oven and bake until the edges are super puffed, browned, and crisp, the center is golden and set, and the blueberries have burst, 15 to 18 minutes.

Serve: Remove the skillet from the oven and let sit for about 5 minutes. The pancake will fall as soon as it comes out of the oven—that's normal! Cut the pancake into quarters, drizzle with maple syrup, and serve.

Brown Butter Corn Muffins

Makes 12 muffins

Special Equipment:
12-cup muffin tin

Melted **butter** and **flour** for the pan

2 cups **corn kernels** (10 oz / 284g), cut from about 2 large ears, or thawed frozen corn kernels

1 stick **unsalted butter** (4 oz / 113g)

3 tablespoons **honey** (2.3 oz / 64g)

1 cup **all-purpose flour** (4.6 oz / 130g)

½ cup medium or coarse **yellow cornmeal** (2.6 oz / 75g)

2 teaspoons **baking powder** (0.28 oz / 8g)

¾ teaspoon **baking soda**

1 teaspoon **Diamond Crystal kosher salt** (0.11 oz / 3g)

2 large **eggs** (3.5 oz / 100g), at room temperature

¾ cup **sour cream** (6.3 oz / 180g), at room temperature

⅓ cup **buttermilk** (2.8 oz / 80g), at room temperature

⅓ cup **sugar** (2.3 oz / 66g)

I have gone on record as saying that I am not a big muffin lover because muffins are lying to us. They're made to seem healthy with conspicuous mentions of ingredients like oats and bran, but let's be clear: Muffins are in fact nothing more than unfrosted cupcakes. If I want cake, I'll just eat cake! For this reason I only have two muffins in this book: vegan **Seedy Maple Breakfast Muffins** (page 216), which are *actually* relatively wholesome and healthy, and these corn muffins. I make an exception for these corn muffins because they're only slightly sweet, packed with the flavor and pop of real corn, and rich with nutty browned butter. They're moist and cakey without being cake. Smeared with salted butter when hot and fresh or griddled in butter when day-old, they disappear fast.

Preheat the oven: Arrange an oven rack in the center position and preheat the oven to 400°F.

Prepare the pan: Use a pastry brush to coat the 12 cups of a muffin tin with a thin layer of melted butter. Add a few pinches of flour to each muffin cup and shake the pan to coat the cups with flour. Tap out the excess and set the pan aside. ❶

Brown the butter and cook the corn: Have the corn kernels nearby (if using thawed frozen corn, pat the kernels dry to avoid sputtering). In a small saucepan, cook the butter over medium-low heat, stirring and scraping the bottom and sides constantly with a heatproof spatula until the butter sputters, foams, and eventually the solid bits turn dark brown, 5 to 7 minutes. ❷ Add the corn to the saucepan carefully to avoid splatter, then add the honey. Continue to cook over medium heat, stirring occasionally, until the corn is tender, about 5 minutes (if using thawed frozen corn, the kernels will only take 2 or 3 minutes). Remove the saucepan from the heat and set aside to cool.

Mix the dry ingredients: In a large bowl, whisk together the flour, cornmeal, baking powder, baking soda, and salt to combine. Set aside.

Mix the wet ingredients: In a medium bowl, whisk the eggs until no streaks remain, then add the sour cream, buttermilk, and sugar and whisk vigorously until the mixture is smooth. Slowly add the cooled browned

---

DO AHEAD
The muffins, stored airtight at room temperature, will keep up to 3 days but are best served the day they're made.

❶ I like to butter and flour the pan for these muffins because it gives them a tasty, golden brown crust, but use muffin liners if you want to save time and cleanup. Just note that you won't be able to fit quite ½ cup of batter in each cup, meaning you'll have a bit of leftover batter after filling the tin.

❷ Don't walk away from the butter as it's browning, otherwise it'll start to sputter violently. Make sure to stir it constantly to prevent the milk solids from sticking to the pan and burning.

butter/corn mixture (it can be warm, just not hot), whisking constantly to incorporate. Make sure you scrape all the golden bits out of the saucepan!

Mix the wet ingredients into the dry: Make a well in the center of the dry ingredients, then pour in the wet ingredients and gently mix with a flexible spatula, starting in the center and working outward, until no streaks of flour remain and the batter is smooth and well combined.

Fill the muffin pan and bake: Use a ½-cup measure to scoop equal portions of batter into the prepared muffin cups. Bake the muffins until the tops are slightly domed and light golden brown and the centers spring back when pressed, 15 to 20 minutes. [3] Remove the muffins from the oven and let them cool for 5 minutes in the pan, then turn them out onto a wire rack, set them upright, and let cool completely.

[3] These muffins won't dome dramatically during baking. Even though I like the look of a high, tight dome on a muffin, often that's achieved by adding more flour to the batter, which can produce a dry, tasteless muffin. Rather than increase the flour, I try to encourage a dome shape by baking these at 400°F, a relatively high temperature (a hot oven sets the edges of the muffin faster, so the batter rises upward rather than outward). Even so, weaker ovens will produce flatter tops. If yours come out flat, try increasing the temperature by 25°F the next time.

Classic English Muffins

Makes about 8 muffins

Special Equipment:
Instant-read thermometer, stand mixer, 3½-inch round cutter (optional), griddle or large skillet (preferably cast-iron)

1½ cups **whole milk** (12.7 oz / 360g)

2 tablespoons **unsalted butter** (1 oz / 28g)

2 tablespoons **honey** (1.5 oz / 43g)

1 teaspoon **active dry yeast** (0.11 oz / 3g)

2¾ cups **bread flour** (12.7 oz / 360g)

¼ cup **whole wheat flour** (1.2 oz / 35g)

2 teaspoons **Diamond Crystal kosher salt** (0.21 oz / 6g)

Neutral oil, for the bowl and baking sheet

Cornmeal, for dusting

These English muffins are cooked entirely on the stovetop rather than baked and come out looking surprisingly similar to the packaged ones but taste a million times better. One of the keys is an old-fashioned step called "scalding" the milk, meaning bringing it to a temperature just under boiling. This denatures the whey proteins in the milk, and when added to a dough, scalded milk helps improve the gluten network and increases moisture retention (both important if you want to achieve the telltale nooks and crannies of an English muffin). This recipe requires an overnight rest in the refrigerator, which is helpful if you want English muffins fresh for breakfast the next morning, and makes the very wet and sticky dough easier to handle. I like to punch out clean rounds with a cutter, so all the muffins are uniform, but if you don't have a cutter or don't want to discard any dough scraps, see note. ① It's helpful to have a griddle for cooking all the English muffins simultaneously, but it's also very doable in batches in a skillet.

Scald the milk: In a small saucepan, heat the milk over medium heat just until it starts to steam and a skin forms on the surface. You might see some tiny bubbles form around the sides, but don't let the milk come to a full boil. Maintain the milk at this temperature, decreasing the heat slightly if needed, for about 30 seconds, then remove it from the heat. Whisk in the butter and honey and set aside, whisking occasionally, until the mixture is warm but not hot, 10 to 15 minutes (you're going to use the scalded milk to proof the yeast, and if it's too hot, the yeast will die; it should feel lukewarm and register around 105°F on an instant-read thermometer).

Proof the yeast: Combine the yeast and 2 tablespoons of the milk mixture in a small bowl and stir to dissolve the yeast. Let sit until the mixture is foamy, about 5 minutes.

Mix the dough: In a stand mixer fitted with the dough hook attachment, combine the bread flour, whole wheat flour, salt, milk mixture, and yeast mixture and mix on low just until the flour is incorporated into the liquid. Increase the speed to medium-high and continue to mix, occasionally scraping down the sides with a flexible spatula or scraper until the dough is smooth, elastic, and climbing up the hook but still very wet and sticky, 8 to 10 minutes. (continues)

DO AHEAD
The English muffins are best eaten the day they're made but will keep, stored airtight at room temperature, up to 3 days. English muffins can also be frozen up to 2 months.

① If you don't have a cutter, or if you don't want to discard any scraps, use an oiled bench scraper to cut the slab into free-form pieces measuring about 3½ inches across. The muffins won't be round, but they'll be just as good.

Let the dough rise: Generously oil the inside of a separate large bowl and scrape in the dough. You want it to slide around freely, so shake the bowl and loosen any areas where the dough is stuck to the sides. Cover the bowl tightly with plastic wrap and let rise in a warm spot until the dough is doubled in size and filled with big air pockets, 1 to 1½ hours.

Prepare the baking sheet: While the dough is rising, line a large rimmed baking sheet with parchment paper and generously brush the surface with more oil. Dust with cornmeal and set aside.

Flatten the dough and chill: When the dough has risen, use a dough scraper or spatula to gently loosen the dough from around the bowl and let it gently slide out onto the prepared baking sheet. Try not to knock out too much air as you do this. Generously brush another sheet of parchment paper with oil and place it oiled-side down on top of the dough, then use the palms of your hands to flatten it down into a thin, even slab measuring about ½ inch thick. Leaving the top layer of parchment right where it is, cover the baking sheet with plastic wrap and refrigerate for at least 8 hours and up to 12 (cold dough will not only be easier to handle, but the English muffins will taste better, too). [2]

Form the English muffins: Remove the baking sheet from the refrigerator, uncover, and peel off the top layer of parchment. Use an oiled 3½-inch round cutter to punch out as many rounds as you can from the slab, fitting them close together for as little scrap as possible. The dough will be sticky, so oil your hands as well if needed, and press down firmly with the cutter, twisting once you hit the parchment. Depending on the shape of the slab and how tightly you cut out the rounds, you could get anywhere from 7 to 9 English muffins—if you have large pieces of scrap dough, pinch them together and cut another round. Discard any scraps and make sure the rounds have a little breathing room between them.

Griddle the muffins: Transfer as many rounds as will fit to a cold griddle or large skillet, spacing them ½ inch apart (in a skillet, you'll have to cook them in batches). Heat the griddle or skillet over medium-low heat and cook until the muffins are puffed, the bottoms are crisp and deeply browned, and the surface has gone from shiny to matte, 7 to 10 minutes. Flip the muffins gently, reduce the heat to low, and cook until the second side is deeply browned, another 5 to 7 minutes. [3] If the muffins are cooking faster, reduce the heat—you want them to cook slowly to help form interior nooks and crannies and to ensure that the centers are cooked through. If you're using a skillet, cook the remaining batches over low heat the entire time.

Let cool and then split: Transfer the English muffins to a wire rack as they're done and let them cool completely. Stab the tines of a fork into the pale sides of the muffin at the midway point, puncturing the dough all the way around, then slowly pull the halves apart. Eat fresh or toasted.

---

[2] Don't let the dough sit in the refrigerator for longer than 12 hours. Past this point the gluten network will start to break down due to the dough being very wet, resulting in muffins that are flatter and denser.

[3] Move the muffins around the skillet or griddle to promote even cooking, as sometimes the browning can be a little spotty. If you're using a skillet, you can rotate it around the burner as well.

Brioche Twists
with Coriander Sugar

Makes 8 buns

Special Equipment:
Stand mixer (for the Brioche Dough)

½ cup **demerara sugar**

1 tablespoon **ground coriander** [2]

Pinch of **kosher salt**

½ recipe **Brioche Dough**
(page 352), chilled

All-purpose flour, for rolling out

4 tablespoons **unsalted butter**
(2 oz / 57g), melted

A few recipes in this book call for a half quantity of **Brioche Dough** [1] (page 352), so if perhaps you've made a full batch and you're looking for something to do with the rest, look no further. This is one of those unassuming recipes that might not have much of a glamour factor, but the flavor of the coriander sugar—simply a mix of demerara sugar and ground coriander seed—is unexpectedly delicious. Coriander is usually used in savory recipes, but when combined with sugar it lends a lemony, flowery perfume to baked goods that's reminiscent of chamomile. You can set these twists up in the evening, refrigerate them overnight, and bake them the next morning for a lightly sweet bun that's ideal for dunking in coffee.

Make the coriander sugar: In a small bowl, toss the demerara sugar, coriander, and salt to combine. Sprinkle onto a dinner plate and set aside for assembling the twists.

Divide the dough and prepare the baking sheet: Divide the brioche dough into 8 equal pieces each weighing 2.25 ounces (64g); if you don't have a scale, you can eyeball it. Place the pieces on a parchment-lined baking sheet, cover them with plastic wrap, and refrigerate to prevent the dough from softening (which will make it difficult to work with).

Form the twists one at a time: Remove one piece of dough at a time from the refrigerator and roll it out on the work surface, applying a bit more pressure toward the center, until you have a rope about 10 inches long that's a bit thicker at the ends and thinner toward the middle. In general, it's easier to roll out the dough on an unfloured surface because the friction helps to stretch it, but add just the tiniest bit of flour if needed to prevent sticking. Working on a plate, use a pastry brush to coat the entire rope all over with melted butter, then roll the rope in the coriander sugar to coat completely. Grasping the rope in the center, twist the two ends once or twice around each other to form a keyhole. [3]

Place the twist back on the baking sheet in the refrigerator, tucking it underneath the plastic, and repeat the process with the remaining pieces of dough, melted butter, and coriander sugar. All the back-and-forth in and out of the fridge is to make sure all the twists proof at the same rate. At this point, the twists, covered on the baking sheet, can be refrigerated up to 12 hours. (continues)

DO AHEAD
The baked twists, covered and stored at room temperature, will keep up to 3 days but are best eaten the day they're made.

[1] See **Pigs in a Brioche Blanket** (page 303) and the **Apricot and Cream Brioche Tart** (page 102).

[2] Substitute another spice for the coriander, such as ½ teaspoon ground cardamom, ½ teaspoon ground star anise, or 2 teaspoons ground cinnamon.

Proof the twists: Remove the twists from the refrigerator. Make sure they're all evenly spaced on the baking sheet and let them sit at room temperature, covered, until the twists are puffed and the dough springs back when poked but holds a slight indentation, 55 to 65 minutes.

Preheat the oven: Meanwhile, arrange an oven rack in the center position and preheat the oven to 350°F.

Bake: When the twists are proofed, remove the plastic wrap and bake until they're golden brown, 20 to 25 minutes. Let the twists cool on the baking sheet.

---

3 Form the rope of brioche into any shape you like, such as a simple knot or spiral. Whatever shape you choose, just don't twist the dough too tightly so the brioche has some room to expand in the oven.

Strawberry-Almond Bostock

Makes 8 pastries

¼ cup sliced **almonds**

1 pound (454g) **strawberries**, hulled and thinly sliced lengthwise [1]

2 tablespoons **sugar**

1 loaf baked **Brioche** (page 352) or 1 store-bought brioche or challah bread, cut into eight ¾-inch-thick slices [2]

½ recipe **Honey Almond Syrup** (page 320)

¼ cup good-quality **strawberry jam**

1 cup **Frangipane** (page 329), at room temperature

Bostock, or twice-baked brioche, is a French breakfast pastry that's like a cousin of French toast but with frangipane baked on top (frangipane, or almond cream, is the delicious crunchy stuff you find inside an almond croissant). Bostock checks every box of a great brunch recipe: It's a superb use for day-old bread, easy to assemble ahead of time (once you have the components prepped), and a little chic. This recipe can be made any time of year without the fresh strawberries, but I like the bright note they bring to the recipe.

Preheat the oven and toast the almonds: Arrange an oven rack in the upper third of the oven and preheat to 350°F. Scatter the almonds on a small rimmed baking sheet and bake, shaking halfway through, until they're golden and nutty smelling, 8 to 10 minutes. Remove from the oven and let cool. (Leave the oven on for the bostock.)

Macerate the strawberries: In a large bowl, toss together the strawberries and sugar and set aside while you make the bostock to allow the berries to release their juices.

Assemble the bostock: Meanwhile, arrange the brioche slices on a parchment-lined rimmed baking sheet, spacing them evenly apart. Lightly brush both sides of the bread with the honey almond syrup (you may not use it all). Using a butter knife or small offset spatula, spread the jam on one side of the bread, spreading it very thinly all the way to the edges. Spoon 2 tablespoons of the frangipane over top of the jam on each slice, then carefully spread all the way to the edges. Divide half of the sliced strawberries evenly among the slices, spooning over the frangipane.

Bake the bostock: Transfer the baking sheet to the upper rack of the oven and bake until the frangipane is browned around the edges, the strawberries are soft and juicy, and the bottoms of the slices are golden, 25 to 30 minutes. [3]

Finish and serve: Remove the bostock from the oven and set aside to cool slightly. Top with the remaining strawberries, dividing evenly, and then sprinkle with the toasted almonds.

DO AHEAD
The bostock, covered at room temperature, will keep up to 3 days but are best served on the day they're baked. The bostock can be brushed with syrup and topped with jam and frangipane 1 day ahead; cover with plastic wrap and refrigerate on the baking sheet.

[1] Substitute fresh pitted cherries, blueberries, blackberries, or sliced fresh figs and the corresponding jam flavor to change things up!

[2] Because the size of store-bought bread loaves varies, have extra honey almond syrup, strawberry jam, and frangipane on hand if you're making this with store-bought brioche or challah.

[3] The light brushing of syrup on the bottoms of the bread slices will encourage them to brown, so peek underneath the slices toward the end of the bake time to make sure they're not getting too dark. If you see them taking on lots of color, you can slide another baking sheet under the one in the oven for insulation.

Babkallah

Serves 12

Special Equipment:
Instant-read thermometer

DOUGH

½ cup **whole milk** (4 oz / 113g)

1 (0.25 oz / 7g) envelope **active dry yeast** (about 2¼ teaspoons)

⅓ cup **granulated sugar** (2.3 oz / 66g)

4 large **egg yolks** (2.5 oz / 70g)

1 teaspoon **vanilla extract**

3 cups **all-purpose flour** (13.8 oz / 390g), plus more for kneading

1 teaspoon **Diamond Crystal kosher salt** (0.11 oz / 3g)

1 stick **unsalted butter** (4 oz / 113g), cut into ½-inch pieces, at room temperature, plus more for the bowl

FILLING AND ASSEMBLY

6 ounces (170g) **semisweet chocolate**, finely chopped (about 1 cup)

⅓ cup packed **light brown sugar** (2.3 oz / 65g)

1½ teaspoons **ground cinnamon**

Pinch of **kosher salt**

4 tablespoons **unsalted butter** (2 oz / 57g), melted and cooled

1 large **egg**, beaten

Demerara sugar, for sprinkling the top

The first version of this recipe originally appeared in the 2015 holiday issue of *Bon Appétit* magazine. I wanted to create a mash-up of babka and challah, and my friend and colleague at the magazine, Julia Kramer, coined the name. I've made a few minor changes to the recipe since it ran, but the babkallah remains very much the same. It's a fun recipe to attempt any time of the year (no stand mixer required) and is highly transportable and giftable. A traditional challah is made with oil rather than butter, but I use butter here, making this dough closer to a sweet yeast dough. I opted for a filling that combines chocolate and cinnamon, the two most common flavors of babka, but you could also use jam, chocolate-hazelnut spread, or the cookie butter filling from the **Speculoos Babka** on page 239.

Proof the yeast: In a small saucepan, gently warm the milk over low heat, swirling the pan, just until it's lukewarm but not hot, about 105°F on an instant-read thermometer (you can do this in the microwave, too, but beware of overheating). Pour the milk into a large bowl and whisk in the yeast to dissolve; let the mixture sit until it's foamy, 5 to 10 minutes.

Make the dough: To the yeast mixture, add the granulated sugar, egg yolks, and vanilla and whisk to combine. Add the flour, salt, and butter and mix with a wooden spoon until a shaggy dough forms. Turn the dough out onto a lightly floured surface and knead, adding a bit more flour as necessary to prevent sticking, until the dough is smooth, supple, and no longer shiny, 8 to 10 minutes (you can also do this in a stand mixer fitted with the dough hook; mix on medium speed for 5 to 8 minutes).

Let the dough rise once: Butter the inside of a large clean bowl, then gather the dough into a ball and place it inside. Cover the bowl with plastic wrap and let it sit in a warm place until the dough has doubled in size, 1½ to 2½ hours, depending on the ambient temperature.

Mix the filling: In a small bowl, toss the chocolate, brown sugar, cinnamon, and salt to combine.

Fill the dough: Turn the dough out onto a clean work surface and divide it into 3 equal portions. Shape each portion into (continues)

DO AHEAD
The baked babkallah, well wrapped and stored at room temperature, will keep up to 4 days but is best served on the first or second day.

a rope measuring 12 inches long. Flatten each rope with the heel of your hand, then use a rolling pin to roll out each piece into a 12 × 6-inch rectangle (you shouldn't need any flour to prevent sticking). Brush the surface of each rectangle with the melted butter and then sprinkle with the chocolate mixture, dividing it evenly among the 3 pieces and leaving a ½-inch border uncovered along one long edge of the dough. Starting on the opposite long side, roll up each rectangle to form a spiraled log and pinch along the length of the seams to seal. ①

Assemble the braid: Place the logs seam-side down and side by side on a parchment-lined baking sheet.

Pinch the logs together at one end and braid them. ② Then pinch the opposite ends together and tuck both ends underneath the braid. Cover the babkallah loosely with plastic wrap and set aside in a warm spot until it's expanded to about 1½ times its original size, 1 to 2 hours.

Preheat the oven: Arrange an oven rack in the center position and preheat the oven to 350°F.

Bake: Brush the babkallah with the egg, then sprinkle generously with demerara sugar. Bake until the surface of the dough is deeply browned, 35 to 45 minutes. Let cool completely on a wire rack.

---

① Make sure you seal the chocolate-filled logs of dough very well so they don't unravel as you braid, as this could compromise the spiral of filling in the finished babkallah.

② Leave a little slack in the braid, as lots of tension could cause the strands to split apart down the centerline in the oven, exposing the filling. If this happens, though, it won't adversely affect the final flavor or texture.

Speculoos Babka

Makes 2 babkas [1]

Special Equipment:
Stand mixer (for the Sweet Yeast Dough), two 4½ × 8½-inch loaf pans (measured from the top), instant-read thermometer

Butter for the pans

1 cup **speculoos cookie butter** (9.9 oz / 280g)

2 tablespoons plus 1½ sticks **unsalted butter** (7 oz / 200g), melted and cooled

1 tablespoon plus 2 teaspoons **ground cinnamon**

1 teaspoon **Diamond Crystal kosher salt** (0.11 oz / 3g)

1⅓ cups **all-purpose flour** (6.1 oz / 173g), plus more for rolling out

½ cup packed **light brown sugar** (3.5 oz / 100g)

Sweet Yeast Dough (page 344)

1 large **egg**, beaten

I truly never had any interest in cinnamon babka (the so-called lesser babka), always preferring its chocolate sibling. But after a bit of experimenting, I found that cookie butter, a spread made from speculoos—those light and crisp Belgian spice cookies handed out on Delta flights—might actually make a superior filling. Not only is it an ideal vehicle for cinnamon flavor, but cookie butter spreads beautifully across the dough and stays soft and creamy after baking, adding moisture and richness in a way that chocolate doesn't. I first had cookie butter while I was in culinary school in France before it was common in the United States, but now it's much easier to find. If you can't find the classic Lotus brand of speculoos spread, Trader Joe's also makes a version under its own label.

Prepare the pans: Brush the bottom and sides of two standard loaf pans with a thin layer of melted butter. Line the bottom and two longer sides of each pan with a long piece of parchment paper, leaving an overhang of a couple of inches on either side. Brush the parchment lightly with butter and set the pans aside.

Make the filling: In a small bowl, combine the speculoos cookie butter, 2 tablespoons of the melted butter, 1 tablespoon of the cinnamon, and ½ teaspoon of the salt and stir until the mixture is smooth. Cover and set the cookie butter mixture aside.

Make the brown sugar crumble: In a medium bowl, combine the flour, brown sugar, and the remaining 1½ sticks (6 oz / 170g) melted butter, 2 teaspoons cinnamon, and ½ teaspoon salt. Use a fork to work the butter fully into the other ingredients until you have a uniformly crumbly mixture that holds together easily when squeezed. Set the crumble aside.

Roll out the dough: Turn the dough out onto a lightly floured surface. Divide the dough in half (each piece will weight about 1½ lbs), then cover one half and put it back in the refrigerator. Use the heel of your hand to press down all over the other half of the dough to expel the built-up gas from the first rise. Tugging at the edges to form four corners, stretch the dough to coax it into an even rectangular shape. Dust the top and underside of the dough with more flour and roll it out, dusting with more flour as needed, into a thin rectangle measuring about 18 × 10 inches. [2] (continues)

DO AHEAD
The babkas, well wrapped and stored at room temperature, will keep up to 5 days.

[1] To make a single babka, simply halve all of the above ingredients. See note on page 344 for making a half quantity of **Sweet Yeast Dough**. Note that the bake time of the single babka will be shorter than the bake time for two baked together, so start checking it after 45 minutes.

[2] Work quickly with this dough to prevent it from softening too much, and don't worry if you don't get it into a perfect rectangle when rolling it out. The shaping is forgiving since the babka is baked in a loaf pan, so you're likely to get a nice spiral regardless.

Make sure a long side of the dough is facing you, with the shorter sides to your left and right.

Fill the dough and twist: Scrape half of the cookie butter mixture onto the dough and spread with a small offset spatula in an even layer across the entire surface, leaving a ½-inch border along the long side that's farther from you. Starting at the long side closer to you, roll up the dough like a jelly roll into a tight spiraled log, then pinch firmly along the seam to seal it and rest it seam-side down on the surface. Squeeze the log where it's a bit thicker in the center and tug outward to elongate and even out the thickness. Bring the ends of the dough together, lining up the two sides of the log so they're parallel to each other and bending at the midpoint to maintain the alignment (like the shape of a tuning fork). Twist the lengths of dough around each other twice to form a short, tight corkscrew, then transfer the coil to one of the prepared loaf pans. Press down gently on the twist to flatten it into the pan, then cover with plastic wrap and set aside. Repeat the rolling, filling, and twisting process with the remaining piece of dough and cookie butter mixture.

Proof the babkas: Let the babkas sit covered at room temperature until the dough is very puffy and the babkas are about 50 percent expanded in size, 40 to 60 minutes. [3]

Preheat the oven: Meanwhile, arrange an oven rack in the center position and preheat the oven to 350°F.

Top with the crumble and bake: Uncover the pans and brush the surfaces of both babkas with the egg. Heap the crumble over the dough, breaking up any larger pieces and dividing evenly. Make sure the dough is completely covered, but let the crumbs fall down around the sides if they want. Bake the babkas side by side until the tops are risen, very well browned, and firm to the touch and an instant-read thermometer inserted into the center of each loaf registers 185°F, 55 to 65 minutes. [4]

Let cool and serve: Remove from the oven and let the babkas cool in their pans for 20 to 25 minutes. Use a small offset spatula or paring knife to cut down between the babkas and the shorter sides of the pans, then use the parchment to lift out the babkas and transfer to a wire cooling rack. Let cool completely before slicing and serving.

---

[3] Don't rely on the usual "doubled in size" indicator to judge when the babka is proofed. By that point, it will be overproofed, and the baked babka will lack the light but bready texture you want. Look for the dough to expand by about 50 percent, and know it will rise dramatically in the oven.

[4] I recommend using an instant-read thermometer to check that the babka is fully baked in the center, since it can be difficult to judge from the exterior and a tester will come out clean even before the center is done. After all the effort, you don't want a babka with a doughy core.

St. Louis Gooey Butter Cake

Serves 12

Special Equipment:
Instant-read thermometer, stand mixer, 13 × 9-inch pan (preferably glass), ① pastry bag

CAKE

1 teaspoon **active dry yeast** (0.11 oz / 3g)

½ cup **whole milk** (4 oz / 113g)

⅓ cup **granulated sugar** (2.3 oz / 66g)

3 large **egg yolks** (1.8 oz / 50g)

1 large **egg** (1.8 oz / 50g)

1 teaspoon **Diamond Crystal kosher salt** (0.11 oz / 3g)

2½ cups **all-purpose flour** (11.4 oz / 325g)

1 stick **unsalted butter** (4 oz / 113g), cut into tablespoons, at room temperature, plus more for the pan

TOPPING

¼ cup **heavy cream** (2 oz / 57g), at room temperature

2 tablespoons **light corn syrup** (1.4 oz / 40g)

1 tablespoon **vanilla extract**

10 tablespoons **unsalted butter** (5 oz / 142g), at room temperature

1 cup **granulated sugar** (7 oz / 200g)

¼ cup packed **light brown sugar** (1.8 oz / 50g)

1 teaspoon **Diamond Crystal kosher salt** (0.11 oz / 3g)

1 large **egg** (1.8 oz / 50g), at room temperature

1 cup **all-purpose flour** (4.6 oz / 130g)

Powdered sugar, for serving

I was born and raised in St. Louis, Missouri, a city that boasts quite a few quirky culinary traditions, such as St. Louis-style pizza, toasted ravioli, and, my favorite, gooey butter cake. Gooey butter cake is essentially a coffee cake base topped with a sugary batter that doesn't fully set when baked, staying gooey in some places. Like many celebrated local food specialties, the origins are disputed, but one story I've heard is that gooey butter cake was accidentally invented by a German-American baker in the 1930s who messed up the proportions in a cake recipe and added too much butter. Often, recipes for gooey butter cake call for boxed cake mix as a base and cream cheese in the topping, but I never favored this approach. In order to dial down the sweetness (and to nod to the cake's supposedly German origin), I prefer the combination of a yeasted coffee cake base and buttery topping. In the oven, the topping and base swirl together to form peaks and valleys, while the edges caramelize into a sweet, chewy crust. Note that this cake has an overnight rise in the refrigerator, which sets you up to bake it the next morning.

Dissolve the yeast: In a small saucepan, gently warm ¼ cup water (2 oz / 57g) over low heat, swirling the pan, just until it's lukewarm but not hot, about 105°F on an instant-read thermometer (you can do this in the microwave, too, but beware of overheating). Pour the water into the bowl of a stand mixer fitted with the paddle attachment and whisk in the yeast to dissolve. Set aside until the mixture is cloudy and slightly puffed, about 5 minutes.

Make the yeasted cake batter: To the bowl with the yeast mixture, add the milk, granulated sugar, egg yolks, whole egg, salt, and 2 cups of the flour (9.2 oz / 260g) and mix on low until the ingredients are combined. Increase the speed to medium and continue to beat, scraping down the sides of the bowl once or twice, until you have a smooth, thick batter, about 1 minute. With the mixer still on medium, add the butter one piece at a time, beating thoroughly after each addition. Switch to the dough hook and, with the mixer on medium, add the remaining ½ cup flour (2.3 oz / 65g) 1 tablespoon at a time, mixing until you have a smooth, very soft, somewhat sticky dough that just barely pulls away from the sides of the bowl (you may not need to use all the flour). (continues)

DO AHEAD
The cake, covered and stored at room temperature, will keep up to 4 days but is best served on the first or second day.

① Although I generally don't like to bake in glass, I call for a glass pan here. It's convenient for monitoring how quickly the cake is rising and for gauging doneness in the oven, and it encourages browning around the edges, which is a good thing in this case. If you only have metal, that's fine, just keep in mind that the cake might take a little longer to bake.

Let the cake rise and prepare the pan: Cover the bowl with plastic wrap and let it rise in a warm place until nearly doubled in size, 1 to 1½ hours. Generously butter the bottom and sides of the pan and set aside.

Pat the dough into the pan and chill overnight: Scrape the risen dough into the prepared pan and press it into a single layer, working it all the way into the corners. If the dough sticks to your hands, butter your fingertips and proceed. If your pan is glass, mark the outside with a piece of tape to indicate the starting height of the dough (so you can easily gauge the rise on day two). Tightly cover the pan with a sheet of plastic wrap and refrigerate at least 8 hours and up to 12.

Preheat the oven: Arrange an oven rack in the center position and preheat the oven to 350°F.

Make the topping: In a small bowl, whisk together the heavy cream, corn syrup, and vanilla until combined and set aside.

In a stand mixer fitted with the paddle attachment, beat the butter, granulated sugar, brown sugar, and salt on medium-high, scraping down the sides once or twice, until the mixture is light and fluffy, about 5 minutes. Add the egg and beat just until combined. Reduce the speed to low and add half of the flour, followed by the cream mixture, then the remaining flour, scraping down the sides of the bowl and mixing after each addition just until combined. When the batter is smooth, transfer it to a large pastry bag or 1-gallon resealable bag. Twist or seal the bag to close, pressing out any air, and snip off a 1½-inch opening.

Top the cake: Remove the pan of dough from the refrigerator and uncover. Pipe a wide snake of topping all across the surface of the dough, using the entire amount (you can also just dollop it with a spoon, but piping it gives a more even application). Use the back of a spoon or small offset spatula to spread the topping across the surface in an even layer all the way to the edges. ❷ The dough will likely have already risen to 1½ times its height while in the refrigerator overnight (use the tape as a point of reference), but if it hasn't, cover the pan again and let the cake sit at room temperature until risen.

Bake and cool: Bake the cake (be sure to remove the piece of tape) until the edges are deep golden brown and firm to the touch but the center is still shiny and jiggles slightly when the pan is shaken, 30 to 40 minutes. ❸ Let the cake cool completely in the pan on a wire rack (as it cools, the filling will fall in places, forming gooey valleys in the cake).

Serve: Dust lightly with powdered sugar and cut into squares before serving.

---

❷ Work the topping all the way to the edges so it makes contact with the sides of the pan. These edges will caramelize and become chewy in the oven—this is the best part of the cake!

❸ The surface will be pale in the center even when the cake below is done, so don't wait until the top is deep golden brown before pulling it from the oven. At that point, the cake beneath will be dried out.

Walnut-Maple Buns

Makes 15 buns

Special Equipment:
13 × 9-inch pan (preferably metal), stand mixer (for the Sweet Yeast Dough)

2 cups **walnut halves** or **pieces** (7 oz / 200g) [1]

½ cup **maple syrup** (5.6 oz / 160g)

Seeds scraped from 1 **vanilla bean** or 2 teaspoons **vanilla extract**

½ cup plus ⅓ cup packed **light brown sugar** (5.8 oz / 165g)

8 tablespoons **unsalted butter** (4 oz / 113g)

1 teaspoon **Diamond Crystal kosher salt** (0.11 oz / 3g)

1¾ teaspoons **ground cardamom**

1 teaspoon finely grated **orange zest**

Sweet Yeast Dough (page 344), chilled

All-purpose flour, for rolling out

I ride the fence when it comes to sticky buns or cinnamon buns. I like the *idea* of them: a rich, yeasted dough filled with nuts and warm spices and coated in a sweet-sticky shell. But in reality I always found them too sweet, too heavy, and too dry. I tweaked this recipe quite a bit to get the results I wanted, which meant timing the doneness to make sure the buns stay soft, making the right amount of sticky goo so they're coated but not drenched, and adjusting the combination of flavors so they complement instead of overpower. But the real solve was adding a LOT of well-toasted walnuts, which provide a savory edge that helps balance everything out. Finally, a sticky bun I can get behind.

Preheat the oven and toast the nuts: Arrange an oven rack in the center position and preheat the oven to 350°F. Scatter the walnuts on a small rimmed baking sheet and toast, shaking halfway through, until they're golden brown and fragrant, 8 to 10 minutes. Remove from the oven and set aside to cool. Place the nuts inside a plastic bag and seal, pressing out all the air, then bash the nuts lightly with a rolling pin to crush them into tiny bits. Set aside. (Turn the oven off.)

Make the sticky topping: In a small saucepan, combine the maple syrup, vanilla, ½ cup brown sugar, 4 tablespoons butter, and ½ teaspoon salt. Cook the mixture over medium heat, stirring often, until it comes to a boil. Boil for about 30 seconds, then remove from the heat and pour into the bottom of the pan (reserve the saucepan for melting more butter). Scatter the crushed walnuts evenly over the liquid and set aside.

Prepare the filling: In a small bowl, combine the cardamom, orange zest, and remaining ⅓ cup brown sugar and ½ teaspoon salt and massage with your fingertips until the zest is worked into the sugar and the mixture is fragrant. Melt the remaining 4 tablespoons butter in the reserved saucepan over low heat. Set the butter aside to cool.

Roll out the dough: Turn the dough out onto a lightly floured surface and press down on it all over with the heel of your hand to expel the built-up gas from the first rise. Tugging at the edges to form four corners, stretch the dough to coax it into an even, rectangular shape. Dust the top and underside of the dough with more flour and roll it out, dusting with more flour as needed, into a ¼-inch-thick rectangle measuring about 20 × 9 inches. [2] (continues)

DO AHEAD
The buns, stored airtight at room temperature, will keep up to 4 days but are best served the day they're made.

[1] Use other nuts besides walnuts, such as pecans or peanuts. Whatever you use, just make sure they're well toasted. You can also use cinnamon or another warm spice rather than cardamom in the filling.

[2] Work quickly to prevent the dough from warming and becoming soft and sticky while shaping the buns. If at any point it becomes too soft to handle, you can let it firm up in the refrigerator for 15 minutes.

Form the buns: Brush the cooled, melted butter all across the surface of the dough in an even layer, working all the way to the edges. Scatter the cardamom filling over the dough, rubbing it gently into the dough with your hands so it adheres and spreading into any bare spots so the entire surface is covered. Starting at one of the long sides, roll up the dough like a jelly roll into a tight spiraled log and let it rest seam-side down on the surface. Squeeze the log where it's a bit thicker in the center and tug outward to elongate and even out the thickness.

Cut and place in the prepared pan: Use a serrated knife to trim off a ½-inch-thick slice from each end, revealing the spiral. Try to work quickly while the dough is still cool and easier to slice. Cut the log in half crosswise, then each piece in half again. Cut each piece into thirds so you have 12 more-or-less-equal pieces. Place each piece cut-side down in the prepared pan on top of the walnuts, spacing evenly in a 3 × 4 grid.

Second rise: Cover the pan loosely with plastic wrap and let the buns rise at room temperature until they're about 50 percent expanded in size, 40 to 60 minutes. ③

Meanwhile, preheat the oven: Arrange an oven rack in the center position and preheat the oven to 350°F.

Bake and unmold: Uncover the pan and bake until the buns are puffed and golden brown across the surface, 30 to 35 minutes. Remove the pan from the oven and let the buns rest 5 minutes. Cut between the sides of the pan and the buns with a small offset spatula or butter knife to loosen them, then place a wire rack on top of the buns and invert the entire pan and rack together in one motion—there might be hot leaking caramel, so use caution and work over a sink if you can. Remove the pan slowly and scrape off any nuts that have stuck in the pan and spread them back onto the buns. Let the buns cool on the rack. Serve warm or at room temperature.

③ Be careful that you don't overproof the dough in the pan since this will produce a harder textured bun rather than a soft, bready one. If you wait until the buns hit the usual indicator of "doubled in size," they'll be a bit too far gone. Go with the "50 percent" indicator and trust they will expand dramatically in the oven.

A Little Bit of Everything Bagels

Makes 9 bagels

Special Equipment:
Instant-read thermometer, stand mixer (optional), a large, wide Dutch oven

¼ cup **sesame seeds**

3 tablespoons **poppy seeds**

1½ teaspoons **caraway seeds**, crushed under a heavy saucepan

2 tablespoons dried minced **onion**

1 tablespoon dried minced **garlic**

1 teaspoon **active dry yeast** (0.11 oz / 3g)

2 tablespoons **barley malt syrup** (1.5 oz / 43g), plus several tablespoons for boiling ①

3¾ cups **bread flour** (17.2 oz / 488g), plus more for kneading

½ cup **rye flour** (2.3 oz / 65g)

1 tablespoon **Diamond Crystal kosher salt** (0.32 oz / 9g)

Coarse cornmeal, for dusting

Flaky salt, for sprinkling the tops

You might ask why anyone would bother to make bagels at home when the average city has at least a handful of bagel shops. My answer is because I think the average bagel is generally too big, too doughy, and not chewy or crusty enough. Making them at home not only gives me control over these factors, but I also get to play around with flavors. I'm partial to an everything bagel, but I also quite like the occasional pumpernickel, so I add a touch of rye flour to my bagel dough for that earthy flavor. To prevent any chance of the seeds and spices falling off and burning in the oven, and to bypass the step of patting on the seeds and spices after boiling—yes, a proper bagel is boiled, *then* baked—I mix them right into the dough. It all adds up to a bagel that hits every beat. Note that there's an overnight rise in the refrigerator for this recipe, so remember to plan accordingly. See page 251 for a **Bialy Variation** on the same dough—it's not at all traditional, but very tasty nonetheless.

Make the "everything" mixture: In a small bowl, toss the sesame seeds, poppy seeds, crushed carraway seeds, onion, and garlic to combine. Set aside.

Proof the yeast: In a small saucepan, gently warm 1¼ cups water (10 oz / 283g) over low heat, swirling the pan, just until it's lukewarm but not hot, about 105°F on an instant-read thermometer (you can do this in the microwave, too, but beware of overheating). Pour the water into a medium bowl and whisk in the yeast and 2 tablespoons of the barley malt syrup (1.5 oz / 43g) until both are dissolved. Let the mixture sit until it's foamy, about 5 minutes.

Mix the dough: In a stand mixer fitted with the dough hook attachment (or in a large bowl if making by hand), combine the bread flour, rye flour, and kosher salt. Make a well in the center and pour in the yeast mixture. Mix on low speed until a shaggy dough forms. Increase the speed to medium and continue to mix, scraping down the sides of the bowl as needed, until you have a very smooth, stiff dough, 8 to 10 minutes. (Alternatively, stir with a wooden spoon to bring the dough together and then knead by hand on a clean work surface). The dough should be tacky but not sticky, so add more flour a tablespoon at a time if needed to prevent sticking. (continues)

DO AHEAD
The bagels are best eaten the day they're made but will keep, stored airtight at room temperature, up to 3 days (they will need a toasting to revive them). The bagels can also be frozen up to 1 month in a resealable bag.

① Barley malt syrup imparts a subtle sweetness and malty flavor that is a bagel hallmark. It is usually available at natural foods stores. If you can't track it down, molasses will work as a substitute.

Mix in the seeds and proof the dough: With the mixer on low, add the "everything" mixture to the bowl with the dough and mix until the seeds and spices are evenly distributed. (Alternatively, scatter the seeds across the dough and the work surface and knead until all the seeds are well incorporated.) If you're having a hard time incorporating the seeds into the stiff dough, add a teaspoon of water to help the mixture work in and stick. Gather the dough into a ball and dust it all over with a bit more bread flour. Place the dough in a large clean bowl and cover with plastic wrap. Place it in a warm, draft-free spot and let the dough rise until it's nearly doubled in size, 1 to 1½ hours.

Prepare the baking sheets: Generously sprinkle two large rimmed baking sheets with cornmeal and set aside.

Portion and form the bagels, then chill overnight: Use a fist to punch down the dough and knock out some of the gas that built up during the first rise. Turn the dough out onto a clean, unfloured surface and use a bench scraper to divide the dough into 9 pieces weighing about 4 ounces (113g) each. (If making the **Bialy Variation**, skip to page 251.) Working with one piece of dough at a time and keeping the other pieces covered, roll it into a ball, flatten it slightly, then poke a thumb through the center and out the other side. Work and stretch the dough outward to widen the hole, maintaining an even thickness all the way around, until you have a ring measuring about 4 inches across. Place the ring on the surface and flatten it slightly with the heel of your hand, then place it on one of the prepared baking sheets and cover with plastic wrap. Repeat until you've formed all the pieces of dough into rings and spaced them out evenly across both baking sheets. Make sure the sheets are covered and transfer to the refrigerator to chill for at least 8 hours and up to 12.

The next morning, do the float test: Fill a large, wide Dutch oven about halfway with room-temperature water. Remove one of the baking sheets from the refrigerator—the bagels will have puffed slightly. Uncover the sheet and gently transfer one of the bagels to the Dutch oven. If it floats, the bagels are ready to go. Gently pat the test bagel dry, return it to the baking sheet, cover, and place the baking sheet back in the refrigerator until ready to cook. However, if it *doesn't* float, take the second baking sheet out of the refrigerator and let both sheets of bagels sit at room temperature, covered, until a test bagel floats (repeat the test every 15 minutes). At that point, return the covered baking sheets to the refrigerator. Reserve the Dutch oven of water for boiling the bagels.

Preheat the oven and prepare the boiling liquid: Arrange two oven racks in the upper and lower thirds of the oven and preheat to 475°F. [2] Bring the reserved Dutch oven of water to a boil over high heat. Add barley malt syrup to the water a tablespoon at a time, stirring to dissolve, until the water is the color of strong black tea. Fill a large bowl with ice water and set it next to the boiling water along with a wire rack.

Boil the bagels: Remove one baking sheet from the refrigerator and gently drop as many bagels into the boiling water as will comfortably fit. Boil for 30 seconds on the first side, then flip and boil for 30 seconds on the second side. Use a slotted spoon or spider to remove the bagels from the water and transfer them to the bowl of ice water. Turn the bagels a couple of times to cool them off, then transfer to the wire rack. Repeat until you've boiled all the bagels from both sheets and set them on the rack.

Bake the bagels: Dust the same baking sheets with a bit more cornmeal to prevent sticking. [3] Return the bagels to the baking sheets, spacing evenly. Sprinkle all the bagels with flaky salt and transfer to the oven. Bake until the bagels are deeply browned and shiny, 15 to 20 minutes, switching racks and rotating the sheets front to back after 10 minutes. Remove from the oven and let cool completely on the wire rack.

---

[2] Use a baking stone if you have one. Preheat it in the oven and slide the bagels onto it directly. For ease of transfer, place the boiled bagels on a cornmeal-dusted peel or the reverse side of a baking sheet.

[3] Don't line the baking sheets with parchment paper, as the bagel dough after boiling will really want to stick to it, even with a generous layer of cornmeal on top.

VARIATION

Bialys

Makes 9 bialys

ONION FILLING

2 tablespoons olive oil

1 large onion (12 oz / 340g), coarsely chopped

Kosher salt and freshly ground black pepper

2 teaspoons poppy seeds

1 large egg white, beaten

Flaky salt, for sprinkling

Make the bialys and chill overnight: Instead of poking a hole in each 4-ounce portion of dough to make bagels, form each piece into a ball. Flatten each ball of dough and stretch it into a disk with a wide, flat depression in the center. You want a round that is about 4 inches wide with a 2-inch-wide depression. Place the bialys on the cornmeal-dusted baking sheets, spacing them evenly apart, then cover and refrigerate overnight.

The next morning, make the onion filling: In a medium saucepan, heat the oil over medium heat. Add the onion and season with kosher salt and pepper to taste. Cook, stirring often, until the onion pieces are very soft and translucent and browned around the edges, 8 to 10 minutes. Remove the pan from the heat and stir in the poppy seeds. Let the mixture cool completely.

Fill and proof the bialys: Remove the baking sheets from the refrigerator, uncover, and fill the depression of each bialy with a generous tablespoon of onion filling. Cover again and let the bialys sit at room temperature until the outer edge of dough is puffed and a finger poked into the side leaves only a slight impression, 45 minutes to 1 hour 15 minutes longer.

Meanwhile, preheat the oven: While the bialys are proofing, arrange two oven racks in the upper and lower thirds of the oven and preheat to 475°F.

Brush with egg white and bake: Uncover the bialys and brush the surface of the dough with the egg white. Sprinkle with flaky salt and more black pepper. Bake until the bialys are deeply browned and shiny and the onions have darkened all over, 15 to 20 minutes, switching racks and rotating the sheets front to back after 10 minutes. Remove from the oven and let cool completely on a wire rack.

DO AHEAD
The bialys are best eaten the day they're made but will keep, stored airtight at room temperature, up to 3 days. The bialys can also be frozen up to 1 month in a resealable plastic freezer bag.

Spelt Croissants

Makes 8 croissants

Special Equipment:
Instant-read thermometer, spray bottle filled with water

1 teaspoon **active dry yeast** (0.11 oz / 3g)

3 cups **bread flour** (13.8 oz / 390g), plus more for rolling out

½ cup **spelt flour** (2.3 oz / 65g)

3 tablespoons **unsalted butter** (1.5 oz / 43g), melted and cooled

2 tablespoons **sugar** (0.9 oz / 25g)

2½ teaspoons **Diamond Crystal kosher salt** (0.21 oz / 6g)

12 ounces (340g) salted **European-style butter**, cut into tablespoons, chilled

2 tablespoons **heavy cream**

1 large **egg yolk** (0.6 oz / 16g)

Croissant-making is a sensitive process—it's one of the many doughs that can "smell fear." I made a lot of sub-par test batches of croissants, some overproofed, some rolled too tightly, and many underproofed, before I dialed in a method that reliably turned out burnished, shattering, light-as-a-feather croissants. It's a project, no doubt, but one that's also magical and exciting. Many thanks to Laurie Ellen Pellicano, a friend and talented food stylist (who helped style many of the recipes for this book), for helping me troubleshoot this recipe. Laurie Ellen used to work at the famed bakery Tartine in San Francisco, where she made probably thousands of croissants, so I sought her wisdom and incorporated some of it here. The addition of spelt flour makes these croissants extra flavorful, even a little savory. Note that this recipe requires an overnight rest in the refrigerator and several hours the next morning to proof the croissants.

Dissolve the yeast: In a small saucepan, gently warm ¼ cup water (2 oz / 57g) over low heat, swirling the pan, just until it's lukewarm but not hot, about 105°F on an instant-read thermometer (you can do this in the microwave, too, but beware of overheating). Pour the water into a large bowl and whisk in the yeast to dissolve. Set aside until the mixture is cloudy and slightly puffed, about 5 minutes.

Make the dough: To the bowl with the yeast, add ¾ cup room temperature water (6 oz / 170g), then add the bread flour, spelt flour, melted unsalted butter, sugar, and salt. Mix with a wooden spoon or spatula until a shaggy dough forms, scraping down the sides, then switch to your hands and knead inside the bowl until the dough comes together. Turn the dough out onto a clean work surface and knead until you have a very smooth, supple, and firm dough, 8 to 10 minutes. The dough should not be sticky at all, nor should it be so dry that it holds cracks. Add more flour or a few drops of water to adjust the consistency as needed.

Proof the dough: Form the dough into a smooth ball and dust it lightly with flour all over. Place the dough inside a medium bowl, cover it, and let sit at room temperature until nearly doubled in size, 1 to 1½ hours.

Make the butter block: While the dough is rising, place the pieces of cold salted butter in a mound on a sheet of parchment paper, then place another sheet on top. Use a rolling pin to beat the butter firmly (continues)

DO AHEAD
The croissants, stored airtight at room temperature, will keep up to 2 days but are best served the day they're made.

① Return the dough to the refrigerator whenever it feels like the butter is getting warm and the dough becomes soft and sticky, or if it's stubbornly springing back

on you as you roll. Always try to work quickly with the dough, but don't try to rush the process.

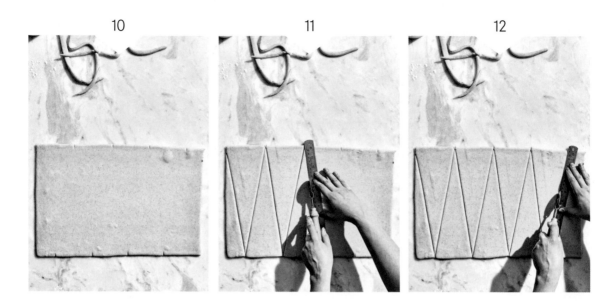

but gently, flattening it into a single layer about ½ inch thick (beating the cold butter makes it pliable without also making it soft and sticky). Remove the top sheet of parchment paper and use a small offset or regular spatula to spread the butter into an approximately 7-inch square, squaring off the corners and straightening the edges, too. Fold the bottom layer of parchment around the butter to completely enclose it (like you're wrapping a gift), eliminating any air pockets, and creating a neat square packet. Turn the packet over so the folds of the parchment are facing down and roll across the butter block in both directions with your rolling pin to flatten and even out the thickness to about ¼ inch. Refrigerate the butter while the dough is rising.

Punch down and chill the dough: When the dough has nearly doubled, use a fist to lightly punch it down to expel some of the gases produced during the first rise. Line a small rimmed baking sheet with plastic wrap. Transfer the dough to the lined sheet and flatten it into a square shape (the dimensions aren't important). Cover it with plastic wrap and freeze until the dough is very firm but not frozen, about 10 minutes.

Enclose the butter block: Remove the dough from the freezer and the butter block from the refrigerator.

Uncover the dough and place it on a lightly floured surface. Roll it out, stretching it with your hands if needed, until you have about an 8-inch square. The dimensions aren't important as long as the thickness is even and the dough is slightly larger than the butter block all the way around.

Note that the following numbered steps (1 through 9) correspond to the photographs on page 260.

[1] Unwrap the butter just so the top is exposed and, using the sides of the parchment paper, turn the block over and place it on top of the dough, positioning it so it looks like a diamond set onto the dough square, with the points of the butter aligning with the midpoints of the sides of the dough. Peel off the parchment paper and discard.

[2,3,4] Fold each of the four corners of the dough inward one at a time toward the center of the butter block. They should easily meet and overlap slightly in the center and along the sides. Pinch the dough together firmly along all the seams so they seal.

Do the first "turn:" [5] Use the rolling pin to lightly beat the dough to flatten and lengthen slightly, then roll out the dough, working it both toward and away from you, to elongate it into a rectangle that's about three times longer than it is wide and between ¼ and ½ inch thick (somewhere around 20 inches long and 7 inches wide is good, but the exact dimensions aren't important). Do your best to keep the edges squared off and dust with more flour if needed. ①

[6,7] With a short side facing you, fold the dough in thirds like a letter, first lifting up the bottom third and pressing it into the center, then folding down the top third. This rolling and folding process is called a "turn," and it creates the layers of butter and dough that make a flaky pastry. Wrap the dough in plastic and refrigerate for 45 minutes to allow the gluten to relax.

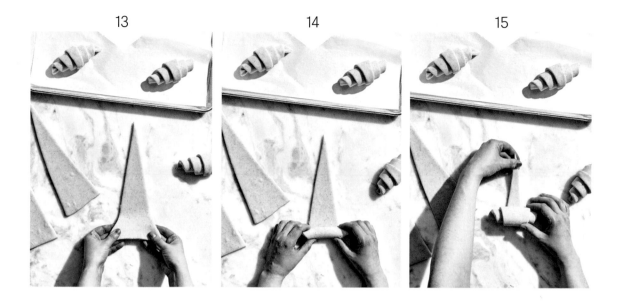

Do two more "turns": [8,9] Unwrap the chilled dough and place on a lightly floured surface so the flap is facing up and the edge of the flap is on the right (if you were to unfold the dough, you would open it to your left like a book). Roll out the dough again into a long rectangle just as you did before, dusting underneath with more flour if needed, and fold into thirds again. Try to keep the edges as square as possible in order to keep the layers aligned.

Wrap in plastic and refrigerate again for 45 minutes, then repeat the rolling and folding process one more time so you have performed three turns total.

Roll into a slab and chill: After completing the third turn, roll out the dough into a thinner slab until it starts to spring back (again, the size isn't important). Wrap the slab in plastic, place on a rimmed baking sheet, and refrigerate at least 8 hours and up to 12. [2]

The next day, prepare the pans: Line two baking sheets with parchment paper and set aside.

Note that the following numbered steps (10 through 15) correspond to the photographs above.

Roll out and cut the dough: Remove the dough from the refrigerator and roll it out on a very lightly floured surface into a large rectangle measuring slightly larger than 18 × 12 inches. This will take some elbow grease, but try to work as quickly as you can to prevent the butter from softening and making the dough sticky. Once the dough is rolled out, dust off any excess flour. Use a wheel cutter or sharp knife to trim the dough on all four sides to square it off so you have an 18 × 12-inch slab.

[10] Along one of the long sides, use a ruler and a paring knife to make small notches, spaced 4 inches apart, in the dough. Along the opposite long side, make the same marks every 4 inches but begin 2 inches in from the edge, so that the marks are offset from the first side. [11,12] Starting at one end, use a ruler to connect the notches from one side to the other, cutting along the straightedge of the ruler with the wheel or knife in a zigzag pattern, to form 8 long triangles. (You will have 2 half-triangles left over.) [3]

Form and proof the croissants: [13,14,15] Working with one piece of dough at a time, tug gently along the short side of the triangle to widen it (continues)

---

[2] I don't recommend forming the croissants the night before and letting the crescents rest overnight in the refrigerator, as this tends to encourage them to proof more slowly and unevenly.

[3] Hold onto the dough scraps, rolling the half-triangles left over from either end of the dough slab into smaller croissants. Proof and bake along with the regular croissants.

slightly, then starting at that end, roll up the triangle into a snug crescent shape (you don't want it loose, but also not stretched tightly around itself). Place each croissant on the prepared baking sheets so it's resting on the point. Keep the baking sheets covered with plastic wrap as you work to prevent the dough from drying out. Once you have all the croissants formed and evenly spaced across the two baking sheets, uncover and spritz the pans lightly with water, avoiding the croissants themselves. Cover again and let proof at room temperature, spritzing with water one more time halfway through, until the croissants are doubled in size, extremely airy, and wobble when the sheets are shaken, 3 to 4 hours.

Preheat the oven: Toward the end of the proofing, arrange two oven racks in the upper and lower thirds of the oven and preheat to 400°F.

Egg wash the croissants: In a small bowl, beat the heavy cream and yolk with a fork. Gently brush the egg mixture over the croissants, coating every surface of the croissants but taking care not to brush the cut sides where the layers are exposed.

Bake and cool: Uncover the pans and transfer them to the oven, placing one on the lower rack and one on the upper. Bake the croissants until they are dramatically puffed, deeply browned, and shiny, 20 to 25 minutes, switching racks and rotating the pans front to back after 15 minutes. Remove from the oven and let cool completely on the baking sheets.

Kouign-amann

Makes 24 muffin-sized kouignettes

Special Equipment:
Instant-read thermometer, two standard 12-cup muffin tins ①

1 teaspoon **active dry yeast** (0.11 oz / 3g)

3¼ cups **all-purpose flour** (14.6 oz / 423g), plus more for rolling out

3 tablespoons **unsalted butter** (1.5 oz / 43g), melted and cooled

1½ teaspoons **Diamond Crystal kosher salt** (0.16 oz / 5g)

1¼ cups **sugar** (8.8 oz / 250g)

12 ounces (340g) salted **European-style butter**, cut into tablespoons, chilled

Butter and **sugar** for the muffin tins

Like a caramelized, slightly denser croissant, *kouign-amann* is a pastry from the Brittany region of France that's as difficult to make as it is to pronounce (it's "kween-ah-mahn," for the record), but for my money, there is no better pastry out there. Making *kouign-amann* requires a technique known as lamination, a process of enveloping butter inside dough and then rolling and folding the dough several times to create lots of buttery layers that puff during baking. It's tricky, especially when you add sugar and yeast to the mix as you do here, so you'll want to rely on the refrigerator and freezer to keep the dough cold and therefore workable. *Kouign-amann*, or *kouignettes*, as the individual pastries are called, are all about the flavor of butter, so try to seek out a European-style salted butter, such as Kerrygold, which has a higher butterfat percentage (it's available in most large grocery stores).

Dissolve the yeast: In a small saucepan, gently warm ¼ cup water (2 oz / 57g) over low heat, swirling the pan, just until it's lukewarm but not hot, about 105°F on an instant-read thermometer (you can do this in the microwave, too, but beware of overheating). Pour the water into a large bowl and whisk in the yeast to dissolve. Set aside until the mixture is cloudy and slightly puffed, about 5 minutes.

Make the dough: Add ¾ cup room temperature water (6 oz / 170g) to the bowl, then add the flour, melted unsalted butter, salt, and ¼ cup of the sugar (1.8 oz / 50g). Mix with a wooden spoon to combine all the ingredients until you have shaggy pieces. Knead the dough by hand in the bowl several times to bring it together, then turn it out onto a clean work surface and continue to knead by hand, adding a sprinkle of flour only if the dough is sticking to your hands and/or the surface, until you have a very smooth, supple, and soft dough, 10 to 12 minutes.

Proof the dough: Gather the dough into a smooth ball and dust lightly with flour. Place it inside a medium bowl and take a photo so you can more easily gauge how the dough rises over time. Cover it with a damp kitchen towel and let it sit until the ball has nearly doubled in size, 1 to 1¼ hours.

Make the butter block: While the dough is rising, place the cold pieces of salted butter in a mound on a sheet of parchment paper, then place another sheet on top. Use a rolling pin to beat the butter firmly but gently, flattening it into a single layer about ½ inch thick (continues)

DO AHEAD
The *kouignettes* are best served the day they're baked but will still be absolutely delicious 3 or even 4 days later. Store well wrapped at room temperature.

① Don't use a dark muffin tin if you can help it because a dark pan will caramelize the sugar on the outside of the *kouignettes* quickly and possibly cause them to burn. A light-colored pan is always best for even baking.

(beating the cold butter makes it pliable without also making it soft and sticky). Remove the top sheet of parchment paper and use a small offset or regular spatula to spread the butter into an approximately 7-inch square, squaring off the corners and straightening the edges, too. Fold the bottom layer of parchment around the butter to completely enclose it (like you're wrapping a gift), eliminating any air pockets, and creating a neat square packet. Turn the packet over so the folds of the parchment are facing down and roll across the butter block in both directions with your rolling pin to flatten and even out the thickness to about ¼ inch. Refrigerate the butter while the dough is rising.

Punch down and chill the dough: When the dough has nearly doubled, use a fist to lightly punch it down to expel some of the gases produced during the first rise. Line a small rimmed baking sheet with plastic wrap. Transfer the dough to the lined sheet and flatten it into a square shape (the dimensions aren't important). Cover it with plastic wrap and freeze until the dough is very firm but not frozen, about 10 minutes.

Enclose the butter block: Remove the dough from the freezer and the butter block from the refrigerator. Uncover the dough and place on a lightly floured surface. Roll it out, stretching it with your hands if needed, until you have about an 8-inch square. The dimensions aren't important as long as the thickness is even and the dough is slightly larger than the butter block all the way around.

[1] Unwrap the butter just so the top is exposed, and, using the sides of the parchment paper, turn the block over and place it on top of the dough, positioning it so it looks like a diamond set onto the dough square, with the points of the butter aligning with the midpoints of the sides of the dough. Peel off the parchment paper and discard.

[2,3,4] Fold each of the four corners of the dough inward one at a time toward the center of the butter block. They should easily meet and overlap slightly

in the center and along the sides. Pinch the dough together firmly along all the seams so they seal.

Do the first two "turns": Dust more flour underneath and on top of the dough, which should now completely encase the butter block.

[5] Use the rolling pin to lightly beat the dough to flatten and lengthen slightly, then roll out the dough, working it both toward and away from you, to elongate it into a rectangle that's about three times longer than it is wide and between ¼ and ½ inch thick (somewhere around 20 inches long and 7 inches wide is good, but the exact dimensions aren't important). Do your best to keep the edges squared-off and dust with more flour if needed.

[6,7] With a short side facing you, fold the dough in thirds like a letter, first lifting up the bottom third and pressing it into the center, then folding down the top third. This rolling and folding process is called a "turn," and it creates the layers of butter and dough that make a flaky pastry.

[8,9] Rotate the dough 90 degrees counterclockwise, dust with a bit more flour if needed, and repeat the rolling out and folding process. This is your second turn. ②

Chill the dough: Wrap the dough in plastic and freeze it for 10 minutes to rapidly cool it down, then transfer it to the refrigerator and chill for 1 hour.

Do the final two "turns" with sugar: Orient the chilled dough on a lightly floured surface so the flap is facing up and the edge of the flap is on the right (if you were to unfold the dough, you would open it to your left like a book).

[10,11,12] Roll out the dough again into a long rectangle just as you did before, dusting underneath with more flour if needed. Sprinkle several tablespoons of sugar from the remaining 1 cup over the surface of the dough. Fold it into thirds again, then rotate 90 degrees. (continues)

---

② Work as quickly as you can when rolling the dough and return it to the refrigerator or freezer as needed if it becomes soft and sticky. It will become more difficult to work with once you start to add sugar during the third and fourth turns because the sugar crystals tear at the increasingly thin sheets of dough. If any butter pokes through, causing the dough to stick to the surface or rolling pin, pat a bit of flour into the spot and press on. Bottom line: Work quickly!

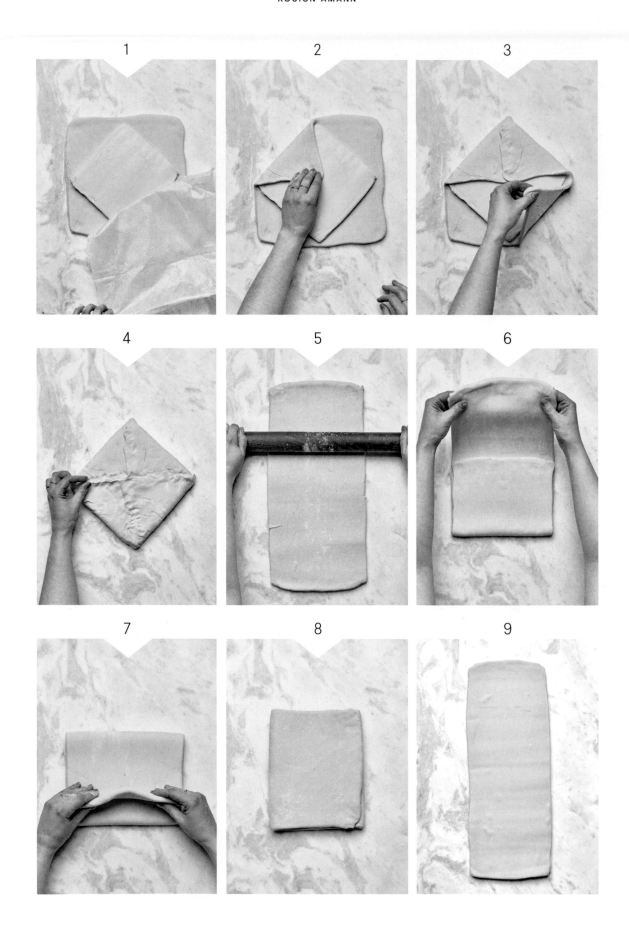

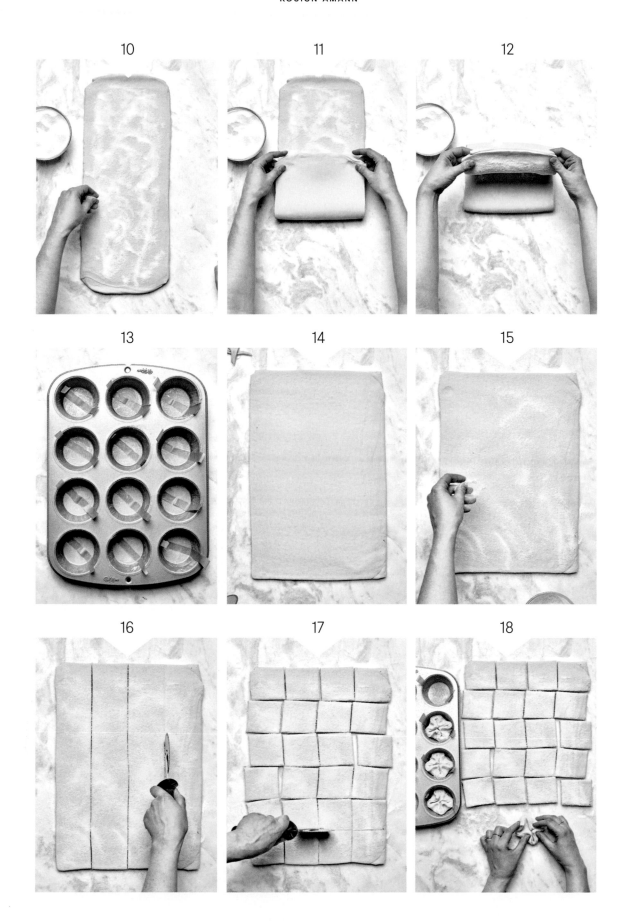

Remove any excess sugar from the work surface, dust underneath the dough with more flour, and roll out again. Sprinkle the surface of the dough with more sugar and fold into thirds one final time.

Chill the dough: Wrap the dough in plastic and freeze for 10 minutes to rapidly cool, then transfer it to the refrigerator and chill for 1 hour.

Prepare the pans: ③ [13] Brush 24 cups of two standard muffin tins with a generous layer of cooled, melted unsalted butter. Cut 24 strips of parchment paper, each measuring about 5 inches long and ¼ inch wide, and lay a strip flush across the bottom and up the sides of each muffin cup. Brush the parchment strips with more butter, sprinkle a generous pinch of sugar inside each muffin cup, then set the pans aside.

Roll out and cut the dough: [14,15] Remove the cold dough from the refrigerator and roll it out on a very lightly floured surface into a large rectangle measuring slightly larger than 18 × 12 inches. This will take some elbow grease, but try to work as quickly as you can to prevent the butter from softening and making the dough sticky. Once the dough is rolled out, use a pastry brush to dust off any excess flour. Use a wheel cutter or large chef's knife to trim the dough on all four sides to square it off. Sprinkle the remaining sugar underneath and on top of the dough, pressing gently on the surface of the dough to encourage the sugar to stick.

[16,17] Cut the dough into twenty-four 3-inch squares (6 x 4 grid).

Fill the pans and proof: [18] Working with one square at a time, fold all four corners inward toward the center of the square so they meet, then press gently so the corners stay in place.

Place the folded-up square inside a muffin cup and repeat until you've folded all the squares and filled the pans. Cover the pans loosely with plastic and let them sit at room temperature until the *kouignettes* are puffed and the layers of dough and butter have visibly separated, 35 to 45 minutes. (Alternatively, the covered pans can be refrigerated up to 12 hours. Do not let them rise at room temperature before baking, as the rise will happen slowly in the refrigerator. Transfer them directly to the preheated oven.)

Preheat the oven: Arrange two oven racks in the upper and lower thirds of the oven and preheat to 400°F.

Bake and cool: Uncover the pans and transfer to the oven. Immediately reduce the temperature to 350°F and bake until the *kouignettes* are risen and deep golden brown, 25 to 30 minutes, switching racks and rotating the pans front to back after 18 minutes. Remove the pans from the oven and let them sit for 5 minutes. Tug on the ends of the parchment strips to dislodge the caramelized *kouignettes* from the pans (don't let them cool any longer in the pans, as the caramelized sugar will make them stick). Transfer them to a wire cooling rack and let cool completely.

---

③ You can make this recipe with only one muffin pan and simply do two rounds of baking. Roll out the dough and cut into 24 squares as written, but transfer half the squares to a cutting board or rimmed baking sheet, cover with plastic wrap, and refrigerate. Fold the remaining squares of dough, fill the pan, proof, and bake. Remove the *kouignettes*, wash and prepare the pan, then repeat the proofing and baking process with the cold squares. Alternatively, after baking 12 *kouignettes*, you could use the remaining half of the squares to make a half recipe (12) of **Cherry Cream Cheese Danishes** (page 263).

Cherry Cream Cheese Danishes

Makes 24 small Danishes [1]

CHERRY COMPOTE

1 tablespoon fresh **lemon juice**

2 teaspoons **cornstarch**

1 pound (454g) fresh or frozen pitted **sweet cherries**

¼ cup **sugar** (1.8 oz / 50g)

Finely grated **zest of 1 lemon**

ASSEMBLY

6 ounces (170 g) full-fat **cream cheese**, preferably Philadelphia, at room temperature

1 large **egg yolk** (0.6 oz / 16g)

Kouign-amann dough (page 257), cut into 24 squares as directed and unbaked

A treat for me as a kid was walking from my house to the St. Louis Bread Company, a family-owned, fast-casual bakery and café (later sold and turned into the Panera chain), and buying a snack from the pastry case. Sometimes I would get a banana-nut or pumpkin "muffy," which was just the muffin top (genius!), but more frequently I would get one of their cherry and cheese Danishes. It felt like a very fancy treat then, and that's still how Danishes feel to me now. I didn't attempt them at home for a long time because true Danish pastry dough is both yeasted and laminated, and thus complicated. But once I successfully developed and got comfortable with the recipe for **Kouign-amann** (page 257), another pastry made from a similar style of dough, Danishes were only a couple of steps away. It's not exactly a recipe for the timid baker, but it yields an extremely delicious and special treat.

Make the cherry compote: In a small bowl, use a fork to stir together the lemon juice and cornstarch and set aside.

In a small saucepan, combine the cherries, sugar, lemon zest, and ¼ cup water (2 oz / 57g) and cook over medium heat, stirring occasionally with a wooden spoon or heatproof spatula, until the cherries have released their juices and the mixture comes to a boil. Continue to cook, stirring, until the cherries are soft and tender and the juices have started to thicken, about 5 minutes.

Stir the cornstarch mixture to recombine, then add it to the saucepan with the cherries. Bring the mixture to a boil, stirring, and cook for about 30 seconds to activate the cornstarch so it thickens the liquid. Remove the compote from the heat and let it cool completely. Transfer the compote to a bowl, cover with plastic wrap, and refrigerate until you're ready to assemble the Danishes.

Make the cream cheese mixture: In a small bowl, mash together the cream cheese and egg yolk until you have a smooth mixture. Set aside.

Strain the cherry mixture: Set a sieve over a bowl. Drain the cooled cherries in the sieve and reserve the juices and cherries separately. (continues)

DO AHEAD
The Danishes, stored airtight at room temperature, will keep up to 3 days but are best served the day they're made (the pastry will soften over time). The cherry compote, covered and refrigerated, will keep up to 1 week.

[1] If you don't want 24 Danishes, make a half recipe, halving the amounts for the cream cheese mixture and the cherry compote. Use the other half of the dough to make 12 **Kouign-amann** (page 257), requiring just one muffin tin. I don't recommend trying to freeze the dough, since the sugar in it will make the dough too sticky to handle after it thaws.

Assemble and proof the Danishes: Line two baking sheets with parchment paper. Divide the 24 squares of unbaked *kouign-amann* dough between the baking sheets, spacing them evenly. Use the tines of a fork to prick the centers of each square in three places. Dollop a scant tablespoon of the cream cheese mixture in the center of each square of pastry (you can also pipe it using a pastry bag or resealable plastic bag with a corner cut off), then press 3 or so drained cherries over the top of the cream cheese. Cover the baking sheets with plastic wrap and let the Danishes sit at room temperature until the dough is puffed and the layers of dough and butter have visibly separated on the sides, 30 to 40 minutes.

Preheat the oven: Meanwhile, arrange two oven racks in the upper and lower thirds of the oven and preheat to 400°F.

Bake the Danishes and drizzle with juices: [2] Uncover the pans and transfer to the oven, placing one on the lower rack and one on the upper. Immediately reduce the temperature to 350°F and bake until the pastries are deep golden brown, 20 to 25 minutes, switching racks and rotating the pans front to back after 15 minutes. Remove the pans from the oven and let the Danishes cool completely on the baking sheets. Drizzle some of the reserved cherry juices over the warm pastries and serve warm or at room temperature.

[2] Don't open the oven during the first 15 minutes of baking; the dough needs sufficient time to rise and start to set so the final Danishes will be light and flaky.

Breads and Savory Baking

While a chapter of breads and savory baking recipes might seem out of place in a book titled *Dessert Person*, a person cannot live on dessert alone. I have a particular affinity for the recipes here because they best demonstrate the transformational nature of baking. In the **Soft and Crispy Focaccia** (page 289), for example, an incredibly wet, sticky dough goes into the oven and emerges a golden, light, airy bread. It's nothing short of miraculous. This chapter demonstrates not only how dramatic baking can be, but also how flexible, diverse, and adaptable it is. We all know that pie dough can be used to make make a sweet galette, but did you know it can also serve as the base for a **Caramelized Endive Galette** (page 278) that's topped with fresh dressed greens? Now you do. So go ahead, try some savory recipes and flex those baking muscles.

TOMATO, GARLIC, AND THYME
FOCACCIA, PAGE 293

Loaded Corn Bread

Serves 12

Special Equipment:
10-inch ovenproof skillet (preferably cast-iron)

7 tablespoons **unsalted butter** (3.5 oz / 100g), plus more for serving

3 ounces (85g) sliced **bacon** (3 or 4 slices), coarsely chopped

2 cups **corn kernels** (10 oz / 284g), cut from about 2 large ears, or thawed frozen corn kernels

4 **scallions**, chopped

1 medium **Fresno** or **jalapeño chile**, halved, seeded, and finely chopped

1 cup **all-purpose flour** (4.6 oz / 130g)

½ cup **yellow cornmeal** (3 oz / 85g), preferably coarse

1½ teaspoons **baking powder** (0.21 oz / 6g)

1½ teaspoons Diamond Crystal kosher **salt** (0.16 oz / 5g)

¼ teaspoon **baking soda**

½ teaspoon freshly ground **black pepper**

¼ teaspoon **cayenne pepper** ①

2 large **eggs** (3.5 oz / 100g), at room temperature

1 cup **sour cream** (8.2 oz / 232g), at room temperature

½ cup **buttermilk** (4.2 oz / 120g), at room temperature

2 tablespoons **sugar**

¼ cup finely chopped **fresh cilantro**

I know that real Southern corn bread uses all cornmeal (no flour) and is made intentionally dry in order to best accompany saucier foods. Still, I can't help but prefer the bastardized recipe my mom used to make from the *New Basics Cookbook*: moist, light, and bulked up with chile and other aromatics. My corn bread is a side dish in itself, loaded with bacon and scallions and lots of fresh corn. It might be heresy to a Southerner, but it's also super delicious.

Preheat the oven: Arrange an oven rack in the center position and preheat the oven to 425°F.

Brown the bacon: In the ovenproof skillet (preferably cast-iron), heat 5 tablespoons of the butter over medium heat until foamy. Add the bacon and cook, stirring often, until the fat is rendered and the bacon is crisp, 5 to 7 minutes.

Cook the corn and aromatics: To the skillet with the bacon, add the corn (if using thawed frozen corn, pat the kernels dry first), scallions, and chile and cook, stirring often, until the corn is tender and aromatics are soft, 5 to 7 minutes (if using frozen corn, the kernels will already be soft due to freezing and thawing, so only cook the mixture for as long as it takes for the aromatics to soften). Remove the skillet from the heat and set aside to cool.

Mix the dry ingredients: In a large bowl, whisk together the flour, cornmeal, baking powder, salt, baking soda, black pepper, and cayenne to combine. Set aside.

Mix the wet ingredients: In a medium bowl, whisk the eggs until no streaks remain. Whisk in the sour cream, buttermilk, sugar, and cilantro until the mixture is smooth. Set aside.

Mix the wet ingredients into the dry: Switch to a flexible spatula and make a well in the center of the dry ingredients. Pour in the wet ingredients, then scrape in the cooled corn and aromatics mixture (it's okay if it's slightly warm); reserve the skillet for baking the corn bread. Gently mix with the spatula, starting in the center and working outward, folding just until the batter is evenly mixed.

DO AHEAD
The corn bread, well wrapped and stored at room temperature, will keep up to 3 days but is best served the day it's made.

① Omit the cayenne if you don't want a corn bread with a slow-building heat. On the flip side, if you like quite a bit of heat, feel free to leave the seeds in the chile and/or add more cayenne.

Miso Buttermilk Biscuits

Makes 16 biscuits

½ cup **sweet white miso** (4.8 oz / 136g) [2]

1¼ cups **buttermilk** (10.6 oz / 300g), chilled

3¼ cups **all-purpose flour** (15 oz / 423g), plus more for rolling out

1 tablespoon **baking powder** (0.42 oz / 12g)

1 tablespoon **sugar** (0.46 oz / 13g)

¼ teaspoon **baking soda**

2 sticks **unsalted butter** (8 oz / 227g), cut into ½-inch pieces, chilled, plus 2 tablespoons (1 oz / 28g), melted, for brushing

Freshly ground **black pepper**

Most people know miso from Japanese miso soup, but they might not be aware of all the incredible applications this salty, funky umami-rich paste (made from fermented soybeans) has in cooking and baking. I've played around with it in sweet recipes with only limited success, but Chris Morocco from the *Bon Appétit* test kitchen has made a convincing case that it's definitely possible (check out his miso almond butter cookies recipe on bonappetit.com). In these flaky, fluffy, savory biscuits, I mash a staggering ½ cup sweet white miso, one of the milder varieties, into cold buttermilk and mix it into the dough. The miso both seasons the dough and contributes an almost cheesy flavor. It makes a fantastic biscuit that works just as well served with scrambled eggs as it does as the base for a katsu sandwich. Or you can just do as I recommend and serve them warm with miso butter. [1]

Preheat the oven and prepare the baking sheet: Arrange an oven rack in the center position and preheat the oven to 425°F. Line a large rimmed baking sheet with parchment paper and set aside.

Mix the miso and buttermilk: Place the miso in the bottom of a medium bowl and pour in a couple of tablespoons of the buttermilk. Mash with a fork until smooth, then add a few more tablespoons of buttermilk and continue to mash until you have a smooth, lump-free paste. Repeat the process until you've worked about half of the buttermilk into the miso and you have a smooth, pourable mixture (working the buttermilk in just a bit at a time helps prevent lumps). Whisk in the rest of the buttermilk until smooth. Refrigerate while you assemble the rest of the ingredients.

Mix the dry ingredients: In a large bowl, whisk together the flour, baking powder, sugar, and baking soda to combine.

Work in the butter: Add the pieces of butter to the bowl with the flour mixture and toss to coat. Then use your fingertips to quickly smash all the pieces into the flour mixture, flattening them and breaking up into bits.

Mix in the miso buttermilk: Stirring the mixture constantly with a fork, drizzle the buttermilk mixture into the bowl with the (continues)

DO AHEAD
The biscuits are best served the day they're made but will keep, stored in an airtight container at room temperature, up to 3 days. Rewarm the biscuits before serving. The unbaked biscuits can be covered with plastic wrap on the baking sheet and refrigerated up to 24 hours or frozen up to 1 month. No need to thaw before baking (frozen biscuits may take a few minutes longer in the oven).

[1] To make miso butter to serve with the biscuits, mash together room temperature unsalted butter and miso with a fork in a small bowl until smooth—how much miso you add is up to your own taste, but I like about 1 part miso to 2 parts butter.

flour mixture. Using a flexible spatula or bench scraper, fold the mixture several times inside the bowl to bring the dough together and ensure that it's evenly combined. It will be a bit wet and sticky.

Form the biscuits: Turn the dough out onto a lightly floured surface. Use floured hands to pat it into a rectangle about ½ inch thick. Use a bench scraper or knife to cut the dough in half lengthwise and again crosswise to create quadrants. Stack the quadrants one on top of the other, dust a bit more flour on top and underneath the dough, and then roll out the stack with a rolling pin into a square measuring about 8½-inches across (this stacking and rolling step creates flakiness).

Cut and chill the biscuits: Using a sharp knife, trim the edges to straighten so you have a neat 8-inch square. Then cut the square into sixteen 2-inch squares (a 4 x 4 grid). Transfer each square to the prepared baking sheet, spacing evenly. Place the baking sheet in the freezer for about 15 minutes to allow the butter to firm up.

Brush with butter and bake: Brush the tops of the chilled biscuits with the 2 tablespoons melted butter and top with black pepper. Transfer the baking sheet to the oven and reduce the temperature to 375°F. Bake until the tops of the biscuits are browned and the bottoms are golden brown, 20 to 25 minutes. Remove from the oven and let cool on the baking sheet.

[2] Use any variety of miso if you like, but keep in mind that darker varieties are typically aged longer and will be both saltier and more pungent. There's no need to add additional salt to the dough—the miso is plenty salty on its own and will season the dough throughout.

Tomato Tart
with Spices and Herby Feta

Serves 8

Special Equipment:
Food processor (optional)

2½ pounds (1.13kg) **heirloom** or **beefsteak tomatoes**

1 medium **shallot**, cut into thin wedges

5 **garlic** cloves, unpeeled

2 large sprigs **fresh thyme**, plus
1 teaspoon fresh thyme leaves

¼ cup **extra-virgin olive oil** (2 oz / 57g),
plus more for drizzling

½ teaspoon **coriander seeds**, crushed
with the flat side of a knife

¼ teaspoon **crushed red pepper flakes**

¼ teaspoon **cumin seeds**

¼ teaspoon **fennel seeds**

Kosher salt and freshly ground black **pepper**

Flaky All-Butter Pie Dough (page 333) [1]

All-purpose flour, for rolling out

8 ounces (227g) **feta cheese** [2]

¼ cup **mayonnaise** (2.2 oz / 60g)

2 tablespoons finely chopped
fresh **oregano** leaves, plus more leaves
for topping

This tart is inspired by one of my favorite ways to use a ripe tomato: sliced on top of a toasted everything bagel with cream cheese. With that flavor combination in mind, I developed this tomato tart: a mix of fresh and roasted tomato slices with lots of olive oil and sizzled spices, layered over an herby feta and mayo schmear on a flat, free-form pastry base. Using both cooked and raw tomatoes gives the tart the best of both flavor worlds: juicy and fresh as well as deep and concentrated. I wait all year for tomato season, picking any and all wan, orangish-pink slices off salads and sandwiches until I can really savor a juicy, deep red tomato. In the Northeast, this means holding out until August, at which point I make sure to incorporate tomatoes into every meal until they disappear in October.

Preheat the oven: Arrange an oven rack in the center position and preheat the oven to 400°F.

Bake the tomatoes: Core half of the tomatoes and use a serrated knife to cut them into ¼-inch-thick slices. Scatter the sliced tomatoes, the shallot wedges, garlic, and thyme sprigs across a rimmed baking sheet. Drizzle with ¼ cup of olive oil and sprinkle with the coriander seeds, red pepper flakes, cumin seeds, and fennel seeds. Season everything with salt and pepper. Roast until the tomatoes are sizzling, darkened around the edges, and very fragrant, 35 to 40 minutes, rotating the pan halfway through. Remove the pan from the oven (leave the oven on). Carefully loosen the tomatoes with a metal spatula in case they've stuck. Remove the thyme sprigs and crumble the crispy thyme leaves over the tomatoes (discard the stems). Transfer the tomatoes, garlic, shallots, and any oil or spices left on the baking sheet to a plate and set aside to cool. Clean the baking sheet, line it with parchment paper, and set it aside to bake the crust.

Roll out and bake the crust: Let the pie dough sit at room temperature for about 5 minutes to soften slightly. Place the dough on a lightly floured surface and use a rolling pin to beat the dough all across the surface to make it more pliable. Roll out the dough, dusting with more flour as needed to prevent sticking, until you have an oblong slab that's a little more than ⅛ inch thick. (Don't worry about the **(continues)**

DO AHEAD
The tart will keep, loosely covered, for 1 day at room temperature and up to 3 days in the refrigerator (the crust will soften over time and the fresh tomato slices might turn mealy when chilled). The baked crust and roasted tomato mixture, both covered and stored separately at room temperature, can be made 1 day ahead. The feta mixture, covered and refrigerated, can also be made 1 day ahead. Assemble just before serving.

shape—irregular is fine, good even!) Transfer the pastry to the parchment-lined baking sheet and prick all over with the tines of a fork. If the pastry has softened and is a little sticky, chill it briefly until it's firm, about 10 minutes. Bake the pastry until it's deep golden brown all over, 20 to 25 minutes. Remove from the oven and set aside to cool.

Make the herby feta: In a food processor, combine the feta, mayonnaise, chopped oregano, and 1 teaspoon thyme leaves. Squeeze the reserved roasted garlic cloves out of their skins and into the food processor. Season lightly with salt and pepper and process until the mixture is light and smooth. (Alternatively, you can simply mash all the ingredients together in a medium bowl with a fork until well combined; it just won't be super smooth.)

Assemble the tart: Slice the remaining tomatoes and season with salt and pepper. Scrape the feta mixture directly onto the cooled pastry and spread it with a small offset spatula or the back of a spoon all across the surface to the edges, leaving a thin border. Layer the fresh and cooked tomato slices over the feta. Top with fresh oregano leaves, drizzle with more olive oil, and serve.

---

① You can also use a sheet of thawed, store-bought frozen puff pastry in place of the homemade pie dough. Just make sure to let it thaw in the refrigerator overnight, roll it out with a bit of flour to flatten any creases, and prick it very well with a fork before baking. If it puffs up during baking, flatten it with the back of a spoon. I recommend Dufour brand, but any brand labeled "all-butter" will work.

② Always look for the feta cheese that comes as a block packed in brine rather than the pre-crumbled stuff. It will whip up much lighter and smoother. There are lots of varieties, but I prefer the extra-tangy sheep's milk feta.

Gougères

Makes about 70 bite-sized puffs

Special Equipment:
Stand mixer (optional), pastry bag
(optional)

Pâte à Choux (page 346)

½ teaspoon **ground nutmeg** (preferably
freshly grated)

½ teaspoon **sweet paprika**

Generous pinch of **kosher salt**

Pinch of **cayenne pepper**

10 ounces (283g) **Gruyère** or other
semi-soft cheese, coarsely grated
(about 1½ cups)

1 large **egg**, beaten

Pulling a tray of hot, golden brown gougères out of the oven when I have friends over is my best party trick. Everybody loves a cheese puff, they're both fun to make and easy to prepare in large quantities, and you can do all the work ahead of time. The base is *pâte à choux* with a few spices and lots of grated cheese beaten in, then piped and baked into toasty, savory, soft-crispy cheese puffs. Gruyère is the classic flavor, but feel free to use pretty much any semi-soft cheese you like, such as sharp cheddar or smoked Gouda.

Preheat the oven: Arrange two oven racks in the upper and lower thirds of the oven and preheat to 425°F.

Make the gougères dough: Prepare the *pâte à choux* through the step of beating the eggs into the dough. With the mixer on low, beat in the nutmeg, paprika, salt, and cayenne. Slowly add 6 ounces (170g) of the grated cheese to the bowl a bit at a time, waiting for each addition to incorporate into the batter before adding the next. Reserve the remaining 4 ounces cheese for topping the gougères.

Transfer to a pastry bag: Scrape the batter into a large pastry bag or resealable plastic bag. Twist or seal the bag to close, squeezing out as much air as possible. Snip a ½-inch opening in the bag.

Bake the puffs: Follow the directions for preparing the baking sheets and piping plain cream puffs on page 347. Brush with the egg, then sprinkle the remaining 4 ounces (113g) grated cheese over top, dividing it evenly between the mounds. Bake and cool as directed for cream puffs. [1]

DO AHEAD
The gougères, stored airtight at room temperature, will keep up to 2 days or can be frozen up to 1 month. They will soften if made ahead, so to recrisp, bake the gougères uncovered on a baking sheet at 400°F for 5 to 8 minutes and let cool. The gougères dough can be made and stored in the pastry bag in the refrigerator for 1 day. Let it come to room temperature before piping. The dough can also be portioned onto the lined baking sheets and frozen up to 1 month. Let the uncovered mounds of dough freeze solid, then wrap them well on the baking sheet. Brush the frozen mounds with egg, top with more cheese, and bake (starting from frozen, they'll take a few minutes longer in the oven).

[1] It's sometimes possible to revive collapsed gougères—which can happen if they're not sufficiently baked—by putting them back in a 400°F oven for 5 to 8 minutes as soon as you see the puffs start to deflate. The blast of heat *might* reinflate a flat, underdone puff.

Caramelized Endive Galette

Serves 6 as a snack, 4 as a main course

6 large **Belgian endive**
(1 lb 13 oz / 822g)

2 ounces (56g) **Parmesan cheese**

2 tablespoons plus ¼ cup **extra-virgin olive oil** (3 oz / 85g)

2 medium **yellow onions** (1 lb / 453g), halved and thinly sliced

1 teaspoon **fresh thyme leaves**, plus more for sprinkling the top

2 teaspoons plus 1 tablespoon **white wine vinegar**

Kosher salt and freshly ground **black pepper**

Flaky All-Butter Pie Dough
(page 333)

All-purpose flour, for rolling out

1 large **egg**, beaten

½ small **shallot**, very finely chopped

1 tablespoon **Dijon mustard**

1 teaspoon **honey**

1 small **radicchio**, leaves separated and torn ①

¼ cup **fresh flat-leaf parsley leaves**

This galette is a slightly more refined take on one of my favorite mash-ups: salad pizza! The contrast between the thin, buttery, caramelized base and the bright, bitter, crunchy salad is everything I could want in a meal. It's hard evidence that just because a recipe is baked in the oven doesn't mean it can't feature raw, fresh, seasonal ingredients.

Prep some of the ingredients: Starting from the leafy end, slice 5 of the endive crosswise into ½-inch-thick pieces, discarding the core, which can be very bitter, and set aside. Take the remaining endive and separate the leaves; refrigerate the leaves under a damp towel. Finely grate 1 ounce of the Parmesan, then shave the remaining ounce with a vegetable peeler. Set both aside.

Make the caramelized endive filling: In a medium skillet, heat 2 tablespoons of the olive oil over medium-high heat until shimmering. Add the onions and sliced endive in a few batches, stirring after each addition until wilted enough that you can fit the next batch in the skillet. Cook, stirring occasionally, until the onions are translucent, about 5 minutes. Reduce the heat to medium-low and continue to cook, stirring occasionally and adding a splash of water if the onions begin to stick, until the endive and onions are golden brown, 35 to 40 minutes (they'll take on more color in the oven). If the mixture is taking a very long time to caramelize, increase your heat slightly. Stir in the thyme and cook until the mixture is fragrant, about 1 minute, then stir in 2 teaspoons of the white wine vinegar. Season the mixture with salt and pepper to taste and remove the skillet from the heat. Let the filling cool completely.

Preheat the oven and prepare the baking sheet: Arrange an oven rack in the center position and preheat the oven to 350°F. Line a rimmed baking sheet with parchment paper and set aside.

Roll out the pastry: Let the pie dough sit at room temperature for about 5 minutes to soften slightly. Place the dough on a lightly floured surface and use a rolling pin to beat the dough all across the surface to make it more pliable. Dust the top and underside of the dough with more flour and roll it out, dusting with more flour as needed, into a rectangle measuring about 9 × 13 inches.

DO AHEAD
The galette, covered and stored at room temperature, will keep up to 3 days but is best served the day it's made while the pastry is still crisp. If baking ahead of time, wait until just before serving to

assemble the salad and top the galette. The caramelized endive filling can be made 3 days ahead. Transfer to an airtight container and refrigerate.

① Use any type of bitter lettuce you like in the salad, such as Treviso, or—the most photogenic of all lettuces— pink-striped Castelfranco radicchio.

Assemble the galette: Transfer the pastry to the parchment-lined baking sheet. Sprinkle half of the grated Parmesan evenly across the surface, leaving a 1½-inch border all the way around. Dollop the cooled caramelized endive filling over the cheese, then spread in an even layer.

Fold up the pastry: Brush the border of the pastry with the beaten egg and then, using the parchment paper to help you, fold the four sides up and over the filling, leaving the center open and pleating the dough at the corners. Press firmly on the pleats to help the pastry adhere to itself, then brush the top of the pastry with more egg. Sprinkle the remaining grated Parmesan around the edges of the crust, then top the entire galette with more black pepper.

Bake the galette: Bake the galette until the pastry is a deep golden brown, 45 to 55 minutes. Remove from the oven and let cool for at least 30 minutes.

Make the vinaigrette: [2] While the galette is baking, in a small bowl, whisk the shallot, mustard, honey, and remaining 1 tablespoon vinegar to combine. Slowly stream in the remaining ¼ cup olive oil, whisking constantly, until you have a thick and glossy vinaigrette. Season with salt and pepper and set aside.

Toss the salad and finish the galette: In a large bowl, combine the radicchio, parsley, whole endive leaves, and shaved Parmesan. Drizzle with the vinaigrette, season the salad with more salt and pepper, and toss gently with clean hands to coat all the leaves. Cut the galette into squares and pile the salad on top. Sprinkle with fresh thyme leaves and serve.

---

[2] Make a double or even triple recipe of this vinaigrette and keep it in a jar in the refrigerator for making salads. Though this is a fairly classic, all-purpose vinaigrette, it's a bit heavy on the honey— the added sweetness is to balance out the bitterness of the lettuces—so feel free to tweak it to your taste.

Season: All | Active Time: 1 hour (not including making the Flaky Olive Oil Dough) | Total Time: 2 hours, plus time to cool
Difficulty: 2 (Easy) | Vegan

Crispy Mushroom Galette

Serves 6 as a snack, 4 as a main course

7 tablespoons **extra-virgin olive oil** (7 oz / 200g), plus more for assembling

2 large **leeks** (1 lb 8 oz / 680g), dark green tops discarded, white and light green stalks split lengthwise, rinsed, and chopped

1 tablespoon grainy **Dijon mustard** (0.63 oz / 18g)

Kosher salt and freshly ground **black pepper**

1 pound (454g) **shiitake**, **cremini**, **oyster**, and/or **maitake mushrooms**, sliced or torn into 1-inch pieces

5 **garlic** cloves, 4 smashed and peeled, 1 finely grated

2 **fresh rosemary** sprigs, plus 1 tablespoon coarsely chopped fresh **rosemary** leaves

Flaky Olive Oil Dough (page 341)

All-purpose flour, for rolling out

2 tablespoons **panko bread crumbs**

2 teaspoons **nutritional yeast**

This mushroom galette has everything going for it: a base of melty leeks, rosemary-laced mushrooms, garlicky bread crumbs, and flaky pastry. It also happens to be vegan while sacrificing nothing, and makes for an impressive main course. If you prefer a buttery crust and don't mind the dairy, feel free to use **Flaky All-Butter Pie Dough** (page 333) instead.

Preheat the oven and prepare the baking sheet: Arrange an oven rack in the center position and preheat the oven to 350°F. Line a rimmed baking sheet with parchment paper and set aside.

Make the melted leek base: In a medium skillet (preferably cast-iron), heat 2 tablespoons of the olive oil over medium heat until shimmering. Add the leeks and cook, stirring often, until softened and translucent, 5 to 8 minutes. Reduce the heat to low and continue to cook, stirring occasionally and adding a splash of water to the skillet as needed if the leeks are starting to brown, until they're very tender and starting to break down, another 15 to 20 minutes. Remove the skillet from the heat and stir in the mustard. Season with salt and pepper. Scrape the mixture into a medium bowl and set aside to cool. Wipe out the skillet and set it back on the stove for the mushrooms.

Cook the mushrooms: Add 2 tablespoons of the olive oil to the same skillet and heat over high heat until shimmering. Add half of the mushrooms, 2 of the smashed garlic cloves, and 1 of the rosemary sprigs. Toss the mushrooms once just to coat in oil, then let them cook undisturbed until they're browned in spots, about 3 minutes. Continue to cook, tossing occasionally, until the mushrooms are browned all over, have released their liquid, and are tender, 5 to 8 minutes longer. ① Season the mixture with salt and pepper. Scrape into a separate medium bowl and set the bowl aside to cool. Repeat the process in the same skillet with 2 more tablespoons of oil, the remaining mushrooms, 2 smashed garlic cloves, rosemary sprig, and more salt and pepper. Reserve the skillet again for toasting the panko.

Roll out the dough: Unwrap the dough, place it on a lightly floured surface, and lightly dust the top with more flour. Roll out the dough, dusting with more flour as needed to prevent sticking, into a round about

DO AHEAD
The galette, covered at room temperature, will keep up to 3 days but is best served the day it's made (the pastry will soften over time). The leek mixture, covered and refrigerated, will keep up to 4 days.

① Wait to salt the mushrooms in the skillet until after they're nicely seared, since salting draws out the moisture and will prevent them from browning. Because they're not seasoned to begin with, the mushrooms require a generous amount of seasoning later on, so don't be shy with the salt!

DESSERT PERSON
280

12 inches in diameter. If it starts to shrink back as you're trying to roll it, cover the dough and let it rest on the surface for 10 minutes, then proceed.

Assemble the galette: Transfer the dough to the prepared baking sheet. Spread the cooled leek mixture across the surface of the dough, leaving a 1½-inch border all the way around. Scatter the cooked mushrooms and garlic (discard the rosemary) over the leeks.

Fold up the crust: Using the parchment paper to help you, fold the sides of the pastry up and over the mushrooms, leaving the center open and creating a series of evenly spaced pleats all the way around. Press firmly on the pleats to help the pastry adhere to itself, then brush the exterior of the pastry with more olive oil. Sprinkle more salt and pepper across the entire surface of the tart.

Bake the galette: Bake the galette until the pastry is golden brown and the tops of the mushrooms are crispy, 45 to 55 minutes.

Make the garlicky bread crumbs: While the galette is baking, heat the remaining 1 tablespoon oil in the skillet over medium heat. Add the panko, nutritional yeast, grated garlic, and rosemary leaves and cook, stirring constantly, until the panko is golden brown and the mixture is very fragrant, about 4 minutes. Remove the skillet from the heat, season the mixture with salt and pepper, and scrape it onto a paper towel-lined plate to cool.

Finish the galette and serve: Remove the galette from the oven and let it cool before topping with the garlicky panko and cutting into slices. Serve warm or at room temperature.

Creamy Greens Pie
with Baked Eggs

Serves 6

Special Equipment:
10-inch ovenproof skillet (preferably cast-iron), pie weights or 4 cups dried beans or rice (for parbaking)

Flaky All-Butter Pie Dough (page 333)

All-purpose flour, for rolling out

Diamond Crystal kosher salt

8 cups loosely packed torn **Tuscan kale leaves** (stripped from 2 medium bunches, about 1 lb / 454g total)

8 cups loosely packed torn **green or rainbow Swiss chard leaves** (stripped from a 1 lb / 454g bunch)

3 tablespoons **unsalted butter** (1.5 oz / 42g)

2 large **shallots** (4 oz / 113g), finely chopped

1 tablespoon **all-purpose flour** (0.28 oz / 8g)

1 (10 oz / 283g) package frozen **spinach,** thawed and squeezed to remove all moisture

Freshly ground **black pepper**

7 large **eggs** (12.3 oz / 350g), at room temperature

⅔ cup **heavy cream** (5.6 oz / 160g), at room temperature

2 ounces (57g) finely grated **Parmesan cheese** (about ½ cup)

1 tablespoon finely chopped **fresh dill**

¼ teaspoon **ground nutmeg** (preferably freshly grated)

Hot sauce, for serving

This recipe, like many others in this book, represents my attempt to combine a few ideas into one ultra-satisfying dish. Inspired by the Italian dish *torta pasqualina*, a thin double-crust tart filled with greens and eggs, this open-faced version also takes a few cues from my favorite steakhouse side dish, creamed spinach. Tons of hardy greens are cooked down into a Parmesan-y, nutmeg-y filling that's studded with eggs and baked inside a buttery pastry shell until the whites are set but the yolks are still jammy. It's an all-in-one brunch, lunch, or dinner dish.

Preheat the oven: Arrange an oven rack in the center position and preheat the oven to 400°F.

Roll out the pastry and line the skillet: Let the pie dough sit at room temperature for about 5 minutes to soften slightly. Place the dough on a lightly floured surface and use a rolling pin to beat the dough all across the surface to make it more pliable. Dust the top and underside of the dough with more flour, then roll it out, dusting with more flour as needed, into a 12-inch round. Transfer the pastry to the ovenproof skillet (preferably cast-iron) and press it down into the bottom and up the sides. Trim off any overhang so the pastry is flush with the top of the skillet. Prick the bottom of the pastry all over with the tines of a fork.

Bake the pastry: Press a double layer of foil onto the pastry and fill the skillet with pie weights, dried beans, or rice. Bake until the edges of the pastry are golden, 20 to 25 minutes. Carefully remove the skillet from the oven, lift out the foil with the weights, and set aside. Reduce the oven temperature to 350°F (baking it again at this lower temperature minimizes shrinkage, helping to prevent cracks). Return the skillet to the oven and bake until the pastry is golden across the surface, 15 to 20 minutes longer. Remove from the oven and set aside. ❶ (Leave the oven on and increase the temperature to 400°F.)

Blanch and chop the greens: Bring a large saucepan of water to a boil over medium-high heat. Toss in a generous amount of salt, then plunge the kale into the water and cook just until the leaves are bright (continues)

DO AHEAD
The pie is best served the day it's made because the baked eggs don't keep well. The baked pie crust, covered and stored at room temperature, can be made 1 day ahead. The cooked greens

filling can be made 1 day ahead, covered, and refrigerated. Let it come to room temperature before spreading into the baked crust.

❶ Don't be too concerned if the crust has some cracks in it after baking and before you add the filling. The filling is thick, so there's no risk of leaking.

green and tender, about 2 minutes. Use a slotted spoon or spider to transfer the greens to a sieve and rinse under cold water, tossing, until they're no longer warm. Shake off the excess water, then gather the greens in a bundle between your hands and squeeze as tightly as you can to wring out as much water as possible. Place the kale on a cutting board and set aside. Repeat the cooking, rinsing, and wringing process with the Swiss chard. Finely chop the greens and set aside.

Cook the greens mixture: In a separate medium skillet, heat the butter over medium heat until foamy, about 30 seconds. Add the shallots and cook, stirring often, until softened and translucent, about 3 minutes. Stir in the flour until all the bits of shallot are coated, about 1 minute, then stir in the reserved chopped cooked greens and the spinach. Season with ¾ teaspoon salt and lots of black pepper and continue to cook, stirring often, until the skillet is dry and the mixture has cooked down, about 5 minutes. Remove the skillet from the heat and set aside for a few minutes to cool.

Mix the filling: In a medium bowl, beat 1 of the eggs until no streaks remain, then stir in the heavy cream, Parmesan, dill, and nutmeg. Scrape the slightly cooled greens mixture into the bowl and stir until the filling is evenly mixed. [2]

Fill the pie, crack the eggs, and bake: Scrape the filling into the baked pie crust and spread it into an even layer. Use the back of a spoon to make six large, evenly spaced indentations throughout the filling. Crack the remaining eggs into the indentations and season the tops with more salt and pepper. Carefully transfer the pie to the oven and bake until the whites are opaque and set and the yolks are still soft, 25 to 30 minutes. [3]

Serve: Remove the pie from the oven and let cool for 15 minutes before slicing into wedges (1 egg per slice). Serve with hot sauce.

---

[2] Make sure to let the greens cool several minutes before adding them to the cream and egg mixture, otherwise they might cook the eggs. The filling can be warm when you scrape it into the baked crust.

[3] Keep a watchful eye on the eggs while they're in the oven, especially after you hit the 20-minute mark—the whites will look raw and jiggly for most of the bake time, then turn opaque and set quickly. Try not to overcook them, otherwise the yolks will be dry.

Clam and Fennel Pizza
with Gremolata

Serves 4

CLAM AND FENNEL PIZZA

½ recipe **Soft and Pillowy Flatbread** dough (page 349), or 1 lb store-bought pizza dough

½ cup dry **white wine**

4 pounds (1.8kg) **littleneck clams**, scrubbed

¼ cup **extra-virgin olive oil**, plus more for assembling and serving

12 **garlic** cloves, smashed and peeled

1 large bulb **fennel** with stalks and fronds (12.6 oz / 357g), bulb halved, cored, and thinly sliced; thick stalks thinly sliced; fronds reserved for gremolata (below)

½ teaspoon **crushed red pepper flakes**, plus more for serving

FENNEL GREMOLATA

3 tablespoons very finely chopped **fresh flat-leaf parsley**

3 tablespoons very finely chopped **fennel fronds**

1 **garlic** clove, finely grated

2 teaspoons finely grated **lemon zest**

Diamond Crystal kosher salt

The smell of sliced garlic frying in olive oil is one of my earliest food memories. This was a frequent smell in my house growing up, and was usually a sign that my dad was making linguine and clams. It's a dish my family has cooked and shared for years and something I crave regularly. This pizza translates all the taste memories of that dish into pizza form (plus a welcome addition in the form of fennel, a great bedfellow of bivalves). Like the pasta original, this dish is all about the clams and calls for a whopping 4 pounds. Anything less just felt skimpy, and this quantity guarantees a clam in every bite. This pizza is every bit as craveable as the pasta version and, similarly, makeable on a weeknight if you use store-bought dough. **1**

Have the dough ready: Set up the flatbread dough for its first rise (if you want to make a full recipe of flatbread dough, use the other half to make flatbreads). While the dough is rising, prepare the clams and aromatics.

Steam the clams: In a medium Dutch oven or large saucepan, bring the wine to a boil over medium-high heat, then add the clams and cover. Cook for about 7 minutes, then remove the lid and use tongs to transfer any clams that have opened to a large bowl. Give the unopened clams in the Dutch oven a toss, cover, and continue to cook, checking every couple of minutes and transferring clams as they open to the bowl. Cook until all the clams are open (discard any shells that don't open after 15 minutes). Set the clams aside to cool, then slowly pour ¾ cup of the cooking liquid into a heatproof measuring cup and set aside. **2** (Discard any remaining liquid, then rinse and dry the Dutch oven.)

Cook the aromatics: In the same Dutch oven, heat the olive oil over medium-high heat until shimmering. Add the smashed garlic and cook, stirring often, until golden, about 3 minutes. Add the sliced fennel bulb and stalks and red pepper flakes and cook, stirring often, until the fennel is soft and browned in some places, 8 to 10 minutes. Add the reserved clam liquid to the Dutch oven, scraping the bottom to dissolve any browned bits. Continue to cook, stirring occasionally, until the bottom of the Dutch oven is nearly dry, about 5 minutes. Remove from (continues)

---

1 To use store-bought pizza dough in place of homemade, start at the step where you stretch the dough on the baking sheet, then make your fennel and clam topping while the dough sits covered at room temperature. Store-bought pizza dough is typically less active than yeast dough made at home, so you likely won't see a lot of puffing or other evidence of proofing. It'll still turn out great!

2 The liquid from the clams is gray and murky, which is totally normal. Just make sure when you pour it off you do it slowly, which will make sure any grit released from the clams stays in the Dutch oven and not on your pizza.

the heat and set aside to cool. Taste the fennel mixture—it probably doesn't need salt because the clam liquid is very salty, but add a pinch if you think it could take it.

Add the clams: Pick the cooled clams from their shells and toss into the Dutch oven with the fennel mixture (discard the shells).

Preheat the oven: Arrange an oven rack in the center position and preheat the oven to 500°F.

Stretch and proof the dough: When the dough is risen, uncover and use your fist to punch it down lightly to expel some of the gases that built up during the first rise. Generously drizzle a large rimmed baking sheet with olive oil and turn the dough out onto the baking sheet. Turn the dough to coat in oil and gently stretch it across the baking sheet into a thin oval that measures about 15 inches long and 10 inches wide. (If the dough springs back stubbornly, cover it with an oiled sheet of plastic wrap and let it rest 5 minutes before trying again.) Cover the stretched dough with an oiled sheet of plastic wrap and let it sit at room temperature until puffed, 20 to 25 minutes.

Make the gremolata: While the dough is proofing on the baking sheet, in a small bowl, toss together the chopped parsley, chopped fennel fronds, grated garlic, and grated lemon zest. Season with salt and set aside.

Parbake the pizza: Uncover the dough and bake until the surface is bubbled and browned in spots around the edges, 5 to 7 minutes. Remove from the oven (but leave the oven on).

Top and bake again: Sprinkle the fennel and clam mixture evenly across the surface of the dough, leaving a 1-inch border. Bake again until the bottom of the crust is browned and crisp, another 5 to 7 minutes. Remove from the oven and let the pizza cool slightly. Sprinkle with the gremolata, drizzle with olive oil, and top with more red pepper flakes, if desired. Cut the pizza into squares or wedges and serve immediately. [3]

---

[3] You can also spread the fennel and clam topping and gremolata on baked **Soft and Crispy Focaccia** (page 289) or on grilled bread slices for delicious clam toast.

Garlic and Rosemary Focaccia Topping

¼ cup **extra-virgin olive oil**

4 **garlic** cloves, very thinly sliced

2 tablespoons fresh **rosemary** leaves

Flaky salt, for sprinkling the top

Prepare the garlic-rosemary mixture: In a small bowl, stir together the olive oil, garlic, and rosemary and set aside.

Top the focaccia: After the focaccia has finished its second rise, spoon the garlic and rosemary mixture over the dimpled dough, then drizzle with any oil left in the bowl. Sprinkle the surface generously with flaky salt. Bake as directed.

Charred Cauliflower Focaccia Topping

⅓ cup plus 3 tablespoons **extra-virgin olive oil**

2 pounds (907g) **cauliflower** (about 1 medium) florets, grated on the large holes of a box grater, stem and core coarsely chopped

½ teaspoon **Diamond Crystal kosher salt**

½ teaspoon **hot paprika**

½ teaspoon **crushed red pepper flakes**

½ cup finely chopped **fresh flat-leaf parsley**

3 tablespoons **capers**

4 **garlic** cloves, very thinly sliced

Flaky salt, for sprinkling the top

1 **lemon**, for finely grating on top

Prepare the charred cauliflower mixture: Heat a large skillet (preferably cast-iron) over high heat. Add ⅓ cup of the oil and swirl to coat. Add the cauliflower in three batches, cooking and stirring in between batches until the cauliflower has softened before adding the next. Stir in the kosher salt and continue to cook the cauliflower over high heat, stirring only occasionally to allow the bottom layer to brown, until the mixture is browned all over. Stir in the hot paprika and red pepper flakes and remove the skillet from the heat. Scrape the cauliflower into a medium bowl and let sit until no longer hot, stirring once or twice, about 10 minutes. Stir in the parsley, capers, garlic, and remaining 3 tablespoons olive oil and set aside.

Top the focaccia: After the focaccia has finished its second rise, scatter the cauliflower mixture across the dimpled dough and sprinkle with flaky salt. Bake as directed. Immediately after the focaccia comes out of the oven, finely grate the lemon zest over the top.

VARIATION 3

Tomato, Garlic, and Thyme Focaccia Topping

2 medium **beefsteak tomatoes** (about 1 lb / 454g), halved horizontally

¼ cup **extra-virgin olive oil** (2 oz / 57g)

3 **garlic** cloves, very thinly sliced

½ teaspoon **crushed red pepper flakes**

½ teaspoon **Diamond Crystal kosher salt**

8 ounces (227g) **cherry, Sun Gold**, or other small **tomatoes**, halved (about 2 cups)

Leaves from 3 sprigs **fresh thyme**

Flaky salt, for sprinkling the top

Prepare the tomato mixture: Grasp the rounded side of a tomato half in your palm and squeeze to force out the seeds and surrounding jelly (discard). Repeat with all the halves. Working over a medium bowl, grate the cut sides of the tomatoes on the large holes of a box grater and keep going until all that's left are the skins (discard—and watch out for your knuckles). You should have about ¾ cup grated tomato flesh. Stir in the olive oil, garlic, red pepper flakes, and salt and set aside.

Top the focaccia: After the focaccia has finished its second rise, spoon the tomato mixture over the dimpled dough. Press the cherry tomato halves into the dough all over. Sprinkle with thyme leaves and a light dusting of flaky salt. Bake as directed.

VARIATION 4

Purple Potato Focaccia Topping

Special Equipment:
Mandoline

12 ounces (340g) small **Yukon Gold** and/or **purple potatoes**, scrubbed

1½ teaspoons **Diamond Crystal kosher salt**

1 large **shallot** (2 oz / 57g), thinly sliced crosswise

¼ cup **extra-virgin olive oil**

¼ cup thinly sliced **chives**

Freshly ground **black pepper**

Flaky salt, for sprinkling the top

Prepare the potato mixture: Working over a large bowl filled with room temperature water, very thinly slice the unpeeled potatoes on a mandoline—you want them thin enough that the raw slices are flexible and will bend without breaking. Drain the potatoes in a colander, then rinse them under running water to remove any surface starches. Return to the same bowl and fill it with warm tap water. Add 1 teaspoon of the kosher salt to the bowl and let the potatoes sit in the salted water for 10 to 15 minutes. Drain and pat the potatoes dry. Dry the bowl, return the potatoes to it, and add the shallot, olive oil, chives, and remaining ½ teaspoon kosher salt and toss until all the slices are evenly coated. Set aside.

Top the focaccia: After the focaccia has finished its second rise, scatter the potato mixture across the dimpled dough, overlapping the slices. Top generously with black pepper, sprinkle with flaky salt, and bake as directed. Note that the potatoes will largely cover the surface of the dough and prevent it from browning, but another doneness indicator is that the edges of the potato slices will brown and curl.

Honey Tahini Challah

Makes 2 medium challahs

1½ teaspoons **active dry yeast** (0.18 oz / 5g)

½ cup **honey** (6 oz / 170g)

½ cup **tahini** (4.5 oz / 128g)

3 large **egg yolks** (1.8 oz / 50g), at room temperature

⅓ cup **extra-virgin olive oil** (2.6 oz / 73g), plus more for the bowl

3 large **eggs** (5.3 oz / 150g), at room temperature

4⅓ cups **bread flour** [1] (19.9 oz / 563g), plus more for kneading

2 teaspoons **Diamond Crystal kosher salt** (0.21 oz / 6g)

Sesame seeds, for sprinkling the top

I love to bake challah but hardly ever made it the same way twice. I always added extra-virgin olive oil and honey for flavor, but constantly changed everything else, trying to find the formula that would produce a flavorful loaf with a bready but light crumb and super shiny crust. In pursuit of this goal, one day I added tahini to the dough on a whim. It imparted a subtle sesame flavor—a natural fit for challah since I like to load the top with sesame seeds—but also such silky richness that I decided I'd only ever make challah with it again. For anyone looking to get more comfortable baking with yeast, this recipe is a good place to start. There's no mixer required, and the only necessary skill is forming a three-strand braid (if you don't know how, look it up on YouTube!).

Dissolve the yeast: In a small saucepan, gently warm ¼ cup water (2 oz / 57g) over low heat, swirling the pan, just until it's lukewarm but not hot (if you have an instant-read thermometer, it should register about 105°F). You can warm the water in the microwave, too, but beware of overheating. Pour the water into a medium bowl and whisk in the yeast to dissolve. Set aside until the mixture is cloudy and slightly puffed, about 5 minutes.

Make the dough: To the bowl with the yeast mixture, add the honey, tahini, egg yolks, olive oil, 2 of the whole eggs, and ½ cup room temperature water (4 oz / 113g) and whisk to combine. In a large bowl, whisk 4⅓ cups of the flour (22.2 oz / 630g) and salt just to combine. Make a well in the center of the flour and pour in the egg mixture. Mix with a wooden spoon, starting in the center and working outward to incorporate the flour, until you have a shaggy dough. Knead the mixture inside the bowl several times until you have a cohesive dough with a few floury spots. Turn the dough out onto a generously floured work surface and knead, adding more as necessary to prevent sticking, until the dough is very soft, smooth, supple, and just a little bit tacky, 5 to 10 minutes (when you poke a finger into the ball of dough and remove it, the dough should cling to it gently and then release). [2]

Let the dough rise one time: Form the dough into a tight ball. Lightly coat the inside of a large bowl with olive oil and place the dough inside. Cover the bowl with a damp towel and let the dough rise in a warm place until it is about doubled in size, 1½ to 3 hours. When you poke it with a finger, the dough should feel very airy and spring back, holding a (continues)

DO AHEAD
The challahs, wrapped well and stored at room temperature, will keep up to 3 days or can be frozen up to 2 months.

[1] Using bread flour ensures that your challah has a pull-apart texture, but you can use all-purpose if that's all you have.

[2] To speed up this process, you can assemble the dough in a stand mixer and mix with the dough hook attachment on medium speed for 5 to 8 minutes. It's not a very sticky dough, though, and is easy to work by hand.

slight impression. (At this point, the dough can be covered with plastic wrap and refrigerated up to 12 hours.)

Portion the dough: Uncover the dough and use your fist to punch it down lightly to expel some of the gases that built up during the first rise. Turn the dough out onto a clean, unfloured surface. Divide the dough in half and then divide each half into 3 equal pieces to get 6 portions. ❸ Roll out each portion into a strand about 16 inches long, pressing down on the ends as you roll to create a rope that's thicker in the midsection and tapers off at the ends (the unfloured surface provides traction for the dough so it stretches more easily). Dust the dough strands lightly with flour and roll to coat, then place 3 of the dough strands side by side on a parchment-lined baking sheet and the other 3 on another parchment-lined sheet (the dusting of flour will keep the strands more defined in the baked challahs).

Braid the challahs: Working with one loaf at a time, begin to braid the strands starting in the middle, lifting and moving the outer strand to the center, alternating from left to right with each pass and tugging on the strands lightly to make a tall, three-dimensional braid. Pinch the ends together to seal and tuck them underneath the braid, then reverse the process with the other half of the strands. Pinch and tuck the other end. Repeat with the remaining dough strands to make the second loaf.

Let the dough rise a second time: Cover the two braids loosely with plastic wrap and let them sit in a warm place until they have expanded to about 1½ times their original size, 1 to 2 hours (if the dough was refrigerated overnight, this step could take 30 minutes to 1 hour longer).

Preheat the oven and make the egg wash: Arrange two oven racks in the upper and lower thirds of the oven and preheat to 350°F. In a small bowl, beat the remaining egg with a fork until smooth.

Finish the challahs and bake: Uncover the dough and brush the surfaces of both loaves with the egg. Sprinkle generously with sesame seeds and bake the challahs until the surfaces are shiny and deep golden brown, 25 to 35 minutes, switching racks and rotating the pans front to back after 20 minutes. Let cool completely on the baking sheets.

---

❸ You could divide the dough in thirds and make one giant loaf instead of two smaller ones. Keep in mind it will take longer on the second rise and longer in the oven. Use the same size and color indicators to guide you on doneness.

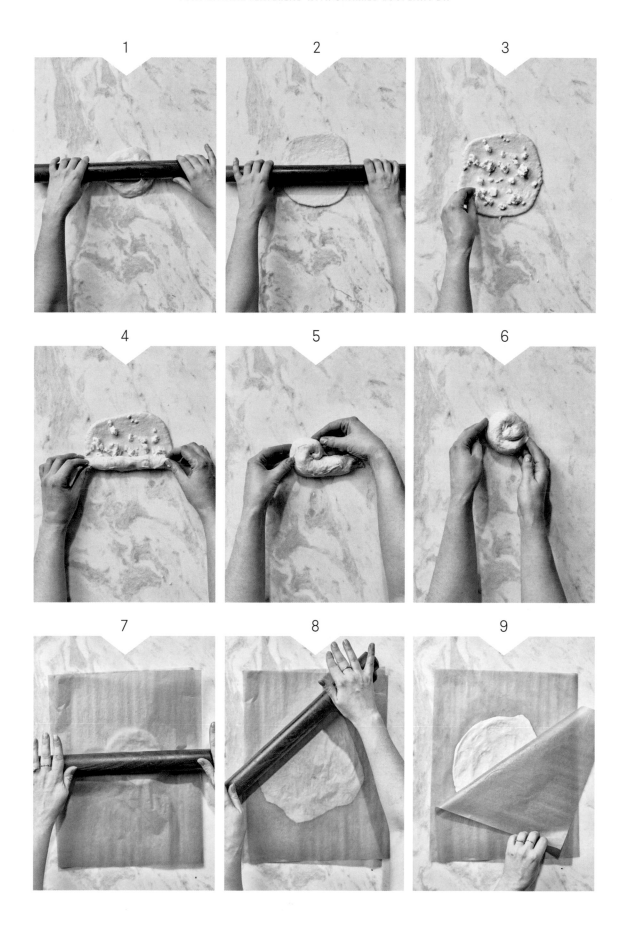

Pigs in a Brioche Blanket

Makes 48 bite-sized pieces

Special Equipment:
Stand mixer (for the Brioche Dough)

PIGS IN BRIOCHE

½ recipe **Brioche Dough** (page 352), chilled ①

All-purpose flour, for rolling out

8 **all-beef hot dogs** (about 2 oz / 57g each), patted dry, pricked all over with the tip of a paring knife ②

1 large **egg**, beaten

1 tablespoon **sesame seeds**

CREAMY MUSTARD DIP

¼ cup **spicy brown mustard** (2.8 oz / 80g)

⅓ cup **sour cream** (3 oz / 86g)

1 teaspoon **honey**

Pinch of **kosher salt**

Pinch of **cayenne pepper**, or more to taste

While working full-time in the test kitchen at *Bon Appétit* for many years, I heard a lot of food editors argue over a lot of opinions, yet there was broad consensus around one core belief: that there exists no finer hors d'oeuvre than pigs in a blanket. To create my own best version of the classic finger food, I replaced the usual puff pastry with brioche (in a nod to another favorite of mine, the French dish *saucisson en brioche*). It's still buttery and rich like classic pigs in a blanket, but whereas the typical puff pastry wrapper has a tendency to stay flabby in places after baking, the yeasted brioche cooks all the way through. Not only are they insanely snackable, but I love how the dish is basically hot dogs baked *in their buns*. Cut into pieces and served with a stir-together creamy mustard dip, it truly is the ultimate party food.

Portion the dough: Use your fist to lightly punch down the brioche dough to expel some of the gases that built up during the first rise. Turn the dough out onto a clean work surface. Use a bench scraper to divide the dough into 8 equal pieces each weighing about 2.25 ounces / 64g (eyeball it if you don't have a scale). Arrange the pieces on a rimmed baking sheet, spacing them evenly, then cover with plastic wrap and refrigerate to keep them cold (cold dough is easier to maneuver around the hot dogs).

Preheat the oven and prepare the baking sheet: Arrange an oven rack in the center position and preheat the oven to 350°F. Line a second rimmed baking sheet with parchment paper and set aside.

Roll out the dough: Remove a piece of dough from the refrigerator and roll it out on an unfloured surface into a thin rope measuring about 22 inches long (the unfloured surface provides traction for the dough so it stretches more easily; if it starts to stick, dust it with a pinch of flour). Return the rope to the baking sheet in the refrigerator, tucking it back underneath the plastic, and repeat the rolling process with the remaining pieces of dough one at a time. The point here is to keep the brioche cold so the dough is easier to work with and all the pieces proof at the same rate.

(continues)

DO AHEAD
The pigs in a blanket are best eaten the day they're made but will keep, covered and refrigerated, up to 3 days. The hot dogs can be wrapped in brioche, covered on the baking sheet, and refrigerated for several hours before proofing and baking.

① Go ahead and double the recipe if you're really feeding a crowd, using a full recipe of brioche and 16 dogs!

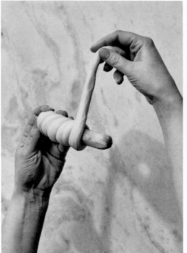

Cover the hot dogs: Remove the baking sheet from the refrigerator. Working one piece at a time, lightly dust a hot dog with flour to coat, then take a piece of brioche and, starting from the midpoints of both, wind the dough around the hot dog until you reach one end. Tug gently to stretch the dough and overlap it onto itself as you wind, then wrap the rest of the rope around the other end of the hot dog. Pinch the ends so the brioche seals to itself. Place on the parchment-lined baking sheet and cover with plastic wrap while you repeat the process with the remaining dogs and pieces of brioche.

Proof the pigs in a blanket: Once all the hot dogs are in their blankets and covered on the baking sheet, let them sit at room temperature until the dough is puffed and springs back but holds a slight imprint when poked with a finger, 25 to 35 minutes.

Egg wash, sprinkle with sesame, and bake: Uncover the dogs and gently brush every surface of the dough with the egg. Sprinkle the sesame seeds evenly over top. Bake the pigs in a blanket until they're deep golden brown all over, 25 to 30 minutes. Remove from the oven and let cool on the baking sheet.

Make the dipping sauce: In a small bowl, stir the mustard, sour cream, and honey until smooth. Season with the salt and cayenne.

Slice and serve: Cut each of the cooled pigs in a blanket crosswise into 6 pieces and serve them on a platter with the dipping sauce.

---

2 Use any brand of hot dog you like, from an old standby like Hebrew National to a fancy artisanal dog, as long as each dog weighs around 2 oz. Keep in mind you might need to wind the brioche a bit tighter around a hot dog that's on the longer and skinnier side to make it stretch the full length. (Alternatively, you could have a bit of extra brioche if using a more petite brand, in which case just pinch off the excess.) Whatever you use, don't forget to prick them all over, otherwise they could potentially burst in the oven.

Ricotta and Broccoli Rabe Pie

Serves 10

Special Equipment:
9-inch springform pan

1½ teaspoons **Diamond Crystal kosher salt** (0.16 oz / 5g), plus more for the saucepan

1 bunch **broccoli rabe** (13 oz / 368g), stem ends trimmed

16 ounces **whole-milk ricotta cheese** (about 1¾ cups / 454g)

4 ounces (113g) low-moisture **mozzarella cheese**, coarsely grated (about 1 cup)

2 ounces (57g) finely grated **Parmesan cheese** (about ½ cup)

4 **anchovy fillets** mashed with the flat side of a knife into a paste

3 **garlic** cloves, finely grated

1 teaspoon finely grated **lemon zest**

Generous pinch of **crushed red pepper flakes**

4 large **eggs** (7 oz / 200g)

1 cup pitted **Castelvetrano olives** (5 oz / 142g) [1]

2 recipes **Flaky Olive Oil Dough** (page 341)

All-purpose flour, for rolling out

Bitter, multitextured broccoli rabe is high on my list of favorite vegetables. I was looking for a way to bake with it, and this savory ricotta pie was the answer. I combine the broccoli rabe with all the flavors I like to use when I cook with it: garlic, anchovies, lemon, Parmesan, and briny, buttery Castelvetrano olives. Not only is the flavor of the **Flaky Olive Oil Dough** complementary here, but it's sturdier than pie dough and can stand up to the hefty ricotta filling. This pie makes an excellent lunch, dinner, picnic, or snack, and keeps well for several days.

Blanch the broccoli rabe: Fill a medium bowl halfway with ice water and set aside. Bring a large saucepan of salted water to a boil over high heat. Add the broccoli rabe and submerge. Cook the broccoli rabe until it's tender and the tines of the fork slide easily into the stems, about 2 minutes. Use tongs to transfer the broccoli rabe to the bowl of ice water and agitate so it cools down quickly.

Drain and chop the broccoli rabe: Remove the broccoli rabe from the bowl and squeeze firmly to wring out as much water as possible. Pat the pieces dry on paper towels or on a clean kitchen towel (you want it really dry to avoid watering down the filling) and place on a cutting board. Slice the broccoli rabe crosswise into ½-inch pieces and set aside.

Make the filling: In a medium bowl, stir together the ricotta, mozzarella, Parmesan, anchovies, garlic, lemon zest, red pepper flakes, 1½ teaspoons salt, and 3 of the eggs with a flexible spatula until the mixture is smooth and the anchovies and garlic are distributed throughout. Fold in the olives and chopped broccoli rabe, then set the filling aside while you preheat the oven and roll the pastry.

Preheat the oven and beat the remaining egg: Arrange an oven rack in the center position and preheat the oven to 425°F. In a small bowl, beat the remaining egg with a fork until no streaks remain and set aside.

Roll out the pastry: Remove both pieces of the olive oil dough from the refrigerator and unwrap. Use a knife or bench scraper to lop off about one-third of one piece of dough and press it onto the other piece (you want one smaller piece of pastry for the top of the pie and one larger for the bottom). (continues)

DO AHEAD
The ricotta pie is best served on the first or second day but will keep, covered tightly and stored at room temperature, up to 3 days.

[1] Use any kind of olives you like, although I prefer the buttery, mild flavor of Castelvetrano olives.

Roll out the smaller piece of dough between two sheets of parchment paper, occasionally lifting and repositioning the parchment and turning the dough to prevent wrinkling, until you have a 10-inch round. Lift the dough off the parchment and lay it back down to allow it to contract if that's what it wants, then place the base of the springform pan on top of the dough. Cut around it with a wheel cutter or paring knife so you have a smooth round (discard the scraps). Transfer the round to a plate and refrigerate. Roll out the second piece of dough the same way you did the first until you have a 13-inch round.

If the pastry starts to shrink back as you're trying to roll it, let it rest between the sheets of parchment on the surface for 10 minutes, then try again. [2]

Assemble the pie: Peel the top layer of parchment paper off the dough for the bottom crust. Place the base of the springform pan on the work surface, then use the bottom layer of parchment to invert the dough onto the base. Remove the parchment paper and make sure the pan base is centered beneath the dough round. Fold the edges of the dough in toward the center, making large folds like a galette, so all

the pastry is sitting inside the base. Lock the outer ring of the pan onto the base and unfold the dough, pressing it into the bottom and up the sides all the way around, smoothing any creases, to line the pan (see photographs on pages 310–311 for a visual guide). Scrape the filling into the pan, working it into an even layer. Remove the dough round from the refrigerator and place it over the filling, pressing to eliminate any air pockets, then brush the top of the pastry with the beaten egg. Fold the edges of the bottom layer of pastry down and over the top layer, pressing to seal them together. Brush around the perimeter with more egg and use the tip of a paring knife to cut a few slits in the top.

Reduce the oven temperature and bake: Transfer the pan to the oven and decrease the temperature to 350°F. Bake until the pastry is puffed and deep golden brown across the surface and pulling away from the sides, 1 hour 10 minutes to 1 hour 20 minutes. Let the pie cool completely in the pan, which will take several hours. Remove the outer metal ring from the pan and cut into wedges to serve.

---

[2] This dough is prone to shrinking, so stop rolling if you feel it start to resist. You want to roll it out thin, and a relaxed dough will roll out more easily and won't contract as much during baking.

Fortunately, the olive oil dough can sit at room temperature for long periods without compromising the texture, unlike butter-based pie dough.

All Allium
Deep-Dish Quiche

Serves 8

Special Equipment:
9-inch springform pan, pie weights or
4 cups dried beans or rice (for
parbaking), standard or handheld
blender (optional)

Flaky All-Butter Pie Dough (page 333)

All-purpose flour, for rolling out and
making a bit of paste for patching

4 large **eggs** (7 oz / 200g), at room
temperature

1 medium **yellow onion** (8 oz / 227g),
peeled and halved through the root end

Neutral oil, such as vegetable or
grapeseed, for brushing

2 tablespoons **unsalted butter** (1 oz / 28g)

4 ounces (113g) **pancetta** or **bacon**,
chopped

4 **garlic** cloves, smashed and peeled

5 **scallions**, chopped

1 large **shallot** (2 oz / 57g), coarsely
chopped

1 medium **leek** (10 oz / 283g), dark
green tops discarded, white and light
green stalk split lengthwise, rinsed, and
chopped

1½ teaspoons **Diamond Crystal kosher
salt** (0.16 oz / 5g), plus more as needed

Freshly ground **black pepper**

2 teaspoons **white wine vinegar**

2 cups **half-and-half** (17 oz / 482g), at
room temperature

A quiche is simple in concept, yes, but this recipe has a difficulty rating
of 4 because it's actually quite a technical process. The pastry must
be thoroughly weighted down and baked before the filling is added to
prevent sogginess and ensure the structural integrity of the tall sides
(how many times have you had a quiche with a less-than-crisp, sad, pale
bottom?). However, this also makes it prone to cracking, which leads to
the liquidy filling running out of the crust. I try to protect against leaks by
diligently patching the crust and setting it with a bit of egg wash before
adding the custard, but if it springs a leak, your quiche will still taste
great and look impressive. I like this take with a little pancetta and a
whole lot of cooked-down oniony things.

Preheat the oven: Arrange an oven rack in the center position and
preheat the oven to 425°F.

Roll out the pastry and line the pan: Remove the pie dough from the
refrigerator and let it sit at room temperature for about 5 minutes to
soften slightly. Place the dough on a lightly floured surface and use
a rolling pin to beat the dough all across the surface to make it more
pliable. Dust the top and underside of the dough with more flour, then
roll it out, dusting with more flour as needed to prevent sticking, into
a 13-inch round. Slide the base of the springform pan underneath the
dough round, centering it. Fold the edges of the dough inward, letting it
overlap onto itself, so the entire pastry is sitting inside the metal base.
Snap the outer ring into place around the base, then unfold the dough
and press it firmly against the sides (see the photographs on pages
310–311 for a visual guide). The dough will fold onto itself in a few places,
which is fine; just press firmly over the folds to even out the thickness all
the way around. Transfer the pan to the freezer and chill until the pastry
is very firm, about 10 minutes.

Bake the crust: Remove the pan from the freezer, line the bottom and
sides with a double layer of foil, and fill the pan with pie weights, dried
beans, or rice. ① Place the pan on a foil-lined baking sheet and bake
until the edges of the pastry are golden, 20 to 25 minutes. (continues)

DO AHEAD
The quiche, covered and refrigerated, will
keep up to 3 days but is best served the
day it's made (the pastry will soften over
time). Rewarm the quiche, uncovered on
a baking sheet, in a 300°F oven.

① Make sure the double layer of foil
beneath the pie weights is very sturdy
since you must use it to lift the hot,
heavy weights out of the hot crust. If the

weights were to bust through the foil, it
would be a huge mess to clean up (and
a huge pain). If you're in doubt, reinforce
with a third layer of foil.

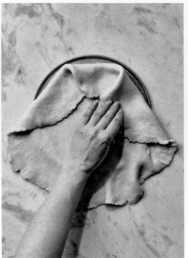

Remove the pan from the oven and carefully lift out the foil and weights. Reduce the oven temperature to 325°F (baking it again at this lower temperature minimizes shrinkage, helping to prevent cracks). Return the baking sheet to the oven and bake until the pastry is golden all over, 30 to 35 minutes longer. Remove from the oven and set aside. (Leave the oven on.)

Patch, egg wash, and bake the crust again: In a small bowl, thoroughly mix a couple tablespoons of flour with a bit of water until you have a thick, smooth paste. Smear the paste into any cracks or crevices like it's spackle to patch them, especially focusing on where the bottom meets the sides (this will help prevent leaks). [2] Beat one of the eggs in a small bowl with a fork until streak-free, then brush the bottom and sides of the pastry with the egg (reserve the leftover egg for the filling). Return the baking sheet to the oven and bake just until the egg is set, about 5 minutes. Remove from the oven and set aside to cool. (Leave the oven on.)

Make the decorative onion petals (optional): If skipping this step, coarsely chop the onion and proceed to the next step. Preheat a medium skillet (preferably cast-iron) over medium-high heat. Brush the cut sides of the onion with a bit of oil and place them in the pan oiled-side down. Cook the halves undisturbed until the inner layers of the onion have blackened all over (the outer layers will lift away from the skillet), about 5 minutes. Use a spatula to carefully remove the onion halves from the skillet (the blackened parts might stick). Transfer them to a cutting board to cool and remove the skillet from the heat but reserve it for the filling. When the onions are cool enough to handle, pull out the inner layers and separate them into "petals." Set 7 or 8 petals aside, then chop the rest of the onion.

Cook the allium mixture: Set the skillet over medium heat, add the butter, and heat until it's melted and foamy, about 30 seconds. Add the pancetta and cook, stirring often, until the pieces are browned and

---

[2] Definitely take some time to patch the crust, but know that leaks happen and it's not a big deal. Any egg that seeps through the crust cooks quickly against the hot pan and eventually seals itself, so the filling won't continue to leak out as the quiche bakes.

crispy and the fat has rendered, about 4 minutes.
Use a slotted spoon to transfer the crispy pancetta
to a small bowl, leaving the fat in the skillet. To the
skillet, add the garlic, scallions, shallot, leek, and
chopped onion and cook, stirring often, until the
onion is very soft and translucent and many of the
bits are browned around the edges, 12 to 15 minutes.
Season the mixture lightly with salt and a generous
amount of black pepper, then stir in the vinegar.
Remove the skillet from the heat and set aside
to cool.

Make the custard: In a blender (or in a bowl using a
handheld blender or a whisk), combine the half-
and-half, remaining 3 eggs, leftover beaten egg,
and 1½ teaspoons salt (0.16 oz / 5g) and blend until
completely smooth.

Assemble the quiche: Scatter the allium mixture and
pancetta across the surface of the crust, then slowly
pour in the custard, filling as high as the crust will
allow (depending on the height, you might have to
leave a bit out). Scatter the onion petals across the
surface of the custard, making sure a little bit of
custard fills the petals like a cup.

Bake the quiche: Carefully transfer the quiche to the
oven and bake until the center is just a bit wobbly
when you shake the pan but looks set across the
surface, 50 to 60 minutes. Remove from the oven
and let the quiche cool completely in the pan.

Slice and serve: Once the quiche is cool, remove the
ring (if a bit of the custard leaked, slide a paring knife
between the crust and the pan to loosen the quiche,
then remove the ring). Cut into slices and serve.

Pull-Apart Sour Cream and Chive Rolls

Makes 24 rolls

Special Equipment:
Stand mixer, instant-read thermometer, 13 × 9-inch pan (preferably metal)

½ cup plus 2 tablespoons **whole milk** (5 oz / 142g)

5⅓ cups **bread flour** (1 lb 8.4 oz / 693g), plus more for dusting

1½ teaspoons **active dry yeast** (0.18 oz / 5g)

1 cup **sour cream** (8.2 oz / 232g), at room temperature

¼ cup **sugar** (1.8 oz / 50g)

4 teaspoons **Diamond Crystal kosher salt** (0.42 oz / 12g) ①

3 large **eggs** (5.3 oz / 150g)

8 tablespoons **unsalted butter** (4 oz / 113g), cut into pieces, at room temperature

½ cup very finely chopped **chives** (0.71 oz / 20g)

Flaky salt and freshly ground **black pepper**

I don't care much for dinner rolls unless we're talking about the soft, buttery, pull-apart Parker House variety—then they're pretty much all I care about! This recipe is inspired by Parker House rolls but manages to make ones that are even more pillowy, thanks to a technique borrowed from Japanese milk bread that uses something called a *tangzhong*. A *tangzhong* is a cooked paste made from flour, milk, and water that, when added to a dough, increases the ability of that dough to hold onto moisture. The resulting texture is ultrasoft and tender. Add the tang of sour cream and the mild oniony flavor of chives, and you have dinner rolls so good they make it very hard not to fill up on bread.

Make the *tangzhong*: In a small saucepan, whisk ½ cup of the milk (4 oz / 113g), ⅓ cup of the flour (1.5 oz / 43g), and ½ cup water (4 oz / 113g) until smooth. Set the saucepan over medium heat and cook, whisking constantly, until you have a very stiff paste that resembles mashed potatoes, about 2 minutes. Remove the saucepan from the heat and scrape the mixture into the bowl of a stand mixer fitted with the dough hook attachment.

Proof the yeast: Gently warm the remaining 2 tablespoons milk in the same saucepan over low heat until it's lukewarm but not hot, about 105°F on an instant-read thermometer. Remove from the heat and whisk in the yeast until dissolved. Set the saucepan aside until the mixture is foamy, about 5 minutes.

Mix the dough: To the bowl with the *tangzhong*, add the sour cream, sugar, kosher salt, 2 of the eggs, 4 tablespoons of the butter (2 oz / 57g), and the remaining 5 cups bread flour (22.9 oz / 650g). Scrape in the yeast mixture and mix on low until a shaggy dough forms. Increase the speed to medium and mix, scraping down the sides occasionally with a flexible spatula or dough scraper and adding more flour by the tablespoon if the dough is very sticky, until the dough is very smooth and supple, 8 to 10 minutes.

Let the dough rise once: Scrape the dough out of the bowl and onto a clean work surface. Form it into a smooth ball and dust lightly with flour. Place the dough inside a separate large, clean bowl and cover tightly with plastic wrap. Let it sit in a warm place until roughly doubled in size, 1 to 1½ hours. (continues)

DO AHEAD
The rolls are best eaten the day they're made but will keep, stored airtight at room temperature, up to 3 days. The rolls can be formed, placed in the prepared pan, covered, and refrigerated 1 day

ahead (do not let them rise first). Remove from the refrigerator and let rise at room temperature before baking (because they're starting from cold, this could take up to 3 hours).

① Trust the amount of kosher salt in the recipe—4 teaspoons might seem like a lot, but without it, the rolls will taste flat. (Note: If you're using Morton kosher salt, you should use half this amount.)

[3,4] Starting at one end, fold up the dough several times, enclosing the chives in a loose roll. Flatten the roll with the heel of your hand into a long rectangle.

[5] Dusting with more flour as needed, roll out the dough again into a 16 × 6-inch rectangle.

[6] Use a wheel cutter or bench scraper to cut the dough into twenty-four 2-inch squarish pieces (8 × 3 grid).

Form the rolls: [7] Working with one piece of dough at a time, gather all the edges and pinch them together to form a teardrop shape. Place the piece of dough seam-side down on the work surface.

[8,9] Holding your fingers in a cupped position like you're playing the piano, place your hand on top of the piece of dough and drag the dough across the surface, moving your hand in a rapid circular motion, to form it into a tight ball. Do not add flour, as this step requires friction between the dough and the surface. Place the ball of dough in the prepared pan and repeat with the remaining pieces of dough, spacing them in a 4 × 6 grid.

Do the second rise and preheat the oven: Cover the pan with plastic wrap and let sit at room temperature until the rolls are nearly doubled in size, 45 to 60 minutes. Meanwhile, arrange an oven rack in the center position and preheat the oven to 375°F.

Brush with egg and bake: Beat the remaining egg in a small bowl with a fork until no streaks remain. Uncover the pan and gently brush the tops of the rolls with the egg, then sprinkle with flaky salt and black pepper. Bake the rolls until the tops are deep golden brown, 25 to 30 minutes.

Brush with more butter and let cool: Remove the pan from the oven and immediately brush the tops of the hot rolls with the remaining 2 tablespoons butter. Let the rolls cool in the pan for 15 minutes. Cut around the sides of the pan to loosen the rolls, then slide a metal spatula underneath to loosen the bottom. Slide the entire grid of rolls out and onto a wire rack to cool. Serve warm or at room temperature.

Prepare the pan: While the dough is rising, smear 2 tablespoons of the butter across the bottom and sides of a 13 × 9-inch pan, preferably metal (it will be a generous layer of butter, which is what you want). Set the pan aside.

Add the chives and portion the dough: [2] [1] Uncover the dough and use your fist to punch it down lightly to expel some of the gas that built up during the first rise. Turn the dough out onto a lightly floured surface and stretch it into a square.

[2] Roll it out into about a 12-inch square, dusting with more flour underneath as needed to prevent sticking, and sprinkle the chives evenly across the dough.

---

[2] Try to work quickly when you're forming the dough into individual rolls—if the dough sits on the counter too long it will start to proof, and you want to make sure all the rolls rise together at the same rate. Because 24 little rolls are a lot to get through, enlist help from a friend!

1

2

3

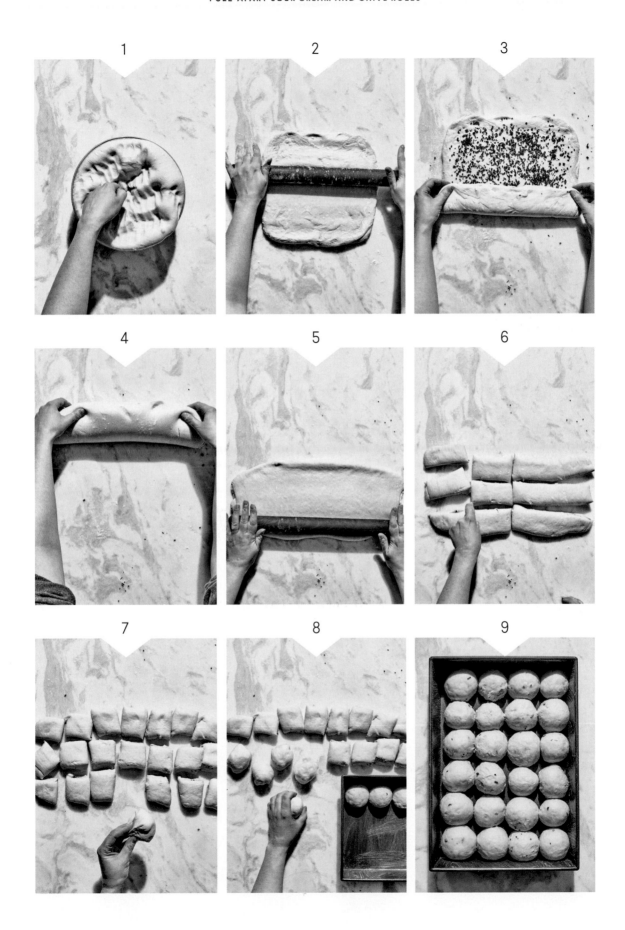

4

5

6

7

8

9

Foundation Recipes

On one hand, the recipes in this chapter are not stand-alone; they are used as components in other recipes elsewhere in the book. On the other, they exist independently, since recipes like **Pastry Cream** (page 321) or **Sweet Yeast Dough** (page 344) can be applied outside of this book in the general baking realm. I hope you get familiar with the doughs, fillings, and frostings in this chapter and eventually mix and match them on their own. That's when the possibilities become truly endless, and that's what baking is all about.

CREAM WHIPPED TO
SOFT PEAKS, PAGE 23

All-Purpose Crumble Topping

Makes about 3 cups

1 cup **all-purpose flour** (4.6 oz / 130g)

1 cup old-fashioned **rolled oats**
(3 oz / 90g)

⅓ cup packed **light brown sugar**
(2.3 oz / 65g)

1 teaspoon **ground cinnamon**

½ teaspoon **Diamond Crystal kosher salt**

10 tablespoons **unsalted butter**
(5 oz / 142g), cut into ½-inch pieces,
chilled

This is a very riffable basic crumble recipe that works as a topping on a variety of pies, tarts, and cakes.

Make the crumble: In a medium bowl, toss together the flour, oats, brown sugar, cinnamon, and salt until combined. Add the butter and toss to coat, then use your fingertips to work the butter into the flour mixture until no visible pieces of butter or floury spots remain. It should naturally clump together and hold its shape when squeezed. Cover and refrigerate the crumble until ready to use.

VARIATIONS

· **Almond Crumble:** Substitute 1 cup sliced almonds for the oats.

· **Buckwheat Crumble:** Replace ¼ cup of the all-purpose flour (1.2 oz / 33g) with ¼ cup buckwheat flour (1.2 oz / 33g).

DO AHEAD
The crumble mixture, covered and refrigerated, will keep up to 4 days.

Honey Almond Syrup

Makes about 1 cup

½ cup **honey** (6 oz / 170g)

½ teaspoon **almond extract**

Pinch of **kosher salt**

Congratulations, you have found the easiest recipe in this book! It's a simple syrup made with honey instead of granulated sugar and used as a soak to add moisture to pastries and cakes. I like the hint of almond flavor from the extract, which becomes subtler once it's incorporated into another recipe, but you could substitute vanilla extract or a tablespoon of rum, whisky, or brandy, if you prefer. Save any leftover syrup and use it for making cocktails.

DO AHEAD
The syrup, covered and stored in the refrigerator, will keep up to 3 weeks.

Make the syrup: In a 1-pint jar or plastic container, combine the honey, almond extract, and salt. Add ½ cup hot tap water (4 oz / 113g) and seal the jar or container. Shake vigorously until the honey is dissolved. Cover and chill until ready to use.

Pastry Cream

Makes about 2½ cups

2 cups **whole milk** (16 oz / 456g)

Seeds scraped from ½ **vanilla bean** or 1½ teaspoons **vanilla extract** or paste

½ teaspoon **Diamond Crystal kosher salt**

½ cup **sugar** (3.5 oz / 100g)

¼ cup **cornstarch** (1 oz / 30g)

5 large **egg yolks** (2.8 oz / 80g)

6 tablespoons **unsalted butter** (3 oz / 85g), cut into ½-inch pieces, chilled

Pastry cream is a type of custard made on the stovetop from milk, eggs, and sugar that's thickened with cornstarch. That probably doesn't sound like a great sell, but scented with vanilla and enriched with butter, it's one of the most delicious things I know how to make. Pastry cream is used everywhere as a filling—in tarts, éclairs, cream puffs, cakes, and pies, to name a few— so if there is one recipe to master besides pie dough, it's this one.

Set up the sieve: Place a fine-mesh sieve over the top of a large heatproof bowl and set aside.

Infuse the milk: Combine the milk, vanilla seeds and pod, and salt in a medium, heavy-bottomed saucepan. ① Set the saucepan over medium-low heat and let the mixture come slowly to a simmer, whisking occasionally, to allow the vanilla to infuse the milk.

Beat the sugar, cornstarch, and yolks: While the milk is heating, combine the sugar, cornstarch, and yolks in a large bowl. Whisk vigorously until the mixture is very pale, light in texture, and thick, about 2 minutes (it will seem too thick to whisk at first but will thin out as you work it). Using a ladle and whisking constantly, slowly stream about half of the hot milk into the bowl with the egg mixture (this gradually raises the temperature of the eggs so they don't curdle). Whisking constantly, quickly stream the egg mixture back into the saucepan with the remaining warm milk.

Cook the pastry cream: Increase the heat to medium and continue to cook, whisking constantly, until the foam has subsided and the pastry cream is thick like pudding and easily holds the marks of the whisk, about 3 minutes (but possibly several minutes longer depending on the strength of your stove and the sturdiness of your saucepan). It's important that the mixture comes to a boil in order to activate the cornstarch, but at the same time you don't want to overcook the pastry cream—when you pause whisking for about 5 seconds, a few thick bubbles should form beneath the surface and then pop. If this isn't happening or the cream isn't thickening, raise the heat slightly and keep whisking, pausing every 30 seconds to check if it's bubbling.

Strain and incorporate the butter: Scrape the cooked pastry cream into the mesh sieve and use the whisk to press the mixture through the mesh into the bowl below (discard any solids). Whisk the cold butter into the hot pastry cream one piece at a time until smooth. Press a sheet of plastic wrap directly onto the surface of the pastry cream and refrigerate until it's cold, at least 4 hours.

DO AHEAD
The pastry cream, covered and refrigerated, will keep up to 5 days.

① Use the heaviest saucepan you have, as anything with a very thin bottom or sides could lead to scorching.

VARIATIONS

- **Chocolate Pastry Cream:** After incorporating the butter, whisk 4 ounces (113g) finely chopped semisweet chocolate into the hot pastry cream until melted and smooth.

- **Black Sesame Pastry Cream:** After incorporating the butter, whisk ⅔ cup black tahini (5 oz / 140g) into the hot pastry cream until smooth. If the tahini is separated, make sure to stir it well to reincorporate the solids and oil and eliminate lumps before adding it to the pastry cream (warm the tahini if necessary to break up stubborn lumps). If you don't love the bitter taste of black sesame or if you're not sure, consider starting with ½ cup tahini and adding more to taste.

- **Coconut Pastry Cream:** Pour a 13.5-ounce (383g) can unsweetened full-fat coconut milk, well shaken, into a small saucepan and simmer over medium heat, whisking occasionally, until reduced to 1 cup, 15 to 20 minutes. Replace 1 cup of the milk in the pastry cream with the reduced coconut milk, then replace the 6 tablespoons butter with 4 tablespoons virgin coconut oil (1.9 oz / 55g) and follow the recipe as instructed.

Classic Cream Cheese Frosting

Makes about 4½ cups

Special Equipment:
Stand mixer

2 sticks **unsalted butter** (8 oz / 227g), at room temperature

1 pound (454g) full-fat **cream cheese**, preferably Philadelphia, at room temperature ①

Generous pinch of **kosher salt**

1 pound (454g) **powdered sugar** (about 3½ cups), sifted if very lumpy

Seeds scraped from 1 **vanilla bean** or 2 teaspoons **vanilla extract**

In all my years of cake making, I have yet to try a plain or vanilla-flavored European buttercream that beats the deliciousness of good old American cream cheese frosting. Don't give me a piece of carrot cake, red velvet, or coconut cake covered with anything else. This recipe is sweet but not saccharine, and well balanced by the tang of the cream cheese. Between the classic version, the flavor variations below, and **Silkiest Chocolate Buttercream** (page 359), I never need another frosting.

Make the frosting: In a stand mixer fitted with the paddle attachment, beat the butter and cream cheese on medium-high, scraping down the sides of the bowl occasionally, until the mixture is completely smooth. Turn off the mixer, add the salt and all of the powdered sugar, and cover the bowl of the mixer with a clean kitchen towel (to shield you from powdered sugar plumes). Pulse the mixer on low several times to incorporate the sugar, then remove the towel and beat the frosting on medium-high, scraping down the sides once or twice, until the frosting is light, thick, and very smooth, about 1 minute. Beat in the vanilla seeds. The frosting is now ready to use.

VARIATIONS

- **Chocolate Cream Cheese Frosting:** Add 6 ounces (170g) melted and cooled unsweetened chocolate to the mixer bowl after adding the vanilla. Beat, scraping down the sides once or twice, until the frosting is smooth and streak-free.

- **Brown Butter Cream Cheese Frosting:** In a medium saucepan, cook the 2 sticks unsalted butter over medium heat, stirring and scraping the bottom and sides constantly with a heatproof spatula, until the sputtering subsides, the butter is foaming, and the solid bits turn brown, 6 to 8 minutes. Scrape the butter and all the toasted bits into the bowl of the stand mixer and set it aside until the butter is completely cooled and solidified (you can stir it over an ice bath to speed up this process, but don't let the butter harden). Proceed with the recipe. If the consistency of the frosting is very loose and it won't hold a peak, place the bowl in the refrigerator and stir every 10 minutes with a flexible spatula until it's thickened and spreadable.

DO AHEAD
The frosting, stored airtight in the refrigerator, will keep up to 1 week. Let it come completely to room temperature, then beat again in the bowl of a stand mixer with the paddle attachment to smooth out the frosting before using.

① Make sure the butter and cream cheese are both completely at room temperature (and, by extension, the same temperature), otherwise the colder of the two will form lumps. If this happens, take about ¼ cup of the lumpy mixture and warm it gently in the microwave until liquefied, then return it to the mixer bowl and beat until the frosting is smooth. The warm mixture should bring up the total temperature of the frosting slightly, smoothing out the colder lumps.

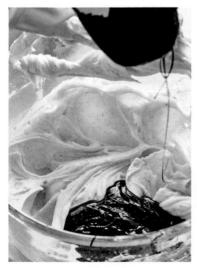
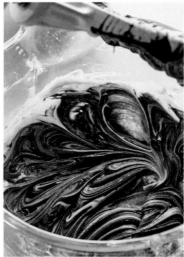

Graham Cracker Crust

Makes one 9-inch tart or pie crust

Special Equipment:
Food processor, 9-inch pie plate,
9-inch removable-bottom tart pan, or
9-inch springform pan

6 ounces (170g) plain **graham crackers**
(9 or 10 sheets), broken into pieces

2 tablespoons **demerara sugar**

½ teaspoon **Diamond Crystal kosher salt**

6 tablespoons **unsalted butter**
(3 oz / 85g), cut into pieces, at room
temperature

1 large **egg yolk** (0.6 oz / 16g)

You can use any cookie or cracker you like for this recipe, but be sure it's thin and wafer-like with a very crisp and light texture (recommended: Lars Own Swedish Ginger Snaps). Thicker cookies with more moisture will produce a crust that's hard and dense rather than dissolve-in-your-mouth crisp. The egg yolk is slightly atypical, but it helps bind the crust and makes for a sturdier base.

Preheat the oven: Arrange an oven rack in the center position and preheat the oven to 350°F.

Make the crumb mixture: In a food processor, combine the graham crackers, demerara sugar, salt, butter, and egg yolk and process in long pulses until the crackers have broken down into fine crumbs and the mixture looks like moist sand. ① It should easily hold together when squeezed.

Press the mixture into the pan: Transfer just shy of half the mixture to a 9-inch pie plate, 9-inch removable-bottom tart pan, or 9-inch springform pan. Push the mixture outward to create an even ring around the perimeter, then use a straight-sided 1-cup dry measure to press the mixture firmly against the sides. Scatter the remaining crumb mixture across the bottom of the pan and use the bottom of the measuring cup to flatten the crumbs into an even layer with no bare spots. Place the pie plate or pan on a foil-lined baking sheet.

Bake the crust: Bake the crust until it's fragrant, firm to the touch, and the outer edges are darkened in color, 13 to 15 minutes.

DO AHEAD
The baked crust, wrapped airtight and stored at room temperature, will keep for 1 day. The crumb mixture can also be pressed into the pan, covered, and refrigerated up to 1 day before baking.

① Stop processing the mixture just at the point where it looks damp but not greasy, otherwise the crust will be more likely to slump in the oven. You could also make this without a food processor by very finely crushing the graham crackers in a 1-gallon resealable plastic bag with all the air pressed out. Roll back and forth over the pieces with a rolling pin to pulverize them, then sift the mixture into a medium bowl. Place any larger pieces back in the bag and pulverize again, then add to the bowl. Add the remaining crust ingredients and work the mixture with your fingertips until the butter disappears and the mixture feels like wet sand.

VARIATION

Speculoos Crust: Break up 6 ounces (170g) Biscoff cookies with your fingertips into small pieces, then transfer to a food processor and process in long pulses until you have fine crumbs (don't overprocess or the mixture will be too wet). Transfer the crumbs to a bowl, then add the demerara sugar, salt, yolk, and only 4 tablespoons unsalted butter (2 oz / 57g). Work the mixture with your fingertips until the butter disappears and the mixture feels like wet sand (doing this part in the food processor would make it too wet to handle). Proceed as directed for pressing into the pan and baking.

Frangipane

Makes about 1½ cups

Special Equipment:
Food processor

1 cup sliced **almonds**, preferably
unblanched (4 oz / 113g) [2]

⅓ cup **sugar** (2.3 oz / 66g)

½ teaspoon **Diamond Crystal kosher salt**

6 tablespoons **unsalted butter**
(3 oz / 85g), cut into ½-inch pieces, chilled

1 large **egg** (1.8 oz / 50g), at room
temperature

1 large **egg yolk** (0.6 oz / 16g), at room
temperature

½ teaspoon **almond extract**

2 tablespoons **all-purpose flour**
(0.56 oz / 16g)

Frangipane, aka almond cream, is a versatile pastry component that's typically used as a filling. The preparation is simple, but there are a thousand interpretations of the recipe. Some versions call for almond flour, some use almond paste. I prefer to start with sliced almonds because they toast quickly (and toasting adds a huge amount of flavor to the frangipane), plus they grind to a fine powder. Sliced almonds (the ones that are flat, not slivered) are easy to find, and the entire recipe comes together in less than 2 minutes in the food processor. While almond is classic, frangipane can be made using almost any kind of nut, or you can substitute almond flour for the sliced almonds and make the mixture by hand. [1]

Preheat the oven and toast the almonds: Arrange an oven rack in the center position and preheat the oven to 350°F. Scatter the almonds on a small rimmed baking sheet and toast, shaking halfway through, until they're golden and nutty smelling, 8 to 10 minutes. Remove from the oven, transfer to a plate or cutting board, and let the almonds cool completely.

Grind the almonds: In a food processor, combine the sugar, salt, and cooled toasted almonds and process in long pulses until the almonds are finely ground.

Make the frangipane: Add the butter to the processor and pulse until the mixture is smooth. Add the whole egg, yolk, and almond extract and pulse until completely incorporated and the mixture is smooth. Scrape down the sides of the bowl, then add the flour and pulse just until the flour disappears. Scrape the mixture into a lidded container, cover, and refrigerate until ready to use.

VARIATION

Chocolate-Hazelnut Frangipane: Substitute an equal weight of blanched hazelnuts for the sliced almonds and toast them using the method above. Proceed with the recipe as written, adding 4 ounces (113g) chopped semisweet chocolate to the food processor with the nuts, sugar, and salt and finely grinding. Use vanilla extract in place of the almond extract.

DO AHEAD
The frangipane, stored airtight in the refrigerator, will keep up to 4 days. Let it come to room temperature before using.

[1] To make the frangipane by hand, replace the sliced almonds with 1 cup (4 oz / 113g) almond flour (skip the toasting step) and start with room temperature butter: In a medium bowl, beat the butter and sugar with a flexible spatula until light and creamy, then add the whole egg, yolk, and almond extract and beat until incorporated. Add the almond flour, all-purpose flour, and salt and mix until smooth.

[2] Use an equal weight of untoasted shelled pistachios, pecans, walnuts, or blanched hazelnuts in place of the almonds. Be sure to first toast them thoroughly. Replace the almond extract with vanilla extract, if desired.

Lemon Curd

Makes about 2½ cups

¾ cup **sugar** (4.6 oz / 150g)

Finely grated **zest of 2 lemons** [1]

4 large **egg yolks** (2.5 oz / 70g)

1 large **egg** (1.8 oz / 50g)

¾ cup fresh **lemon juice** (6 oz / 170g), from 5 to 6 large lemons

½ teaspoon **Diamond Crystal kosher salt**

1 stick **unsalted butter** (4 oz / 113g), cut into ½-inch pieces, chilled

1 teaspoon **vanilla extract**

Lemon curd is what's called a "stirred custard," meaning it's a mixture of eggs, sugar, and lemon juice that's cooked on the stovetop until thickened. It's one of the first recipes I remember making on my own, and I took extreme care, anxiously cooking it over a double boiler as the recipe instructed to prevent the eggs from curdling. While lemon curd does require some tending to make sure the eggs cook to a smooth consistency, now I generally streamline the process and assemble it directly in a saucepan (to absolutely no ill effect). It's a great recipe to learn, not just for the technique but for the myriad uses you can put it to: lemon bars, lemon meringue pie, lemon tarts, etc.

Beat the eggs and sugar in the saucepan: In a small, heavy-bottomed saucepan, [2] combine the sugar and lemon zest and use your fingertips to massage the zest into the sugar until the mixture is fragrant and looks like wet sand. Add the egg yolks and whole egg to the pan and whisk vigorously, making sure no unincorporated sugar is trapped around the sides, until the mixture is very pale, light in texture, and thick, about 2 minutes.

Add the lemon juice and cook the curd: Slowly stream in the lemon juice, whisking constantly and scraping around the sides, until the mixture is smooth. Whisk in the salt. Place the saucepan over medium-low heat and cook, whisking constantly, until the curd turns opaque yellow, is thick enough to coat the back of a spoon, and barely holds the marks of the whisk (it will also register 170°F on an instant-read thermometer), 7 to 10 minutes. Immediately remove the saucepan from the heat.

Whisk in the butter and vanilla: Whisk in the butter one piece at a time, waiting for each piece to disappear into the curd before adding the next, until all the butter is incorporated and the mixture is smooth. Whisk in the vanilla. [3]

Chill the curd until set: Scrape the curd into a medium glass or plastic bowl or container and press a sheet of plastic wrap directly onto the surface (this will prevent a skin from forming). [4] Refrigerate until the curd is cold and set, at least 3 hours.

VARIATION

Meyer Lemon Curd: Decrease the quantity of sugar to ⅔ cup (4.6 oz / 130g) and replace the regular lemon zest and juice with Meyer lemon zest and juice.

DO AHEAD
The curd, covered and refrigerated, will keep up to 5 days.

[1] Finely grate the zest from the lemons *before* you juice them; it's much easier than trying to zest juiced halves.

[2] Using a heavy saucepan with a thick bottom and sides will prevent the curd from heating unevenly and possibly overcooking in places. If you only have a thin, flimsy saucepan, you can still make this curd by stirring it in a large heatproof

bowl set over a large saucepan filled
with 1 inch of simmering water (don't let
the bottom of the bowl touch the water).
Just note the curd will take longer to
thicken because of the gentler heat.

3 I don't strain lemon curd because
straining removes the flavorful zest. But if
for any reason you have lots of solid bits
(where the egg likely curdled), it's best to
go ahead and strain.

4 Don't store the curd in a metal bowl, even
one that's nonreactive or stainless steel,
as the curd will eventually acquire a
metallic taste.

Season: All | Active Time: 25 minutes for the dough, plus another 30 minutes for a par- or fully baked crust
Total Time: 3 hours for the dough (includes 2 hours 30 minutes for chilling), plus another 1 hour 20 minutes to 1 hour 30 minutes
for a par- or fully baked crust | Difficulty: 2 (Easy)

Flaky All-Butter Pie Dough

Makes enough for one 9-inch pie or tart crust [1]

Special Equipment:
Pie weights or 4 cups dried beans or
rice (for parbaking)

1 stick plus 2 tablespoons **unsalted butter**
(5 oz / 142g), chilled

1½ cups **all-purpose flour** (7 oz / 200g),
plus more for rolling out

1 tablespoon **sugar** (0.46 oz / 13g)

¾ teaspoon **Diamond Crystal kosher salt**

For a recipe with so few ingredients, pie dough is one of those essential pastry preparations that no two people make the same way. I prefer to make a relatively dry dough, using as little water as possible to bind the flour, because I find that a drier dough from the outset bakes into a flakier, more tender crust that holds its shape and browns faster (which is especially useful for wetter fillings). If your dough feels a tad crumbly and still has a few floury spots, that's okay. It will continue to hydrate as it rests in the refrigerator, plus the rolling and folding technique—something I learned from baker extraordinaire and overall incredible human Tara Jensen—will further help to bring it together. This recipe makes a generous amount of dough for one standard 9-inch pie plate, which means you have a little extra to work with in case you're not a master with the rolling pin.

Prepare the ice water and slice some of the butter: Fill a 1-cup liquid measure with ice water and refrigerate it while you assemble the pie dough. Cut a 5 tablespoon block of the butter (2.5 oz / 71g) crosswise into ⅛-inch-thick slices (so you have lots of thin butter squares) and refrigerate.

Mix the dry ingredients: In a large bowl, whisk together the flour, sugar, and salt to combine.

Work the butter into the dry ingredients: Cut the remaining 5 tablespoons butter (2.5 oz / 71g) into ½-inch cubes and toss in the flour mixture to coat. [1] Quickly and firmly use your fingertips to smash the butter pieces into the flour, flattening them and working into smaller bits until the largest pieces are no bigger than a pea. [2] [2,3] Remove the butter slices from the refrigerator, add them to the flour mixture, toss to coat, then flatten between your thumbs and fingertips into thin sheets, letting them break apart if that's what they want to do. Once you've worked in all the butter, you should have a very coarse, slightly yellowed mixture filled with some larger pieces of butter and some very small bits.

Bring the dough together: [4] Slowly drizzle 5 tablespoons of the ice water (avoiding any ice) into the mixture, tossing constantly with a fork to incorporate. [5] Switch to your hands and toss the mixture   (**continues**)

DO AHEAD
The dough, wrapped tightly in plastic and refrigerated, will keep up to 3 days or can be frozen up to 2 months (place in a resealable plastic bag before freezing). Let the frozen dough thaw overnight in

the refrigerator before using. The par- or fully baked crust, covered and stored at room temperature, will keep for 1 day.

[1] Double this recipe and make two pieces of pie dough at a time, even if you only need one (see the instructions for the **Double Crust** variation on page 337). It's always a good idea to keep an extra frozen crust for an emergency or a rainy day.

several times until shaggy pieces of dough form, then knead the mixture inside the bowl a few times to bring it together (the dough will look very clumpy and dry, with loose bits). Line the work surface with a sheet of plastic wrap, then transfer any large clumps of dough to the plastic. [6] Tossing again with a fork, drizzle more ice water 1 teaspoon at a time into the bowl with the remaining flour mixture until only a few dry spots remain, then knead with your hands to bring it together into a dough. Transfer the last bits of dough to the plastic wrap.

Wrap and chill the dough: [7] Pat the dough into a ¾-inch-thick square or rectangle. [8,9] Wrap tightly in the plastic, pressing out any air, and press down on the dough with the heel of your hand to flatten it further and force it into the corners of the plastic. Refrigerate for 2 hours. The pie dough is technically ready to use at this point, but proceed through the next step, which will make it extra flaky.

Roll out and fold the dough: Let the dough sit on the counter for 5 minutes to soften slightly. Unwrap it and place on a lightly floured surface. Use a rolling pin to beat the dough all across the surface to make it more pliable. [10] Dust the top and underside of the dough with more flour, then roll it out, dusting with more flour as needed, into a rectangle that's about three times longer than it is wide and between ¼ and ½ inch thick. ③ [11,12] Fold the dough in thirds like a letter (this makes more butter layers, which create a flaky texture), then wrap tightly in plastic. Refrigerate the dough until it's relaxed, at least 30 minutes and up to 3 days. It's now ready to use. If the recipe calls for a lined pie plate, a parbaked crust, or a fully baked crust, follow the directions below.

If baking, preheat the oven and prepare a baking sheet: Arrange an oven rack in the center position and preheat the oven to 425°F. Line a rimmed baking sheet with foil and set aside.

Line a 9-inch pie plate: Let the pie dough sit at room temperature for about 5 minutes to soften slightly, then beat it across the surface again with a rolling pin to make it more pliable. [13] Dust the top and underside of the dough with more flour, then roll it out, dusting with more flour as needed, into a 13-inch round that's about ⅛ inch thick. Roll the pastry onto the rolling pin.

[14,15] Unroll the round onto a 9-inch pie plate, preferably glass, letting the pastry slump gently down the sides into the bottom. Firmly press the pastry into the bottom and up the sides of the plate, ensuring contact everywhere and taking care not to stretch it. ④

[16] Use scissors to trim around the edge of the pastry, leaving a ½-inch overhang (discard the scraps).

[17] Tuck the overhang underneath itself all the way around so you have a lip of double-thick pastry resting just around the rim of the pie plate.

[18] Press down firmly around the rim to seal, then crimp the crust all the way around, using the thumb of one hand and the thumb and forefinger of the other, flouring your fingers if needed to prevent sticking. Instead of a crimp, you can also use the tines of a fork to create hash marks around the rim.

Bake the weighted crust: Freeze the lined pie plate until the dough is very firm, about 10 minutes, then prick the bottom of the pastry in several places with a fork to prevent the crust from puffing up. Line the inside of the pie plate with two pieces of foil, arranged perpendicularly, so the overhang of the foil completely covers the edge of the crust. Fill the pie plate with pie weights, dried beans, or rice and place on the prepared baking sheet. Bake in the center of the oven until the edge of the crust is set and starting to turn golden when you peek under the foil, 25 to 30 minutes. Remove the plate from the oven and carefully lift the foil and pie weights out of the crust. Reduce the oven temperature to 350°F. ⑤ (continues)

---

② Work quickly while you're smashing the butter into the flour so it stays cold; if it starts to soften, place the whole bowl in the freezer to chill for several minutes.

③ If you try to roll out the dough straight from the refrigerator, it will likely crack. However, if tempered dough cracks while rolling, it might be underhydrated. Dribble 2 teaspoons of cold water across the surface, or spritz it a couple of times

with water using a spray bottle, then fold the dough in half, wrap it in plastic, and refrigerate for 30 minutes. This should make it easier to roll out.

1

2

3

4

5

6

7

8

9

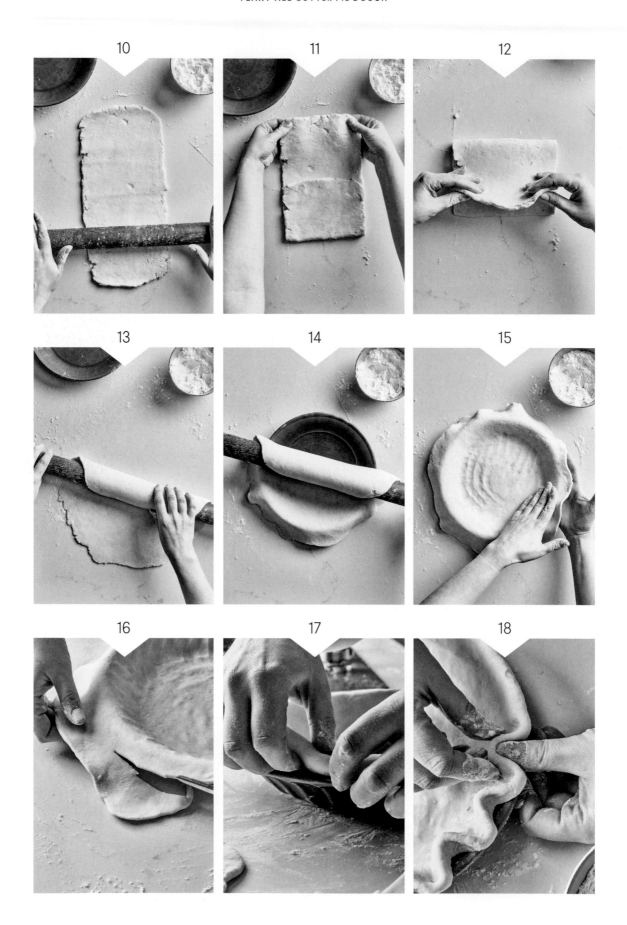

To par- or fully bake the crust: Return the pan to the oven and bake until the crust is golden brown all over, another 20 to 25 minutes for a parbaked crust, or until deep golden brown all over, 10 to 15 minutes longer, for a fully baked crust. ⑥ Set the crust aside to cool.

VARIATIONS

- **Almond Pie Dough:** Replace ⅓ cup of the all-purpose flour (1.6 oz / 45g), with ⅓ cup almond flour (1.4 oz / 40g). Note that the dough will require less ice water to come together because the almond flour is much less absorbent than all-purpose.

- **Whole-Grain Pie Dough:** Replace ⅓ cup of the all-purpose flour (1.6 oz / 45g) with ⅓ cup of any whole-grain flour (1.6 oz / 45g) such as wheat, spelt, rye, or buckwheat, and follow the recipe instructions. Note that whole-grain flour absorbs more water than all-purpose, so you will need slightly more ice water to bring the dough together. Expect this version to be ever so slightly denser and crumblier than the original.

- **Double Crust:** For a double-crust pie, double all the ingredients. Cut half the butter (10 tablespoons / 5 oz / 142g) crosswise into ⅛-inch-thick slices and then cut the rest into ½-inch cubes. Start by adding ½ cup ice water (4 oz / 113g) to the bowl and proceed with the method as written to bring the dough together. Wrap the entire amount of dough in plastic, forming it into a square, and refrigerate. Cut the square of dough in half to create two single crusts and proceed with the rolling and folding method for each one.

---

④ Press the dough firmly and thoroughly into the pie plate or pan with your palms and fingertips, and firmly anchor the edges to the lip of the pie plate. This will help prevent shrinkage in the oven and encourage better browning.

⑤ Don't forget to reduce the oven temperature from 425°F to 350°F when baking the crust again after removing the pie weights. Baking a second time at a lower temperature helps prevent cracking and shrinkage, which could cause problems later on (especially if the pie has a liquidy filling).

⑥ If you're preparing the crust for a custard pie, such as the **Caramelized Honey Pumpkin Pie** (page 93), make sure that the crust is fully baked through and at the very least a deep golden brown across the bottom before you add the filling. Liquidy custards generate steam while they bake, which mostly prevents the crust beneath from taking on any additional color. The edge of the crust may have developed a few dark spots by the time the pie is done, but it's worth it to prevent a soggy bottom.

Sweet Tart Dough

Makes one 9- or 10-inch tart

Special Equipment:
Food processor, 9- or 10-inch removable-bottom tart pan or springform pan

⅓ cup **almond flour** (1.4 oz / 40g) ①

1 cup **all-purpose flour** (4.6 oz / 130g), plus more for hands

¼ cup **powdered sugar** (1 oz / 30g)

½ teaspoon **Diamond Crystal kosher salt**

1 stick **unsalted butter** (4 oz / 113g), cut into ½-inch pieces, chilled ②

1 large **egg yolk** (0.6 oz / 16g)

½ teaspoon **vanilla extract**

This sweet tart dough, aka *pâte sucrée*, is a cousin of pie dough but with a consistency that's less flaky and more uniform and shortbready (a result of incorporating the butter much more thoroughly into the flour). While I won't kick flaky pie dough out of bed, wetter fillings just work better with this style of tart dough. Toasted almond flour gives this recipe a bit more character than the average tart dough, and using a press-in method means you don't have to bother with rolling out or weighting the dough before baking. Note that this quantity of dough will work for a 9-inch or 10-inch tart; the latter will just have a slightly thinner crust.

Preheat the oven and toast the almond flour: Arrange an oven rack in the center position and preheat the oven to 350°F. Spread the almond flour in an even layer on a small rimmed baking sheet and bake, stirring with a heatproof spatula once or twice, until the almond flour is fragrant and golden brown, 6 to 9 minutes. Transfer the almond flour to the bowl of a food processor and let cool. (Turn the oven off.)

Make the dough: Add the all-purpose flour, powdered sugar, and salt to the food processor, then pulse several times to combine. Add the butter and process in long pulses until the pieces of butter are no larger than a pea, about 10 pulses. In a small bowl, beat the egg yolk, vanilla, and 4 teaspoons cold water with a fork until smooth. Remove the food processor lid and drizzle all of the yolk mixture evenly over the flour mixture (use a flexible spatula to scrape out every last drop). Replace the lid and process in long pulses until a ball of dough forms around the blade and no floury spots remain, about 10 pulses. Scrape the dough out of the food processor and onto a sheet of plastic wrap. Pat the dough into a ½-inch-thick disk, then wrap in plastic and refrigerate at least 30 minutes and up to 3 days.

Press the dough into the pan: ③ [1] Unwrap the chilled dough and use a knife or bench scraper to cut it in half, then cut one half into 6 strips. [2] Roll the strips beneath your palms on the work surface to form ropes that are about ½ inch thick, then arrange the ropes around the inside perimeter of the tart or springform pan, pressing into place and

---

DO AHEAD
The tart dough, wrapped tightly in plastic and refrigerated, will keep up to 3 days or can be frozen for up to 2 months (place in a resealable plastic bag before freezing). Let the frozen dough thaw overnight in the refrigerator before using. The parbaked or fully baked crust, covered and stored at room temperature, will keep for 1 day.

① Replace the almond flour with an equal weight of whole roasted almonds, if that's what you have. Add the whole almonds to the food processor along with the flour, sugar, and salt and pulse until the nuts are very finely ground, then proceed with the recipe as written.

overlapping slightly so there are no gaps. [3] Using a lightly floured, straight-sided 1-cup dry measure, press the dough against the sides in an even thickness all the way around. If using a tart pan, press until the dough extends slightly above the edge of the pan. [4] Using lightly floured hands, press the other half of the dough into and across the bottom of the pan in an even layer. Where the bottom meets the sides, smooth and press the dough together to seal. [5] For an extra-smooth surface or if you notice any unevenness, use the floured measuring cup to flatten the bottom. (continues)

---

[2] Use cold butter straight from the fridge, otherwise the dough won't form a ball around the blade. Cold butter also helps the dough chill down faster in the refrigerator.

[3] Don't try to roll out this dough with a rolling pin into a round to line the pan. It's a fragile, brittle dough (thanks to the lack of gluten development), so pressing it in is the best option.

Chill the crust: Freeze the lined pan until the dough is completely hardened, 15 to 20 minutes.

Preheat the oven: While the dough is chilling, preheat the oven to 350°F.

Smooth the edge and line with foil: Remove the pan from the freezer. [6] If using a tart pan, hold a paring knife parallel to the work surface and slice horizontally along the rim of the pan, removing excess dough and creating a smooth edge flush with the top of the pan. Reserve the scraps of raw dough to patch any cracks in the crust after baking. If using a springform pan, you can leave the edge unfinished or trim around it with a paring knife to create a smooth edge with an even height. Place the pan on a rimmed baking sheet and prick the bottom all over with the tines of a fork. Press a layer of foil directly onto the surface of the dough and up the sides, especially working it into the space where the bottom and sides meet (this will help prevent the dough from slumping as it bakes—no dried beans or pie weights needed—a tip I picked up from pastry legend Lindsey Shere).

Bake the foil-lined crust: Bake the tart crust until the edge is golden brown (peek under the foil to check), 15 to 20 minutes. Remove the sheet from the oven and carefully peel off the foil.

To par- or fully bake the crust: Return the pan to the oven and bake until the crust is golden all over, another 15 to 20 minutes for a parbaked crust, or until deep golden brown around the edges, 10 to 15 minutes longer, for a fully baked crust. Set the crust aside to cool.

Patch any cracks and cool: Use the reserved dough scraps to patch any cracks. Let cool completely.

VARIATION

Nut-Free Tart Dough: Replace the almond flour with ¼ cup all-purpose flour (1.2 oz / 30g) and skip the toasting step.

Flaky Olive Oil Dough

Makes one 9-inch pie or tart crust

1¾ cups **all-purpose flour** (8 oz / 227g)

1 tablespoon **sugar** (0.46 oz / 13g)

1 teaspoon **Diamond Crystal kosher salt** (0.11 oz / 3g)

¼ teaspoon **baking powder**

7 tablespoons **extra-virgin olive oil** (3.4 oz / 96g)

As a baker I prize all that butter, with its flake-making properties and rich flavor, brings to the table, so I was surprised to learn that olive oil can, in fact, produce a tender, flaky, vegan alternative to classic pie dough. In order to create flakiness in the absence of butter (which contains water, which turns to steam in the oven, which produces a puffing effect), this recipe relies on two things: The first is a bit of baking powder for leavening. The second is a technique similar to the one used in making Chinese scallion pancakes: The dough is rolled out thinly, brushed with oil, then folded and rolled out again. This produces a crust with the same layered texture as an all-butter pastry. Because the crust is redolent of olive oil, I think it works best in savory recipes, but for a version that pairs well with sweet, see the coconut oil variation on page 343.

Mix the dry ingredients: In a medium bowl, whisk together the flour, sugar, salt, and baking powder to combine. Make a well in the center of the dry ingredients.

Work in the oil: [1] Pour 6 tablespoons of the oil (2.9 oz / 83g) into the well and use a fork to incorporate some of the flour from around the sides of the bowl until you have shaggy pieces. [2] Break up the pieces with your fingertips so they're no larger than a pea.

Bring the dough together: [3,4] Drizzle ¼ cup cold tap water (2 oz / 57g) into the bowl, stirring constantly with a fork, then switch back to your hands and knead the mixture inside the bowl until a dough comes together. Transfer the dough to a work surface, leaving any floury bits behind in the bowl, then add more water 1 teaspoon at a time to the bowl to bring the rest of the dough together; add it to the rest of the dough.

Knead and chill: Knead the dough a few times just until it's smooth (you don't want to work the dough too much, although the oil does help prevent gluten development, thus protecting it against toughness). [5] Press the dough into a ½-inch-thick square, wrap it tightly in plastic, and refrigerate for 1 hour.

Roll in more oil to create flakiness: ① Roll out the dough between two large sheets of parchment paper, periodically peeling off and repositioning each piece of the parchment, one at a time, for wrinkle-free rolling, to a ⅛-inch-thick square. ② (continues)

DO AHEAD
The dough, wrapped tightly and refrigerated, will keep up to 3 days or can be frozen up to 1 month (place in a resealable plastic bag before freezing). Let the frozen dough thaw overnight in the refrigerator before using.

① You can skip the step of brushing the dough with more oil and rolling it up if you want to save time—the baked dough will still turn out flaky, just not *as* flaky.

② Use a firm hand to roll out the dough—this is not as delicate a pastry as pie dough, nor is it as prone to stickiness, since there's no butter to soften. If the dough isn't rolling out easily and stubbornly springs back, cover it and let it rest on the surface for 10 minutes before going over it again with the rolling pin.

[6] Remove the top sheet of parchment paper and brush the remaining 1 tablespoon oil across the surface of the dough

[7,8] Starting at the side closest to you, fold up the dough into a flat, loose roll.

[9,10,11,12] Flatten the roll with the heel of your hand across the entire length. Roll out the dough into a rough rectangle that's about ¼ inch thick, then bring the left and right sides of the dough inward to fold it in thirds (this step ensures lots of flaky layers).

Wrap the dough in plastic, pressing out any air, and press down on the dough with the heel of your hand to flatten it into a ½-inch-thick disk. Refrigerate the dough until it's relaxed, at least 30 minutes and up to 3 days. It's now ready to use.

VARIATION

Sweet Coconut Oil Crust: Place ⅔ cup virgin or refined coconut oil (5.3 oz / 150g) in a small bowl and refrigerate until very solid, 20 to 30 minutes. (If you like the flavor of coconut, use virgin coconut oil; for a more neutral flavor, go with refined.) Use the chilled coconut oil in place of the 7 tablespoons olive oil in the dough, cutting it into the flour mixture using a pastry blender or two knives (to avoid melting the oil with your fingertips) until you have pieces no larger than a pea. Proceed with the recipe, but note that you'll likely need a couple additional tablespoons ice water to bring the dough together. After chilling, let the cold dough sit at room temperature for 15 minutes to allow it to soften before rolling out (this dough will be more crumbly than the olive oil version). Brush the surface of the rolled-out dough with 1 tablespoon melted coconut oil in place of the remaining 1 tablespoon olive oil, then proceed as written above.

Sweet Yeast Dough

Makes enough dough for 12 large buns or 2 babkas

Special Equipment:
Stand mixer

1 cup **whole milk** (8 oz / 227g)

1½ teaspoons **active dry yeast**
(0.18 oz / 5g)

4½ cups **all-purpose flour** (20.6 oz / 585g),
plus more for the work surface and bowl

⅓ cup **sugar** (2.3 oz / 66g)

1½ teaspoons **Diamond Crystal kosher
salt** (0.16 oz / 5g)

10 tablespoons **unsalted butter**
(5 oz / 142g), cut into 1-inch pieces, chilled

3 large **eggs** (5.3 oz / 150g)

This is a versatile dough that can be used to make all types of sweet buns and breads—I use it for the **Walnut-Maple Buns** (page 245) and **Speculoos Babka** (page 239). ❶ The texture is light and tender but not quite as rich as brioche. Fortunately, the process of making it is also faster and less technical than brioche, with the mixer doing basically all of the work.

Warm the milk and proof the yeast: In a small saucepan, gently warm the milk over low heat, swirling the pan, just until it's lukewarm to the touch but not hot (about 105°F on an instant-read thermometer). Pour about ¼ cup of the warm milk (2 oz / 57g) into a small bowl and whisk in the yeast until it's dissolved. Let the yeast mixture sit until it's foamy, about 5 minutes.

Make the dough: In the bowl of a stand mixer, combine the flour, sugar, salt, and butter and toss to coat the butter pieces. Make a well in the center of the bowl and pour in the eggs, yeast mixture, and remaining warm milk. Set the bowl on the mixer and attach the dough hook. Mix on low speed until all the flour is moistened, then increase to medium and continue to mix until the butter is incorporated (the warm milk will soften it eventually) and you have a soft, sticky dough, about 5 minutes. Stop the mixer, scrape down the sides of the bowl, then mix on medium-high until the dough pulls cleanly away from the sides, gathers almost completely around the hook, and is very smooth and supple, about 5 minutes longer. It will still be very soft and might start to stick to the bowl when the mixer is at a lower speed, but if the dough sticks on medium-high then add more flour by the tablespoon until it pulls away and is slightly tacky but no longer sticky.

Proof the dough and then chill: Turn the dough out onto a lightly floured surface and gather it into a ball. Dust the dough all over with a bit more flour, then place inside a medium bowl. Cover the bowl tightly with plastic wrap and let it sit at room temperature until it's about 50 percent expanded in size, 1 to 1½ hours. ❷ Transfer the bowl to the refrigerator where the dough will finish the first rise, eventually doubling. Chill until cold, at least 4 hours, though 8 to 12 is better (not only will refrigerating the dough make it firmer and easier to handle, it will improve the flavor as well).

DO AHEAD
The sweet yeast dough, covered, can be refrigerated up to 16 hours (refrigerating it longer will lead to overproofing and should be avoided).

❶ Make a half recipe of this dough if, for example, you only want to make a single **Speculoos Babka** (page 239). All of the quantities are simply halved except for the sugar and the eggs. To make it easy, use 3 tablespoons sugar and 1 whole egg plus 1 yolk for the half recipe. A half recipe will come together faster than a full recipe, 5 to 8 minutes total on medium speed.

❷ This dough is sensitive to temperature, so don't stress if it seems to be rising faster or slower than the given time frame. Keep an eye on it and move it to a warmer spot (like inside the oven with the light turned on) if the dough seems to be rising slowly.

Pâte à Choux

Makes 60 to 70 bite-sized puffs

Special Equipment:
Stand mixer (optional), pastry bag (optional)

½ cup **whole milk** (4.4 oz / 125g)

1 tablespoon **sugar** (0.46 oz / 13g)

½ teaspoon **Diamond Crystal kosher salt**

7 tablespoons **unsalted butter** (3.5 oz / 100g), cut into pieces

1 cup **all-purpose flour** (4.6 oz / 130g)

6 large **eggs** (10.6 oz / 300g)

Of all the tasty raw doughs and batters that exist, from chocolate chip cookie to brownie, I think I like eating *pâte à choux* the most. It's weird, I know, but there's something about the slightly sweet, slightly salty, very silky dough I find extremely delicious. *Pâte à choux*, a basic cream puff dough, is unique because it's precooked on the stovetop before being enriched with a very high proportion of eggs, which helps the dough puff in the oven. It's one of those very classic, very French pastry preparations that sounds harder than it is.

Heat the liquid ingredients: In a small saucepan, combine the milk, sugar, salt, butter, and ½ cup water (4 oz / 113g). Bring the mixture to a lively simmer over medium-low heat, stirring with a wooden spoon to melt the butter.

Stir in the flour and cook the dough: When you see active bubbling on the surface, add the flour all at once and stir slowly to incorporate it into the liquid. Once all the flour disappears, stir vigorously until all the ingredients come together into a soft dough and a light film forms around the sides and across the bottom of the saucepan. [1] Continue to cook the dough over medium heat, using the spoon to smack it against the sides, until the dough is smooth and firm and holds together in a ball, and the film on the bottom of the saucepan has been reabsorbed into the dough, about 3 minutes. The most important thing here is to make sure the dough has a chance to dry out and the flour loses its raw taste, so don't rush it.

Beat in the eggs: Scrape the dough into the bowl of a stand mixer fitted with the paddle attachment (or into a large bowl if making by hand). ❶ [2] Let it rest for about a minute to cool slightly, then turn the mixer on medium and add 5 of the eggs, one at a time, beating thoroughly after each addition. It will look separated at first but will smooth out with mixing. (If making the dough by hand, just stir the mixture vigorously with a wooden spoon.) After each egg, the dough should look glossier and looser than before. Keep beating in the eggs one at a time until the mixture is very glossy, smooth, and thick enough to hold its shape but loose enough that it leaves a thin V-shaped trail as it falls off the end of the paddle or spoon. You might not need to add all 5 eggs, so stop once the mixture reaches this point (if you're making **Gougères**, page 277, mix in the spices and cheese now).

DO AHEAD
The *pâte à choux*, stored in the pastry bag in the refrigerator, can be made 1 day ahead. Let it come to room temperature before piping. The dough can also be piped onto the baking sheets and frozen solid, uncovered, then wrapped well and kept frozen up to 1 month. Bake the dough straight from the freezer (they'll take a few minutes longer in the oven). The baked puffs, stored airtight at room temperature, will keep up to 2 days or they can be frozen up to 1 month. The puffs will soften if baked ahead, so to recrisp the exterior, space them out on a baking sheet and bake in a 400°F oven for 5 to 8 minutes (depending on the number of puffs), and let cool.

1   2   3

Transfer to a pastry bag: Scrape the batter into a large pastry bag or resealable plastic bag. ② Twist or seal the bag to close, squeezing out as much air as possible. The dough is now ready to use.

If baking, preheat the oven: Arrange two oven racks in the upper and lower thirds of the oven and preheat to 425°F.

Prepare the baking sheets: Line two large rimmed baking sheets with parchment paper. Trace around a 1-inch-diameter cutter (or bottle cap), making rows of circles spaced about 1½ inches apart. You want about 35 circles per sheet, so arrange the circles in a 5 × 7 grid. Turn the parchment over so the ink side is down (you should still be able to see the circles) and set the baking sheets aside.

Pipe the puffs: Snip a ½-inch opening in the pastry bag filled with the dough. [3] Working over the prepared baking sheets, center the opening of the bag inside a circle and squeeze gently, without moving the bag, to extrude a mound of dough, filling the circle. Continue piping until you've filled all the circles on both sheets.

Brush with egg: Beat the remaining egg in a small bowl with a fork until streak-free, then use a pastry brush to dab it gently over all the dough mounds (if you're making the **Croquembouche**, page 211, omit this step and use the *craquelin*).

Bake the puffs: Transfer the baking sheets to the upper and lower racks and immediately reduce the oven temperature to 375°F. Bake until the puffs are risen and deep golden brown, 30 to 35 minutes, switching racks and rotating the pans front to back after 20 minutes.

Cool the puffs and poke holes: Turn off the oven and allow the puffs to cool inside with the door propped open for 15 minutes. Remove from the oven and use the tip of a paring knife to poke a small hole in the bottom of each puff to allow steam to escape (trapped steam can sometimes cause the puffs to deflate as they cool). Let the puffs cool completely on the baking sheets.

---

① Make sure you wait several beats before mixing the first egg into the dough once it comes out of the saucepan. It will be very hot and could cook the egg, leading to little unwanted curds throughout your dough.

② Don't have a pastry bag or a resealable plastic bag? You can simply use two spoons to drop heaping tablespoon-sized mounds of batter onto the baking sheets. Your puffs will still puff, they'll just be a bit more free-form.

Soft and Pillowy Flatbread

Makes eight 7- to 8-inch flatbreads [1]

Special Equipment:
Instant-read thermometer, griddle or large skillet (preferably cast iron)

1 **russet potato** (about 8 oz / 227g), peeled and cut into 1-inch pieces

1 teaspoon **active dry yeast** (0.11 oz / 3g)

3¼ cups **all-purpose flour** (15 oz / 423g), plus more for the work surface

2 tablespoons **extra-virgin olive oil** (1 oz / 28g), plus more for the bowl

2 teaspoons **Diamond Crystal kosher salt** (0.21 oz / 6g)

Flaky salt, for sprinkling the top

As far as yeast doughs go, flatbread (yes, it still contains yeast) is extremely forgiving and therefore a great recipe for people who think they can't bake bread. This dough contains a secret ingredient—mashed potato—which keeps these flatbreads soft and pliable. I learned this trick from Hanna Rose Strauss (aka Nano), former *Bon Appétit* Deputy Editor Julia Kramer's great-grandmother, whose famous recipe for *schnecken*, or cinnamon rolls, calls for cooked potato. Making Nano's *schnecken* was the first time I'd added potato to any dough that wasn't for potato bread, and I was pleasantly surprised at just how soft it made both the dough and the final product. Thanks, Nano!

Cook and mash the potato: Place the potato in a small saucepan and cover with cold water just until the pieces are submerged. Bring the water to a boil over medium-high heat and cook until the potato is very tender and a fork easily slides into the center of a piece, 12 to 16 minutes. Remove the saucepan from the heat and use a slotted spoon to transfer the potatoes to a medium bowl; reserve 1 cup of the cooking liquid. Mash the potatoes inside the bowl with a large fork or potato masher until no lumps remain and set aside. [2]

Proof the yeast: Let the reserved potato cooking liquid cool until it's lukewarm but not hot (it should register about 105°F on an instant-read thermometer; refrigerate it to speed up the cooling process if necessary). Combine ¼ cup of the luke warm potato cooking liquid (2 oz / 57g) and the yeast in a large bowl and whisk to dissolve the yeast. Let the mixture sit until foamy, about 5 minutes.

Mix the dough: Add the remaining ¾ cup potato cooking liquid (6 oz / 170g) to the bowl with the yeast, then add the flour, olive oil, kosher salt, and the mashed potato. Mix with a wooden spoon until you have a shaggy dough, then scrape everything onto a lightly floured surface. Knead the dough, adding a bit more flour as needed if it's very sticky, until the dough is very soft and elastic and slightly tacky—it might stick to your hands slightly but should pull away from the surface   (continues)

DO AHEAD
The cooked flatbreads are best eaten right away, although you can wrap them in foil while still warm and hold them in a 200°F oven up to 1 hour. The dough, portioned after the first rise and covered on the baking sheet, can be refrigerated up to 16 hours.

[1] You can make a half recipe of dough if you only want 4 servings. You can also make a full recipe and portion just half of the dough to make flatbreads, then cover and refrigerate the other half of the dough before the second rise to make the **Clam and Fennel Pizza with Gremolata** (page 285) the next day.

[2] You can use leftover baked potato instead of mashed boiled potato to make the flatbreads. Scoop and mash 8 ounces (227g) of flesh and use tap water in place of the potato cooking liquid.

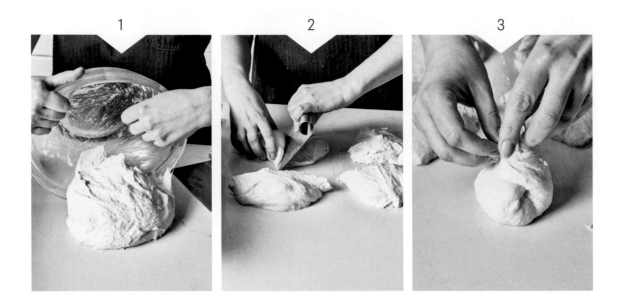

cleanly—10 to 12 minutes. You can also mix the dough in a stand mixer fitted with the dough hook on medium speed until the dough is barely pulling away from the sides, adding more flour as needed, 8 to 10 minutes.

Let the dough rise one time: Wash and dry the bowl you used to mix the dough, then lightly oil the inside. Gather the dough into a ball, place it inside the bowl, and turn to coat. Cover the bowl with a damp towel and let sit at room temperature until the dough is doubled in size, 1 to 1½ hours. If you're making the **Clam and Fennel Pizza with Gremolata** (page 285), prepare the dough through this step.

Prepare a baking sheet: Line a large rimmed baking sheet with parchment paper and lightly oil the parchment. Set aside.

Portion and shape the dough: Uncover the dough and use your fist to punch it down lightly to expel some of the gases that built up during the first rise.

[1,2] Turn the dough out onto a clean surface and use a bench scraper or knife to divide it into 8 equal pieces.

[3,4] Working with one piece of dough at a time, gather all the edges and pinch them together to form a teardrop shape. Place the piece of dough seam-side down on the work surface.

[5] Holding your fingers in a cupped position like you're playing the piano, place your hand on top of the dough and drag the dough across the surface, moving your hand in a rapid circular motion, to form it into a tight ball. Do not add flour, as this step requires friction between the dough and the surface.

[6] Place the ball on the prepared baking sheet and cover with plastic wrap. Repeat the forming process until you've shaped all 8 pieces of dough and placed them underneath the plastic on the baking sheet. (At this stage, the dough, tightly covered on the baking sheet, can be refrigerated up to 16 hours.)

Let the dough rise a second time: Let the dough sit at room temperature until the balls are nearly doubled in size, 40 to 50 minutes (note that if you refrigerated the dough, the second rise will slowly take place in the refrigerator, but if pieces haven't doubled, let them sit at room temperature before proceeding). Transfer the baking sheet with the risen dough balls to the refrigerator. If you're making the **Feta-Za'atar Flatbread with Charred Eggplant Dip** (page 299), prepare the dough through this step.

4

5

6

Roll out the flatbreads: Remove a piece of dough from the baking sheet, keeping the rest covered and in the refrigerator, and place it on an unfloured work surface. Roll out the dough to a thin round about 7 or 8 inches in diameter (roundish is okay; the shape isn't important!). The dough will be very relaxed and should only require a small amount of pressure with the pin, but don't add any flour since the friction with the surface will help the dough extend.

Preheat the skillet: Heat a large, dry skillet (preferably cast-iron) or griddle over medium heat for several minutes.

Cook the flatbread: Peel the flatbread carefully off the work surface and transfer it to the preheated skillet. Cook until the bottom is lightly charred all over and the surface of the dough has bubbled up and gone from shiny and sticky to matte and dry, 1 or 2 minutes. Turn the flatbread and cook on the second side until the dough is cooked through, about another 30 seconds. Transfer to a cooling rack and sprinkle immediately with flaky salt.

Roll and cook the remaining flatbreads: Remove one piece of dough at a time from the refrigerator and repeat the rolling and cooking process until all the flatbreads are cooked. Serve warm or at room temperature.

VARIATION

Sweet Potato Flatbreads: Substitute an equal weight of sweet potato for the russet potato and cook as directed. Because the sweet potato flesh is wetter and less starchy than that of a russet, the sweet potato dough will be softer and require a few additional tablespoons of flour during kneading.

Brioche Dough

Makes 2 loaves [1]

Special Equipment:
Instant-read thermometer, stand mixer (optional, but recommended), two 8½ × 4½-inch loaf pans (if baking into loaves)

DOUGH

¼ cup **whole milk** (2 oz / 57g)

1 teaspoon **active dry yeast** (0.11 oz / 3g)

4 cups **all-purpose flour** (18.3 oz / 520g), plus more for the surface and dusting

¼ cup **sugar** (1.8 oz / 50g)

2 teaspoons **Diamond Crystal kosher salt** (0.21 oz / 6g)

6 large **eggs** (10.5 oz / 300g), at room temperature

2 sticks **unsalted butter** (8 oz / 227g), cut into 8 pieces, at room temperature [2]

FOR BAKING

Butter for the pans

1 large **egg**, beaten

Brioche is a super delicious, super eggy, super buttery French bread. It's only slightly sweet, making it an essential pastry component in both desserts and savory dishes. Brioche is made by mixing all the ingredients except the fat until smooth and supple, then incorporating room temperature butter slowly and piece by piece so it emulsifies into the mixture to form a very soft, rich dough. While I like the tactile sensation of making dough by hand, I usually opt for the stand mixer when it comes to brioche because things can get very sticky and a little messy. If you do take this recipe on by hand, see the variation on page 354 and make sure you have a generous amount of work space, a bowl scraper, and patience.

Proof the yeast: In a small saucepan, gently warm the milk over low heat, swirling the pan, just until it's lukewarm but not hot, about 105°F on an instant-read thermometer (you can do this in the microwave, too, but beware of overheating). Pour the milk into a small bowl and whisk in the yeast to dissolve. Set aside until the mixture is foamy, about 5 minutes.

Combine the ingredients: In the bowl of a stand mixer, combine the flour, sugar, and salt. Make a well in the center of the flour mixture and pour in the yeast mixture, followed by the eggs.

Mix the dough in a stand mixer: Set the bowl on the mixer and attach the dough hook. Mix on low speed until a shaggy dough forms, about 1 minute. Increase the speed to medium and mix until a dough comes together around the hook. Continue to mix, scraping the dough from the hook occasionally, until the dough is very supple, soft, and cleanly pulls away from the sides of the bowl (it will still stick to the bottom), adding an additional tablespoon or two of flour if the dough continues to stick to the sides, 8 to 10 minutes.

Work in the butter: With the mixer still on medium, add the butter one piece at a time, allowing each piece to fully incorporate into the dough before adding the next. Be patient, as working in all the butter can take about 15 minutes or more. (continues)

DO AHEAD
Following the first rise, the brioche dough can be refrigerated up to 24 hours (refrigerating it longer will lead to overproofing and should be avoided). The baked loaves, covered at room temperature, will keep up to 4 days but are best served on the first or second day.

[1] Halve the ingredients to make a half recipe of dough, which is the amount used in a number of recipes in this book, including **Pigs in a Brioche Blanket** (page 303) and **Brioche Twists with Coriander Sugar** (page 229). The dough takes some effort, though, so I usually make the full amount and bake the other half in a loaf or reserve it for another use.

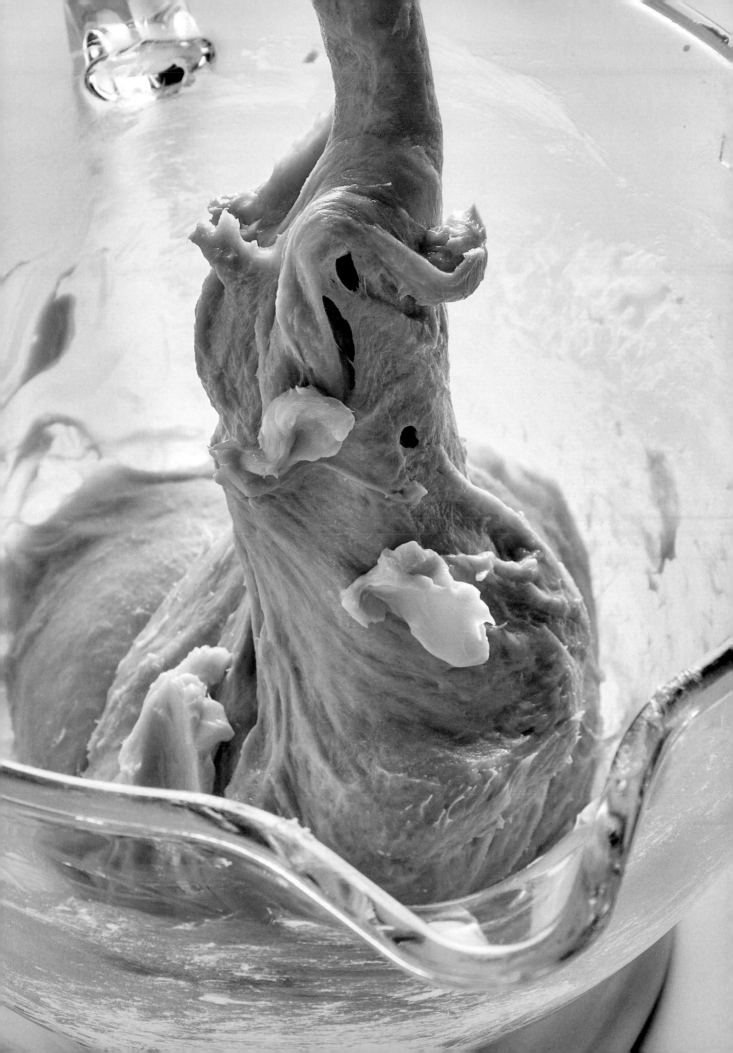

Let the dough rise once and chill: Gather the dough, which at this point will be extremely soft and supple, into a ball and lightly flour it all over. Place the dough inside a large bowl and take a photo so you have a point of comparison as it rises. Cover it with plastic wrap and let the dough sit at room temperature until it has nearly doubled in size, 1 to 1½ hours. **③** Place the bowl in the refrigerator and chill for at least 8 hours and up to 24 (not only will refrigerating the dough make it firmer and easier to handle, it will improve the flavor as well). At this point, the dough is ready to be used in another recipe, or it can be formed into loaves and baked.

Prepare the pans to bake the loaves: Lightly butter the bottom and sides of two 8½ × 4½-inch loaf pans. Line the bottoms and two longer sides with parchment paper, leaving an overhang of several inches on both sides. Lightly butter the parchment paper and set the pans aside.

Form the dough into loaves: Scrape the cold dough onto a lightly floured surface and use your fist to punch it down lightly to expel some of the gas that built up during the first rise. **④** Divide the dough in half with a bench scraper or knife. Use the heel of your hand to pat each half into a rectangle measuring about 8½ × 6 inches. Starting from one of the long sides, roll up the dough into an 8½-inch-long log and place it inside the loaf pan seam-side down. Repeat with the second piece of dough.

Let the dough rise a second time: Cover both pans with a damp towel and let them sit at room temperature until the dough has swelled to fill out the bottom of the pans, 1 to 1¼ hours.

Preheat the oven: Arrange an oven rack in the center position and preheat the oven to 350°F.

Bake the loaves: Uncover the loaves and brush the surfaces of the dough with the beaten egg. Bake side by side until the tops of the loaves are a deep golden brown, 30 to 35 minutes, switching the position of the pans and rotating them front to back after 20 minutes.

Cool the loaves: Remove the loaves from the oven and let them cool in their pans for 15 minutes, then use the parchment paper to lift the loaves out of the pans and transfer to a cooling rack. Peel off the parchment paper and let cool completely.

VARIATION

Mix the dough by hand: In a large bowl, combine the sugar, salt, and flour. Make a well in the center and pour in the yeast mixture and eggs. Stir with a wooden spoon until a shaggy dough forms. Turn the dough out onto a lightly floured surface and knead to bring it together into a single mass. Continue to knead until it becomes very sticky, then, using a bench scraper and your other hand, lift the dough off the surface and slap it back down again. Continue to lift and slap the dough, adding a tablespoon or two of flour to the surface if it continues to stick, until the dough is very soft, supple, and quite tacky but not sticky, 10 to 15 minutes. Place it on the work surface and smear one piece of the butter across the dough with your fingers. Continue using the same lifting and slapping motion until the butter is completely incorporated into the dough, then repeat with the remaining butter pieces, working them in one at a time, until the dough is soft, smooth, and supple (expect this to take upward of 15 minutes).

---

② Make sure the butter is completely room temperature, otherwise it won't incorporate easily into the dough. It should be soft and very spreadable but not greasy looking (butter that is too warm isn't good either). I recommend leaving the butter at room temperature for several hours and even overnight before making the dough, but you can also quickly temper cold butter by zapping it in the microwave in 20-second intervals on 30 percent power.

③ Avoid letting the dough rise in a very warm spot, otherwise the butter will start to melt and ooze out of the dough.

④ Don't let the dough sit too long at room temperature when you're forming it, as this will soften the butter and make the dough sticky. If that happens, work quickly and dust with a bit more flour. You can also return it to the refrigerator as often as needed to firm it up.

Rough Puff Pastry

Makes enough pastry for two 10-inch crusts

3 sticks **unsalted butter** (12 oz / 340g), chilled

3½ cups **all-purpose flour** (16 oz / 455g), plus more for rolling out

2 tablespoons **sugar** (0.9 oz / 25g)

1½ teaspoons **Diamond Crystal kosher salt** (0.16 oz / 5g)

This recipe, a hybrid of pie dough and traditional puff pastry, relies on a series of rapid folds to flatten slices of butter into thin sheets within the dough, which then release steam during baking and produce a flaky, layered effect. It mimics the more formal pastry technique known as lamination, used to make **Kouign-amann** (page 257) and **Spelt Croissants** (page 253), but without a lot of fuss. The key to the flakiest pastry is to keep it very cold, so feel free to return the dough to the refrigerator as frequently as needed while you work.

Freeze some of the butter and the dry ingredients: Place 1½ sticks of the butter (6 oz / 170g) in the freezer until very firm but not frozen solid, 10 to 15 minutes (this will make it easier to grate). In a large bowl, whisk the flour, sugar, and salt and place in the freezer until the butter has firmed up.

Slice the remaining butter and prepare ice water: Thinly slice the remaining 1½ sticks butter (6 oz / 170g) crosswise into ⅛-inch-thick slices and place them on a plate in the refrigerator. Prepare about 1 cup of ice water and refrigerate.

Grate the frozen butter into the flour mixture: Remove the butter and flour mixture from the freezer and toss the whole butter sticks in the flour mixture to coat. [1] Working quickly to prevent your hands from warming the butter, grate the flour-coated butter on the large holes of a box grater directly into the flour. ➊ Use a fork to toss the butter bits in the flour to thoroughly coat them.

Add the sliced butter and bring the dough together: [2] Remove the butter slices from the refrigerator and toss them in the flour mixture to distribute. [3] Gradually drizzle ½ cup of the ice water (4 oz / 113g) into the bowl, tossing constantly with a fork, until you have shaggy pieces of dough. [4] Using your hands, knead the dough a couple of times in the bowl to bring it together in large pieces. Place a large sheet of plastic wrap on your work surface and transfer the large pieces of dough onto it, leaving the floury bits behind in the bowl. Drizzle more ice water into the bowl by the teaspoon, tossing with the fork, just until the remainder of the dough holds together in a mass when squeezed (the dough will still seem very dry, which is normal). [5] Place every last bit of dough on top of the plastic wrap and pat it down into a ½-inch-thick square, pressing firmly on any dry spots to compact. (continues)

DO AHEAD
The rough puff pastry, well wrapped and refrigerated, will keep up to 2 days or can be frozen up to 2 months (let the dough thaw in the refrigerator overnight before rolling out).

➊ You could also use the grating disk of the food processor to very quickly grate the partially frozen butter instead of using a box grater. Place 2 tablespoons of the total flour in the bowl of the food processor first so it coats the butter shreds and keeps them separated.

10

11

12

[6,7] Wrap tightly in plastic, eliminating air bubbles, then use the rolling pin or the heel of your palm to flatten the dough further, pushing it into the corners of the plastic. Refrigerate for 2 hours.

Roll out and fold the pastry twice: Let the dough sit at room temperature for about 5 minutes to soften. Unwrap and place on a lightly floured surface. Use a rolling pin to beat the dough all across the surface to make it more pliable. [8] Roll out the pastry, dusting the top and underside with more flour as needed, into a long rectangle that's about three times longer than it is wide and ¼ inch thick. [9,10] Fold the dough in thirds like a letter, first lifting up the bottom third and pressing it into the center, then folding down the top third. [11,12] Rotate the dough 90 degrees. Using more flour as needed, roll out the dough into another long rectangle and fold in thirds again. Cut the dough in half crosswise, wrap each half tightly in plastic, and refrigerate at least 1 hour. The pastry is now ready to use. [2]

---

[2] Don't try to use the pastry right after performing the series of folds, even if it still seems cold and workable. The back-to-back rolling and folding will develop gluten, which will cause the pastry to spring back when you try to roll it (and then shrink during baking). It needs to rest at least 1 hour in the refrigerator so the gluten can relax.

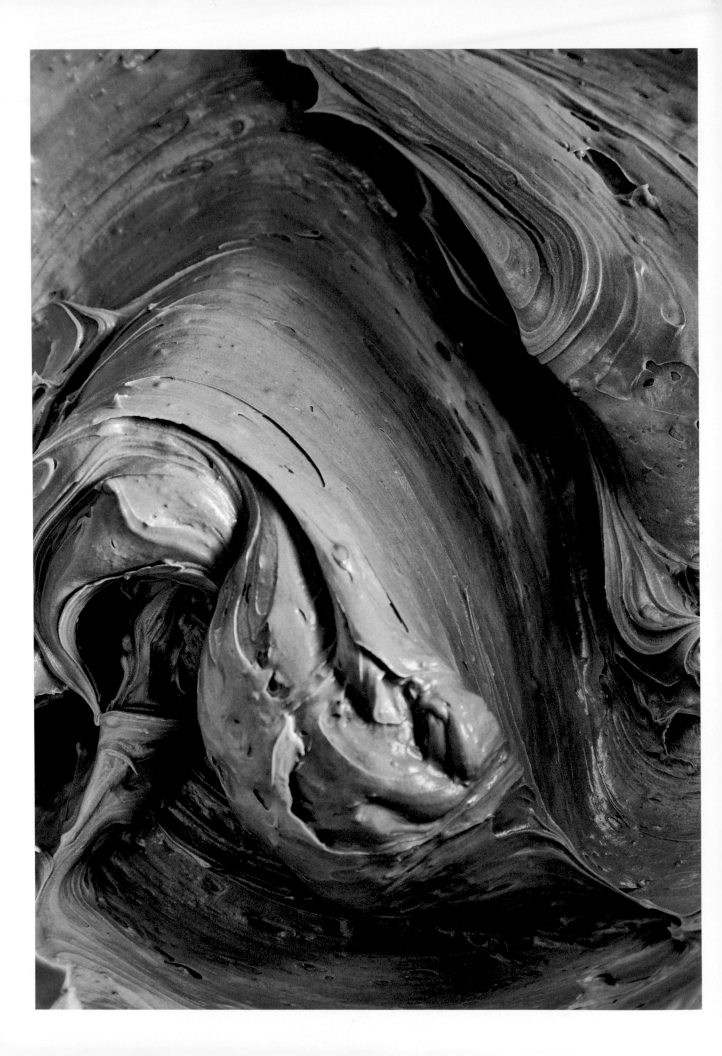

Silkiest Chocolate Buttercream

Makes about 4 cups

Special Equipment:
Instant-read or candy thermometer, stand mixer

2 large **eggs** (3.5 oz / 100g), at room temperature

2 large **egg yolks** (1.1 oz / 32g), at room temperature

¾ cup **sugar** (5.3 oz / 150g)

2½ sticks **unsalted butter** (10 oz / 283g), cut into tablespoons, at room temperature

8 ounces (227g) **semisweet chocolate** (preferably 68 to 70% cacao), melted and cooled [1]

1 teaspoon **Diamond Crystal kosher salt** (0.11oz / 3g)

2 teaspoons **vanilla extract**

This is technically a French-style buttercream, one of several types of European, egg-based buttercreams, and it requires a bit of choreography. The method involves streaming a hot sugar syrup, cooked to a precise temperature, into whipped eggs, then beating in butter and melted chocolate to form a smooth, stable emulsion. I can understand if any of that puts you off, but also know it might be the best chocolate frosting you'll ever try. When making any kind of European buttercream, I prefer to flavor it with semisweet chocolate—a lot of it, actually—since the bitterness offsets all the fat and sweetness. If you want a less fussy frosting, there's always the chocolate variation of the **Classic Cream Cheese Frosting** (page 324).

Have all of your ingredients ready to go: Since the first part of making the buttercream requires simultaneous operations, have all the ingredients measured out. Put the whole eggs and yolks in the bowl of a stand mixer and attach the whisk. In a small saucepan, combine the sugar and 3 tablespoons water (1.5 oz / 43g) and set aside. Make sure your butter is thoroughly at room temperature and your chocolate is melted and cooled.

Start to beat the eggs: Turn the mixer on medium-low just to break up the eggs, then add the salt and increase to medium speed. Continue to beat until the mixture is very light and pale and it falls off the end of the whisk and onto itself in a slowly dissolving ribbon, about 5 minutes. While you're waiting for this, pivot to the sugar.

Cook the sugar syrup: Heat the sugar mixture over medium-high heat, stirring with a heatproof spatula until dissolved and you have a clear syrup. Stop stirring when the mixture comes to a boil, then use a wet pastry brush to brush down the sides of the pan, dissolving any sugar crystals. Using an instant-read thermometer or clipping a candy thermometer to the side of the pan, boil, swirling the pan occasionally, until the mixture registers 230°F. Reduce the heat to medium-low and continue to cook, swirling the pan, until the syrup hits 238°F. While all this is happening, keep an eye on the eggs and stop the mixer if they've formed a ribbon. Don't walk away! You want the sugar and eggs to be ready at the same time. (continues)

DO AHEAD
The buttercream, refrigerated in an airtight container with plastic wrap pressed directly onto the surface, will keep up to 1 week or can be frozen up to 1 month (let it thaw for 24 hours in

the refrigerator). Before using, let the buttercream sit at room temperature for several hours until it's spreadable, then put it back in the stand mixer and beat with the paddle attachment on medium speed until smooth.

[1] Use a good-quality chocolate, preferably one that comes in a block or in disks. I like the following brands: Guittard, Callebaut, or Valrhona. Don't use chocolate chips, which often have added stabilizers.

1

2

3

4

Stream the sugar into the eggs: [1] When the syrup reaches 238°F, remove it from the heat immediately. If you've stopped the mixer, turn it on medium-high and slowly and carefully stream the syrup down the side of the bowl into the egg mixture. Avoid pouring onto the whisk because this will splatter sugar around the bowl; aim for the point just where the eggs meet the side of the bowl. Continue to steadily pour in the syrup until you've added it all. The eggs should get thicker, paler, and denser.

Beat until cool: Increase the mixer to high and continue to beat until the egg mixture is very light and dense and the sides of the bowl are completely cool to the touch, 5 to 8 minutes.

Beat in the butter, then beat some more: [2] When the egg mixture is very room temperature, add the butter one piece at a time, making sure each piece incorporates smoothly into the mixture before adding the next. If the eggs are still a bit warm when you start to add the butter, the residual heat will cause the butter to melt and your buttercream will look soupy. If this happens, just keep beating the mixture. If the butter is too cold, it won't emulsify smoothly into the eggs and the buttercream will have a curdled look. [3] In either case, just keep beating to let the temperature equalize. I promise the buttercream will come back together. Scrape down the sides of the bowl often and keep gradually adding the butter until it's all incorporated and you have a smooth, glossy, light buttercream.

Beat in the chocolate: ② [4] Stop the mixer, scrape down the sides, and add the chocolate and vanilla. Beat on medium speed until no streaks remain, scraping the bottom and sides again if needed. The buttercream is now ready to use. ③

---

② Make sure the chocolate is completely cooled before adding it to the buttercream, otherwise it will warm the butter and deflate your hard-earned buttercream. At the same time, it should still be very liquid (I know, it's a dance!). If the chocolate has started to set, it could form tiny hardened bits when it hits the cool buttercream, marring the smooth finish of the frosting. It's not as delicate as it sounds, since melted chocolate can sit at room temperature for quite a while before it sets, so just don't melt it too far in advance.

③ It is possible to overwhip buttercream, which will make it so fluffy and filled with air bubbles that it will be difficult to smooth over a cake. If this happens, put it back in the mixer and beat with the paddle attachment on medium for a few minutes, which will knock out some of the air.

Acknowledgments

I could not have written this book without Harris, my love. Thank you for feeding me throughout the entire process, especially on the days when I was tired from recipe testing and cranky from only eating sugar. Thank you for tasting all my recipe tests, giving me honest feedback (even when I got mad at you for it), and cheering me on through the many meltdowns, high points, and deadlines. You kept me going, and I will always be grateful.

To my family: my mom, Sauci, my dad, Jeff, and my sisters, Emily and Jane. All of you have always treated my passion for cooking with seriousness and respect, even when I wasn't sure how to pursue it as a career. Your excitement and support around this book helped propel me to the finish. I am especially indebted to my mom, who washed countless dishes, shopped for ingredients so I could write, and assisted me tirelessly in the kitchen while I tested recipes.

My deepest gratitude goes to my friend Sue Li, who styled the recipes in this book beautifully while also working as my life coach and creative director (kidding! But not really). She is a force, and never wrong. The same to my friend and photographer, Alex Lau, for his incredible talent and charm. I'm grateful to Astrid Chastka, who created the visual world in which *Dessert Person* exists and is herself a fount of inspiration.

This book would not have happened without David Black, my literary agent, who gave endlessly of his time and wisdom. My appreciation also goes to Matt Belford, Emma Peters, and Ayla Zuraw-Friedland at the David Black Agency, for their exceptional care and attention.

I had the great fortune to work with Raquel Pelzel at Clarkson Potter. Every first-time author needs an editor like her: kind, compassionate, and a total pro. Thanks also to Doris Cooper, for her valuable input, and Stephanie Huntwork and Mia Johnson at Clarkson Potter for their work to develop the design and visual identity of this book.

I am indebted to Annie Kramer for providing extraordinary support and organizational skills throughout the writing and production of *Dessert Person*. My sincere thanks to Laurie Ellen Pellicano, Emily Tylman, Susan Kim, Veronica Spera, and Catherine Yoo for their hard work and superb skills both as recipe testers and stylists behind the scenes. Thanks also to Nancy Jo Iacoi for lending her expertise and guidance in planning our many photo shoots, and to Rhoda Boone, Janice Gilman, Jessica Miller,

and Allison Ochiltree at Condé Nast for helping us coordinate our studio space.

Special thanks to the following:

Julia Kramer, Emily Graff, David Tamarkin, and Kate Heddings, for their enthusiastic belief in this project. You are all my favorite dessert people.

Chris Morocco, Andy Baraghani, Gaby Melian, Brad Leone, Rick Martinez, Carla Music, Molly Baz, Amiel Stanek, Christina Chaey, Alex Beggs, Sohla El-Waylly, Sarah Jampel, and all my friends at *Bon Appétit*. Nobody I know loves food or cooking more.

Dan Siegel, Kevin Dynia, Tyré Nobles, Mike Guggino, and Jon Weigell from the *Bon Appétit* video team, for your kindness and understanding (especially when I was late and blamed it on the book).

Vincent Cross for his video and editing know-how, and for shining his light behind the scenes of the making of *Dessert Person*.

All of my friends and family who tested recipes. There are too many of you to name, but the generosity you showed with your time and energy helped me immensely.

Somsack Sikhounmuong and Lori Brown at Alex Mill, for inviting me to work with them to design a perfect apron, and for making me look good (and feel good) during my shoots.

Emily Eisen for lending inspiration and her stellar sense of taste.

Sophie Neuhaus, for her careful eye and tremendous editing skills, and the entire Neuhaus family for their warm support.

Rick Osofsky and John LeSauvage from Ronnybrook Dairy, for supplying superlative product, and Nick Contess and Lillian Berliner for their multiple forms of help.

My neighbors Ann Marie Janeway, Brant Janeway, and Nayla Della Penna, for magnanimously taking countless pastries off my hands.

And a final, very warm thanks to everyone who has watched "Gourmet Makes" and followed *Bon Appétit* in print and online. Your support also made this book possible.

Index

Published in the United States by Clarkson Potter/
Publishers, an imprint of Random House, a division
of Penguin Random House LLC, New York.
clarksonpotter.com

CLARKSON POTTER is a trademark and POTTER
with colophon is a registered trademark of
Penguin Random House LLC.

Library of Congress Cataloging-in-Publication
Data has been applied for.

ISBN 978-1-9848-2696-1
Ebook ISBN 978-1-9848-2697-8

Printed in China

Book and cover design by Mia Johnson
Cover photographs by Alex Lau

10 9 8 7 6 5 4 3 2 1

First Edition

Claire Saffitz is the host of Bon Appétit's *"Gourmet Makes" and is a contributor to the magazine. She studied French cuisine and pastry in Paris after graduating from Harvard. Originally from St. Louis, Claire lives in New York City.*